AF531163

Human Rights and War Through Civilian Eyes

PENNSYLVANIA STUDIES IN HUMAN RIGHTS

Bert B. Lockwood, Jr., Series Editor

A complete list of books in the series is available from the publisher.

HUMAN RIGHTS AND WAR THROUGH CIVILIAN EYES

Thomas W. Smith

UNIVERSITY OF PENNSYLVANIA PRESS

PHILADELPHIA

Published by
University of Pennsylvania Press
Philadelphia, Pennsylvania 19104-4112
www.upenn.edu/pennpress

Printed in the United States of America on acid-free paper
10 9 8 7 6 5 4 3 2 1

Library of Congress Cataloging-in-Publication Data
ISBN 978-0-8122-4863-0

For Golfo

CONTENTS

PREFACE

The prohibition against directly targeting civilians in war may be the strongest norm in all international relations. Nevertheless, civilian devastation remains a hallmark of today's armed conflicts. Terrorists and zealots and "unlawful enemy combatants" routinely kill and maim innocent people. But so do state militaries that profess to follow the laws of war, also known as international humanitarian law, or IHL. The image of modern humanitarian law is the judge advocate in the war room surveying the battlespace and advising the generals on the legality of particular tactics and targets. It's not the war room of *Dr. Strangelove* with its jingoistic antics and blinking "big board." Far from it. Humanitarian law genuinely strives to limit the destructiveness of war, particularly as regards the treatment of noncombatants. The legal notion that civilians should be spared the hard hand of war is not absolute, however. It is designed to mitigate civilian harm while upholding, within limits, the prerogative of states to pursue military necessity and strategic advantage. It weighs the lawfulness of war from the standpoint of the state's actions and intentions, not from the standpoint of war's collateral victims.

I propose that in thinking about war we expand our moral field of vision and focus much more on the effects of war on civilians. This book adopts the conceptual framework and moral resolve of human rights to try to do justice to the civilian experience. The argument is philosophical in the sense that it recognizes the intrinsic value of human life and human dignity. But it is also vividly empirical. One of the book's central themes is that the depth and detail of rights helps to constitute civilians and civilian protections around extra-military human rights norms. The specificity of rights conveys the terror and anguish of people whose lives are shattered by war. We see the overt violence of artillery fire or bomb strikes, of breaking down doors in the middle of the night, of arbitrary roundups and detention, of torture and abuse, and of the destruction of civilian property; as well as the insidious and long-term effects of shattered economies, rent social fabrics, collapsed public health, and constricted lives. Rights offer a rich account of the history of contemporary armed conflict. More importantly, they capture how most people today experience war. Hence the notion of human rights and war "through civilian eyes."

When I talk about human rights and war, I mean all of human rights: the right to life; the right to be spared cruel, inhuman, or degrading treatment and arbitrary arrest or detention; the right to due process; the right to feel safe in one's home; the right to work, to family life; the right to physical and mental health; the right to food, clothing, and housing; the right to freedom of movement; the right to cultural and religious freedom; the right to self-determination; the rights of asylum seekers and refugees, and so on. This is not to claim that all these entitlements can or must be honored while the bombs are falling, but rather that rights provide a ready litany for what is at stake for those caught in the crucible. To invoke human rights is also to tap into the elaborate practice and politics of the movement. The rights revolution empowered individuals to make legitimate claims against those who wield power over them. Civilians are not just objects of pity or of rescue, but can be agents and advocates in their own cause. Increasingly we see civilians adapting universal conceptions of rights to local conditions and culture.

The book comes at a time when liberal states are rethinking the ethics of war as they seek to extricate themselves from unjust or unwise conflicts, while acknowledging a responsibility to intervene, possibly even militarily, to stave off the slaughter of innocent people. Some analysts worry that international humanitarian law has failed to keep pace with today's wars, or that the encroachment of "lawfare" is starting to criminalize legitimate acts of self-defense. When states say the Geneva Conventions are outmoded or quaint, it's almost always because they want to loosen the rules. By drawing attention to rights I hope to push the debate in a pro-civilian direction. The ethics of war aren't limited to complying with humanitarian law. Even if the conduct of war is technically legal under IHL, are the human rights costs prohibitive? Conversely, in a case like Syria, where a war straight out of Thomas Hobbes's state of nature has uprooted half the country's population, do the human rights costs of inaction outweigh the violence and destruction that intervention will inevitably entail? By addressing these questions from the standpoint of rights I hope to raise expectations for civilian protections and to push back against the complacent view that civilians always die in wars and there isn't much we can do about it.

CHAPTER 1

Human Rights and the Norms of Modern Warfare

> What has changed above all since the wars of earlier centuries is our growing consciousness of what it means to be human.
> —Mary Kaldor (2009)

> Waging war is no excuse for ignoring human rights.
> —Kenneth Roth (Human Rights Watch 2004a)

The laws and customs of war have changed markedly over the centuries. The traditional focus on interstate wars has broadened to include civil wars, insurgencies, and other armed conflicts. Some criteria have faded (just intention, formal declarations of war), while others (discrimination, proportionality) have taken their place. In the 1970s, the whole body of law concerning the conduct of war was rechristened "international humanitarian law," or IHL. Humanitarian law continues to evolve. This shouldn't be surprising. The character of war has changed—and continues to change—in ways that demand more attention to the protection of individuals caught in its path.

Unfortunately, the law of war hasn't changed nearly enough. Its focus is too narrow. It demands that we ask whether belligerents are justified in entering a war, and, if so, how they should comport themselves during the war's execution. These questions are critical to any legal or moral evaluation of war. However, it is not my aim to address these, at least not directly. I propose instead that we focus much more on the earth-shattering ways war affects those directly impacted by it: soldiers, but especially civilians. It's not as if IHL doesn't calculate the effects of war on civilians. It does. However, it does so largely from the perspective of the state's actions, not from the perspective of those who are terrorized or killed or have their lives thrown into disarray by war. As the Hague Conventions put it, the goal is "to diminish the evils of war so far as military requirements permit."[1] The law was designed as a process of weighing and judging humanity in light of military necessity. It demands "no *unnecessary* damage, not one more civilian than necessary" (Kennedy 2006b:90). This approach diminishes and demeans those individuals whose lives are destroyed or disrupted by war.

We have at hand the conceptual and moral tool to give civilians their due: the notion of human rights. The suggestion that human rights apply in war isn't entirely new, of course. International lawyers routinely say that rights apply alongside or in addition to the laws of war. Geoffrey Best (1980), Theodor Meron (2006), Ruti Teitel (2011), and others have described the growing influence of human rights on the substance and style of humanitarian law. War crimes courts and tribunals routinely leaven humanitarian law with human rights ideas and norms. Human rights agencies and advocates enthusiastically take up the cause of rights in war zones. But we have yet to see a systematic account of human rights as an independent body of war norms. This book sets out to make that case. I don't suggest that human rights should sweep aside humanitarian law altogether. But I do think a rights framework conveys the impact of war on innocent and vulnerable people more vividly than humanitarian law does. This vantage, I hope to show, is crucial as we assess the justification and conduct of modern wars.

Rights have purchase on a wide range of armed violence committed by state militaries as well as non-state rebels, militias, and terrorists. Soldiers wield raw power over civilians and other soldiers, and the potential for abuse is frightful. The more wars depart from the classical assumptions of humanitarian law, the more relevant rights become. Adherence to IHL is envisioned largely in terms of reciprocity, or the mutually assured compliance of belligerents of roughly equal capabilities. Rights, by contrast, are designed exactly for conditions of unequal power. Compliance derives from public shaming and civil society campaigns; monitoring, exposure, and sanctions by national governments and international organizations; and the threat of national or international prosecutions.

A human rights model doesn't simply enjoin combatants to observe the rights of noncombatants. Rights also anchor humanitarian expectations and strengthen the status of civilians. A framework of dignity and sympathy turns our attention from high politics and strategy to the individual experience of war. Rights bore into details of everyday life, helping us to see—really see—civilians. This is no small feat when death and destruction are euphemized into "collateral damage" to "civilian objects," or are reduced to "gains" and "losses" on the strategist's ledger (see Rothbart et al. 2012). Rights claims also reverse the traditional order of agency in war. Unlike chivalry or just war, the idea of rights doesn't hinge on the beneficence or mercy of the sovereign; civilians aren't simply spared by belligerents or rescued by international peacekeepers. Rights become a vehicle for individual agency and identity, as those who bear the brunt of war adapt human rights ideas to local conditions and carry out their own documentation, monitoring, and public reporting.

The specificity of human rights lends a bracing realism to our grasp of war. While humanitarian law provides a list of principles to guide decision making (discrimination, proportionality), human rights provide a list of ends to be attained (right to life, free speech, free movement) (see Koller 2005:245). Rights increasingly give form and definition to general concepts in IHL. Humanitarian law prohibits torture, for example, but doesn't define it. For that, we turn to the Convention against Torture and Other Cruel, Inhuman and Degrading Treatment or Punishment (1985). The specificity and concreteness of rights makes them harder to evade than general humanitarian injunctions, and requires the warring parties to explain why particular rights should be overridden in particular cases. These same details propel the narratives and images that have become the stock in trade of human rights advocacy.[2]

Two caveats are in order. First, I don't claim that the full suite of rights can be achieved in the midst of armed conflict all or even most of the time. Human rights treaties allow signatories to opt out of certain provisions in time of war or other national emergency. But there is far more room for rights than conventional wisdom suggests. Many legal scholars say we can't rely on human rights because war is "far too complex and brutal a phenomenon to be capable of being constrained by rules designed for peacetime" (Christopher Greenwood, quoted in Quénivet 2008:11). This strikes me as too sweeping. War is many things, some of which clearly can and should be constrained by rules designed for peace. Sometimes war isn't even war: governments often try to skirt human rights duties and tap into more permissive laws of war by claiming they're fighting for their survival. The "war on terror" or the "long war," for example, would turn the state of exception into the norm. Modern militaries are more vulnerable to human rights scrutiny than we might think. Human rights abuses can exact a heavy price in terms of public support, institutional reputation, and the legitimacy—and success—of the mission. Concern for rights increasingly colors the strategic and tactical choices that states make. Scores of non-state armed forces have also signed human rights "deeds of commitment" as a way to burnish their humanitarian bona fides.[3]

Second, the categorical nature of human rights makes them resistant to trade-offs with other goods, but not *too* resistant (Griffin 2008:37). Rights are rarely absolute. Indeed, taking rights seriously means weighing the human rights costs and benefits of an act—even if that act happens to be war or occupation or a drone-based missile strike. The fact that an army is fighting a defensive war, or a war of liberation or self-determination, carries moral weight as well. Human rights and war are often associated with humanitarian intervention or the responsibility to protect, or "R2P" as it's colloquially called. Most human rights advocates recognize that sometimes it will be necessary to sacrifice lesser rights in the quest for greater rights. But it's hard to brook humanitarian warriors who systematically trample human rights on the way to victory. I address these dilemmas in detail in Chapter 6. For now, suffice it to say that specific rights claims weigh heavily in this calculus, emphasizing humanitarian concerns in the planning and execution of specific military operations as well as the overall aims of war.

Human Rights as War Norms

Human rights rest on the idea that people should be treated as ends and not as means. Immanuel Kant argued that this was a categorical imperative for us to act as though we were legislators in the "universal kingdom of ends" (Reiss 1996:19). That moral idea has been transformed into modern legal and political obligations. Today we think of rights as legitimate claims or entitlements to certain standards of treatment, usually on the part of governments. These tend to be regarded as important and weighty claims not easily dismissed or traded away. Maurice Cranston (1967:51–52) described them as matters of "paramount importance" responding to "a grave affront to justice." Many people view human rights claims as "political trumps" that take precedence over other claims, some say over *all* other claims (Dworkin 1978:xi).

Scholars still debate where rights come from and why we should observe them. Rights are endowed by a Creator or reflect a vision of human dignity that is "ineliminably religious" (Perry 1998:11); or they are *droits de l'homme*, seized on the barricades and avowedly of this world. Natural rights theorists say rights are pre-political or pre-institutional claims that are given in nature; legal positivists say rights are no more or less than "claim[s] as recognized by law and maintained by governmental action" (Martin 1980:396, and see Hart 1955). Rights are universal norms that exist by virtue of our humanity; or they are Western cultural mores imposed on everyone else. Advocates of "thin" human rights emphasize classic rights of life, liberty, and security. Proponents of "thick" human rights count economic, social, and cultural claims within the compass of rights.

The idea of rights has nevertheless proved remarkably resilient. "Yes, we agree about the rights, but on condition that no one asks us why," said the Catholic social theorist Jacques Maritain, who labored alongside his secular counterparts to draft the Universal Declaration of Human Rights (1948) (Joshua Cohen 2004:193–94). A similar pragmatism underpins the practice of rights. As Charles Beitz notes, the idea of human rights shapes much of the normative discourse of world politics today. Rights have developed a "doctrinal and institutional complexity" that "commands the energy and commitment of large numbers of people and organizations." While the scope and content of human rights aren't fixed, they are widely accepted as a "distinctive class of norms as reasons . . . for an array of modes of action" (Beitz 2009:9–10). This isn't the El Dorado of universal right, but it's a compelling norm nonetheless. As the Argentine philosopher Eduardo Rabossi put it, human rights are an undisputed "fact of the world" (quoted in Rorty 1993:134). That fact is not lost on would-be offenders. As Jeremy Waldron notes (1987:155), "there is now scarcely a nation on earth which is not sensitive to or embarrassed by the charge that it is guilty of rights-violation."

The strength of right stems from its connection to duty. Right implies duty: the negative duty to forbear (to refrain from arbitrary detention or torture, for example), as well as the positive duty to act (to provide social security or health care, for example). In either case, rights demand to be satisfied, not just intended. If a well-meaning city housing official fails to secure fair housing for me, I still have the right—and he or she the obligation—to see that I get it. It is this moral and psychological purchase that rights have on other people that is so empowering. As Hugo Slim notes (2008:283), "feeling that one has a right to something is a much more powerful feeling than simply feeling that one needs or wants something. It automatically implies that someone has a duty to give it to you and politicizes this relationship immediately and irrevocably."

As politics, human rights provide an organizing idea, a moral language, and a legal strategy. An army of activists help to press the case: human rights must be one of the most networked, NGO'd ideas in history. Thomas Risse and Kathryn Sikkink (1999:18) describe human rights as a model global social movement, "bound together by shared values, a common discourse, and dense exchanges of information and services." Hundreds if not thousands of national and transnational human rights organizations, as well as national, state, and local government agencies, document abuses, frame debates, set standards and agendas, lead educational and lobbying campaigns, shame abusers, cajole policymakers, push reforms, offer solutions, and monitor implementation (Keck and Sikkink 1998:201).

Practitioners have converged on substantive as well as practical norms. NGOs have developed protocols and handbooks that cover everything from prison visits, to refugee relief, to the treatment of indigenous peoples, to helping physicians recognize the marks of torture on the human body. The Council of Europe has published a series of citizen's handbooks that cover each of the major subject areas of the European Convention on Human Rights. International conferences, degree and certificate programs, wikis and listservs, and professional societies, as well as an academic publication—*Journal of Human Rights Practice*—buttress an elaborate global practice. With some allowance for cultural differences, human rights practitioners use roughly the same vernacular and methods in Krakow as they do in Dhaka.

Rights have always been on the march. The movement was invented out of revolutionary ideas and social movements, and continues to foment what Human Rights Watch (HRW) (2000) calls "an evolution in public morality." There is no a priori boundary that rights cannot cross (Meron 1995:80–81). Jack Donnelly (2003:61) argues that rights should address the "principal systematic public threats to human dignity in the contemporary world," whatever realm of life they happen to fall in. Still, major NGOs tend to choose their battles pragmatically. Human Rights Watch, for example, sets its priorities based on "the severity of the crimes being committed, the numbers of those affected, and our potential to have impact" (Human Rights Watch n.d.). Rights advocates and agencies certainly have agendas (and sometimes bureaucratic pathologies), and some issues catch fire while others die out (Tomaskovic-Devey et al. n.d.). But rights groups usually pivot to confront new crises. In her study of Amnesty International, Ann Marie Clark (2001:16) found that the "principled norms" of human rights groups are rooted in fact finding and expertise. But the lifeblood of the movement was the ability to "to form new concepts about human rights based on collected facts."

Addressing war is a particularly pragmatic turn. Traditionally, rights protected people from their own governments, fending off what John Stuart Mill (1859:53) called "the dungeon and the stake." But activists have always dreamed of breaching the citadel and bringing to heel the state at its most powerful. War, after all, is the classic *force majeure*, voiding normal peacetime obligations. On the home front, states invoke war powers to flout individual rights, suspending habeas corpus or censoring news, for example. Threats to rights increase exponentially in war zones. UN Secretary-General Kofi Annan underscored "the intimate connections between systematic and widespread violations of the rights of civilians and breakdowns in international peace and security" (UN Security Council 1999:6). Human Rights Watch observed that "almost without exception, the world's worst human rights and humanitarian crises take place in combat zones" (Human Rights Watch 2004b:1). The annual "top ten" humanitarian crises compiled by Médecins sans Frontières/Doctors Without Borders (MSF) are almost all war-related.

Françoise Bouchet-Saulnier, legal adviser to MSF, says that civilian protection begins with the recognition "that individuals have rights and that the authorities who exercise power over them have obligations" (quoted in S. Gordon 2010:89). That relationship can't be short-circuited for the sake of expedience. The nature of contemporary warfare has forced the issue. Former NATO commander Sir Rupert Smith argues (2007:6) that contemporary military engagements take place "in the presence of civilians, against civilians, in defence of civilians." Managing civilians has become a singular concern for liberal militaries: anticipating and attending to refugees, coordinating relief efforts with humanitarian agencies and NGOs, overseeing public works projects, organizing communities, weaning people away from radicalism, getting society back on its feet. An army's conduct vis-à-vis civilians has become a litmus test for the legitimacy of its mission.

Traditionally, human rights was the law of peace and IHL the law of war. That dichotomy is fading fast. The blurring of classic human rights violations and war-related breaches has made clear that the traditional separation cannot (and ought not) be sustained. Many rights groups found their calling in the "dirty wars" of the 1970s and 1980s. Amnesty International cut its teeth fighting political murder and disappearance in Central America, repression and killing in the Southern Cone, and torture in Northern Ireland. From their inception, Americas Watch (1981), Africa Watch (1988), and Middle East Watch (1989) dealt with insurgency, civil war, and other armed conflicts. In 1997, HRW amended its mission statement, pledging "to protect people from inhumane conduct in wartime."

The internecine conflicts of the 1990s thrust rights into the foreground. "New wars"—an imperfect term that encompasses post-Cold War ethnic, religious, and nationalist strife, violent struggles over natural resources, and contemporary insurgencies and other informal conflicts—are every bit orchestrated mass violations of rights as they are organized armed violence (Kaldor 2001). Human rights advocates have never been more animated, pushing war norms far beyond the traditional bounds of humanitarian law (Clapham 2006:288–89). NGOs accustomed to writing polite letters to interior ministers asking them to free their dissidents are now grappling with failed states, civilianized wars, sexual violence, child soldiers, and public health disasters. Global rights groups deploy their own researchers or cultivate local networks to file reports from the killing fields. This vocal defense of civilians complements the more discreet approach of the ICRC, which prefers to intercede with belligerents privately rather than shame them publicly.

Human rights take a catholic view of the effects of armed conflict—the immediate and direct impact of violence as well as the long-term fallout on physical infrastructure, public health, social fabric, economics, environment, and culture. As Karima Bennoune, a former legal advisor to Amnesty International, notes (2004:173), "the human impact of an armed conflict is much larger than a sum of violations of the Geneva Conventions." Media attention tends to focus on headline atrocities, but the lion's share of the misery and abuse is submerged in the daily privations of war. Strikingly little collateral damage involves noncombatants caught in the crossfire between combatants. As Hugo Slim pegs it (2008:91), "most people die *from war* rather than *in battle*."

Reliable data are scarce and there is great variation across conflicts, but recent estimates set the ratio of indirect to direct killing of civilians at between 3:1 and 9:1.[4] Infrastructure crumbles, economies collapse, the flow of goods and services is interrupted, states fail, and societies unravel; people are displaced, deported, and detained; social costs like rising crime, domestic violence, and divorce kick in. Even "low-intensity" conflicts can wreak havoc on civilians and civilian life. One study of war-related deaths in sub-Saharan Africa during the 1980s noted that "the four horsemen of the apocalypse—famine, pestilence, death, and war—ride out together" (Slim 2008:90).

Researchers in the field of health and human rights have increasingly turned their attention to the epidemiology of war (Garfield et al. 2003; Thoms and Ron 2007). Death and disease have long been seen as part of the natural history of war. Thucydides (1881:127–28) described how refugees were swallowed up by famine and plague during the Peloponnesian War. "They perished in wild disorder. . . . The dead lay as they had died, one upon another, while others hardly alive wallowed in the streets and crawled about every fountain craving for water." A 1939 medical journal noted that war offered "a splendid opportunity for the devastating virus, the bold bacillus, or the enterprising entamoeba" (Wigham 1939:49). People suffer from unhygienic conditions, polluted water, rapid exposure to multiple pathogens, rape, and sexually transmitted diseases; others endure emotional trauma of fear, pain, separation, and loss; soldiers are poisoned by toxic battlefields or tormented by post-traumatic stress (Smallman-Raynor and Cliff 2004:5). War exacts a double toll, spreading disease while simultaneously disrupting and diverting medical care. When humanitarian aid is available, it is often leveraged in exchange for political or military support (S. Gordon 2010:76). The aftershocks can affect public health and human development for decades (Ghobarah et al. 2002). Again, right implies duty. Growing healthcare capacities have given rise to new obligations to address indirect and long-term effects of war.

Lest the truism that "war" kills civilians absolve commanders or soldiers of their misdeeds, it should be stressed that human rights disasters flow predictably from certain means and modes of war. The Dirty War Index, for example, measures the effects on civilians of particular classes and uses of weapons (Hsiao-Hicks and Spagat 2008). An "armed violence morality index" models the risks associated with the kind and number of arms, the intent of belligerents, and the relative vulnerability of victims (Taback and Coupland 2005). Attacks on "dual-use" infrastructure, such as bridges and roads, electrical grids, or water purification plants, also erode public health and raise mortality rates in ways that can be modeled and measured. The fallout can settle far from the actual fighting. A 1991 *Lancet* article foretold the aftershocks of the Gulf War: "Bomb now, die later" (Kandela 1991).

Rights is also the thread that runs from *jus in bello* to *jus post bellum*, or justice in the wake of war (see, e.g., Bass 2004; Patterson 2012). Brian Orend notes (2000:219) the "overwhelming emptiness" of humanitarian law with regard to the ending of wars. Only the Hague Laws deal with war termination, and some of the provisions concerning trumpeters, buglers, and white flags read like rules at a Boy Scout camp.[5] The pursuit of human rights in the wake of war is often fraught, but in many ways rights offer more relevant and realistic norms to govern post-conflict truth, justice, reconciliation, and compensation, providing a clear, liberal, blueprint for a new or reconstituted society (Stahn 2007:928). Rights also spell out the residual obligations belligerents hold in the wake of war and occupation. If a just peace is the goal of a just war, human rights help to define what that end state looks like. Here, too, there is greater room for rights than is usually supposed. The conventional wisdom cautions that human rights demands can make conflicts more intractable and peace more elusive because they raise the moral stakes and narrow the room for negotiation (for an overview of the claims see Sriram, Martin-Ortega, and Herman 2009). But recent research shows that "naming and shaming" media coverage appears to lead to shorter wars and a higher incidence of negotiated peace deals (Burgoon et al. 2015).

There is a great deal of interplay between human rights and humanitarian law. Still, the two regimes evolved independently, and these disparate origins are reflected in the letter and spirit of each field. Human rights emerged from the struggle between oppressed or disadvantaged people and their rulers. The laws of war sprang from customary practices of belligerents and, later, the legal conventions concluded between sovereign states. Rights were domestic norms that were then codified in international law; IHL was international from the start (Oberleitner 2015:10). Philosophically, human rights are universal in nature, while IHL leans toward a statist ethic and national security framework. Rights are founded on religious teaching, moral principles of humanism, liberal and socialist political theory, and a burgeoning body of legal doctrine and practice. They are animated by the voices of victims declaring that their rights have been violated and demanding justice. The laws of war are ameliorative rather than absolute, seeking a space for charity and mercy amid the brutal necessities of war. Traditionally, they governed just cause (*jus ad bellum*) as well as just conduct (*jus in bello*) through the principles of proportionality, distinction between combatants and noncombatants, and the economy of violence. Human rights, by contrast, set out a list of specific ends to which civilians are entitled. Interpretations and applications of IHL vary widely. The International Committee of the Red Cross stresses its commitment to humanity, while many states follow a more technical legalism that directs the discussion toward operational questions of targeting and proportionality and away from the concrete human suffering wrought by war.

Both regimes observe proportionality, but each weighs the economy of violence on a different scale. Under the laws of war the anticipated harm to civilian life or property must be consonant with the anticipated military advantages. In human rights, violence is allowed only to advance other, greater, rights. Military or operational concerns may enter in, as in the case of humanitarian intervention, but have no currency of their own. Proportionality is a core concept in IHL. It is confidently invoked by belligerents, yet "images of an almost scientific balancing of opposing interests on finely tuned scales of humanitarian justice, masks a much more complex and unclear reality" (Watkin 2005:4). Article 52(2) of Protocol I of the Geneva Conventions states that attacks must be limited strictly to military objectives, defined as "those objects which by their nature, location, purpose or use make an effective contribution to military action and whose total or partial destruction, capture or neutralization, in the circumstances ruling at the time, offers a definitive military advantage." Commanders and soldiers are meant to apply the rule directly, but a number of key questions are unresolved: What relative values are to be assigned to mission goals and civilians and civilian objects? What constitutes excessive force? What defines a military advantage? Are they incommensurate ends in the first place? No "proportionometer" exists to gauge whether or not the principle has been honored (see Fenrick 2001; Holland 2004:47–48). It can be a wobbly, subjective principle, liable to be bent and abused when the stakes seem high enough. This isn't to suggest that human rights have mastered the art of proportionality. Human rights advocates remain sharply divided over the question of humanitarian intervention, for example, but in general rights offer a steelier norm in the face of military demands.

Which Rights Apply?

Human rights don't have free range in war. Even core rights are filtered through IHL. Humanitarian law is widely regarded as *lex specialis*, or "special law," derived explicitly for the circumstances of armed conflict and designed to be compatible with the pursuit of military ends. These special rules are usually thought to trump the more general rules of human rights. In its 1996 advisory opinion in the *Nuclear Weapons* case, the International Court of Justice ruled that human rights law "does not cease in times of war" except when the states parties formally derogate from certain limited provisions. But it was up to the law of war to determine what human rights meant in this context. No one could arbitrarily be deprived of the right to life, for instance, but defining what was arbitrary fell, according to the ICJ, to "the applicable *lex specialis*, namely, the law applicable in armed conflict" (International Court of Justice 1996: para. 25).

Humanitarian law isn't as special or human rights as general as this approach suggests. When it comes to civilian protections, the laws of war revolve around malleable concepts of discrimination, military advantage, and proportionality. On issues such as detention and torture, adequacy of investigations, fair trials, and criminal punishment, and in internal conflicts generally, it is *human rights* that arguably serve as *lex specialis* (see, e.g., Doswald-Beck 2006; Koller 2005; Droege 2008). Granted, the rhetoric of rights tends to soar. If IHL bars belligerents from directly attacking civilians, human rights protect us all from being subsumed by Homer's "blood-stain'd God of War" (Homer 1866:191). As noted, rights elevate personal dignity and worth over fear and degradation. Respect for individuals offsets the war powers of states, the secrecy and censorship, the coercion of patriotism, and the high cost of dissent. Rights seek to end conflicts justly and rebuild societies rent by violence.[6]

But these general goods are observed by way of specific laws and norms. As James Nickels suggests (2007:7), human rights today are "specific and numerous, not broad and abstract"; they are (apologies to my philosopher friends) "the rights of the lawyers, not the rights of the philosophers." Most of the civil and political rights listed in the United Nations Universal Declaration of Human Rights (1948) apply in wartime as well as in peacetime:

- freedom from discrimination;
- right to life, liberty and security of the person;
- freedom from slavery or servitude;
- freedom from torture or cruel, inhuman or degrading treatment;
- recognition as a person before the law;
- equality and equal protection before the law;
- right to an effective remedy before a national tribunal;
- right of personhood and equality before the law;
- prohibition of arbitrary arrest, detention or exile;
- right to a fair and public trial;
- presumption of innocence until being proven guilty;
- freedom from interference in family and private life and communications;
- freedom of movement and residence, including the right to abandon one's own country;
- right to asylum from persecution;
- right to a nationality;
- freedom of thought, conscience, and religion;
- freedom of opinion and expression;

- freedom of peaceable assembly and association, and the freedom not to be compelled to belong to an association;
- right to own property and the right not to be deprived of it arbitrarily.

Many of the social and economic rights elaborated in the Universal Declaration also apply: the right to work, the right to a standard of living adequate for the health and wellbeing of self and family; the right to education; the right to practice and preserve one's culture. To these sources of wartime rights we can add the European Convention for the Protection of Human Rights and Fundamental Freedoms (1950); the Convention on the Prevention and Punishment of the Crime of Genocide (1951); the Convention Relating to the Status of Refugees (1951), the Convention against Torture and Other Cruel, Inhuman or Degrading Treatment or Punishment (1985); the International Covenant on Civil and Political Rights (1966); the American Convention on Human Rights (1969); the International Covenant on Economic, Social and Cultural Rights (1976); the Convention on the Elimination of All Forms of Discrimination against Women (1979); the African [Banjul] Charter on Human and Peoples' Rights (1986); the Convention on the Rights of the Child (1989); and the Rome Statute of the International Criminal Court (2002).

Unless states lawfully suspend, or "derogate" from, their obligations, or the circumstances at issue lie outside the treaty's competence or jurisdiction, all apply. The list of non-derogable rights, which cannot be skirted for any reason, including *raison de guerre*, is growing. The extraterritorial reach of human rights conventions is expanding as well (Milanović 2011b). In 2004, the United Nations Human Rights Committee, which monitors compliance with the International Covenant on Civil and Political Rights, noted that state signatories to the treaty are required to "respect and ensure the rights laid down in the Covenant to anyone within the power or effective control of that State Party."

> The enjoyment of Covenant rights is not limited to citizens of States Parties but must also be available to all individuals regardless of nationality or statelessness, such as asylum seekers, refugees, migrant workers and other persons, who may find themselves in the territory or subject to the jurisdiction of the State Party. This principle also applies to those within the power or effective control of the forces of a State Party acting outside its territory, regardless of the circumstances

> in which such power or effective control was obtained. (UN Human Rights Committee 2004)

Even this language has the ring of the state to it. Effective control of territory echoes the Hague Laws regarding the duties of commanders toward populations living under occupation. The standard has been espoused by virtually every major human rights body. Today, however, obligation is shifting from a spatial model of jurisdiction to a personal model of jurisdiction: effective control over people rather than places. Human rights standards run closest to absolute in sub rosa wars of detention, torture, and targeted killing. Here the perpetrators have the greatest degree of control over the bodies of those being detained, tortured, or killed, and the threat of harm to others is lowest.[7]

The European Court of Human Rights has developed this paradigm in cases concerning detention or torture but also in some instances involving active warfare. Strictly speaking, only the parties to a treaty are bound by its provisions. But basic humanitarian protections increasingly apply to everyone as a matter of customary law. This includes clandestine operatives, intelligence services, non-state armed forces, and private security companies whose representatives never attended a treaty conference or signed or ratified any conventions (Zegveld 2002; Conte 2013). This is a signal normative turn. If duty falls to the formal exercise of power over others, not just to governments with respect to their citizens, then soldiers carry human rights obligations with them wherever they go.

Agencies, Institutions, and Courts

Skeptics will say that trying to leverage human rights in a battle zone is naïve or even reckless. Human rights activists are often accused of overreaching. Critics say that making human rights the *in bello* standard is worse than futile; that norms will drift into irrelevance if they come unmoored from the grim reality of war (Watkin 2004:24). Some worry that the supposed clarity of IHL will be muddled by the introduction of human rights (Garraway 2010). Or that conflating the two will erode protections in peacetime, as states seek to weaken general human rights provisions to ensure their militaries a free hand in wartime (Matheson 1997). Others contend that human rights and humanitarian law are working fairly well as it is, so each ought to stay in its own corner. René Provost, for example, concludes that each set of laws "displays a peculiar normative richness and resilience likely to be weakened . . . by over-simplistic or overenthusiastic attempts to recast one in terms of the other." Provost welcomes some overlap between the regimes, but concludes that "each performs a task for which it is better suited than the other" (Provost 2002:349–50).

Human rights and humanitarian law are not two stone tablets, one we consult in war, the other in peace. The regimes often borrow and trade ideas. Nor are human rights as absolute or otherworldly as critics claim. The movement is hardly pacifist. For every human rights activist calling for an end to war there are two clamoring for armed intervention to protect rights. The responsibility to protect has easily been assimilated to the culture of rights. Virtually all mainline rights groups promote some version of R2P, accepting the possibility that military force can serve humanitarian ends. Human rights choices are not always black and white in any case. Rights advocates sometimes cooperate and compromise with perpetrators of violence, leveraging compliance by appealing to self-interest and welcoming even half-measures if they ease the suffering of innocents.[8]

The growing array of agencies, institutions, and courts that invoke human rights in war tend to be pragmatic as well. The greater the disparity of power and risk between soldiers and civilians, the more these bodies tend to emphasize the human rights of civilians as against the war rights of belligerents. The rule of thumb is that the scope of obligations is relative to the degree of control. As conditions come under greater control, expectations grow from negative rights (freedom from arbitrary killing, freedom from torture, freedom of speech or religion) to positive freedoms (economic well-being, educational or cultural rights) (Cerone 2006:1504–5). Expectations are highest when armed forces exercise "effective control" over people, property, or territory (Turkey in Northern Cyprus, Israel in the West Bank, Britain in Southern Iraq, etc.).

Human rights courts have been judging the conduct of war for half a century. Some of the earliest cases decided by the European Commission of Human Rights (today the European Court of Human Rights, ECtHR) dealt with the British counterinsurgency in Cyprus.[9] The ECtHR has since adjudicated hundreds of combat and occupation cases, all stemming from "intractable" ethnic, separatist, or insurgent conflicts: Northern Ireland, Cyprus (again), Turkey, Chechnya, Armenia, and Azerbaijan. More than 3,000 petitions arising from the 2008 South Ossetia war have been lodged with the Court, most by ethnic Russians claiming they were abused by Georgian troops. The Court has recently taken up several cases arising from the war in Iraq.

The ECtHR tends to apply human rights law directly to the conduct of war, scarcely mentioning IHL at all. On the right to life, for instance, the Court does not categorically forbid killing in the context of armed conflict; no human rights treaty does that. Rather, no one shall *arbitrarily* be deprived of the right to life. The Convention holds that killing may result only "from the use of force which is no more than absolutely necessary" (Art. 2(2)). The Court has applied this single standard to clashes between rioters and police officers, small armed attacks (a PKK ambush in Eastern Turkey), major battles (a thousand irregular fighters arrayed against Russian troops in Chechnya), and a counter-terror operation in which plainclothes SAS forces surveilled and then killed three IRA operatives on city streets in Gibraltar (see Abresch 2005:753).

The ECtHR grants member states a wide margin of appreciation in determining the existence of a state of emergency and the appropriateness of derogations. Nonetheless, the Court's decisions have unsettled some of the basic assumptions of militaries at war. It has set a high threshold for the use of lethal force and has rebuffed many of the necessity and fog-of-war defenses available in IHL. The Court has breathed rigor into the concepts of discrimination and proportionality, and set strict criteria for the conduct of investigations, a point that is critical given that many courts-martial fail (or are never convened) because shoddy or on-the-fly investigations can't support the prosecution of alleged atrocities. The Court has examined, inter alia, the right to life of soldiers and civilians, the adequacy of operational planning, the definition of military advantage, arbitrary detention, torture and forcible return, admissibility of evidence obtained under torture, the rule of law in low-intensity conflicts, state responses to terrorism, and "rendition," or transferring a prisoner to another country for interrogation.[10]

Some of the most closely watched decisions have involved the Iraq War. In April 2004, British Armed Forces Minister Adam Ingram argued that Iraqi civilians couldn't petition the ECtHR because they held "no rights" under the Convention (Bowring 2008:74). That defense was quickly dispelled. Not only did human rights apply in war, but they applied when State Parties engaged in war on the territory of non-State Parties.[11] The Court ruled that the UK violated the Convention when it transferred detainees from British custody in Basra into the hands of an Iraqi court where they potentially faced the death penalty.[12] Other cases have run the gamut of wartime violence. British troops have been tried for illegally killing Iraqis while on patrol, during a raid, and in a cross-fire incident; illegally detaining an Iraqi-Briton; beating an Iraqi suspect and then forcing him to swim across a river, where he drowned; and torturing a detainee to death.[13]

As noted, the Court has replaced the spatial model of effective control with an individual model of jurisdiction, as the "exercise of physical power and control over the person in question."[14] This is quintessential human rights language, evoking the torturer looming over the shackled prisoner, or the dissident being snatched off the street and bundled into a van. The judges conceded that applying the Convention within a controlled British military compound in Iraq was "exceptional," but 40 years of jurisprudence on extraterritoriality and the British Army's clear control over the detainees placed the military base within the legal space of the Convention. Remarkably, the Court held in the *Al-Skeini* case that soldiers in Iraq could also be bound by the Convention when they ventured outside the compound walls as they conducted "patrols, arrests, anti-terrorist operations, policing of civil demonstrations, protection of essential utilities and infrastructure and protecting police stations." Even in kinetic military operations (e.g., a gunfight during a patrol), the "United Kingdom, through its soldiers engaged in security operations . . . exercised authority and control over individuals killed in the course of such security operations."[15]

The regime that has grown up around the American Convention on Human Rights (1978) has examined the protection of human rights in states of emergency, armed invasions, civil strife, civil wars, state terrorism, and military demobilizations. The Inter-American Commission on Human Rights has ruled that human rights and humanitarian law "share a common nucleus of non-derogable rights and a common purpose of protecting human life and dignity."[16] Calling the provisions of Common Article 3 of the 1949 Geneva Conventions "pure human rights law," the Commission has directly applied IHL, even weighing in on specific violations of the Geneva Conventions.[17] As for the duty to prevent and protect, the Americans are a step ahead of the Europeans. In a series of cases arising from the protracted civil war in Colombia, the Inter-American Court imposed "special obligations" on the government in Bogotá to safeguard vulnerable groups from anti-government insurgents as well as pro-government paramilitaries (Burgorgue-Larsen and Úbeda de Torres 2011:156).

Grievants in the regional courts sue governments, and only governments. This has prompted jurists to look up the chain of command to rules of engagement and other policy decisions taken at the seat of power (T. Smith 2010:33–34). Other courts have embraced individual criminal responsibility. The ad hoc tribunals such as the International Criminal Tribunal for Yugoslavia (ICTY) and the International Criminal Tribunal for Rwanda (ICTR); hybrid courts like the Special Court for Sierra Leone (SCSL) and the Extraordinary Chambers in the Courts of Cambodia (ECCC); as well as domestic ad hocs such as the Iraqi High Criminal Court, enforce a mix of international human rights and war crimes conventions and customs as well as domestic statutes. The International Criminal Court (ICC) is fundamentally a human rights court. The Rome Treaty applies whether violations are committed in international or domestic conflicts, during humanitarian or non-humanitarian missions, or even during peacetime; no nexus with war is required. These courts have internalized much of the language and many of the assumptions of rights. One of the judges on the Iraqi High Criminal Court noted that the court's rulings on war crimes were every bit pronouncements on human rights principles (Global Justice Center 2008:2).

Protecting civilians has emerged as a defining goal at the United Nations as well. Up until the 1960s the UN stuck to the Charter principle of non-interference in the internal affairs of states. In the wake of the 1967 Six-Day War, the UN General Assembly (1967) resolved that "essential and inalienable human rights should be respected even during the vicissitudes of war." The 1968 Teheran Conference on Human Rights decried the failure of the Hague and Geneva Laws to deter or prevent war, declaring that "peace is the underlying condition for the full observance of human rights and war is their negation" (Human Rights in Armed Conflict 1968). The Teheran Proclamation (1968) noted that "Massive denials of human rights, arising out of aggression or any armed conflict with their tragic consequences, and resulting in untold human misery, engender reactions which could engulf the world in ever growing hostilities. It is the obligation of the international community to cooperate in eradicating such scourges." In September 1970 the Secretary General concluded that human rights instruments "may prove of value in regard to periods of armed conflict," thus anticipating the reporting practices of the Human Rights Committee. That December the General Assembly affirmed that "Fundamental human rights, as accepted in international law and laid down in international instruments, continue to apply fully in situations of armed conflict" (Droege 2008:505).

During the 1970s "human rights in armed conflicts" became "one of the most popular phrases in the United Nations political vocabulary" (Suter

1976:394). Reflecting general humanitarian sentiment but not the details of rights, the idea helped to rally diplomatic support for the 1977 Additional Protocols. In the 1980s human rights protections were wedded to the expanding peacekeeping efforts. The Declaration of Turku (1990), a private initiative geared toward "situations of internal violence, disturbances, tensions and public emergency" was integrated into UN rhetoric and sometimes practice.[18] The Declaration saw human rights and humanitarian law as the warp and woof of norms designed to "protect the rights of groups, minorities and peoples, including their dignity and identity" (Declaration of Minimum Humanitarian Standards 1995; Droege 2008:7). More recently, "human security" (as opposed to national security) has been the coin of the realm. Since 2000, the UN has adopted more than 300 resolutions upholding human rights in the midst of armed conflict, and UN agencies continue to affirm the salience of human rights laws to the conduct of war and occupation (Doswald-Beck 2013:140).

While the UN has instituted some enforcement mechanisms, it generally has proceeded cautiously, elaborating IHL rather than supplanting it with new human rights laws.[19] States still dominate the process. Several UN human rights treaties allow individuals to lodge complaints against states, though only if the target state recognizes the competence of the UN to receive individual complaints. The UN is often slow to recognize and respond to crises. The Security Council did not adopt a thematic resolution on civilian protections until 1999, at the end of a decade marked by ethnic cleansing and genocide. Since then, Secretaries-General Kofi Annan and Ban Ki-moon both have criticized the UN failure to adapt to the changing character of war, though the issue remains shackled to the broader question of humanitarian intervention and the protection of civilians, or "PoC." Even as the UN extols the civilian idea, its own humanitarian aid missions often "struggle over what it means for a peacekeeping operation to protect civilians, in definition and in practice" (Roberts 2009:47).

The trajectory is similar at the Human Rights Commission, the principal forum for UN human rights diplomacy. The Commission was established in 1946 and reconstituted as the Human Rights Council in 2006. For years, the Commission saw and heard no evil. Out of deference to member states it failed to condemn genocide in Cambodia, mass murder in Uganda, and state terror in the Central African Republic. Sotto voce criticism of the Tiananmen Square massacre and Sudan's genocidal murders brought the Commission no honor either. But in other cases the Commission/Council has deputized a stream of special rapporteurs, experts, and others to investigate human rights abuses in war. Rapporteurs have been barred entry, deported, harassed, and denounced. They've also made a difference, spotlighting specific allegations as well as general themes: distinction and proportionality, targeted killing, drones, airstrikes, blockades, mercy killings, cluster bombs, perfidy, human shields, urban counterinsurgency, and reparations (Report of the Special Rapporteur on Extrajudicial, Summary or Arbitrary Executions 2010; Alston, Morgan-Foster, and Abresch 2008). The Council is still dogged by controversy, most recently over the Goldstone report on the Gaza war and, to a lesser extent, the Alston report on drone warfare. But overall its calendar looks like Max Weber's slow boring of hard boards: seeking to curb the use of child soldiers, diminish sexual violence during armed conflict, rein in abuses by mercenaries, stop summary executions, end forced displacement of populations, strengthen national human rights institutions, and develop a body of law to bind private military and security companies to protect human rights.[20]

Constituting Civilians

Human rights norms don't merely shore up noncombatant immunity against military necessity. They also constitute civilians around extramilitary human rights norms, establishing the identity and status of civilians within a rights framework. The Oxford English Dictionary defines constitutive principles as those "having the power of constituting, establishing, or giving formal, definite, or organized existence to something." Human rights norms, like all norms, establish what Ward Thomas (2001:17) calls "matrices of meaning" that help us make sense of the world. "Hard" laws and institutions as well as "soft" social ideas and practices fix boundaries and set expectations. People who were exposed to violence are now protected. Acts once considered unremarkable are set firmly beyond the pale.

The idea that civilians should be protected in wartime is, at least in the abstract, an undisputed norm. Derived from classical ideas of mercy and restraint and given moral depth by the just war tradition, protecting civilians has arguably become the linchpin of modern humanitarian norms. Clearly, this isn't enough. The laws of war have been refined and reinforced, and humanitarian sentiment is running high, yet civilians continue to bear the brunt of war. New wars have become the new killing fields. Since 1990, some eight million civilians, most of them in central Africa, have died from the direct and indirect effects of war.[21] As many as 100 million people have been driven from their homes or countries. According to the Office of the UN High Commissioner for Refugees (UNHCR), at the end of 2014, 60 million people, half of them children, were displaced by war and persecution. A record 14 million people—many from Syria, South Sudan, the Central African Republic, Ukraine, Pakistan, and Myanmar—were newly displaced in 2014 (Sengupta 2015).

The scale of violence and dispossession reflects the persistence of anti-civilian ideologies as well as the sheer vulnerability of noncombatants in modern conflicts. From Bosnia to Burundi, civilians have become instruments and objects of violence: as strategic targets, targets of intimidation and terror, victims of collective punishment and reprisal, or of racial or ethnic hatreds. While the overall number of armed conflicts has declined since the early 1990s, one-sided violence against civilians, mostly committed by states, has grown (Stepanova 2009; Eck and Hultman 2007:237). Liberal militaries that ostensibly distinguish between soldiers and civilians also kill large numbers of noncombatants. Daniel Rothbart (2012:115) argues that the militaristic framing of war fuels "civilian objectification," often with lethal results. Martin Shaw (2004) says that "direct killing of civilians by Western forces has become a normal feature of recent campaigns." New tactics and technologies, the allocation of risk between combatants and noncombatants, and expansive definitions of what constitutes active participation in hostilities all put pressure on the civilian idea. In high-mobility operations there often isn't time to warn civilians of impending attacks; airstrikes penetrate ever deeper into densely populated urban spaces; the power of explosives keeps expanding; bomber aircraft, land mines, mortars, and machine guns have proliferated; counterinsurgencies are fought in close civilian quarters (Fellmeth 2008:455).

The toll also reflects the shifting boundaries of what constitutes legitimate violence in wartime. Civilian protections have ebbed and flowed, but there is no paradise lost. European set-piece wars are considered the high-water mark in this history, but those too could be nightmares for noncombatants. Most tableaux of the Thirty Years' War, for example, depict uniformed soldiers squaring off on neatly groomed battlegrounds, but Jacques Callot's "Miseries of War" etchings (1633) present a truer picture of the plunder and abuse of noncombatants, the displaced masses huddled in cities, the war-borne disease that depopulated Europe in the seventeenth century. If chivalry wore thin in Europe, it failed completely in overseas wars of conquest and occupation. Industrialized warfare has been horrific, civil wars grim, state-building campaigns brutal. Norms break down as wars wear on. Atrocities spike as one side gains predominance and the other side is less able to retaliate (Dunoff and Trachtman 1999).

The civilian can seem like a pure Platonic form, essential for understanding but forever out of reach. Historians wince at references to civilians as stock, decontextualized figures. Geoffrey Best (1980:285) says the "classic clarity of the textbook categories" can strike soldiers and resistance-minded individuals alike as "incredible." Religious ethicist James Turner Johnson scarcely uses the word in his works on the just war tradition. "The functional role of civilians in war has differed not only over history," he observes, "but also from culture to culture and even, within a culture, from one armed force to another" (Johnson 2000:445). The term was first used in treaty law in a single reference each in Hague II (1899) and Hague IV (1907), in chapters dealing with spies. It appears 28 times in Geneva Convention (IV) Relative to the Protection of Civilian Persons in War (1949), and some 200 times in the Additional Protocols (1977).

While indispensable to any discussion of modern war, "the civilian" has yet to evoke a definition beyond that of a noncombatant: someone who does not take an active part in hostilities, or someone who is not currently taking an active part in hostilities. Civilians are defined in the negative. The Geneva Conventions consider combatants as members of state (or, under the Additional Protocols, non-state) armed forces who are under command control, wear a uniform or other distinctive emblem recognizable from a distance, carry arms openly, and follow the laws and customs of war. People who take up arms to fight off an invading force but who are not yet organized militarily are also considered combatants. Everyone else is a civilian.

Defining civilians as noncombatants comes at a cost. Making combatants the prime referent deprives civilians of a positive identity to buffer them from violence. Upholding the autonomy of civilians is critical as legal interpretations of active participation creep toward non-material and non-military support. A negative definition also heads off serious consideration of the civilian idea itself (Kinsella 2011:6). To be a civilian is to pursue the positive goods of civilian life free of coercion and fear. Finally, the approach narrows what protection means. Merely refraining from targeting civilians as though they were combatants eclipses other, more affirmative interpretations of the law.

Of course, combatants and noncombatants are not always as distinctive as the laws of war suppose. As Helen Kinsella (2011) wonderfully puts it, the civilian represents "the image before the weapon"—the soldier's view of the person standing before him. The soldier thinks, "I will not harm you because you do not appear to pose me harm." That view (and the even more myopic view held by state and society back home) is undoubtedly colored by the mode of war, tolerance for risk, and the interests believed to be at stake, not to mention fear and loathing and other pathologies of war. The image rarely reflects the civilian's own account of herself and her case for protection: "I'm studying to be a nurse." "I'm on my way to see a friend." "My family needs me." At that moment, the civilian looks less like a right-holder laying claim against a duty-holder than a subject kneeling before the sovereign, pleading for mercy.[22]

Today, certain ideal types of civilians are safely beyond dispute, at least as objects of direct violence. But others face ambivalence or even hostility. UN Human Rights Council Special Rapporteur on Extrajudicial, Summary or Arbitrary Executions Philip Alston notes "a tendency to expand who may permissibly be targeted and under what conditions" (UN Human Rights Council 2010b). Distinguishing between civilians and soldiers is often presented as a matter of specialized knowledge and expertise, further insulating tactical choices and targeting decisions from critical scrutiny (Winter 2011:506). Belligerents of all types would cast people outside the protection of the law. Many exclusionary practices stem from what Frédéric Mégret (2006:268) calls the "anthropology of savagery." Civilizational or religious wars, and nationalist, ethnic, and separatist strife are framed to exclude even the possibility of rights. Kant himself dismissed "lawless savages . . . devoid of right" (Reiss 1996:165). Unruly subjects are demonized as "rebels," "bandits," or "terrorists" in order to deny them formal belligerent status and restrict protections accorded them (Bhatia 2005). Sometimes the labels fit, but the same broadsides are leveled at sympathizers and supporters, even whole peoples, paving the way for collective punishment.

Particular modes of war further delineate civilians and the rights they ought to hold. The assumptions of set-piece battles differ sharply from those of partisan warfare, peasant uprising, or the *levée en masse*, for example. Turney-High's *Primitive Wars* (1991:23) argued that a proper army is organized and purposeful: "true war" involved tactics, command and control, sustained campaigns, a clear motive, and adequate lines of supply. Informal warfare, on the other hand, entailed little more than "face-painting and sporadic butchery"—something you'd read about in *National Geographic* rather than *Jane's Defence Weekly*.

In contemporary warfare, high strategy and advanced technology continue to frame civilian losses as unavoidable tragedies. After all, the best technology was used to try to avoid these "accidents" (T. Smith 2002b; Owens 2003; Zehfuss 2011). If an army believes that civilians inevitably will be caught up in insurgency or separatist strife, complacency settles over efforts to improve their lot. Strategic-legal categorizations erode the rights of detainees, too, both the meticulous classification of "high-value" suspects and the anodyne treatment of low-value ones. For a time in Iraq, the U.S. adopted the term "person under control," or "PUC." Political philosopher Giorgio Agamben (2005:3) described these people in limbo as "legally unnameable and classifiable being[s]. . . . Neither prisoners nor persons accused, but simply 'detainees,' they are the object of a pure de facto rule."

The Depth and Detail of Rights

The specificity of rights helps to counteract this dehumanization. Rights defenders have always married high principle to a detailed catalogue of abuses. In the sixteenth century, the Dominican friar Bartolomé de las Casas (1552) pleaded for the dignified treatment of indigenous Americans on grounds that they were rational beings in the eyes of God. His theological claims were rounded out with lurid details of the *conquistadores'* crimes, "the horrid and unexampled massacres, butcheries, and all manner of cruelties, that Hell and Malice could invent." This kind of graphic narrative remains the stock in trade of human rights advocacy. Human rights methodologies—site visits, surveys, hospital records, monitoring, and public reporting—are similarly almost ethnographic in their concreteness and detail (O'Flaherty and Ulrich 2010; Jacobsen 2008).

The laws of war set specific rules covering a range of issues, from respect for cultural property, to the treatment of human remains, to the release and repatriation of prisoners of war. However, the closer one gets to core questions of strategy and necessity the more general the rules become (M. Schmitt 2007). But it is also true that international norms are constantly being tested and revisited as general rules collide with particular cases. So it is with the rules of war, where principles of proportionality or military advantage are often hard to square with the actual consequences on the ground (Sandholtz 2008).

Consider the targeting or commandeering of schools by armed forces. Schools are classic civilian structures. But because they tend to be centrally located and solidly built, belligerents often use them as barracks, weapons depots, firing positions, or detention and interrogation centers. The laws of war allow combatants to use schools for military purposes—rendering them military "objects" and thus legitimate targets of attack—as long as the building is not simultaneously being used for educational purposes. Note how quickly and *legally* schools are militarized. By allowing belligerents to transform a school into a barracks or a weapons depot, IHL effectively trumps the children's right to an education. "Guaranteeing the right to education is rarely a priority, or even a consideration, for armed forces and armed groups engaged in fighting," notes the Global Coalition to Protect Education from Attack (2012:55). "Even those armed forces that pride themselves on their knowledge and compliance with the laws of war may be unaccustomed and unfamiliar with the idea of having to take into consideration children's rights or economic and social rights when planning maneuvers and tactics for the battlefield."

This isn't to say that IHL is callous or uncaring. The law forbids categorically deliberately targeting schools as such. But protection ultimately hinges on operational rather than humanitarian demands, in the sense that schools are not protected from being militarized in the first place. By contrast, human rights focuses less on the intentions of those targeting or taking over schools and more on the actual consequences for students, teachers, and the community. A student described to Human Rights Watch how his school in Jharkhand state, India, had been blown up by Maoist fighters in 2009:

> The school has been damaged. There is no education happening here. There are no teachers, no instructors, no benches, no fans, nothing. The whole building has been ruined. The windows are smashed and blown. The floor is cracked, [and] so are the walls and ceiling. Even the door is broken. Everything is in ruins. (Human Rights Watch 2011:5)

Across the wartorn areas of the Middle East and North Africa, 13 million students—40 percent of the school-age population—were out of school in 2015. In Syria, Iraq, Yemen, and Libya, nearly 9,000 schools were closed because they had been damaged or destroyed or seized by belligerents or converted to shelters for the displaced (Gladstone 2015). In Syria the physical and bureaucratic school infrastructure has collapsed, leaving approximately 2 million children out of school. A fifteen-year-old boy noted the irony of seeing his schoolhouse turned into an interrogation center:

> Some men came to our village. I tried to escape, but they took me to jail. Except it wasn't a jail—it was my old school. It's ironic—they took me there to torture me, in the same place I used to go to school to learn. . . . They had taken over the school and made it into a torture center. (Global Coalition to Protect Education from Attack 2012:8)

A Syrian refugee living in Lebanon recalled,

> students don't go to school, because when they did there were shells—I think they targeted the school because shells fell all across it. Students were leaving to go home in the afternoon when it started and two children died—they were both very young. I am in ninth grade but this war stopped me from graduating and now my future is destroyed. (UNESCO 2013)

These impacts have rippled across the region. Among Syrian refugees in Lebanon, Jordan, and Turkey some 700,000 children are not enrolled in school. The High Commissioner for Refugees described "a generation of traumatised, isolated, and suffering Syrian children" (Onishi 2013; UNHCR 2013). Detail and data underscore what is at stake: the safety of students and teachers, school enrollment and retention rates, and successful educational outcomes that open the doors to children's aspirations. As rights tap into this local knowledge the life-shattering effects of war come into focus. Without the structure and path to the future that schools provide, children are more likely to fall into radicalism and violence. Parents are apt to pull girls and young women in particular out of school, and it can take years to make up for lost education and training.

Or take the case of drone warfare. Many humanitarian lawyers have expressed skepticism about the risk-free nature of drone-based missile attacks and the "moral disconnections" of remote killing (O'Connell 2012; Whetham 2012). But the strategic frame of reference is constant: Were the people killed or wounded militants? Was the intelligence accurate? Will the attacks advance the overall war effort? This line of questions framed the discussion in terms of the capabilities of the drones and the intentions of their far-distant operators rather than the actual effects on people on the ground.

Human rights analysts paint a more visceral picture of the violence. U.S. drone activity is most active in Pakistan, Afghanistan, and Yemen. Drone attacks include both "named" strikes that target identified individuals or groups, and "signature strikes" or "Terrorism Attack Disruption Strikes," in which the drones hover overhead while their operators look for suspicious "life patterns" that would indicate planning or participation in terrorism. Both kinds of strikes are conducted with deliberation and care, but there is always a danger of imposing a predetermined pattern on ambiguous circumstances (Cockburn 2015:15–16). Misidentifications and mis-strikes are routine. Wedding parties, family gatherings, and work details have all been struck. To some degree these "accidents" are driven by policy, particularly the working assumption that males of military age found in the vicinity of a suspected militant are themselves involved. Because of a tactic known as the "double tap" in which the targeted site is struck multiple times in relatively rapid succession, people are often afraid to help the wounded or collect the dead.

Life in the shadow of drones narrows. Residents are afraid to go to school, to attend weddings or funerals, or to gather for *jirga* councils. Particular rights are abridged: the right to life, but also the rights to assemble, to work, to be educated, to observe social and cultural traditions, and so on. Authorities rarely investigate attacks, much less acknowledge the harm victims suffer, or provide remedy or redress.

The psychological effects of drone warfare are pronounced. The incessant circling of drones overhead affects everyone under their gaze. (In Gaza, the slang word for drones is "zananas," an Arabic word for a bee's buzz.) The largest human rights survey of drone violence in Pakistan's North Waziristan Agency to date was conducted in 2012 by researchers from the International Human Rights and Conflict Resolution Clinic at Stanford University Law School, and the Global Justice Clinic at New York University School of Law (2012). Witnesses described the "constant and severe fear, anxiety, and stress" of living under drones, especially given the helplessness to ensure their safety (55). A psychiatrist described it as "anticipatory anxiety" (81) over the ever-present possibility of a strike wedded to the impotence to do anything about it. Villagers are at the mercy of the information and technology of the targeteers. One witness said the sound of the drones elicited "a wave of terror." "Children, grown-up people, women, they are terrified . . . .They scream in terror" (81).

> Everyone is scared all the time. When we're sitting together to have a meeting, we're scared there might be a strike. When you can hear the drone circling in the sky, you think it might strike you. We're always scared. We always have this fear in our head. (81)

> Drones are always on my mind. It makes it difficult to sleep. They are like a mosquito. Even when you don't see them, you can hear them, you know they are there. (83–84)

> When [children] hear the drones, they get really scared, and they can hear them all the time so they're always fearful that the drone is going to attack them. . . . Because of the noise, we're psychologically disturbed—women, men, and children. . . . Twenty-four hours, [a] person is in stress and there is pain in his head. (86–87)

> Our minds have been diverted from studying. We cannot learn things because we are always in fear of the drones hovering over us, and it really scares the small kids who go to school. (90)

Amnesty International's interviews with survivors of nine separate drone strikes in North Waziristan also highlighted these psychological impacts. "Children have lost their mental balance, they are afraid all the time," said a resident of the village of Zowi Sidgi, a transit point a few miles from the Afghan border, where eighteen men were killed and at least twenty-two wounded in a drone strike in July 2012 (Amnesty International 2013:33). On October 24, 2012, in Ghundi Kala, a sixty-eight-year-old woman named Mamana Bibi was picking okra in the family field when she was blown to pieces by two Hellfire missiles fired from a U.S. drone aircraft. A second strike followed several minutes later. The aircraft had hovered over the farm for perhaps two hours before unleashing the missiles: not exactly the fog of war. From the perspective of the villagers, the killing was completely arbitrary. "I wasn't scared of drones before," said the woman's eight-year-old granddaughter, Nabeela, "but now when they fly overhead I wonder, will I be next?" (Amnesty International 2013:7).

Terrified children, sleep disorders, traumatic stress, lives arbitrarily snatched away, residents paralyzed by fear: whether the drone strikes were legal or not is almost beside the point. A witness to the killings in Zowi Sidgi pleaded, "At least for the sake of human rights they should stop these drone strikes" (Amnesty International 2013:56).

Rights serve as a touchstone for what is right and wrong amid the turmoil. For its *People on War Report* the ICRC commissioned a survey of 13,000 combatants and civilians across 12 war-torn regions. The norms cited by the respondents centered around notions of human rights, "humanness," and "staying human." Certain kinds of conduct were wrong because they violated human rights and human dignity. Overall, 49 percent based their judgment on rights, by far the most common reason cited. Soldiers in Bosnia-Herzegovina referred to "a human rule . . . basically, human dignity is a stronger rule than any written one." "I know prisoners should be treated as human beings and not as animals"; "God forbid! I think that we're not on the level of such savages"; and "one of the battles we fought in this war was a battle to stay human." In Lebanon, respondents said war brought out "animal instincts," "which meant no respect for human rights" (ICRC 2000:14–15).

In the recent wars in Chechnya, human rights practices became "one of the only ways to recover the dignity Chechens had been so crudely deprived of." Lawyers in Moscow or London publicized abuses and helped victims petition the courts. But ultimately these were the Chechens' own claims. Documenting human rights abuses became "an organizing principle around which fears, anger, and disillusionment could coalesce and find new direction in a search for authenticity and truth" (Gilligan 2010:162). During the war in Sierra Leone (1991–2002), violence and displacement shattered many traditional social arrangements based on religion and patrimonial ties. A kind of creole, or localized rendering of universal right, took their place. This was especially true with regard to the just and fair treatment of "strangers," that is, people who had been displaced from the chiefdom of their birth, such as traders, migrant workers, or refugees.[23] In Pakistan, many victims of drone strikes have filed lawsuits against government officials for failing to protect their rights as citizens, including the right not be assassinated by a foreign government (Shah 2014). In Nepal, where civilians were squeezed between extortionist Maoists and heavy-handed government forces, public discontent has been channeled into a regenerative social movement led by a human rights clearinghouse known as the Informal Sector Service Center.

More surprising, human rights norms can transform the identity and interests of *combatants*. Rights become part of the normative culture in which belligerents think and act. As the reputation, or "audience," costs of violating rights rise, it becomes clear that military attitudes and practices are not completely dyed in the wool of *Realpolitik*. As researchers have shown in the case of the Convention on the Prohibition of the Use, Stockpiling, Production and Transfer of Anti-Personnel Mines (1997), for example, human rights and other civil society actors can mobilize to reverse basic military practices (Price 1998). Security communities can undergo similar transformations. In recent years, middle powers such as Canada and Australia have emerged as arbiters of humanitarian norms; that identity has infused their foreign and military policies. Although it struggled to square ends and means during its high-flying intervention in Libya or on the ground in Afghanistan, even NATO has arguably reinvented itself as a champion of civilian protections.

Normative and pragmatic motivations can also converge on rights. For much of the Iraq War, e.g., the coalition struggled to achieve military goals *and* protect civilians. In Afghanistan, however, civilian security was at the core of the mission. "What are we here for?," Brigadier General Larry Nicholson, the top Marine commander in Afghanistan at the time, shouted to his troops in the run-up to the Marja offensive in February 2010. "The people," the marines yelled (de Montesquiou and Riechmann 2010). This was not just parade ground zeal, but studied doctrine that protecting Afghan civilians from Taliban tyranny as well as from American bombs was the way to win. The quest to protect civilians and ostracize insurgents arguably led straight down the path of human rights—not just security and subsistence rights, but the civil and political rights of Afghans to order their own affairs. Some Pentagon brass sounded like evangelists for the Rights of Man, framing the war on terror as "a historic debate about the rule of law and human rights," as a U.S. marine reserve general put it (Serwer 2009).

This isn't to say that militaries don't push back. They do, sometimes ferociously. For institutions schooled in humanitarian law, the turn to human rights is not obvious. As we will see in the next chapter, states often cry foul, saying the turn to rights constitutes "lawfare," or legal overreach. Indeed, *violations* of human rights can become the norm. In the wake of the September 11, 2001 attacks, a number of signatories to the International Convention on Civil and Political Rights adopted repressive anti-terror policies or rebranded ongoing counterinsurgencies as more aggressive counter-terror operations (Darcy and Collinson 2009:6; International Commission of Jurists 2009). Still, while human rights may struggle for recognition, no serious discussion ignores them altogether. Even if states can legally derogate from certain of their human rights obligations in wartime, they can't escape the residual effect of rights. There's no covering up how people *should be* treated.

Human Rights and New Media

There's no covering up the abuses either. The civilian is a cause tailor-made for the media age. During the Vietnam War, U.S. Army combat photographer

Ronald Haeberle published his iconic photographs of the My Lai massacre 20 months after the killings. Released over the Pentagon's objections, the pictures—of women pleading for their lives, and of the contorted bodies of villagers, some belonging to infants, jumbled together on a dirt levee—first appeared in grainy black and white on the front page of Haeberle's home town newspaper, the Cleveland *Plain Dealer*. Today, digital images of atrocities circle the planet in seconds. A surge of visuality and viral outrage has been dubbed the "Neda effect," after Neda Agha-Soltan, a twenty-six-year-old student who was shot and killed by a pro-government sniper during a June 2009 street protest in Tehran. Several bystanders recorded her dying minute on cell phone cameras. One of the videos focuses on Neda's face. Her eyes turn from wide-open alarm to vacant as she bleeds out onto the pavement. Within hours, the video was uploaded on YouTube. By the end of the day it had become a "trending topic" on Twitter, and Neda's story was quickly picked up by other media. *Time* magazine called it "probably the mostly widely witnessed death in human history" (Mahr 2009). It was one of the sharpest indictments of the ayatollahs in thirty years of Islamic rule. Nicholas Kristof (2009) called the Tehran uprising "the quintessential 21st-century conflict. On one side are government thugs firing bullets. On the other side are young protestors firing 'tweets.'" The incident led to the quip: "Two mullahs gaze out on a crowd of protesters in Tehran. The one says, 'Arrest the correspondents.' To which the despondent reply is: 'But they're all correspondents!'" (Roger Cohen 2009).

New media serve as pathways for new norms. Charli Carpenter (2012) suggests that "the single biggest shift in the sociology of war in the past quarter-century has been not in the way it is fought, but in the relationship between its grim realities and the perceptions of those on the home front . . . the increasing visibility of ordinary warfare." This is partly the visual and narrative product of a new kind of "advocacy journalism" or "journalism of attachment" that isn't shy about taking sides in conflicts (Hammond 2002). But countless nodes of data also provide unprecedented exposure and access (Kaempf 2013). Video (sometimes called the other "air war") and jpegs are backed up by NGO reports, journalistic accounts, Freedom of Information Act (FOIA) documents, leaked or hacked information, data compiled by body-counters scouring news outlets, and up-to-the-minute local content. During the Iraq War an anonymous Baghdad blogger known as Riverbend (2005) became an internet celebrity as she chronicled the occupation through the eyes of ordinary Iraqis. Anyone could download an "Iraqi death estimator" in order to track, like a national debt clock, the mounting civilian toll.

Images have become almost the sine qua non to distinguish particular atrocities from the general tragedy of war. The Haditha killings came to light only after a videotape of the bodies was circulated by the Hammurabi Human Rights Organization, an Iraqi NGO. The notoriety of the case of Baha Mousa, the hotel receptionist tortured to death by British soldiers in Basra, was almost guaranteed by the visual narrative that surfaced. The "before" images consisted of a one-minute movie taken on a soldier's cell phone at the beginning of Mousa's interrogation. The footage showed Mousa, hooded and handcuffed, being screamed at and forced into painful stress positions by the soldiers. The "after" images consisted of 46 autopsy photographs released at the inquest, including a close-up of the grotesquely bruised face of the dead Iraqi, two plastic tubes protruding from his mouth, apparently from an attempt to resuscitate him. Google "Baha Mousa" and that particular image appears, unbidden, on the results page, even before you click any of the links.

Public opinion can pivot on a seminal photograph. During the Yugoslav wars, sympathy for the Bosnian cause was galvanized almost overnight by Roy Gutman's *Newsday* stories and Britain's Independent Television News footage of gaunt Bosnian prisoners peering through the barbed wire of a Serbian concentration camp—echoes of the Holocaust. *New York Times* photographer Tyler Hicks's stunning images of four boys killed by an Israeli airstrike while they played on a beach in Gaza prompted one of the IDF's few formal investigations into the conduct of the war. Some images, such as the Abu Ghraib jpegs, reflect the naïve gaze of the tourist-as-torturer. Others are deliberately composed to create "witnessing publics"—not passive onlookers but responsible, implicated viewers forced to take a moral stand (Torchin 2006). Sharon Sliwinski's description of Francisco de Goya's harrowing etchings of the Napoleonic wars in Spain, "The Disasters of War" (1810–1815), could easily apply to many recent images from Bosnia, Darfur, or Iraq:

> Spectators are positioned to gaze upon these terrors from the viewpoint of a bystander. Each composition is carefully arranged as a fragile bridge between the spectator's perspective and the events occurring in the picture. The sense of proximity transforms the viewer into a witness . . . spectators are called into these scenes, summoned to face these terrible events *as if* they were present. (Sliwinski 2011:51)

This kind of image politics is central to the promotion of human rights. Pictures put a face on abuses, often training attention on individuals in a sea of suffering. Advocacy campaigns increasingly use locally sourced content remixed with global ideas. "See it, film it, change it" is the mantra of the Witness Project, whose "Cameras Everywhere" initiative sought to put movie cameras in the hands of people in the midst of conflicts.

This democratization of access and exposure has unsettled what had been the carefully managed visual landscape of war (L. Kennedy 2009). During the Vietnam War, General William Westmoreland decried the unfiltered television coverage of the first living-room war. "Without censorship," he said, "things can get terribly confused in the public mind" (quoted in Tsouras 2005:65). When the Abu Ghraib story broke in a flurry of digital photographs, U.S. Secretary of Defense Donald Rumsfeld lamented the difficulties of operating "in the information age, where people are running around with digital cameras and taking these unbelievable photos" (quoted in L. Kennedy 2009:817). Rumsfeld was worried that the Abu Ghraib pictures were being circulated in violation of the Geneva Conventions, which protect prisoners of war against "insults and public curiosity." But he was also watching the official narrative of the war slip away. It was impossible to reconcile a "humanitarian" war with photos of prisoners being humiliated and tortured by American M.P.s. (who are mugging it up for the camera). The pictures revealed what is usually unseen and unknown in wartime: the interior environments of detention centers, interrogation rooms, and prison cells, as well as the tools of torture—leashes, black hoods, dogs, chemical light tubes, broomsticks, electrical wire. Glimpses of the banality of abuse in situ made systematic torture seem all the more plausible (Whitty 2010:696).

Cameras are everywhere in today's wars. Overhead, drones, satellites, and remote sensing reveal panoramic effects of conflicts. This "human rights mapping" has identified artillery placed in civilian zones, mass executions and grave sites, homes targeted based on the ethnicity of the inhabitants, political prison camps, the removal of civilian populations, and the destruction of villages (Marx and Goward 2013). The UN monitors humanitarian crises via its proprietary UNOSAT satellite system, sometimes publishing images of events as they unfold—of civilian convoys fleeing Chad's war-riven capital N'Djamena in February 2008, or of pockmarked fields where the Sri Lankan Air Force bombed a civilian "safe haven" in spring 2009. The technological capabilities of NGOs to remotely monitor conflicts now outstrip the capacity of many state governments. Amnesty International's "Eyes on Darfur" project shows before-and-after satellite photographs of villages burned and depopulated by the Janjaweed. Working with experts from the American Association for the Advancement of Science, Amnesty has used similar geospatial technologies to convey displacement and destruction in the Swat Valley in Pakistan, in Kyrgyzstan, New Orleans, Sri Lanka, Chad, Georgia, Lebanon, Burma, Congo, Ethiopia, Nigeria, Syria, and Burundi.

Images from the front line convey the day-to-day reality of war, the visceral as well as the mundane. These are YouTube wars (N. Cohen 2010). Soldiers upload combat videos to the web; e-mail souvenir jpegs to friends; tweet from the war zone; or post text and image on "milblogs." Much of this content humanizes military experience, showing the decidedly anti-heroic life of the enlisted man or woman. But other images show spectacular levels of violence. One clip filmed by U.S. ground troops in Iraq showed two airstrikes on a large, apparently new, mosque that possibly had been used by insurgents as a firing position or a weapons cache—the video gives no context. The first missile flattens the main body of the mosque; the second explodes the minaret. A billow of dust lifts, and nothing but rubble remains. The ground soldiers seem awestruck. "Bad-aaaaas. That was sweeeeeet," says one.[24]

With this much information in play, media management teams can't be far behind. Belligerents marshal evidence and tailor information much like public relations firms. In 2007 the U.S. Department of Defense launched its own YouTube channel, MNFIRAQ (Multi-National Force—Iraq) ("the clips are ours, the conclusions are yours"). The site offered what it called a "boots on the ground perspective on the war," but the propagandist's hand is also evident in the selective focus on American soldiers engaging in clean combat and aiding local Iraqis (Andén-Papadopoulos 2009:923). At the low end, combatants organize on Facebook and proselytize on Twitter. With barriers to entry virtually nil, it's a rare insurgent movement that doesn't have a web site. Heightened visibility has increased the propaganda value of the other side's targeting errors or collateral damage. Davids fighting Goliaths often seem perfectly willing to draw their brothers and sisters into the fight in hopes of making them, willing or not, front-page martyrs for the cause (Skerker 2004).

During the Gaza Wars, Hamas and the Israeli Defense Forces (IDF) waged breaking-news media offenses. Both sides plied the internet with blogs, YouTube, and Facebook. An IDF "vlog," or video blog, provided a running narrative of Israeli restraint and precision in contrast to Hamas's reckless and deliberate endangerment of civilians on both sides of the conflict. In one clip, a Hamas fighter, gun slung over his shoulder, dashes across a street carrying a young boy as a shield against Israeli snipers.[25] In another, unexpectedly gruesome, YouTube skirmish, the IDF and Hamas accused each other of deliberately slaughtering animals in the Gaza Zoo: animal rights meet modern warfare.

Very different sorts of images are found on the so-called "war porn" websites. Billed as an unedited look at war, the sites feature soldiers' photographs of severed arms, legs, or fingers, spilled intestines, or decapitated heads ("headshots," in the posting lingo), often accompanied by crude or flippant remarks ("name this body part"; "that's gotta hurt!") as well as technical chat about what kind of weapon likely caused the damage depicted. This is the digital flotsam of today's wars. But many soldiers who post pictures or contribute comments say the images force viewers to reckon with the true costs of war; that they're a corrective to conventional media coverage that sanitizes war as a matter of decency and taste. "Maybe then the public will not be so rah-rah about killing people," noted a user named "some more gore from the Q" (quoted in Andén-Papadopoulos 2009:924).

Of course, information and images of this sort are easy to manipulate. Iconic photographs mislead by abstraction and saturation. Some images go viral while others languish. Information activism has its moral hazards, too. Susan Sontag (2003) reminds us that a barrage of war images can be overwhelming and paralyzing. The privacy and safety of those uploading pictures can be put at risk (images and audio leave digital traces that can be used to identify the originator). Spin is endemic. While information broadcast by human rights groups usually adheres to certain standards of proof, user-generated and edited content usually doesn't. Images are often shorn of context. Truth can dissolve in a mash-up of borrowed jpegs and bad information. On the user end, shallow "clicktivism" can replace meaningful study and engagement (Witness 2011; Carpenter 2012).

Greater transparency won't of itself lead to greater accountability or better human rights outcomes. But the ubiquity of new media makes it more likely that the truth will out and that we will have a more detailed and less curated grasp on the reality of war. WikiLeaks was able to obtain, decrypt, and post on YouTube a 38-minute audio-video clip filmed from the turret of a U.S. Apache helicopter that showed the killing in July 2007 in the Iraqi suburb of New Baghdad of 18 people, including two Reuters journalists, by a burst of rounds fired from the gunship's 30 mm cannons, followed by attacks on a van attempting to rescue the wounded.[26] The gross disparity of power, combined with the callous banter of the gunners during the killings, makes the video disturbing to watch. Even taking into account the fact that one person on the ground appears to be holding an RPG rocket launcher and that a 3-minute version of the video was misleadingly edited, the episode belied official assurances that all the victims were confirmed militants, and cast doubt on the overarching U.S. narrative about the care and precision of attacks. After Pentagon officials defended the killings as within the rules of engagement (ROE) in force at the time, WikiLeaks posted classified versions of the ROE to suggest that wasn't the case either.

The Power of Human Rights

The obstacles to realizing human rights in war are many: deference to the war powers of executive branches, push-back from militaries, and the view that vital issues of national security are ultimately beyond the reach of "peacetime" laws, just to mention a few. Human rights continue to combat the frankly militaristic idea that an acceptable measure of civilian harm is unavoidable and even expected in contemporary war. The more axiomatic and self-evident that belief becomes, the harder it will be to pursue brighter humanitarian hopes. Still, the currency of rights in international thought and practice is formidable and growing. Naturally skeptical of the exercise of power, unfettered by military mores, and singularly humanitarian in aim, human rights norms defend the continuity of rights in dark times, set a high threshold to infringe the right to life, and show healthy skepticism toward the recourse to war, and distrust, perhaps even incredulity, toward military claims regarding the conduct of operations. Rights bring the long-term and cumulative impacts of war into focus, highlighting the terrorization of people even by lawful attacks, and counting the true cost of war.

CHAPTER 2

Humanizing the Laws of War

> How dangerous it can be to be innocent.
>
> —Hannah Arendt (quoted in Owens 2007:72)

> . . . whatever it is that the law is after it is not the whole story.
>
> —Clifford Geertz (2008:173)

A human rights framework rejects the idea that war is a state of exception governed by a law unto itself. Rights protect human dignity "always and everywhere" (Provost 2002:19). The integrity and autonomy of the individual count in every case. To think of people in this way is to resist Thucydides's tragic maxim that "the dominion of imperious necessities" makes war a "hard master" (Thucydides 1881:222). It is to affirm the intrinsic value of civilians and civilian life. These are people with rights who cannot be used for some military purpose. Soldiers, too, have a right not to be used as cannon fodder (cf. Walzer 1977:137). Juxtapose these categorical imperatives with the more utilitarian designs of humanitarian law, and the law seems wanting. As Louise Doswald-Beck, former head of the ICRC legal division, notes (2004:356), the safeguards afforded by humanitarian law conventions "have now fallen behind the protection provided by HR [human rights] treaties." This is perhaps a *cri de coeur* from a field battered by new wars, but the rigor of rights does set them apart from the qualified protections available under the laws of war.

As noted, the idea that human rights are the law of peace and international humanitarian law is the law of war is hard to sustain given the character of today's conflicts. These tensions still crop up in the form of turf battles between the regimes, but more pragmatic developments are unfolding within the law itself. Considerations of strategy and victory continue to marginalize human rights, but ideas and practices associated with rights are nevertheless seeping into IHL, rendering it less technical and tactical, less deferential to reasons of state, and more in step with the suffering of the individual victims of war. As Marko Milanović puts it,

> The law applicable in war is no longer solely a law between sovereigns who agree out of grace and on the basis of reciprocity to limit themselves in their struggles to reduce the suffering of innocent people. Rather, human beings embroiled in armed conflict retain those rights that are inherent in their human dignity, which are more—not less—important in wartime than in peacetime. (Milanović 2011a:95)

Human rights and the laws of war have been loosely associated for decades, but it was not until the internecine carnage of the 1990s that the details of rights started to take hold in customary, and to a lesser degree, treaty law. The legal gap with regard to intrastate wars created an opening for rights, but so did the changing normative terrain. A web of NGOs, intergovernmental organizations and agencies, and progressive states pressed the issue. Human rights courts and ad hoc tribunals began to draw indiscriminately from both regimes. Law and activism have proved mutually constitutive. For example, a consortium of civil society and state actors lobbied the International Criminal Court into existence, albeit with the Court's legal powers—and its budget—derived through state consent. The ICC now stands both as a forum for adjudicating human rights and war crimes and as a referent for argument and debate about the pursuit of rights in other cases (Roach 2006). As we will see, the legal reach of rights is still hotly contested, particularly in asymmetric conflicts where the power of reciprocity has waned, though here, too, an increasingly coherent and pragmatic movement is pushing the debate in the direction of rights.

Humanity's Law

International humanitarian law has traditionally regulated the use of violence between states, while human rights law has protected people from abuse at the hands of their own governments. But the trend today is to view these two sets of norms and strands of law as complementary, as existing in tandem or in parallel, or as mutually reinforcing, like "belt and suspenders" (Schabas 2007). Human rights courts can adjudicate war crimes that might otherwise go unaddressed, or supplement IHL with extra conditions with respect to the use of force or the protection of noncombatants. Or the two regimes may operate along a continuum in which human rights law applies in milder "law enforcement" situations, but as threats and violence escalate the law of war takes over (T. Smith 2010:25).

Ruti Teitel describes this process of convergence and complementarity as "humanity's law." "The most pronounced change in the international legal system," she writes, is "the dramatic expansion of humanitarian law's reach through its merger with international human rights law" (Teitel 2002:359). This view is widely echoed by legal scholars and jurists. The late Theodor Meron (2006) lauded the humanization of humanitarian law under the influence of human rights. Hans-Joachim Heintze describes (2004:791) human rights law as "an intrinsic part of the legal rules governing wars and other emergency situations." The International Criminal Tribunal for the Former Yugoslavia (ICTY) noted "a slow but profound transformation of humanitarian law under the pervasive influence of human rights."[1] The Court observed in the *Tadić* case that "A sovereignty-oriented approach has been gradually supplanted by a human being-oriented approach."[2]

Enthusiasm sometimes gets ahead of practice, but there is little doubt that human rights now leaven humanitarian law in meaningful ways. The chemistry between the two regimes can be awkward, however. Where, after all, is the common ground between the dignity represented by rights and the tragedy represented by the "necessary" violence—including collateral violence against civilians—that is sanctioned by the laws of war? "On a normative level," notes Audrey Benison, "humanitarian law contemplates a starting point of death, violence, and destruction that is repugnant to the essence of human rights law" (Benison 1999:152). Bill Bowring describes IHL as "intrinsically conservative, taking armed conflict as a given." Human rights are much more eager to shake off the past. The idea of rights is "revolutionary, scandalous in its inception, inspired by collective action and struggle, and threatening to the existing state order" (Bowring 2009:5–6).

Each tradition traces a distinct provenance. From the start, the law of war was *military* law, a "contract between sovereign military powers" (A. Dworkin 2006:224). Book One, Chapter 1 of Grotius's *De Jure Belli ac Pacis* (1625) is titled "On War and Right," referring to the *jus ad bellum* right of states to launch wars. The "combatant's privilege" to take human life is as old as the law of war itself. The primary subject of the *jus in bello* has always been the reciprocal treatment of armed agents of the state and the preservation of their right, within limits, to kill in war. Rights tend to be bottom-up, while IHL tends to be top-down. Cordula Droege notes that humanitarian law "did not emanate from a struggle of rights claimants, but from a principle of charity—'*inter arma caritas*'" (2008:503). It confers protections upon us in the context of state power. As Draper (1998:125) observed of the Hague laws, "the powerful thrust of military considerations" is apparent. The individual is "an object of the law and not . . . a legal *persona* endowed with rights under the law of nations."

In short, IHL is "of" war: the laws that regulate the conduct of hostilities are designed to moderate but also to accommodate the pursuit of legitimate military ends. It revolves around an economy of violence which greatly values military necessity. The ICRC Commentary to the Additional Protocols notes that "necessity is the limit of legality. Any violence which exceeds the minimum that is necessary is unlawful and it is on this principle that all law relating to the conduct of hostilities is ultimately founded" (see Lamp 2011:232). The laws of war categorically forbid directly targeting civilians as such. But the right of civilians to be free from violence, indeed, the right of rights, the right to life, is a relative right, subject to operational demands, military advantage, and proportionality. For military lawyers, the central question with regard to collateral damage is: "Is it worth it?" Can incidental civilian casualties be justified by the military advantage anticipated? Depending on the military advantages at stake, the level of civilian harm can be high indeed.

Most striking is how elastic the idea is in practice, particularly on this question of proportionality. Here is then U.S. Secretary of Defense Donald Rumsfeld:

> Now the word "proportion"—"proportionate" is interesting. And I don't know that it's appropriate. And I don't know that I could define it. But it might be said—and I wouldn't say it—[laughter]—but it might be said by some that to quickly and aggressively repress a prison riot in one location might help dissuade people in other locations from engaging in prison riots and breaking out of prison and killing more people. I don't know if that's true. It might also persuade the people who are still in there with weapons, killing each other and killing other people, to stop doing it. It's—ah—your question's too tough for me. I don't know what "proportionate" would be. (quoted in Carmola 2007:93–94)

Secretary Rumsfeld was not just being coy. Yes, proportionality is a process of balancing, but the elements on the scale—"concrete" military advantage, force protection, the status of people, excessive or "clearly excessive" force—are themselves contested. The benefits and costs are forward-looking and speculative: *anticipated* advantages and *anticipated* casualties. The scale tilts sharply against civilians when belligerents see a mission as imperative or certain tactics as necessary. The apportionment of risk further undercuts the civilian idea. Modern militaries frequently place protection of their own soldiers on the scales, loosening rules of engagement or choosing munitions and tactics that reduce risks to soldiers but increase them for civilians.[3]

Eyal Benvenisti argues that armies construe their obligations narrowly in any case. "Armies interpret the law as granting them wide discretion," he writes. "They wish to limit the commanders' responsibilities rather than increase protection to civilians. They highlight the obligations imposed on the defending army. In applying the test of proportionality, they stipulate that the means used should be measured against the overall aim of winning the military conflict rather than against the particular aim of winning a specific battle. And this overall aim is defined subjectively" (Benvenisti 2006:95–96). Thus, while military lawyers may judge proportionality in terms of discrete attacks, human rights advocates will tally the cumulative effects of attacks or map broader patterns of excess. Land mines, cluster bombs, and depleted uranium munitions, for example, while legal for "approved" military use, can cause immediate as well as long-term bodily harm. Attacks on infrastructure or dual-use facilities having both a military and civilian purpose (communications networks, electrical plants, water treatment facilities) traditionally have been interpreted in immediate IHL terms, not with regard to long-run effects on human rights and public health.

This is not to say that IHL is putty in military hands. Some legal claims are persuasive and square with the current spirit of the law, while others overreach or fall flat. For example, U.S. officials, not very convincingly, have defended the use of targeted killings as necessary given the "imminent threat" posed, but cite a "flexible" or "elongated" concept of imminence to cover threats that are not, in fact, looming (Human Rights First 2013:2). The interests and inclinations of states tend to dominate the enterprise of IHL in any case. As Kretzmer (2009:27–28) notes, the law "never places an undue burden on the Parties to meet military necessity and to pursue their military purposes." States want as free a hand as possible while remaining within the bounds of the law and the aura of legitimacy. The law of war provides just such semi-restraint. As the British *Manual of the Law of Armed Conflict* puts it, "The law of armed conflict is consistent with the economic and efficient use of force. It is intended to minimize the suffering caused by armed conflict rather than impede military efficiency" (quoted in Waters 2008:33).

If the law of war is malleably utilitarian—even instrumental—in nature, particularly with regard to proportionality, it might be tempting to characterize human rights as categorical or deontological. Human rights certainly drive a harder bargain than IHL does. Some acts—torture or inhuman treatment, arbitrary killings, degrading public health, destroying the fabric of civilian life—are never worth it, regardless of the strategic advantages they might produce. But rights are also consequentialist. Like IHL, they, too, involve weighing and judging, only the utility sought is humanitarian and rescue-oriented rather than strategic. The calculus is this: the human rights benefits of using force must outweigh the human rights costs of using force.[4] How this plays out in policy and practice won't always be clear, but this caveat helps to steel the civilian idea. It sets a high threshold for the use of violence and ensures that wars undertaken for humanitarian reasons are waged as humanely as possible from the standpoint of those civilians on the ground who are most affected by it.

Humanitarian law and human rights are not always at loggerheads, of course. The two regimes overlap along a critical range of rights: due process and detainee rights, the prohibition on torture and cruel, inhuman or degrading treatment, and discrimination based on race, sex, language, or religion. But on the military terrain of strategy, human rights struggle to be heard. Not only does humanitarian law tend to be pliant, but its traditional priorities—the economy of violence, noncombatant immunity, the humane treatment of sick, wounded, and captured soldiers—eclipse the new priorities of human rights. Especially in high-tech campaigns, humanitarian law as lingua franca drives the discussion toward military issues of "correct" or "successful" targeting and whether means and methods of attack were sufficiently restrained, and away from the broader suffering wrought by war. What Pentagon press officer wouldn't rather see a story on GPS-equipped missiles than 1,200 words on declining public health or imperiled women's rights?

The interchangeable semantics of "law of war," or "law of armed conflict," and "international humanitarian law" gloss over these differences and contribute to the confusion. The public relations windfall of couching military operations in humanitarian terms is undeniable. But the term "humanitarian law" is ambivalent at best. Given the violence they license, the words are

"Orwellian," says Yale Law School professor Michael Reisman (Kretzmer 2009:21). Some strict constructionists reject the appellation "humanitarian law" in favor of "operational law," a term that captures the primacy of the military mission as well as the functional utility of the rules. As one U.S. judge advocate put it, IHL confuses "the end desired by the warrior with that desired by the humanitarian. True warriors are chivalrous, but their role is not humanitarian" (Morris 1997:13).

These tensions are becoming more acute, not less. An ambitious human rights agenda seeks, as Milanović (channeling Star Trek) says, "to (boldly) take human rights to places, be they extraterritorial situations or those of armed conflict, or both, where . . . no human rights have gone before" (Milanović 2011a:96). The introduction of rights has shaken up the field and weakened the authority of legal experts to define the legitimacy and justice of war. The (in)justice of the Iraq War, for example, was defined as much by the "folk" legal interpretations of global protesters as by the learned opinions of international lawyers (Reus-Smit 2011:340). Even liberal militaries resist "lawfare," or the use or abuse of law, particularly human rights law, in the midst of war. Liberal societies overwhelming expect their soldiers to minimize civilian harm, but often balk at the prospect of those same soldiers having to fight "with one hand behind their backs," as it's often put (more on this at the end of this chapter). Legal scholar Mark Osiel forecasts a "coming clash" between human rights and humanitarian law. Conflicts between the two regimes are "many and increasing," he says. They are "false friends" who have settled on a common humanitarian vernacular, but who hold starkly different ideas regarding the legitimacy and phenomenology of war (Osiel 2009:130, 127).

These differences come to the fore when human rights and military experts delve into specific cases. Noam Lubell (2005:745) notes that the communication barrier "includes not only words and terms, but . . . conceptual differences that can lead to contrasting ways of thinking and differing approaches to situations." Core concepts—the right to life, proportionality, military advantage—can mean one thing in IHL and another in human rights. During the Afghanistan and Iraq wars, Harvard University's Carr Center for Human Rights Policy convened a series of workshops with representatives from human rights NGOs and U.S. military officers and experts. The sessions revealed "a large, and in some important respects, widening, gap between the views of the human rights community and the U.S. military on the practical meaning of international humanitarian law" (Carr Center for Human Rights

Policy 2002:9). The basic vocabulary of IHL—necessity, proportionality, discrimination, military advantage—was often in dispute.

If human rights locate justice in the universal sphere, the law of war drags it back into the national orbit of interests and strategy. Rights seek to protect physical integrity and human dignity in all circumstances, in peace and in war, at home and abroad, in rebellions, uprisings, riots, and other civil disturbances. No category of people is excluded from its writ. The law of war, on the other hand, designates those people who are legitimate targets of violence and those who are not. It "seeks to legally determine who 'matters' and who 'does not,' and how, in situations of armed conflict, necessity operates within this reality" (Barnidge 2010). Making intent the moral fulcrum of war crimes further limits the reach of IHL. Loosely stated, humanitarian law focuses on the mind of the perpetrator, while human rights focus on the body (and mind) of the victim. To rise to the level of a war crime in IHL, an attack must be waged against noncombatants *as such* with deliberate intent to harm them. Human rights highlight civilian harm even in the absence of the *mens rea*, or "guilty mind," of the attacker. According to the 1998 Rome Statute which established the International Criminal Court, the ICC follows a middle path of individual intention and knowledge: "a person shall be criminally responsible and liable for punishment for a crime within the jurisdiction of the Court only if the material elements are committed with intent and knowledge" (Art. 30(1)).

This reliance on intent rather than outcome underpins much of the rhetoric of modern warfare. "Prosecuting targets," "revisiting the area," "softening resistance," "close air support"—this is the legally correct idiom of planners and press officers. A British air commander during NATO's campaign in Yugoslavia suggested that errant bombs had been "seduced off target" (quoted in Coady 2008:132). Even a passing glimpse of war from the perspective of its collateral victims is enough to deflate the pretentions of this kind of target-talk.

Avenues of redress are distinct as well. To the extent that they are adjudicated at all, breaches of humanitarian law are dealt with almost entirely at the state level. Virtually all are addressed within the military command structure, either through administrative channels or, far less frequently, the court martial system (Moffeit and Kane 2004). International war crimes tribunals allow and sometimes even encourage private individuals to submit evidence to international war crimes tribunals. The Office of the Prosecutor at the ICTY, e.g., maintained an e-mail address for tips and other information. But individuals have no standing to lodge or pursue claims of their own. Human rights courts do the exact opposite. They may rely on states for institutional support and funding, but cases brought by individuals against states are the lifeblood of the regime (Bowring 2009:6). At the ECtHR, for example, state-to-state cases are rare, but individual applications flow in by the thousands. The fact that IHL stands at a remove from the people it ostensibly serves has prompted human rights courts to broaden their writ:

> international human rights law benefits from an enforcement machinery that, for all its faults and limits, is still much better developed than what international humanitarian law offers. Victims, and their lawyers, often have no alternative to articulating their cases in human rights terms, as they can only bring them to international courts the jurisdiction of which is defined by human rights treaties. International courts have, rightly, avoided dismissing these cases outright, preferring to broaden the scope of human rights as previously understood. (Verdirame 2008:691)

Humanitarian law leads a double life, regulating war but also constituting war as a legitimate institution. The rush to violence is often clad in legal scaffolding. Kant famously dismissed the international lawyers of his day as "sorry comforters," "dutifully quoted in *justification* of military aggression" (Reiss 1970:103; emphasis in original). Just as chivalry distinguished between honorable and dishonorable uses of violence, modern rules of war prohibit some forms of killing and destruction but permit others. Legal scholar Frédéric Mégret (2012:19) calls IHL "a huge concession to the violence of the world as it is." The principle of noncombatant immunity serves to mitigate civilian harm, not to bar it altogether. The idea allows us to think of war as a legitimate, if tragic, practice (Zehfuss 2012:435). The strategic utility of violence, a principle that is carefully tended in the laws of war but which sits uneasily with human rights, comes through unscathed.

The law is anything but silent in time of war. Critical legal theorists (and International Relations "realists," for that matter) say that humanitarian law is instrumental, designed to burnish military pursuits, particularly those of powerful, technologically advanced states (T. Smith 2002b; Jochnick and Normand 1994). Modern war has become an elaborate legal institution. Lawyers weigh in on strategy as well as tactics. Judge advocates frequently embed with the troops as they make their way into battle. Particularly knotty targeting decisions are taken in close consultation with legal advisers. In this way legal rhetoric has become one of the "staple features of state practice on the use of force, so that when states use force against other states, they also *use* international law to define and defend, argue and counter-argue, explain and rationalise their actions" (Kritsiotis 2004:47). The law stands for moderation and restraint, but it other ways it functions as "part of war's machinery, not a rod in its wheels" (Burke 2007:140).

This fusion of strategy and humanity was codified early on. Consider the Lieber Code, *Instructions for the Government of Armies of the United States in the Field* (1863), adopted during the American Civil War and the first recitation of modern military law. In Lieber, notes James Turner Johnson (1981:305), "can be found a foretaste of future wars in which high moral purpose would be held up as excuse for ignoring some of the most time-honored and basic restraints of the just war tradition." Lieber did bar cruelty, torture, pillage, and rape; declaimed perfidy and bad faith; and protected churches, schools, hospitals, cultural sites, and scientific objects. It called on field commanders to spare unarmed, compliant civilians "in person, property, and honor as much as the exigencies of war will admit" (Art. 22). In the same breath, however, Lieber endorsed strategic necessity as that which is "indispensable for securing the ends of war" (Art. 14). He not only collectivized enemy civilians: "The citizen or native of a hostile country is thus an enemy, as one of the constituents of the hostile state or nation, and as such is subjected to the hardships of war" (Art. 21); but he also invited the decisive, indeed disproportionate, use of violence: "To save the country is paramount to all other considerations" (Art. 5); "military necessity admits of all direct destruction of life and limb of armed enemies, and of other persons whose destruction is incidentally unavoidable" (Art. 15); "the more vigorously wars are pursued, the better it is for humanity. Sharp wars are brief" (Art. 29).

Then, as now, clashes between formal and informal belligerents posed the greatest challenge. Lieber's code marked a bright line between "barbarous armies" and "modern regular wars of the Europeans, and their descendants," noting that "protection was, and still is with uncivilized people, the exception" (Art. 24). (U.S. soldiers accused of atrocities in the Philippines during the Spanish-American War would invoke the Lieber Code in their defense.) Nineteenth-century European law also codified customary restraints on the conduct of war, including the ban on directly targeting civilians, but it, too, privileged formal armies; the combatant's right to kill would not be usurped by amateurs. Those amateurs tended to be people living under the thumb of occupation or colonial rule. Thus, irregulars and insurgents—and with them any right of resistance—were cast outside the law. The French jurist Amédée Brenet wrote in 1902 that "our goal here is to humanize war, by which we mean to regularize it." Legal war would be preserved as a formal state pursuit in contrast to degenerate guerilla warfare, "which constituted a certain atrocity . . . the most terrible aggravation of war" (quoted in Nabulsi 1999:4).

The Hague Conventions (1899 and 1907) struck genuinely humanitarian notes. The Martens Clause in the preamble to Hague II (1899) invokes the "laws of humanity and the requirements of the public conscience." The Conventions, while high-minded, did not break conclusively with nineteenth-century law and practice. Crafted by the great powers in an age of empire, they were international, not universal. They would apply only to people within the "magic circle" of civilization (Mazower 2006:555, quoting Scottish jurist James Lorimer). Europeans fighting other Europeans would be held to a higher standard than Europeans fighting non-Europeans. In this sense, the Hague rules were the legal equivalent of Callwell's classic *Small Wars: Their Principles and Practice* (1899), a handbook for "expeditions against savages and semi-civilised races by disciplined soldiers" (Callwell 1903:1). Historian Stephen Rockel (2009:23) says the idea that "the laws of war could have any relevance in the process of imperial conquest would have been inconceivable to those planning it and carrying it out." That iron rule was not lost on state leaders. Several of the governments seated at the Hague Conferences were simultaneously committing some of the worst imperial atrocities ever recorded—completely out of sight of international law.

Lest the laws of war seem like the last refuge of Realpolitik (Geoffrey Best suggests that "International law writers usually look hard in the other direction whenever *raison d'Etat* is around"), they have made ever greater room for individual integrity and dignity. Best argues that as the law was systematized and codified, it lost touch with the "common stock" of humanity, becoming "increasingly tied to the rigidities of military thought and practice," but that the rising tide of rights has buoyed the humanitarian side of the law (Best 1980:17–18). The 1949 Geneva Conventions adopted a liberal, universal, tone. Common Article 3, for example, provided that civilians in international as well as domestic wars "shall in all circumstances be treated humanely, without any adverse distinction founded on race, color, religion or faith, sex, birth or wealth"; be free from arbitrary judicial sentences and executions; and be protected from "violence to life and person, in particular murder of all kinds, mutilation, cruel treatment and torture; taking of hostages; outrages upon personal dignity, in particular humiliating and degrading treatment."

The Additional Protocols (1977) have been described as "the world of humanitarian law pa[ying] tribute to the world of human rights" (Doswald-Beck and Vité 1993:113). They recast the 1949 Geneva Conventions in terms of rights. States traditionally had resisted international regulation of civil wars in order to maintain as free a hand as possible to quell uprisings and rebellions, and to deny rebels any formal legal status. The 1977 Protocols directly challenged those arguments. The Preamble to Protocol II applicable to non-international conflicts reminded the generals that "international instruments relating to human rights offer a basic protection to the human person, emphasizing the need to ensure a better protection for the victims of those armed conflicts." The Protocols not only strengthened civilian protections, they also extended combatant privileges to people fighting against colonial domination, occupation by outside forces, and racist regimes. Representatives of several national liberation movements were invited to participate in the negotiations (Roberts and Guelff 1982:387–88). All or part of the Additional Protocols have been ratified by 174 countries, with the United States, India, Israel, Pakistan, Iran, and Turkey notable exceptions.

Beyond *Lex Specialis*: The New Pragmatism

I suggested in the previous chapter that human rights are animated by specific ends, such as the right to life or the freedom of movement, while humanitarian law revolves around general principles of discrimination and proportionality. Nevertheless, humanitarian law enjoys pride of place as *lex specialis*, or "special law," the legal doctrine that particular rules trump general ones. The International Court of Justice (ICJ) has argued that rules derived for the special circumstances of armed conflict take precedence over human rights laws that apply in all circumstances. In the *Nuclear Weapons* Advisory Opinion (1996) the Court ruled that the human right to life, for example, does not vanish in time of war, but is fashioned to fit IHL:

> The protection of the International Covenant of Civil and Political Rights does not cease in times of war, except by operation of Article 4 of the Covenant whereby certain provisions may be derogated from in a time of national emergency. Respect for the right to life is not, however, such a provision. In principle, the right not arbitrarily to be deprived of one's life applies also in hostilities. The test of what is an

arbitrary deprivation of life, however, then falls to be determined by the applicable *lex specialis*, namely, the law applicable in armed conflict which is designed to regulate the conduct of hostilities.[5]

The ICJ's 2004 Advisory Opinion on Israel's separation barrier ("the wall") further refined the compass of human rights. The court rebuffed Israel's claim that human rights laws could not be applied in the context of war and occupation. After forty years of largely institutionalized occupation of the West Bank and Gaza Strip, there was little doubt the ICJ would find that Israel effectively controlled the West Bank and couldn't so easily shrug off its human rights obligations. The Court extended the idea of civilian suffering to include curbs on freedom of movement, and barriers to agricultural lands, water sources, means of subsistence, health services, educational establishments, and religious sites. Military strategy and tactics were also fair game. The Court held that the seizure of Palestinian lands to construct the wall was not militarily necessary, since less drastic methods could have achieved the same end. Still, the Wall opinion was clearer on jurisdiction than it was on substance. The exact provisions were left open, as "some rights may be exclusively matters of international humanitarian law; others may be exclusively matters of human rights law; yet others may be matters of both these branches of international law."[6]

The ICJ took an equally enigmatic stance in *Democratic Republic of Congo v. Uganda* (2005). The Court simply noted that "both branches of international law, namely international human rights law and international humanitarian law, would have to be taken into consideration."[7] The *Congo* ruling lists a wide range of applicable conventions—the Hague Laws, the Geneva Conventions, the Additional Protocols, the International Covenant on Civil and Political Rights, the African Charter on Human and Peoples' Rights, the Convention on the Rights of the Child, and the Optional Protocol on the Rights of the Involvement of Children in Armed Conflict—but the Court provided no guidance on how the norms should interact. Nor did the justices infuse IHL with human rights. Rather, they maintained the parallel worlds of the regimes, with human rights remaining in force, alongside, or, perhaps more likely, beneath, IHL.

The sharpest criticism of special law is that it forces human rights to play on the field of IHL. The idea that "the special rule is closer to the particular subject matter and takes better account of the uniqueness of the context" is a time-honored principle of law (Sassòli and Olson 2008:603). But in this case the uniqueness of the context didn't simply refer to the standard of force most apt when the infantry is pinned down by artillery fire or when a civilian approaches a poorly lighted checkpoint manned by a nineteen-year-old soldier hopped up on Red Bull and death metal music. It also means strategic context, military necessity, casualty aversion, risk apportionment, and so on. If we cast human rights in a secondary role, we miss the full impact of war on its victims. The breakdown of everyday life—the erosion of public security, economic suffering, rent social fabrics, failing public health, environmental degradation, displaced persons—becomes the wallpaper of war, a depressingly familiar backdrop to the main event, the "fighting" war in which proportionality and discrimination are more or less observed.

Over-deference to special law can leave states thinking they've shed their human rights duties altogether, even with regard to classic rights like due process, humane detention, and just punishment (Ben-Naftali and Shany 2003:56; C. McCarthy 2008:107). Defending its treatment of detainees in the war on terror, the George W. Bush administration argued that human rights didn't apply extraterritorially, and even if they did, they would be superseded by IHL. Some within the government argued that *humanitarian law* didn't apply because the adversaries were "unlawful enemy combatants," who did not respect the basic decorum of war. The administration eventually settled on special law. Testifying in 2006 before the UN Committee against Torture, John Bellinger, legal advisor to the U.S. Department of State, said, "Our view is simply that U.S. detention operations in Guantanamo, Afghanistan, and Iraq are part of ongoing armed conflicts and, accordingly, are governed by the law of armed conflict, which is the *lex specialis* applicable to those particular operations."[8] Special law was seconded by the U.S. Supreme Court, which ruled in the 2006 *Hamdan* case (a decision that studiously avoided any mention whatsoever of human rights) that Common Article 3 of the Geneva Conventions did apply to the Guantánamo detainees.[9]

Special law can become the rote military response to the turf challenge posed by human rights. "During combat operations," says the official *Rule of Law Handbook* for American judge advocates, "the U.S. regards the law of war as the exclusive legal regime or a *lex specialis* . . . [which] operates to the exclusion of competing legal frameworks such as human rights law" (Judge Advocate General's Legal Center and School 2009: 80). The 1,200-page *Department of Defense Law of War Manual*, published in 2015, has little patience for rights, endorsing the law of war (the manual's preferred nomenclature in place of the softer "humanitarian law") as "the controlling body of law with regard to the conduct of hostilities and the protection of war victims" (U.S. Department of Defense, Office of General Counsel 2015:901). Other times one finds grudging respect for rights. Remarkably, the U.S. Army's chief legal manual from 1956 said that the purpose of the laws of war was to safeguard "certain fundamental human rights of persons who fall into the hands of the enemy, particularly prisoners of war, the wounded and sick, and civilians." The manual concluded that observing human rights would ultimately "facilitate[e] the restoration of peace" (U.S. Army 1956:para. 2(b), 2(c)). Fifty years later, the *U.S. Operational Law Handbook 2006* stated that human rights obligations based on conventional international law "fall within the category of 'aspiration' rather than 'obligation,'" but that "human rights law based on customary international law binds all states, in all circumstances" (Grimes et al. 2006:50). The 2009 *Rule of Law Handbook*, the main resource for the military lawyers knowns as judge advocate generals, or JAGs, seems certain that human rights work: "Irrespective of the specific legal context, rule of law operations should be guided and informed by human rights law purely as a matter of efficacy" (Judge Advocate General's Legal Center and School 2009: 80).

Military views are not monolithic. Commanders have an absolute duty to see that their troops observe IHL, but they have latitude in identifying and handling breaches. Some JAGs see their role as "force multipliers" whose job is to facilitate rather than fetter violence. Lt. Col. Tony Montgomery, the judge advocate who approved the NATO bombing of the Belgrade television station during the Kosovo crisis, said "judges don't lay down the law. We take guidance from our government on how much of the consequences they are willing to accept" ("They are just covering their ass" 2001). Others take a more independent stand. Some of the most dogged critics of the detainee program at Guantánamo were the JAGs assigned to represent them before military commissions. Unit leaders see the law boiled down to rules of engagement, while commanders consider the broader impact of the law on strategic goals.

Proponents of special law say it is the only way to set clear standards for soldiers. The underlying concern is a serious one. Are the soldiers engaged in law enforcement? Military action? Something in between? As D. Kennedy (2006b:133) notes, "in today's asymmetric postcolonial wars, the terrain beneath a soldier's interpretations of what is and is not appropriate is constantly shifting." Then again, how IHL translates into practice isn't self-evident, either. The 2004 U.S. Army counterinsurgency manual noted that "all counterinsurgency operations comply with law of war principles to the extent practicable and feasible" (U.S. Department of the Army 2004:sec. j-4). Note the double dilution: the practicable/feasible qualification as well as the reliance on law of war principles rather than the law of war per se. As we've seen, precise definitions of military advantage and military necessity are elusive. So it's something of a red herring to say that soldiers will be left to translate "Delphic principles" of human rights into military reality (Garraway 2010:507). The image of soldiers entering the fray with copies of ICJ advisory opinions tucked under their helmet bands is misleading. Rather, human rights norms, like the laws of war, inform concrete policies and rules of engagement. These will vary according to the context and mission, but the overall impact is to push the rules toward stronger civilian protections by elevating humanitarian priorities and emphasizing individual dignity and integrity.

Until now, basic tensions between the regimes have meant that something had to give. In light of strategic pressures, institutional preferences, the historical sway of the laws of war, and near-universal public support for troop protection, that something has tended to be human rights. Canada's former Judge Advocate General, Brig. Gen. Ken Watkin (2004:32), for example, sees times when human rights should come into play; but in the end, human rights must bend to IHL. "International humanitarian law has its own standards for assessing the legality of using lethal force, so that human rights advocates will have to become more comfortable with both the scope of that law and its application to conflict." Mark Osiel (2009:130) says the regimes occupy separate "legal universe[s]," adding, "if either body of law has fair claim today to gobble up the other, it is surely humanitarian law, not human rights."

It should be clear by now that it doesn't have to be this way. Nothing in the DNA of humanitarian law makes it superior to human rights. As Orna Ben-Naftali and Keren Michaeli suggest, we should consider specific circumstances and choose the standard that offers the greatest protection to the innocent (Ben-Naftali and Michaeli 2003b:254; also see Sassòli and Olson 2008:603–4). Special law misses this give and take between the regimes. Scholars have argued for years that human rights should carry greater weight in internal conflicts, given the short shrift IHL accords civil wars. For the ICRC, the institutional guardian of humanitarian law, human rights are a cornucopia of humanitarian norms. The term "human rights" appears more than 4,000 times in the ICRC's massive 2005 study of customary law (see Henckaerts and Louise Doswald-Beck 2005a, b). The ICRC *conception* of civilian protections increasingly echoes that of rights as well: "assur[ing] that authorities and other actors respect their obligations and the rights of individuals in order to preserve the lives, security, physical and moral integrity and dignity of those affected by armed conflicts and/or other situations of violence" (ICRC 2008:9).

As a practical matter human rights give form and definition to general concepts of IHL. Rights offer a detailed blueprint of the right to life, fair trials, adequate investigations, and the treatment of detainees, as well as a range of issues affecting civilians living under military occupation or control: free speech, free association, free movement, the freedom to work, the right of asylum, property rights, and so on (see Moir 2003; Cryer 2010; Roberts 2006). With regard to child soldiers, human rights protections have eclipsed IHL. Under Additional Protocol II, children under fifteen may not be recruited or take part in hostilities. Human rights instruments set a minimum age of eighteen.[10] With the exception of the International Military Tribunal for the Far East (the Tokyo Trials), sexual violence and sexual slavery were not explicitly set out in the law of war until the war crimes tribunals for Rwanda and the Former Yugoslavia (Jacobsen 2008:561). Human rights NGOs tend to set sexual and gender-based violence within an additive legal framework of humanitarian law, human rights, and national and international criminal law (see, e.g., Human Rights Watch 2003c; Amnesty International 2004a,c; and Kippenberg 2005).

Human rights groups layer the details of rights onto their renderings of IHL, often stressing impacts of violence that get glossed over by humanitarian law. Human Rights Watch described breaches of IHL in Colombia's grinding civil war in unmistakable human rights terms: "Violations of international humanitarian law—the laws of war—are not abstract concepts . . . but the grim material of everyday life. War bursts into the daily activities of a farm, a village, a public bus, or a school with the speed of armed fighters arriving down a path or in four-wheel drive vehicles" (Human Rights Watch 1998c:1). A survey by Amnesty International of sexual violence against women in Colombia couched abuses in terms of racial, indigenous, and gender rights:

> The civilian population has increasingly become a victim in the internal armed conflict, not simply caught in the crossfire, but purposely targeted. This has above all affected those communities most at risk, whose voices are rarely heard: Afro-descendent and indigenous women, peasants, and shantytown dwellers on the outskirts of cities, many of whom are already displaced. Women's bodies have become marked as military targets, whether because they have not conformed to their "gender role," because they have challenged prohibitions

> imposed on them by the armed groups, or whether they are perceived as the "depositories" of the honour of a particular community and therefore a useful target on which to inflict humiliation on the enemy. (Amnesty International 2004b:8)

The regional human rights courts and the ad hoc criminal tribunals have led the way in articulating human rights standards of conduct. Yet even while ushering new law into the world, the courts have tended to be pragmatic, recasting IHL in terms of rights rather than rejecting or replacing it. Although the ECtHR is often panned for producing "Ivory Tower" rulings, in fact the Court usually tightens rules of engagement and other policies on the use of force that rest on humanitarian law in the first place (Gaggioli and Kolb 2007:124–27). For example, in the *Ergi* case (involving a civilian killed during a firefight between Turkish soldiers and PKK fighters), the Court ruled against Ankara even though the lethal bullet may have come from a PKK gun. Citing "defects in the planning and conduct of the security forces' operation," the Court argued that the responsibility of the state was "not confined to circumstances when there is significant evidence that misdirected fire from agents of the State has killed a civilian. It may also be engaged where they fail to take all feasible precautions in the choice of means and methods of a security operation mounted against an opposing group with a view to avoiding and, in any event, to minimizing, incidental loss of civilian life."[11] In *Isayeva* (relating to Russian air strikes against suspected insurgents traveling close to a column of refugees on a highway in Chechnya), the Court conceded Moscow's need to pursue "exceptional measures" in the war, and agreed that some degree of force was justified. While the attacks were plausible within an IHL framework, the Court concluded that they were not "planned and executed with the requisite care for the lives of the civilian population."[12] In *McCann* (involving the killing of three unarmed members of the Irish Republican Army by British SAS agents during a stake-out in Gibraltar), a divided court ruled that the design of the operation violated the right to life of the victims. Even if the soldiers believed it was necessary, even "absolutely necessary" to use deadly force "in order to safeguard innocent lives," the court's majority said the soldiers' snap decision to shoot to kill "lack[ed] the degree of caution in the use of firearms to be expected from law enforcement personnel in a democratic society, even when dealing with dangerous terrorist suspects."[13]

In other cases, reliance on rights introduces altogether new norms. The Israeli High Court of Justice (now the Supreme Court of Israel) in the

Targeting Killing case (2006) provided detailed guidance on targeted or "named" killings. Citing dozens of human rights precedents, the High Court insisted on discrimination and proportionality with regard to incidental civilian harm, but also went further, economizing violence in order to maximize the rights of all involved: "among the military means, one must choose the means whose harm to the human rights of the harmed person is smallest. Thus, if a terrorist taking a direct part in hostilities can be arrested, interrogated, and tried, those are the means which should be employed. . . . Trial is preferable to use of force. A rule-of-law state employs, to the extent possible, procedures of law and not procedures of force."[14]

Here a liberal rights norm reins in the idea that combatants can be targeted and killed at any time. Even if they comport with IHL, acts of war can't be severed from human rights standards of fairness and due process (Kretzmer 2005:186). Again, rights are not absolute. Apprehension and trial are preferable to targeted killing, but the resort to lethal force is still an option. The case also shows how tentative many of these advances are. Only four years earlier the same Israeli court said bluntly that military operational matters were "non-justiciable," or beyond the reach of the courts (Ben-Naftali and Michaeli 2003a). Nor has reliance on rights ironed out the controversy over such killings. Far from it. Targeted killings carried out by Israel within the 2006 framework remain highly contentious, and usually only scant details are available regarding specific cases.

Human rights advocates can find themselves torn between the utilitarian culture of humanitarian law and the purer ethos of rights. During the dirty wars of the 1970s, rights groups deliberately avoided the world of IHL, with its "strange and ambiguous (at least to human rights people) concepts such as 'collateral damage' and 'military necessity,' so that even something as apparently straightforward as the killing of civilians might, though regrettable, not constitute a violation of international humanitarian law." Relying on IHL could have unintended moral and legal consequences. In Northern Ireland, for example, human rights groups resisted condemning the killing of civilians by the IRA as a violation of humanitarian law rather than human rights law, lest this telegraph their approval of the killing of British soldiers, who might conceivably be targeted under the laws of war. Indeed, embracing IHL would signal that the conflict *was* a war, and thus legitimize the British government's "shoot to kill" policy in place of policies geared toward apprehension and arrest (Brett 1998).

Since the mid-1990s, however, a loose pattern has emerged. Human rights groups have tended to view low-end, internecine, conflicts through the lens of rights, while framing high-tech, "Western," wars in terms of IHL. For example, Helsinki Watch (later Human Rights Watch) viewed ethnic conflict in Yugoslavia as part of a chain of human rights violations that unfolded over time—from Serbian nationalists silencing press freedoms, to the early purges of ethnic Albanians in Kosovo, to the rise of paramilitary violence (Anderson 1990; Human Rights Watch 1991:602). Having reported from Yugoslavia across the 1980s under the Helsinki system, HRW did not recognize a clean break from peace to war, from human rights to humanitarian law (Helsinki Watch 1986). Even after the Croatian War broke out in 1991, HRW continued to view abuses largely in terms of rights (Helsinki Watch 1991). Amnesty International, too, translated the generalities of the Bosnian war into the details of rights. "War" or "ethnic cleansing" did not unfold as high strategy or pitched battles, but as a rash of killings, expulsions, disappearances, executions, extortion, terror and fear, illegal detentions, beatings, torture, and rapes, skewed investigations and snap trials, and all the daily harassments and humiliations of intercommunal strife (Amnesty International 1992; Amnesty International 1994; Amnesty International 1996a). Conflicts in Africa have similarly been framed in the language of rights. During the civil war in Burundi (1993–2005), for example, Amnesty and HRW both invoked IHL with regard to specific war crimes, but the driving narrative was the crippling effect on civilians (Human Rights Watch 2003a; Human Rights Watch 1998b). Rights coverage of the wars in the Democratic Republic of Congo (1996–2008) tended to reduce the conflagrations to digestible themes: children shanghaied into militias, rape used as a weapon of war, the vast number of persons displaced, and so on. Advocacy campaigns often focused on the massacre of a single village, or even a single family, lest the human costs of war be lost in a sea of statistics (see, e.g., Amnesty International 2009a; Human Rights Watch 2009b; and Refugees International 2013).

At a minimum, such conflicts "not of an international character" are governed by the Geneva Conventions Common Article 3. Maximalists say that many of the civilian protections of Additional Protocol I have passed into customary law and therefore also apply to all parties regardless how the war is categorized.[15] To be sure, IHL is critical in cases of discrete, prosecutable, war crimes. But in the absence of the kind of organization and command and control that traditional laws of war envision, analysts are drawn to rights. Humanitarian law seems almost too formal or event-specific to capture the extended terror and turmoil of societies engulfed by war. Whom do you court martial for the spread of infectious disease or a spike in infant mortality? Nor does special law do justice to the kind of endemic violence that can thrive in the limbo between war and peace. In Congo, for example, the Goma peace agreement formally ended the war in 2008, but there has been little distinction between war and peace since, especially in North Kivu, which is still rocked by waves of killing, displacement, looting, and sexual violence.

When it comes to modern, high-tech warfare, however, human rights groups have grown noticeably comfortable with humanitarian law. An early example is the Israeli incursion into Lebanon in 1996 known as Operation Grapes of Wrath. Amnesty's assessment of the seventeen-day air and artillery campaign did not discuss human rights at all (Amnesty International 1996b). Human Rights Watch's postmortem cited fundamental guarantees of human rights, but its analysis, too, relied exclusively on IHL. Much of the focus was on the IDF's shelling of the South Lebanon village of Qana, where more than a hundred civilians sheltering in a United Nations compound were killed. Both groups accused the IDF of deliberately displacing hundreds of thousands of civilians in order to pressure the Lebanese government to disarm Hezbollah. Under Article 51(2) of Additional Protocol I, "Acts or threats of violence the primary purpose of which is to spread terror among the civilian population are prohibited." Amnesty argued that the warnings were designed as threats, particularly the charge that "any [remaining] presence in these villages will be regarded as subversive" (Amnesty International 1997:9). Human Rights Watch concluded that the IDF language appeared "expressly intended to terrorize the population in the south" (Human Rights Watch 1997).

Ethnic cleansing on the ground in Bosnia was treated largely as a matter of rights, but NATO's 1998 air campaign was scrutinized mainly in terms of humanitarian law (Amnesty International 2000). Rights analysts often echoed military language and assumptions. Human Rights Watch conducted its first "battle damage assessment (BDA) mission" (HRW's own Pentagonese) to gauge damage to civilians and civilian objects caused by NATO's airstrikes (Docherty and Garlasco 2003:10). Research teams from Human Rights Watch have conducted BDAs in Afghanistan, Iraq, and Gaza as well, gathering ballistics evidence, mapping missile strikes, measuring debris spray and bomb craters, identifying shrapnel and pieces of cluster munitions, and interviewing soldiers and survivors. The technical expertise and detailed reporting that went into *Off Target: The Conduct of the War and Civilian Casualties in Iraq* (2003) were hard to ignore. The report identified patterns of misconduct and failures to exercise due care, but made no mention of human rights proper.

Other rights groups have analyzed accountability for abuses on the military's or CIA's own terms. Human Rights First's *Command's Responsibility: Detainee Deaths in U.S. Custody in Iraq and Afghanistan* (Shamsi and Pearlstein 2006) studied scores of cases of detainees who died in U.S. custody, many of them clearly homicides. The analysts at Human Rights First didn't challenge the prerogative of U.S. military commanders or the CIA inspector general to investigate and punish their own breaches, either under the Uniform Code of Military Justice or by referral to the Department of Justice. Rather, the rights group highlighted a yawning "accountability gap" in U.S. practice and suggested measures for improvement:

> deaths went unreported, witnesses were never interviewed, evidence was lost or mishandled, and record-keeping was scattershot. They also include investigations that were cut short as a result of decisions by commanders—who are given the authority to decide whether and to what extent to pursue an investigation—to rely on incomplete inquiries, or to discharge a suspect before an investigation can be completed. Given the extent of the non-reporting, under-reporting, and lax record keeping to date, it is likely that the statistics reported here, if anything, under-count the number of deaths. (Shamsi and Pearlstein 2006:2)

Today, a sizeable subfield of the human rights movement is devoted to documenting and analyzing the conduct and consequences of war. Leading rights groups have hired specialists in humanitarian law, military weaponry and targeting, arms transfers, counterterrorism, humanitarian emergencies, health and human rights, and international justice. With such expertise and evidence on their side, no one can accuse human rights professionals of abandoning the field to the military's legal mandarins. Rights experts have gained relevance and access, communicating and, at times, collaborating with armed forces in response to humanitarian crises. No doubt some of the ethos of human rights rubbed off on military officials in the process, but perhaps at the cost of some critical distance on the part of human rights. With regard to the Iraq war, for example, most rights groups remained skeptical of the Coalition's *ad bellum* claims—Human Rights Watch flatly denied that the war constituted a humanitarian intervention—but at the same time seemed to endorse the *in bello* manner of war the Pentagon aspired to, namely using sophisticated weapons to destroy physical power and infrastructure while limiting civilian casualties (Roth 2004).

Civilians in New Wars

The recent attention to "new" wars has led many analysts to say that the old rules no longer apply. In such conflicts, material capabilities, strategy and tactics, and ethics and etiquette differ sharply between the warring parties. What is lacking above all, say humanitarian lawyers, is the moderating force of reciprocity. Reciprocity in this case refers to the promise of shared norms as well as the threat posed by roughly equal capabilities. In asymmetric warfare one side's competitive advantage may be heavy bombing, while the other's is planting homemade improvised explosive devices, or IEDs. Any restraint that tit for tat might have engendered evaporates. If they're not playing fair, why should we? As reciprocity has waned, so has confidence in IHL. One skeptic suggests the laws of war may have been relevant in an age of "knights and chivalry" but are ill suited to govern today's wars (quoted in Cardenas 2010:1). White House counsel Alberto Gonzales (2002) advised President George W. Bush that the war against terrorism was "a new kind of war" that rendered the Geneva Conventions "quaint."

Arguments about asymmetry usually portray states as the vulnerable victims of non-state violence (Winter 2011:495). However, embedded in this language of alarm are certain assumptions about civilians as well. One of the leading tropes of asymmetric wars is the blurring of combatant and noncombatant identities. Belligerents often describe noncombatants as "not really civilians" or "not only civilians" (Slim 2008:183). "There are civilians all over the battlefield," notes David Kennedy (2006b:113–14). "Not only insurgents dressed as refugees, but special forces dressing like natives, private contractors dressing like Arnold Schwarzenegger, and all the civilians running the complex technology and logistical chains 'behind' modern warfare . . . civil affairs officers run after the troops dispensing compensation and apologetic words in a campaign for hearts and minds." Adam Roberts (2009:19) describes the status of civilians as "multi-faceted and complex: they are both agents and victims; both co-players in the theatre of war and objects of propaganda; both participants in the war economy and protected persons in the laws of war."

These characterizations are surely true, but they can read too much ambiguity into today's wars. It's a rare civilian who is plagued by divided identities or mired in complicity and guilt. The ICRC *People on War Report* describes the "total engagement" of societies in war, though more as victims than as perpetrators. A third of the respondents to the ICRC survey reported that their dwellings had been seriously damaged in fighting. A third were driven from their homes. In Somalia, two-thirds of respondents were displaced. In Afghanistan, the figure was 83 percent. Noncombatants reported that sometimes they were "recruited and pushed and compelled to join with combatants, often from all sides," and were frequently pressured to provide food or other material support to combatants (ICRC 2000:viii). But very few moonlighted as soldiers. Most were hapless bystanders or unarmed refugees with few options.

As contests between professional soldiers turn into contests for hearts and minds, civilian loyalties are implicated. This is guerrilla warfare redux. "The inhabitant in his home is the center of the conflict," wrote Col. Roger Trinquier (1964:29), a French commander during the Battle of Algiers. "Like it or not, the two camps are compelled to make him participate in the conflict; in a certain sense, he has become a combatant too." Michael Walzer notes that the U.S. rules of engagement in Vietnam had "only the appearance of recognizing and attending to the combatant/noncombatant distinction. In fact, they set up a new distinction: between loyal and disloyal, or friendly and hostile noncombatants" (Walzer 1977:193). "You can't tell the difference between these people at all," said Marine Sgt. Matt Mardan. "They all look Arab. They all have beards, facial hair. Honestly, it'll be like walking into China and trying to tell who's in the Communist party and who's not. It's impossible" (Hedges and Al-Arian 2008:46).

Collective punishment waits in the wings. "For every offense punish someone; the guilty, if possible, but someone," suggested British strategist James Maloney Spaight in 1911.[16] State behavior hasn't improved all that much since, treating populations at best as suspect collectives, at worst as chattel. Strategy scholar Colin Gray (2005:223) contends that "irregular warfare almost invariably drives the regular belligerent to behave terroristically towards the civilian populace that provides, or might provide, recruits or support for the guerillas." Even the most humane counterinsurgency strategies call for the physical control, and often removal, of civilians. In the 1950s, British troops "regrouped" hundreds of thousands of ethnic Chinese in Malaysia, and forced similar numbers of ethnic Kikuyu into "emergency villages" during the Mau Mau revolt in Kenya. In Algeria, the French army mapped out territory in an administrative grid (*quadrillage)* and "raked" (*ratissage*) the population. In Vietnam, civilians were herded into "*agrovilles*" by the French and "strategic hamlets" by the Americans. In Sri Lanka, hundreds of thousands of Tamil civilians were corralled into "welfare villages." "Peace walls" in Belfast and "T-walls" in Baghdad helped control people *in situ*. During the

Iraq War entire villages in the Sunni Triangle were encased in barbed wire, and their residents given retinal scans and ID cards and forced to pass through checkpoints as they came and went (see Filkins 2003; Janega 2007).

Humanitarian law anticipates this kind of management of civilians. Additional Protocol II allows the relocation of civilian populations for their own security or for "imperative military reasons" and specifies that "all possible measures" be taken to ensure "satisfactory conditions of shelter, hygiene, health, safety and nutrition" for those displaced (para. 17(1)). But the law can't possibly guarantee that people won't be severed from the physical space and the fabric of their lives. During the PKK (Partiya Karkerên Kurdistan/Kurdistan Workers' Party) insurgency in Turkey in the 1990s, Ankara forcibly removed hundreds of thousands of Kurds from their ancestral villages and into new "consolidated villages." Many more washed up in the shantytowns known as *gecekondus* ("night condo": they spring up overnight) surrounding Turkey's large cities. The Turkish government blamed the displacements on the PKK, an accusation that was at least partly true: Kurds who were unsympathetic to the separatists often faced retribution. Though carried out in the language of military necessity, the removals were also driven by longer-term strategies of cultural hegemony, state-building, and regional development (Ayata 2011; Çelik 2005).

Legal debate today hinges on the meaning of "direct" or "active" participation in hostilities. The ICRC and the T.M.C. Asser Institute toiled for years to try to define direct participation in a way that held the line on traditional noncombatant protections yet remained plausible to belligerents waging nontraditional wars. The study suggested that protections are forfeited when a person acts in a "continuous combat role" (ongoing involvement in preparing, executing, or commanding combat acts) or takes a direct part in hostilities (carrying out acts that adversely affect military operations or capabilities of the enemy; or which harm civilians or civilian objects). In either case the act would have to be a *direct, military* act of warfare. Indirect acts—recruiting, financing, propaganda, and public relations—may sustain the war effort, but that doesn't make their authors legitimate targets of attack (Meltzer 2009).

This is a far cry from how states usually interpret direct participation. Civilians may not be targeted as such, but they're often targeted as something else—suppliers, supporters, sympathizers. During the Kosovo conflict, for example, NATO attacked political and business allies of Milosevic in hopes that they would sever political and financial support. Belligerents often pressure families of militants for information, or destroy family homes or other buildings that are connected to militant violence. Again, humanitarian law does not define military and civilian objects in terms of inherent qualities; rather, the status of a person or object is determined by the use to which they are put. This lends "abstract ambiguity" to the principle of discrimination, and confers conceivable military advantages on all manner of civilian objects (S. Gordon 2010:77). The strategic doctrine of the U.S. Air Combat Command, for example, envisions airstrikes on political leadership, essential industries, communications, and transport infrastructure (Cornish 2007). Civilians are also subject to "effects-based" or "network-centric" targeting that aims to stun and demoralize entire enemy populations into conceding victory (Coward 2009). *The Commander's Handbook on the Law of Naval Operations* (2007) says that military objectives extend to those entities that are "war-sustaining," and therefore "economic objects of the enemy that indirectly but effectively support and sustain the enemy's war-fighting capability" may be attacked (quoted in M. Schmitt 2012:94). As noted earlier, the targeting of dual-use facilities is susceptible to sophistry. Under Protocol I (Art. 52), dual-use facilities may be attacked if their destruction will make an "effective contribution to military action" or produce "a definite military advantage," though military lawyers often regard those advantages in potential and indeterminate ways (Human Rights Watch 1998a).

Tactical pressures also undercut the civilian idea. Even in discriminate warfare, hard-charging "kinetic" raids lower the threshold for violence and transfer risk from soldiers to civilians. Belligerents often designate "military zones," shifting the burden to civilians to evade attack and foisting some measure of guilt or responsibility onto people who fail to clear out of the way, albeit sometimes after issuing public warnings. Even when they have little choice in the matter, civilians are blamed for "allowing" insurgents into their midst. Many civilians are snared in generalized round-ups. Being a "military-aged man," or "MAM" in Pentagon jargon, doesn't exactly make one a target, but it's widely used as a marker of suspicion. Belligerents often assume for statistical purposes that unidentified victims are combatants rather than civilians (Amnesty International 2013:46).

When belligerents say they can't tell who's who in these conflicts, it is often part of an exculpatory narrative to excuse or justify harming civilians, not as a prod to greater caution on their behalf. Convinced that compliance is impractical or impossible, militaries may start to deploy unapologetically anti-civilian tactics (Slim 2003:498). The mere assumption that war is war and innocent people are going to die increases the carnage. Truisms harden into policy. The expectation that bystanders will suffer inordinately in counter-insurgencies, for example, normalizes civilian harm. Why invest heavily in civilian protections in such a conflict? Casualties become part of the "cost of doing business," as the Department of Defense's Bargewell Report on the Haditha killings described the attitude of many U.S. marines in Iraq (Bargewell 2006:22).

The civilian seems caught in a perfect storm. Liberal ethicists like Henry Shue (2008:101) note "a complex spectrum between the paradigm combatant and the paradigm civilian." Security hardliners like Alan Dershowitz (2006b) say the idea of the civilian has grown "increasingly meaningless." Dershowitz describes a "continuum of 'civilianity' ": "Near the most civilian end of this continuum are the pure innocents—babies, hostages and others completely uninvolved; at the more combatant end are civilians who willingly harbor terrorists, provide material resources and serve as human shields; in the middle are those who support the terrorists politically, or spiritually" (Dershowitz 2006a). Anchoring the rules of armed conflict in human rights won't completely lift the fog of war (or the fog of law), but it does resist these erosions and confusions.

Human Rights as Lawfare

The political project to interject human rights into the conduct of war has been contentious, to put it mildly. Armed forces are naturally leery of external constraints and scrutiny. To have a chorus of human rights do-gooders second-guessing their decisions is seen as an affront to military professionalism and good faith. Jean Pictet, one of the prime movers behind the humanization of the laws of war under the auspices of the ICRC, reportedly said, "If we cannot outlaw war, we can make it too complex for the commander to fight!" (Rockwood 2007:161). Distrust of current-day Pictets has left modern armies wary of "lawfare" or "legal encirclement" (Waters 2008), the fear, that like Gulliver in the hands of legal Lilliputians, they'll be paralyzed by laws devised by people who've never see the flash of an enemy muzzle. The term "lawfare" was coined during NATO's bombing campaign in Yugoslavia to suggest derisively that the operation was being run by lawyers rather than generals. It has come to mean "juridical warfare," or "the instrumentalization or politicization of the law to achieve a tactical, operational or strategic effect" (Dunlap 2008; Stephens 2010). The Hoover Institution's Peter Berkowitz (2010) calls it "the march of politics under the banner of law."

Already apprehensive about the legalization of war, defense officials worry that human rights will tie their hands ever more tightly. After Gen. Stanley McChrystal strengthened the rules of engagement in Afghanistan, many soldiers questioned the move. "The ROE, lawyers, and bureaucrats are killing us," said one intelligence officer. "We're fighting a cultural battle we have yet to come to grips with." An Army special operations soldier who served in Afghanistan put it this way: "If soldiers in contact need an air strike or a fire mission, give it to them. Don't deny them illumination or smoke because a canister might land on a civilian. . . . If a Taliban runs into a deserted house after clacking off an IED killing Americans, don't disallow the attack on the house because it is a civilian dwelling. If the same guy who just shot at you, hides his weapon, walks out and gives you the finger, don't let him go because he's an unarmed civilian. The enemy knows our ROE and is using it against us. If we are going to turn war into a joke—get out" (quoted in Scarborough 2010).

The British Army increasingly must operate within the strictures of the European Convention on Human Rights, prompting anti-lawfare activists to decry "coroners' courts, judicial oversight and the imposition of civilian 'duty of care' standards on the armed force" (Tugendhat and Croft 2013:22). Admiral Lord Boyce, Britain's chief of defense at the time of the 2003 Iraq invasion, told the House of Lords:

> The Armed Forces are under legal siege. . . . They are being pushed by people not schooled in operations but only in political correctness. They are being pushed to a time when they will fail in an operation because the commanding officer's authority and his command chain has been compromised with tortuous rules not relevant to fighting and where his instinct to be daring and innovative is being buried under the threat of liabilities and hounded out by those who have no concept of what is required to fight and win. (quoted in Waters 2008:26)

This is only one side of the legalization of warfare. Lawfare is also a tool of the powerful. As Philip Trimble (1990:833) has argued, "A quick look at the 'rules' of international law shows why governments love [it]. . . . International law confirms much more power and authority than it denies." International law upholds sovereignty, and protects territorial claims and border controls, economic, regulatory, and tax sovereignty, control over airspace, sea lanes, and natural resources, often explicitly denying status and standing to non-state actors. As we have seen, the law gives wide berth to the military prerogatives of states. On the battlefield, it ensures the basic right of combatants to kill. In the lock up, states often twist the law to silence claimants, denying even the possibility of a writ, or hobbling advocates within systems of military justice (Luban 2008:1986). One of the aims of the accusation of lawfare is exactly to defang legal claims brought by informal militaries. Hence, human rights lawyer William Schabas's definition of lawfare as "a word coined within the United States military and subsequently adopted by right-wing ideologues as a way of stigmatizing legitimate recourse to legal remedies, particularly within an international law context" (Schabas 2010:309).

Still, skeptics say that lawfare "weaponizes human rights" (Meyer 2010). The specter of legal encirclement has become a favorite foil of the "new sovereigntists," who see international law and the "global potentates" of NGOs and international institutions usurping the authority of states (Spiro 1996/1997). They say lawfare inflates the original purpose of human rights. Human rights groups, activist lawyers, NGOs, and IGOs have all been targeted as threats to national security (Gordon 2014). Humanitarian groups are accused of smuggling a "peacenik agenda" into the law (PoKempner et al. 2003:112; Goodman 2010). The U.S. 2005 National Defense Strategy lumped lawfare with terrorism itself: "Our strength as a nation state will continue to be challenged by those who employ a strategy of the weak using international fora, judicial processes, and terrorism." The tagline to the Lawfare Project is "exposing threats to democracy & freedom." The website lawfareblog.com laments "the depressing reality that America remains at war with itself over the law governing its warfare with others."[17]

Some claim lawfare is a ploy to criminalize the entire Western way of war, placing beyond the pale standoff weapons, air attacks, or drone strikes (see, e.g., Rabkin 2004; Rivkin and Casey 2007). A common refrain is that law-abiding Western states are at a disadvantage in warfare against enemies who are contemptuous of the civilian idea, yet are quick to milk harm to "their" civilians, indeed even invite it, for its propaganda value (Banks 2011:1). On the opinion pages of the *Wall Street Journal* and other conservative outlets, lawfare is pilloried as a tool of terrorists (e.g., al-Qaeda training manuals encourage captured jihadis to claim falsely that they've been tortured). Alan Dershowitz (2004) argued that the Geneva Conventions had "become a sword used by terrorists to kill civilians." The conservative Washington Legal Foundation runs op-ed advertisements in the *New York Times* claiming that terrorists are "hijacking our courts." The American Civil Liberties Union (ACLU) was accused of adapting lawfare for domestic use, waging a "guerrilla legal campaign against national security" ("'Lawfare' Loses Big" 2012).

The UN Human Rights Council is frequently upbraided for interfering in sovereign war prerogatives and posing unrealistic standards of conduct. Special Rapporteur Philip Alston's report on drone warfare and Judge Richard Goldstone's report on the 2008–2009 Gaza War were both criticized on these grounds. In 2011 High Commissioner for Human Rights Navi Pillay was skewered for questioning the killing of an apparently unarmed Osama bin Laden by the U.S. Navy Seals who descended on the al-Qaeda leader's Abbottabad, Pakistan, compound; for denouncing the clumsy execution in October 2011 of Libyan strongman Muammar Qaddafi at the hands of opposition militiamen; and for opposing the drone campaign in Afghanistan and Pakistan. Supporters of the Sri Lankan government dubbed Pillay "terror's diplomat" after she called for a human rights investigation into the conduct of the war against the separatist Tamil Tigers.[18]

Media saturation and heightened humanitarian expectations leave soldiers feeling exposed to legal challenges. A recent survey of British officers found widespread concerns about the effects of international and domestic laws on combat operations. Forty-three percent of officers queried agreed that "recent changes to UK law (incorporating legislation from the International Criminal Court) are damaging the operational effectiveness of units." A similar number said "the utility of mission command had been significantly reduced" for fear of prosecution. Nearly 80 percent of respondents believed that military personnel were "much more likely to be investigated and charged with war crimes than ever before" (Mackinlay 2007). Despite the Rome Treaty's multiple safeguards against politicized prosecutions, it is an article of faith among opponents of the ICC that soldiers who serve honorably may nonetheless end up in the dock in The Hague. Thus, former air force lawyer Jefferson Reynolds argued (2005:69) that the Treaty's provisions were "sufficiently vague to allow and perhaps invite, prosecutions for almost any collateral damage incident."

These fears have trickled down to the rank and file. Although prosecutions are extremely rare, enlisted men and squaddies say that if an operation goes sour they (and not their commanders) will be left dangling in the legal wind. A student of mine who served in the U.S. Army in Iraq told me half-jokingly that "nobody over an E-5" (roughly a sergeant) was likely to be prosecuted in a collateral damage case. A participant in a British on-line forum echoed this distrust. "ROE are pretty clear. You can use lethal force if you feel threatened.

[That the] MOD [Ministry of Defence] reserves the right to drag you through the courts at a later date for political purposes/or just for a laugh seems pretty clear to me" (Waters 2008:29). A brigade-level study conducted by the MOD found that some British soldiers in Iraq were afraid to open fire lest they become embroiled in an investigation in which they would receive "no support from the chain of command" (Rayment 2006). Hardened warriors cringed at the prospect of legal scrutiny and paperwork in the wake of civilian casualties. Soldiers do enjoy strong support from the public, however. American websites such as Defend Our Troops or Defend the Defenders (motto: "Who's got *their* backs?") and UK groups like the British Armed Forces Federation press for more permissive rules of engagement and raise money for soldiers' legal defense teams.

Conclusion

The challenge for human rights is to spotlight the shortcomings of humanitarian law, but also to descend from the mountaintop and suggest concrete ways in which rights can constrain the war machine. The challenge for humanitarian law is to uphold the humanity of the victims of war. As Hersch Lauterpacht once put it:

> We shall utterly fail to understand the true character of the law of war unless we realize that its purpose is almost entirely humanitarian in the literal sense of the word, namely, to prevent or mitigate suffering and, in some cases, to rescue life from the savagery of battle and passion. This, and not the regulation and direction of hostilities, is its essential purpose. Rules of warfare are not primarily rules governing the technicalities and artifices of a game. They have evolved or have been expressly enacted for the protection of actual or potential victims of war. (Lauterpacht 1954:363–64)

Perhaps within the law, buried under militarism and legalism, and suppressed by the heavy hand of the state, are the resources to renew itself. If not, we will have to reinvent it ourselves.

CHAPTER 3

The Implosion of Iraq: "Shock and Awe," Insurgency, and Sectarian Terror

> When Bush "brought the war to the terrorists," he failed to mention he wouldn't be fighting it in some distant mountains or barren deserts: the front line is our homes. . . . the "collateral damage" is our friends and families.
>
> —Riverbend (2005:62)

> Saying who's a civilian, or a "muj" [mujahadin] in Iraq, you really can't. That's how wishy-washy it was. This town did not want us there at all.
>
> —U.S. marine stationed near Haditha (quoted in Broder 2006)

This chapter examines the conduct and consequences of the U.S.-led Iraq War of 2003. Regime change was supposed to reorder the pinnacle of Iraqi society. Instead, the earth opened up and engulfed almost everyone. Even for a country brutalized by Saddam Hussein and reeling from years of war and sanctions, the violence was shocking in its virulence and ingenuity. Society was rent apart by the invasion, the chaotic dismantling of the Ba'athist state, the torture and abuse, the spasms of sectarian kidnapping and killing, the displacement and exile. The walls closed in on everyday life as public order collapsed and infrastructure and vital services failed. U.S. soldiers watched like tourists as looters ransacked and burned government offices, museums, hospitals, libraries, universities, power plants, and private homes. As the mayhem spread, U.S. secretary of defense Donald Rumsfeld blithely observed, "freedom's untidy, and free people are free to make mistakes and commit crimes and do bad things" (U.S. Department of Defense 2003). It looked like occupation without responsibility. As the invasion gave way to counterinsurgency, the American hearts-and-minds strategy descended into crude roundups and reprisals, and lengthy detentions without trial. As the abuses piled up, the legitimacy of the mission ebbed away. At its nadir, the campaign relied on razor wire, lethal checkpoints, neighborhood punishments, night-time raids, and smashing in doors.

As we have seen, humanitarian law tends to view war's fallout from the perspective of the state's action, not from the perspective of those who are terrorized or killed or have their lives uprooted by the conflict. A human rights framework, by contrast, sets the civilian experience front and center: the right to life, the right to be spared cruel, inhuman or degrading treatment, and arbitrary arrest or detention, the right to due process, the right to feel safe in one's home, the right to work, to family life, to physical and mental health, to food, clothing, and housing, to freedom of movement, to cultural and religious freedom, to self-determination. Accounts of the Iraq War tend to be heavy on the memoirs of generals and the heart-of-darkness war stories of U.S. soldiers, but light on portrayals of the conflict through the eyes of ordinary Iraqis. I don't pretend to offer a full people's history of the war, but I do hope to flesh out the systemic effects of sectarian violence and displacement, declining public health, and environmental harm, as well as what the war has cost individuals, families, and communities in Iraq. I hope to illustrate concretely what it means to trade civilian lives for strategic advantages. Iraqis themselves weigh the impact of the war in similarly concrete terms: do they feel safer, freer, more secure? Very few people in Iraq today think life was better under Saddam Hussein, but they nonetheless judge the war harshly with regard to these specific grievances.

The Right to Life

U.S. policies in Iraq effectively de-civilianized ordinary Iraqis. Casualties were prefigured in aggressive rules of engagement and the use of heavy firepower in civilian areas. The civilian toll changed depending on how risk was allocated and how rules of engagement (ROE) were defined. The opening "shock-and-awe" campaign targeted government ministries, military installations, and public works with a plausible military purpose. But the ground war involved area targeting, punishing tank and artillery fire, widespread use of cluster bombs, and heavy reliance on "close air support." As the Coalition grasped for a way forward, calculations of risk drove the choice of military rather than police methods. The Green Zone, the heavily fortified sector of Baghdad that housed many of Saddam's palaces and state ministries, was transformed into the seat of the Coalition Provisional Authority, the Coalition military headquarters, and the American embassy. Meanwhile, most U.S. soldiers existed in their own green zones: dozens of heavily protected "forward operating bases," or FOBs. Walled off from Iraqis, these "sprawling fortress-cities" were better suited for protecting troops than they were for waging an effective counterinsurgency (Partlow 2007). Long periods sequestered on base were punctuated by rapid raids "outside the wire" into what is sometimes referred to as "Indian territory."

A reactive, "kinetic," strategy was marked by hard-charging house raids, belligerent street patrols, and tense checkpoints. The strategy lowered the threshold for the use of violence and transferred risk from soldiers to civilians. A Defense Department analysis of 127 "pacification operations" between May 2003 and May 2005 found that almost all were reactive; only 6 percent were geared toward creating a secure environment for Iraqis. "There was a strong focus on raiding, cordon & search and sweeps ops throughout: the one-day brigade raid is the preferred tactic"; the focus is on "killing insurgents, not protecting the population" (Aylwin-Foster 2005:5). Rules of engagement called for the use of lethal force in response to hostile acts or hostile intent, but the more subjective standard of "perceived threat" became the operative norm, sufficient to warrant a barrage of gunfire. Though the rules generally called for "observed fires," or "eyes on target," "unobserved fires," and indiscriminate "suppressive fire" were routinely used. In the everyday use of terms like "NKIA" (noncombatant killed in action) or "NWIA" (noncombatant wounded in action), the "N" came to mean "neutral" rather than "noncombatant," diminishing the civilian's protected status (Bargewell 2006:15). Words often didn't mean what they said. "Positive identification" of targets, for instance, meant "reasonable certainty that your target is a legitimate military target" (CJT-F U.S. ROE Card n.d). Other times, positive identification simply meant that a house, a neighborhood, or even an entire town had been designated as hostile.

U.S. commanders were concerned to minimize, or at least mitigate, collateral damage. Especially in the case of pre-planned airstrikes, the Pentagon followed a series of "scientifically grounded mitigation steps" known as a

Collateral Damage Estimate (CDE) (McNeal 2014:754). Legal experts judged the legality of the target under IHL, while intelligence teams gathered and analyzed the information underpinning the strike. The heart of the CDE was an algorithm that calculated the physics of the bomb, historical data, and statistical probability in order to model the expected impact of the strike, and to suggest ways to lessen damage to civilians and civilian objects: striking at a different time of day, choosing a weapon with a smaller blast footprint, altering the angle of attack to redirect the debris spray, or fusing the explosive to better contain the blast. Targets that were chosen in advance were subjected to a full CDE, while "fleeting" and "time-sensitive" targets were vetted using an abbreviated protocol. The secretary of defense or the president had to personally authorize strikes with at least a 10 percent chance of harming 30 or more civilians (the "noncombatant casualty cut-off value"). Such permission was sought and given more than fifty times in the early months of the war (Crawford 2013:354–55).

Concern for civilians was awkwardly lashed onto the necessity of striking the target. Many strikes were aborted because the expected collateral damage was deemed too high, but the process was designed to mitigate civilian casualties, not to avoid them altogether. The protocol was undeniably numerical in how it weighed civilian lives against military advantages. Daniel Rothbart and Karina Korostelina suggest (2011:101) that this way of thought leads to a doctrine of "killing civilians in the proper proportion." The exact proportion was changeable. An official at U.S. Central Command told Human Rights Watch that potential collateral damage was reviewed "with excruciating pain": "the primary concern for the conduct of the war was to do it with absolutely minimum civilian casualties. . . . The first concern is having the desired effect on a target. . . . Next is to use the minimum weapon to achieve that effect. In the process, collateral damage may become one of the considerations that would affect what weapon we had to choose" (Docherty and Garlasco 2003:19). As long as a serious effort was made to mitigate civilian harm even marginally, the strike was generally considered legal.

At times, however, the process seemed elastic and artificial, especially given the Coalition's propensity to marry heavy bombing to spotty intelligence. According to defense and intelligence sources interviewed by law professor Gregory McNeal, 70 percent of the instances of collateral damage in Iraq and Afghanistan involved mistaken identification of the target (Crawford 2013:352). The dearth of accurate and current intelligence was a constant challenge. Human Rights Watch criticized targeting that relied on the inexact

GPS coordinates of the Thuraya satellite telephones favored by Ba'athist leaders in Iraq. On April 8, 2003, an airstrike on a house in the affluent Baghdad neighborhood of al-Karada killed thirty-six-year-old engineer Zaid Ratha Jabir and five members of his family. Jabir's two-month-old daughter was blown out of the house by the blast. Both her arms and legs were broken, but she survived. A U.S. Defense Department official told Human Rights Watch that Saddam's half-brother Watban was the intended target of the attack. The misinformation was likely derived from a flawed telephone intercept. Jabir's uncle, Sa'dun Hassan Salih, decried the killing: "I don't know why the house was hit. There was no intelligence, no army nearby, no weapons. Why did Americans tell the world they hit only places of the army? Why did they hit civilian homes?" Salih added that his "family had no dealings with the regime. We hate Saddam" (Docherty and Garlasco 2003:32–34). Residents were often bewildered by the choice of targets, particularly in zones already under American control. Hamziya Ali, a housewife in southern Baghdad, described missile strikes on a vacant dye plant in her neighborhood. "[The Americans] called on us from the tanks to stay at home because they were going to hit targets and they also said: 'If you want to watch our show you can go to the rooftops.'" "But me and my children spent the night shaking. We do not want to be their targets. Yesterday, they hit the factory and open fields which have not been used by any resistance members" (Associated Press 2003).

As insurgent violence increased in the fall of 2003, the U.S. responded with heavy artillery, tanks, attack helicopters, F-16 fighter-bombers, and AC-130 gunships, the fixed-wing workhorse of "close air support," equipped with air-to-surface guided missiles. "Spray and pray," and "clearing rounds"—heavy gunfire or tossing fragmentation grenades into a room in preparation for entry—were also part of the drill. Such tactics in close quarters were guaranteed to kill combatants and noncombatants without distinction. The most dangerous situations still called for stand-off attacks using precision weapons, or, more often, mortars, tank and cannon fire, helicopter gunships, and aircraft. Commanders almost always chose stand-off strikes when the risk of storming a building was deemed too great for the troops. No combination of tactics and weapons was more lethal to civilians. Iraq Body Count documented the circumstances surrounding 23,000 civilian deaths in Iraq between 2003 and 2005. Analysts concluded that "stand-off weapons which put a substantial distance between soldiers and their intended targets are the most likely to cause unintended harm to bystanders" (Iraq Body Count 2005:14).

Data from 2003–2008 suggest that Coalition airstrikes remained highly indiscriminate. This finding is supported by the "Dirty War Index" (DWI) developed by Madelyn Hsiao-Rei Hicks and Michael Spagat (2008). The DWI is a data-driven public health tool that measures unacceptable, undesirable, or illegal combat outcomes such as civilian death, child injury, or torture. The DWI is calculated as follows:

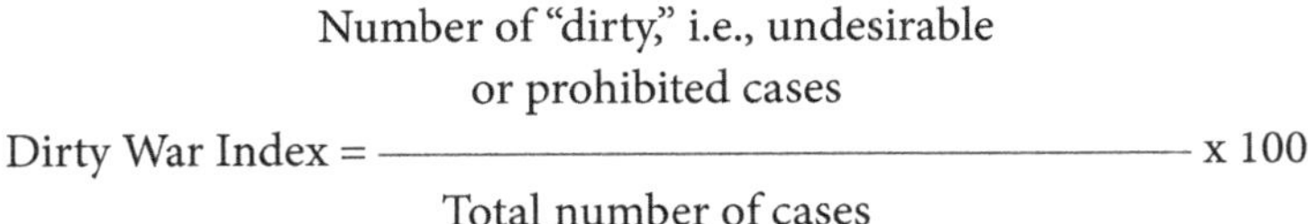

$$\text{Dirty War Index} = \frac{\text{Number of ``dirty,'' i.e., undesirable or prohibited cases}}{\text{Total number of cases}} \times 100$$

The highest average number of civilians killed per attack in which a civilian died were in suicide bombings targeting civilians (19 per lethal event) and Coalition aerial bombings (17 per lethal event). The DWI for the attacks that resulted in the most deaths of women and children were unknown perpetrators using mortar fire (DWI = 79), nonsuicide vehicle bombs (DWI = 54), and Coalition air attacks (DWI = 69). In these attacks, Coalition forces had higher Woman and Child DWIs than Anti-Coalition forces (Hsiao-Rei Hicks et al. 2011).

As Sunni insurgents or Shi'ite militias took control of smaller cities—Fallujah, Samarra, Ramadi, Najaf—the fighting often sank into siege warfare. In Fallujah, Iraq's deeply traditional "City of Mosques," residents quickly soured on the heavy-handed occupation. In April 2003, a group of protestors gathered in front of a school that had been commandeered by the Americans. As the protest turned violent (the exact sequence of events is disputed), U.S. troops opened fire, killing at least fifteen people in the crowd. Then, on March 31, 2004, four American security guards were murdered and mutilated and two of their burned bodies hung from the girders of a bridge over the Euphrates. On April 5, 2004, the U.S. Army 1st Marine Division stormed Fallujah. The rules of engagement transformed the city into a virtual free-fire zone. "Shells and rockets were falling like rain," said one man whose family managed to escape during a ceasefire (Steele 2004). Marines battled house to house, backed by air support from helicopter gunships firing Hellfire and TOW missiles, explosive and fletchette rockets (which release hundreds of lethal darts), and other rounds. Over the course of the April offensive, fixed-wing aircraft flew 1,000 close air support sorties, dropping even heavier bombs (U.S. Army National Ground Intelligence Center 2004:6). Initial reports from Fallujah were that some 600 Iraqis had been killed. U.S. Marine Lt. Col. Brennan Byrne said the Marines had been restrained in use of violence and that almost all the dead were combatants. "What I think you'll find is 95 percent of those were military age males that were killed in the fighting," he said. "The Marines are trained to be precise in their firepower. . . . The fact that there are 600 goes back to the fact that the Marines are very good at what they do" (quoted in Herring and Rangwala 2006:180).

A flood of television images of dead civilians and mosques in flames quickly derailed that narrative. Iraq Body Count (2004) said it documented and cross-checked 800 Iraqi deaths during the April offensive. Between 572 and 616 were civilians and over 300 were women or children. Alice Hills (2006) argues that the battle marked the limits of brute force and a "target-set mentality" in counterinsurgency. Even after eighteen Marines were killed by insurgent RPGs, machine gun and sniper fire, and mortars, many thought the campaign would have succeeded if only they had the political backing to escalate violence, rather than pulling back. Instead, the death and destruction hardened Iraqi opposition to the American presence. Coalition partners objected to the intensity of the attacks, militias stepped up operations in other parts of the country, and the several Sunni members of the Iraqi Governing Council quit, calling the Fallujah offensive "collective punishment" (U.S. Army National Ground Intelligence Center 2004:6). Targeting rules were loosened even further in the November 2004 campaign after most Fallujans were directed to leave the city. The warnings and the exodus that followed surely saved many civilians from harm, but the practice also shifted the burden of protection from combatants to noncombatants, even as the insurgents tried to bar men from fleeing. The director of the city's main hospital, Dr. Rafa'ah al-Iyssaue, said his emergency teams recovered more than 700 bodies from the rubble of the November attack. He said more than 550 of the bodies belonged to women and children, and that the dead men were mostly elderly (IRIN 2005).

Even in relatively controlled environments there were thousands of "escalation of force" incidents involving American troops and Iraqi civilians. During major military assaults, civilians had some control over the dangers they faced: they could flee impending attacks, or perhaps shelter in the inner room of a house. But it was impossible to evade daily traffic control points, or TCPs, and here the risks were controlled almost entirely by the soldiers. The rules of engagement at checkpoints followed an escalating protocol: erect road signs, flash lights and lasers, signal with arm and hands, fire warning shots into the air, fire shots into the engine block of the oncoming vehicle, fire into the vehicle itself. Despite extensive efforts to improve safety, the number of incidents at checkpoints remained high throughout the war. Poor design, lighting, and signage contributed to the accidents. Approaching drivers often didn't realize a checkpoint lay ahead, or were unsure of the protocol to follow. Words and gestures were often misunderstood. Machine gunners were instructed to raise a clenched fist, a military signal that means "stay back," but which was lost on many Iraqis. Gunners would also yell, wave their arms, and throw water bottles before opening fire (Burns 2005b).

Soldiers made snap judgments about oncoming vehicles, knowing that checkpoints were favored targets for terrorist bombers. Many Iraqis said they came under fire with little or no warning. Usually just a second or two elapsed between the warning signals and the time the gunner opened fire, making the distinction between disabling shots and lethal shots academic indeed. Civilian casualties occurred frequently at new and mobile checkpoints. Pentagon officials cited the tactical advantages of these "flying" roadblocks, though ordinary Iraqis, no less than terrorists, could barrel through the stops and draw fire. U.S. troops also employed two-stage checkpoints, the first stage manned by Iraqi soldiers, the second by U.S. troops. Drivers would slow down for the Iraqi contingent, then, thinking they were in the clear, begin to accelerate just as they approached the Americans (Ciezadlo 2005). Or, hearing warning shots, frightened drivers would step on the accelerator, sealing their fate.

Neta Crawford argues (2013:21) that, even when the United States seemed to follow the letter of humanitarian law, "the conduct of operations suggested fatalism about civilian casualties that bordered on indifference." Coalition officials routinely apologized for civilian deaths and offered condolence payments, and many individual soldiers were deeply shaken by the civilian deaths they caused or witnessed. Institutionally, however, the killing was met with a business-as-usual attitude. The internal Pentagon report prepared by Maj. Gen. Eldon Bargewell in the wake of the Haditha killings found a command and field culture that cheapened the value of Iraqi lives. "All levels of command tended to view civilian casualties, even in significant numbers, as routine and as the natural and intended result of insurgent tactics." "Statements made by the chain of command during interviews for this investigation, taken as a whole, suggest that Iraqi civilian lives are not as important as US lives, their deaths are just the cost of doing business, and that the Marines need to get 'the job done' no matter what it takes" (Bargewell 2006:13,22).

Of course, soldiers, too, were brutalized by the war. Four thousand four hundred eighty-eight U.S. soldiers were killed in Iraq, tens of thousands others were physically and psychologically scarred, and "the trace of each bullet, bomb, burn, and brain injury is written on the bodies of survivors and their families" (Crawford 2013:2). Thousands of civilian contractors were also killed or wounded. Iraqi soldiers fared even worse. Conservatively, some 11,000 Iraqi military and police died in the war, and three times as many were wounded (Lutz 2013). Saddam's elite Republican Guard and the Ba'athist paramilitary Fedayeen put up stiff resistance to the initial U.S. invasion. But most Iraqi conscripts wanted nothing more than to escape the advancing forces. Many stripped off their uniforms and fled (some were encouraged by American troops to do so). Others stayed in uniform only because they had heard that Saddam's paratroopers were executing deserters. Even if they were combatants, these soldiers had the right not to be dispatched to needless deaths, or to be buried under American bombs with no chance to surrender. In an encounter in al-Taji, north of Baghdad, two suspected insurgents tried to surrender to a U.S. Apache gunship which had them in its sights. The helicopter pilot radioed a JAG on a nearby base asking whether or not to engage. According to the transcript of the exchange, "Lawyer states they can not surrender to aircraft and are still valid targets." The two Iraqis were then killed with a 30 mm missile (Leigh 2010). A semi-retired Iraqi general, Hussein al-Awadie, said, "there was no honor to be had" in such one-sided killing. Another officer, Mohammed Kahlil Hamid, said, "a whole picture of misery was drawn for us [Iraqi troops] from the start." His own neighborhood was a "disaster scene . . . the wreckage of destroyed tanks and artillery pieces was strewn everywhere. Bombed-out buildings were still on fire. Bodies were rotting in the road. The only signs of life to be seen were the warplanes in the skies and the U.S. soldiers roaming the streets. I felt so helpless when I looked at them, these occupiers. The Kuwaitis looked at us the same way when we invaded there, and they had the right" (Kukis 2011:19–21).

As public order collapsed, civilians faced harrowing chaos, crime, and rising sectarian violence. It was like the *desaparecidos* in Argentina or the drug wars in Bogotá, but on a larger scale. At its peak, in 2006–2007, 3,000 people a month were being killed in raids, bombing, sectarian fighting, abductions, and murders (P. Cockburn 2008). In Baghdad, bodies were dumped in alleyways or garbage bins or pitched into the Tigris. The terror touched nearly everyone. The Baghdad blogger "Riverbend" noted in late 2006 that many Iraqi women had not "shed their black mourning robes since 2003 because each time the end of the proper mourning period comes around, some other relative dies and the countdown begins once again" (Riverbend 2006). The director of a charity that provided Islamic burial services to needy families said the group buried 75–100 bodies a week during the first three years of the occupation, but the weekly number soared to nearly 500 in early 2006 (Kukis 2011:189–90). A 2007 survey found that 26 percent of Iraqi adults had had a family relative murdered in the previous three years, while 23 percent of Baghdadis had had a family relative kidnapped in the previous three years (Global Policy Forum 2007). People were nabbed on the street by militias or kidnappers. Others were disappeared by Iraqi police units, or were swept up by Coalition Forces and delivered into the maw of U.S.-run detention facilities where sometimes even the jailers couldn't find them (Fassihi 2008:150).

In Baghdad, residents frantically traversed the city looking for missing relatives at police stations, hospital emergency rooms, political party offices, military bases, Coalition information centers, and Iraqi jails. For a fee, professional searchers would scour garbage dumps and river banks looking for bodies (al-Khalidi and Tanner 2007:9). The end of the road for many families was the Baghdad central morgue. The morgue processed 28,000 unidentified bodies between 2006 and 2008, about 10,000 of which were never identified. The capacity to conduct large-scale DNA matching was limited. Instead, morgue workers took photographs of thousands of victims. Each picture was assigned a number identifying the burial site in hopes that families could one day claim the remains or visit the grave. The photographs were shown in a public viewing room. Computer monitors and flat screen televisions were mounted on a wall facing rows of benches and cheap plastic chairs. It was grisly cinema. Many of the bodies bore marks of torture—drill holes, cigarette burns, garrote marks. Others were rotting and bloated, or charred beyond recognition. Some photographs displayed parts of bodies that had been torn apart by bombs or hacked to pieces by their killers. Some of the corpses were missing heads. As the images flashed on the screens the visitors craned their necks to try to recognize a face, a body, a scar, or birthmark (Williams and al-Sahly 2009; Freeman 2013). Rajiha Jihad Jassim, searching for her husband, a school watchman who had been kidnapped and whose family could not meet the $30,000 ransom demand, described her peregrinations to the viewing room:

> Hundreds of pictures scrolled on the screens. Thousands. I lost track of how many pictures of bodies I saw looking at those screens for my husband. Only once did I see one that might have been him. One picture showed a body naked except for underwear without a head. The body really seemed like his, but I could not be sure without the head.

> As I looked at the picture wondering whether it was my husband or not I had a nervous breakdown. I went home in a state of shock and stayed there unmoving for days. The body looked so much like his, but I could not bring myself to get the number for his remains. I told myself it was not him, and managed to find enough strength to start going back to the morgue each day after a few days at home. Altogether I went virtually every day for six months to the morgue before stopping. (Kukis 2011:192)

Families were rent emotionally, wanting closure but still hoping their loved one would turn up alive. The search for the missing usually fell to women, since men were often afraid to be seen in public lest they, too, be disappeared or killed. Women whose husbands were missing were cast into social and legal limbo, neither widow nor wife. The cruelest irony was this: with no body, wives often couldn't get death certificates for their husbands, making them ineligible for the modest government subsidies accorded widows. Desperate, some women claimed bodies that they knew did not belong to their husbands in order to receive the pension.

All told, hundreds of thousands of Iraqis died in the war and its aftermath. Iraq Body Count has documented about 165,000 civilian deaths since 2003. A *Lancet* study designed by researchers at Johns Hopkins University concluded that the war caused about 650,000 "excess deaths" between 2003 and 2006.[1] Skeptics say the difference between these two tallies means we really have no idea how many people died. In fact, the two studies measure different things: the first is a count of documented deaths, the second a statistical estimate derived from a sample of Iraqi households. While the *Lancet* study has been criticized on sampling techniques and other issues, biostatisticians generally say that mortality figures extrapolated from large-n household samples in this manner are more accurate than media reports or "sentinel" data collected by hospitals, morgues, or other agencies. Official numbers have always been much lower than estimates modelled by public health researchers. "Six hundred thousand or whatever they guessed at is just, it's not credible," said President Bush in 2006. Gen. George Casey, then the top U.S. commander in Iraq, said that the figure was "way beyond any number that I have seen. I've not seen a number higher than 50,000. And so I don't give it that much credibility at all" (Badkhen 2006).

Most Iraqis probably found the *Lancet* estimate entirely credible. As Riverbend put it, "abductions, militias, sectarian violence, revenge killings, assassinations, car-bombs, suicide bombers, American military strikes, Iraqi military raids, death squads, extremists, armed robberies, executions, detentions, secret prisons, torture, mysterious weapons—with so many different ways to die, is the number so far-fetched?" (Riverbend 2006). The most recent peer-reviewed, population-based survey estimates that there were 460,000 excess deaths between 2003 and 2011. The survey probably improved on earlier studies by including in the sample families that had fled Iraq: nothing drove people into exile more quickly than seeing a family member killed. This estimate, too, is higher than any official number. About 60 percent of the deaths were attributed to direct violence. The rest were blamed on the collapse of infrastructure, secondary health effects of the war, and other indirect, but war-related, causes. Of the direct deaths, 35 percent were attributed to Coalition forces, 32 percent to sectarian militias, 11 percent to criminals, and 21 percent other or unknown (Hagopian 2013).

Illegal Detention and Torture

Under the Fourth Geneva Convention, protected persons (noncombatants) can be interned for "imperative reasons of security."[2] The ICRC insists that internment is meant to be short-lived, but the law itself is vague enough to detain people on the merest pretext and hold them more or less indefinitely. This happened frequently in Iraq. Desperate for intelligence, Coalition forces cast a wide net that ensnared large numbers of innocent people. A former interrogator at Abu Ghraib told me the lion's share of detainees were victims of the "one-block" policy of arresting any military-aged men found in the vicinity of a hostile act. In a February 2004 report prepared for Coalition officials, the ICRC condemned the practice, citing U.S. military intelligence officers who said 70–90 percent of the prisoners had been detained by mistake. The U.S. officers also acknowledged the brutality of many of the arrests, which they blamed on poor training and overzealousness of combat units carrying out what was essentially police work. The arrests, said the ICRC, followed a pattern:

> Arresting authorities entered houses, usually after dark, breaking down doors, waking up residents roughly, yelling orders, forcing family members into one room under military guard while searching the rest of the house and further breaking doors, cabinets and other

> property. They arrested suspects, tying their hands in the back with flexi-cuffs, hooding them, and taking them away. Sometimes they arrested all adult males present in a house, including elderly, handicapped or sick people. Treatment often included pushing people around, insulting, taking aim with rifles, punching and kicking and striking with rifles. Individuals were often led away in whatever they happened to be wearing at the time of arrest—sometimes in pyjamas or underwear—and were denied the opportunity to gather a few essential belongings, such as clothing, hygiene items, medicine or eyeglasses. (Greenberg and Dratel 2005:256–57)

Once in custody, detainees were threatened, insulted, deprived of sleep and food, and injured by over-tight handcuffs or by being shackled to beds or cell bars for long periods. Months before the Abu Ghraib torture photographs became public, the ICRC informed Coalition officials of abuses in the prison's military intelligence section, including prisoners left naked in their cells for days, and prisoners paraded through the corridors handcuffed and unclothed, or with women's underwear on their heads. A military intelligence officer assured the ICRC that such treatment was "part of the process." The ICRC compiled about 50 allegations of ill treatment in the military intelligence wing of Camp Cropper: the use of stress positions (kneeling, squatting, standing with arms raised) for three or four hours; aiming rifles at detainees; striking suspects with rifle butts, slaps, or punches; leaving detainees exposed to the sun for long periods or isolated in dark cells. One detainee said he had been beaten, hooded and cuffed, and threatened to be tortured and killed; that he'd been urinated on, kicked in the head, groin, and kidney area, and had a baseball forced into his mouth and tied in place with a scarf. An ICRC medic examined the prisoner and found hematomas on his lower back, blood in his urine, sensory loss in his hand, and a broken rib (Greenberg and Dratel 2005: 262–65).

A year after the invasion, the Americans held more than 10,000 men and boys (and some women) in jails; the oldest prisoner was seventy-five, the youngest eleven (Gettleman 2004). As the insurgency grew, the number of detainees soared. More than 100,000 people would cycle through the U.S.-run detention system during the course of the war (Paley 2008). Tens of thousands were held at Camp Bucca, then the largest military prison in the world. Although Bucca was expanded and professionalized in the wake of the Abu Ghraib scandal, it, too, faced frequent abuses, riots, and violence, including detainee-on-detainee violence, often by religious extremists meting out punishments decreed by detainee-run sharia courts. The prison became a breeding ground for extremism. An American medical officer described conditions at Bucca as "Camp = men, wire and weapons," adding that the military police told him, "Take care of US—don't care about dets [detainees]" ("Medical Officer/ Preventive Medical Officer Interview Questions" 2004). Detainees in U.S. facilities had virtually no rights. Many were held incommunicado, and almost all were denied lawyers. Some languished for years before hearing the allegations lodged against them, and even then had secret evidence withheld from them. "Ghost prisoners" were carefully kept off lists and hidden from the Red Cross. The practice was not just limited to the CIA's secret "black sites," but became official military policy. The secretary of defense personally ordered some specific prisoners to be hidden (about a hundred ghost prisoners were held at Abu Ghraib). Adil Allami, a lawyer with the Human Rights Organization of Iraq, described the system as "one big Guantánamo" (Gettleman 2004).

Some detainee accounts are worthy of Kafka's *Castle.* Ra'ad Jamal Habib, a long-haul bus driver from Baghdad who was rounded up by U.S. troops in 2007, described being processed for the flight to Bucca, on the Kuwait border: "No one knew what the charges against them were. All the arrest stories were more or less the same. People going about their normal daily lives suddenly surrounded by soldiers and taken away. We were laughing, actually. Because that was exactly how Saddam used to do it." He said interrogators called him by someone else's name and kept asking, "Where are the rocket-propelled grenades?" The detainees were forced to strip for examination. They were humiliated and terrified. They'd all seen the Abu Ghraib photos and feared they'd be sexually tortured, too. Eventually, wearing a yellow jump suit, Ra'ad was packed into the belly of a cargo plane and lined up with scores of other detainees. "Then they strapped us in by stretching a long canvas belt across all of us that they tightened with a wrench, just like we were a bunch of crates" (Kukis 2011:169–71). Once in custody, many of the detainees thought they were in "detention for life," and were mystified by why some got the nod to be released and others did not. The maddening arbitrariness of the process contributed to the riots and unrest in Camp Bucca (Benard et al. 2011; Bill 2010).

The notoriety of Abu Ghraib and a handful of other high-profile cases tended to detract attention from the more routine abuses of Iraqi prisoners. The *Wall Street Journal* reported that American intelligence agents and law enforcement officials stationed in Afghanistan and Guantánamo were authorized to use "a little bit of smacky face" to make prisoners talk. "If you don't violate someone's rights some of the time, you probably aren't doing your duty," a U.S. official was quoted as saying (Bravin and Fields 2003). That attitude quickly migrated to Iraq. An analysis of WikiLeaks documents by the Bureau of Investigative Journalism at City University, London found more than 300 allegations of torture and abuse in the military files between 2005 and 2009, well after the Abu Ghraib scandal. Clearly, not all of these claims were credible, but opportunistic violence against prisoners appears to have been widespread. A sergeant in the U.S. Army 82nd Airborne Division described how soldiers at Forward Operating Base Mercury, near Fallujah, abused prisoners for kicks:

> On their day off people would show up all the time. Everyone in camp knew if you wanted to work out your frustration you show up at the PUC [person under control] tent. In a way it was sport. The cooks were all US soldiers. One day a sergeant shows up and tells a PUC to grab a pole. He told him to bend over and broke the guy's leg with a mini Louisville Slugger that was a metal bat. He was the fucking cook. He shouldn't be in with no PUCs. (Human Rights Watch 2005c)

The sport beatings at Mercury and the high-jinks horrors at Abu Ghraib were amateurish compared to the systematic abuse of suspected "high-value" detainees and people accused of security violations. The abuses were rationalized using the legal rhetoric of proportionality. A secret military-CIA unit known as Task Force 6-26 was headquartered at Camp Nama, next to the Baghdad Airport, and operated an archipelago of interrogation centers in Fallujah, Balad, Ramadi, and Kirkuk. The "black room" at Camp Nama became infamous for its "no blood, no foul" motto. "If you don't make them bleed, they can't prosecute for it," said members of the unit. For a time, even the CIA barred its interrogators from participating in grillings there. The son of one of Saddam Hussein's bodyguards was captured and interrogated at Nama. The son later told investigators that he was punched in the spine until he fainted, planted in front of an air conditioner while cold water was poured on him, and kicked in the stomach until he vomited. An inquiry into the case was eventually shelved because the perpetrators had all used false names and couldn't be identified (the unit said it had lost most of its files from the period in question) (E. Schmitt and Marshall 2006).

A Pentagon official, shaken by what he'd heard about Nama, said, "the reality is, there were no rules there" (E. Schmitt and Marshall 2006). But that wasn't quite right, either. In fact, these were highly bureaucratized, rubric-driven, inquisitions:

> There was an authorization template on a computer, a sheet that you would print out, or actually just type it in. And it was a checklist. And it was all already typed out for you, environmental controls, hot and cold, you know, strobe lights, music, so forth. Working dogs, which, when I was there, wasn't being used. But you would just check what you want to use off, and if you planned on using a harsh interrogation you'd just get it signed off. . . . I never saw a sheet that wasn't signed. It would be signed off by the commander, whoever that was, whether it was 03 [captain] or 06 [colonel], whoever was in charge at the time. . . . When the 06 was there, yeah, he would sign off on that. . . . He would sign off on that every time it was done. (Human Rights Watch 2006:12)

One axiom of state torture is that once harsh measures are sanctioned, they tend to degenerate into even harsher actions: the slope *is* slippery (Rejali 2009). That happened here, as more extreme physical abuses—hitting, slapping, beating—were added to the regimen. A military interrogator at Nama told Human Rights Watch that after he and several colleagues complained about the abuses, "a team of two JAG officers, JAG lawyers, came and gave us a couple hours slide show on why this is necessary, why this is legal, they're enemy combatants, they're not POWs, and so we can do all this stuff to them" (Human Rights Watch 2006:2). As violence against U.S. troops grew, so did the number of people who merited torture. Tony Lagouranis, a U.S. Army interrogator at Abu Ghraib and other sites in Iraq in 2004–2005, spelled out the logic:

> Once introduced into war, torture will inevitably spread because the ticking bombs are everywhere. Each and every prisoner, without exception, has the potential to be the one that provides the information that will save American lives. So if you accept the logic that we have to perform torture to prevent deaths, each and every prisoner is deserving of torture. In a situation like Iraq, it wasn't just a few abstract lives that might be saved somewhere, at some future time. The mortars came almost every day. The life in question was my very own.
>
> Once we accepted that any prisoner might be holding information that could save lives, we gladly used everything in our toolbox on

> everyone. This resulted in an expansion of the class of people who could be tortured. Now it included people who had been picked up for questioning but were not suspected of being insurgents, and it included people who were picked up on hunches—people against whom we had no solid evidence—and it included relatives of real targets. Again, I see the spread of torture to these groups as natural and inevitable. At the same time, I barely noticed it happening. (Lagouranis and Mikaelian 2008:245)

It bears repeating that most of the Iraqis rounded up by Coalition and Iraqi forces were *civilians*—technically under humanitarian law they were "civilian internees." These detentions reverberated across Iraqi society. It could take panicked families weeks and months to locate detainees. Sometimes they never found them. Nearly a year into the war, the ICRC chastised American officials, "there is still no satisfactory system of notification to the families of captured or arrested persons, even though hundreds of arrests continue to be carried out every week" (Greenberg and Dratel 2005:389). Some prisoners were released relatively quickly, but most were not. The average internment lasted 11 months (Rubin 2008).

It was a classic state of exception. Thousands of people languished in U.S. custody because American panels deemed them "imperative threats," but not criminals or terrorists (Welch 2010). After an initial interrogation, most detainees were deemed to be of little intelligence value, and were never interrogated again (Bill 2010:419). Due process was minimal. A dossier on each prisoner was evaluated periodically by a review board that would recommend release or continued detention. Prisoners could write appeals to include in their files, but generally did not appear in person. Brian J. Bill, a Navy JAG and legal adviser to Task Force 134, which ran detainee operations, says the reviewers were conscientious, but given the crushing number and backlog of cases, the appraisals were often cursory. RAND Corporation researchers who visited detention sites in 2007 and 2008 found the detainee files in "serious disorder," with nearly 3,000 files unaccounted for (Benard et al. 2011:59). Combined Review and Release Boards were added in 2004. The boards were made up primarily of Iraqis drawn from the ministries of justice, interior, or human rights, along with several U.S. military officers. Yet, because of U.S. secrecy rules regarding foreign nationals, any secret evidence was withheld not just from the detainees, but from the Iraqi members of the review boards—that is, the majority of the panelists (Bill 2010:423). Nor did the reviewers grow noticeably more adept at distinguishing people who posed a threat from those who did not. Maj. Gen. Douglas M. Stone, who took command of U.S. detainee operations in Iraq in 2008 and is credited with improving conditions and winning victories on the "battlefield of the mind," guessed that about one-third of the internees were "genuinely continuing and imperative security risks. . . . But that means two-thirds are not, or at least remain a question mark" (Rubin 2008).

In 2007, at the height of the communal violence, the U.S. held about 26,000 prisoners, including over 950 minors between the ages of 10 and 17 (UNICEF 2008:11). Despite the passage of national amnesty laws and stepped up releases, 30,000 prisoners were still being held in 2010, two-thirds of them now under Iraqi control. Conditions at U.S. prisons had improved over the years with the addition of civics lessons, vocational training, and an emphasis on "engagement" with moderate Islam as an alternative to extremism. As U.S. forces prepared to withdraw from Iraq, however, they began transferring thousands of prisoners into the Iraqi prison system, where conditions were usually abysmal, and the treatment of detainees likely to worsen. This was especially true for Sunni prisoners being held by what had effectively become a Shi'ite state. Iraqi prison officials often threatened detainees with indefinite detention if their families didn't pay a hefty tribute. In some cases, Iraqi security forces arrested innocent people for the sole purpose of extorting money from their families (Amnesty International 2010:16). Families had to bribe officials to learn where their loved ones were being held, or to have them moved to a better facility. As early as 2005, HRW noted that the new Iraq looked a lot like the old Iraq, as "unlawful arrest, long-term incommunicado detention, torture and other ill treatment of detainees (including children) by Iraqi authorities have become routine and commonplace" (Human Rights Watch 2005a).

Some of the worst abuses were carried out by Iraqi police commando units overseen by the Interior Ministry. The American civilian advisor to the units was retired U.S. general James Steele, who had trained counterinsurgency commandos in El Salvador during the dirty wars of the 1980s. The "Salvador option" included neighborhood raids, mass roundups, and, as it spiraled out of the control of advisers, growing torture and abuse (Maass 2005). The commandos ran a prime-time reality television program, *Terror in the Grip of Justice*, which broadcast the forced confessions of terrorists and Ba'athists. The show aimed to diminish and discredit the insurgency by publicly humiliating its members. The subjects, many of them displaying "bruised, swollen faces and hunched shoulders," were depicted as cowardly, criminal, and, often, gay: many confessed to being homosexuals and pedophiles (Fontan 2008:149). The inquisitor was almost always Shi'ite and the confessor Sunni. U.S. State Department officials wanted to rein in the commando units, especially the notorious Wolf Brigade. But military leaders, though troubled by the commandos' methods, apparently thought them effective, and reportedly supplied the units with the names of people they wanted arrested. Sometimes Coalition forces rendered arrestees directly to the commandos for interrogation. Typical entries from the WikiLeaks documents read: "All 5 detainees were turned over to Ministry of Interior for further questioning" (November 29, 2004), or "The detainee was then turned over to the 2nd Ministry of Interior Commando Battalion for further questioning" (November 30, 2004) (Leigh and O'Kane 2010). As the units were increasingly tinged with Shi'ite extremism, even Gen. Steele worried the abuses would fuel a civil war (Moss 2006).

U.S. troops uncovered several off-the-books detention centers run by the police commandos. Brig. Gen. Karl Horst personally discovered 169 malnourished, diseased, and battered detainees housed in a secret bunker on the grounds of the Interior Ministry. "OK, there were signs of torture," conceded interior minister Bayan Jabr, a former commander in the Iran-backed Badr Brigade. "And for that we will punish those responsible. But there were no killings and no beheadings, as some have said" (Daniszewski 2005). As many as a thousand Sunnis were detained in a secret facility at Muthanna Air Base reportedly operated by prime minister Nuri al-Maliki's military office. Like the American "ghost detainees," the prisoners were hidden or moved in advance of visits by Iraqi and international human rights officials. After they were freed, scores of the prisoners, some still bearing marks of abuse, were interviewed by human rights groups. They described being handcuffed and hung on metal bars, kicked and beaten, whipped with heavy cables, having plastic bags forced over their heads ("oxygen," in prison slang), electric shocks applied to their genitals, fingernails and toenails wrenched out, fingers broken, acid and cigarette burns, and prisoners sodomized with broomsticks and pistol barrels. Men were told that if they did not confess, their mothers or sisters would be raped in front of them. Several younger detainees were reportedly raped by interrogators and prison guards ("Iraq: Human Rights Watch Interviews Detainees from Secret Prison" 2010). Prime Minister al-Maliki called the charges "lies" and a "smear campaign," but he also invoked the U.S. treatment of detainees at Abu Ghraib: "The American government took tough measures, and we are doing the same, so where is the problem and why this raucousness?" (Dagher 2010).

U.S. officials were clearly disturbed by the abuses, but seemed unsure of their obligation to stop them. At a Pentagon press conference Secretary of Defense Donald Rumsfeld sparred with Chairman of the Joint Chiefs Gen. Peter Pace:

> SEC. RUMSFELD: Obviously, the United States does not have a responsibility when a sovereign country engages in something that they disapprove of; however, we do have a responsibility to say so and to make sure that the training is proper and to work with the sovereign officials so that they understand the damage that can be done to them in the event some of these allegations prove to be true.
>
> Q: And General Pace, what guidance do you have for your military commanders over there as to what to do if—like when General Horst found this Interior Ministry jail?
>
> GEN. PACE: It is absolutely the responsibility of every U.S. service member, if they see inhumane treatment being conducted, to intervene to stop it . . . .
>
> SEC. RUMSFELD: But I don't think you mean they have an obligation to physically stop it; it's to report it.
>
> GEN. PACE: If they are physically present when inhumane treatment is taking place, sir, they have an obligation to try to stop it. (U.S. Department of Defense 2005)

The Coalition's decision not to investigate such abuses was formalized in June 2004 in secret Frago 242. A "frago" is a fragmentary order that summarizes a more detailed directive. U.S. personnel in Iraq were secretly ordered not to investigate any breach of IHL unless it directly involved Coalition forces. Abuses were to be reported but not pursued: "no further investigation required." The WikiLeaks war logs record hundreds of such cases reported up U.S. channels, some of them brief notices, others elaborated with sworn statements and photographs. The *Guardian* noted that the reports "reflect the fertile imagination of the torturer faced with the entirely helpless victim—bound, gagged, blindfolded and isolated—who is whipped by men in uniforms using wire cables, metal rods, rubber hoses, wooden stakes, TV antennae, plastic water pipes, engine fan belts or chains. At the torturer's whim, the logs reveal, the victim can be hung by his wrists or by his ankles; knotted up in stress positions;

sexually molested or raped; tormented with hot peppers, cigarettes, acid, pliers or boiling water" (Davies 2010). Every branch of the Iraqi security apparatus was implicated—soldiers, police officers, prison guards, and border police.

U.S. commanders routinely rebuked Iraqi units for abuses, particularly as the handover to the Iraqis approached. U.S. Army Police Transition Teams conducted human rights training with Iraqi police forces, conducted snap inspections of Iraqi jails, and in some cases refused to turn over detainees who they suspected would be abused (Burns 2005a; E. Schmitt and Shanker 2005). One Transition Team that had uncovered "evidence of unchecked torture" at an Iraqi jail (electric shock wires, rubber hoses, a pool of blood on the floor) spent the night at the facility to deter further abuse ("Suspected Detainee Abuse in Husaybay" 2006). Progress was slow. In 2009, the Ministry of the Interior stepped up investigations of allegations of torture and mistreatment, and in recent years has prosecuted and convicted a number of perpetrators, including some high-ranking officials (U.S. Department of State, Bureau of Democracy, Human Rights, and Labor 2010). The Iraqi Human Rights Ministry has identified hundreds more allegations of abuses by personnel within the ministries of interior and defense, and by the Kurdish armed forces, the *peshmerga*. Amnesty International suggests (2010:32) that "this almost certainly represents no more than the tip of a very large iceberg."

Narrowing Civilian Life

Many Iraqis were spared the direct violence of the war, but no one could escape the descent into anarchy, the looting and burning, the shortages and inflation, the shuttered shops, the school closures, the chaos at state agencies, the lack of basic services. Baghdad blogger Al-Araji summed up the early weeks of the war as "dust, bombardment, no electricity, imprisonment at home, a curfew, family and relatives leaving town, and a mysterious, unknown future" (*Iraq War Blog* 2008:19). She was stunned by how naïve and arrogant the invading troops were. She criticized Coalition efforts to stifle hostile media outlets, and scoffed at U.S. forces arresting hapless souls off the street and yelling at them, "Where is Saddam Hussein?" (2008:41).

Al-Araji and other bloggers wrote a lot about traffic conditions: tank treads shredding the pavement, military convoys careening through intersections, drivers getting wedged behind a Humvee filled with soldiers waving rifles and yelling, and helicopters buzzing the roadways. Driving too fast was dangerous, but so was driving too slow. Idling cars were considered suspect. For a time taxis became targets. At checkpoints, people were blinded by spotlights as though they were criminals, were ordered out of cars, had their belongings searched, or were spoken to coarsely. Early in the occupation many Iraqis were embarrassed by having to raise their hand in a sort of salute as they passed by an American tank.

Al-Araji described an incident when she was stuck in traffic behind an American vehicle:

> There was something strange in the middle of the truck. The soldiers were sitting to the left and to the right with their guns aimed and there was something in the middle I couldn't identify at first. It moved and I thought it was some sort of animal. I couldn't believe it—an animal? What would the troops be doing with an animal? I continued driving my car slowly with my gaze stuck on the truck. In a moment, I realized the strange creature was actually a human. A human sitting on his knees with his hands tied behind his back and a rough sack on his head.
>
> I thought of the possible destination of this person. Would he disappear for months in their detainee camps for questioning? These idiotic policies are creating an air of animosity against the American presence, and the people can't be blamed. If that man with the bag on his head had been surrounded by Iraqi police, I would have felt sympathetic to his situation. But when American troops surround an Iraqi civilian it's a provocative sight and one word jumps to mind: occupation. And you feel anger and insult. (*Iraq War Blog* 2008:123)

Insecurity crept into everyday life. "Chaos is raking our lives, shattering our unity. We have become like strangers, each afraid of the other's betrayal," said Al-Araji. "The rhythm of life is worrying, scary, and gloomy. Security dwindles day by day. Constant explosions and assassinations" (*Iraq War Blog* 2008:56, 50). Kidnappings and killings became perversely normal. Ala'a Alzobeidi, who ran a successful international calling center in Baghdad, was snatched off the street in September 2005. He was freed after his family paid a ransom of $50,000 and a block of gold. "The day they released me, I was hooded with a scarf and driven a short distance," Alzobeidi recalled. "They gave me a small amount of pocket money as the car came to a stop. Taxi fare, they said. I was ordered to walk ten paces from the car before taking off the hood. I did as they said and then removed the scarf. I found myself at an intersection on the far outskirts of Baghdad. I saw no car around, just people walking. No one seemed to think it was strange to see someone emerge from a car hooded and walk ten paces as his ride sped away" (Kukis 2011:205).

As the war evolved from regime change to counterinsurgency, Coalition forces adopted more invasive and punitive measures. During the hunt for Ba'ath Party operatives (the "deck of cards"), tactics became more, not less, generalized. Troops carried out sweeping arrests and detentions, mass layoffs, checkpoints and road closures, destruction of civilian homes, sealing off towns and villages, house searches and summary detentions, round-ups and reprisals. "This is absolutely humiliating," said an elementary school teacher whose town, Abu Himsha, was encased in razor wire and its men given retinal scans and issued English language identity cards. "We are like birds in a cage" (Filkins 2003). U.S. soldiers often took out their frustration and fear on Iraqis in general, or "Hajjis," as they were referred to in the day-to-day language of the troops. "An Iraqi came up to me and said it pisses them off to have to wait for military traffic," a U.S. soldier noted. "I told him, 'If you wouldn't blow us up with car bombs, we'd let you pass us.' Shitheads" (Packer 2005:330). An American officer recounted how patrols had deteriorated into "guys kicking dogs, yelling at grown men twenty years older than they are, and pushing kids into parked cars to keep them from following and bothering them" (Packer 2005:247). Dehumanizing stereotypes were hard-wired into the conduct of the war. "You have to understand the Arab mind," said Capt. Todd Brown, an American company commander with the Fourth Infantry Division. "The only thing they understand is force—force, pride and saving face" (Filkins 2003).

Counterinsurgency doctrine primed U.S. troops to see terrorists in every shadow. The 2004 U.S. Army's Counterinsurgency Operations manual acknowledged that "it is nearly impossible for US forces to accurately identify friend from foe from disinterested." While its members may appear to carry on perfectly normal lives, many will lead "second, clandestine lives for the insurgent movement" (U.S. Army 2004:4-4, 1–3). It was tempting to treat all civilians, at least all military-aged men, as enemies or potential enemies. "The US troops view things in very simplistic terms," noted one British officer based near Basra. "It seems hard for them to reconcile subtleties between who supports what and who doesn't in Iraq. It's easier for their soldiers to group all Iraqis as the bad guys. As far as they are concerned Iraq is a bandit country and everybody is out to kill them" (Rayment 2004). Coalition spokesmen regularly suggested that Iraqi civilians bore some responsibility for their plight because they withheld information or allowed insurgents to move in their midst, or simply because they were "anti-occupation." Even the routine designation of "enemy civilians" weakened the principle of distinction: it is doubtful that "friendly civilians" would have been treated in the same way.

Village and tribal ties became proxies for guilt. Relatives of suspects were seized and held as leverage. Houses were demolished as punishment for attacks on Coalition troops. Curfews and checkpoints restricted free movement; schools were shuttered; the flow of labor was disrupted; people were deported or displaced; many were denied due process or compensation; property was sealed or demolished; crops and orchards were wrecked; public life was paralyzed and city services halted; unsympathetic media were intimidated and hostile civil society groups pressured. The tactics reached deep into the Sunni community. Long the rulers of Iraq, the Sunnis became a *sha'ab biduun*, a people without (Shadid 2005:221). Sunnis claimed they were actively targeted by Coalition and Iraqi troops. Typically hundreds of people would be arrested in village sweeps. Even for those released within a few days, the experience was an affront to Sunni rights and honor. And while the Americans clashed with Sunni and Shi'ite militias alike, Iraqi government troops targeted Sunnis almost exclusively. Iraqi General Rashid Flayeh, head of the paramilitary police units, said the arrests were "punishment for those who sympathise with the terrorists," adding, "the fire burns the wet leaves as well as the dry ones. The innocent suffer alongside the guilty" (Al-Taee and Negus 2005).

The walls closed in as much of the country was plunged into violence. Insurgency and counterinsurgency looked increasingly like a Sunni-Shi'ite civil war. The strife bolstered the radical cleric Muqtada al-Sadr, whose messianic Mahdi Army (Jaish al-Madhi) was launched in 2003 with training from Hezbollah in Lebanon and the Badr Brigade, the armed wing of the Iran-aligned Supreme Council for Islamic Revolution in Iraq (SCIRI). Sunni extremists congregated around the Association of Muslim Scholars in Iraq and the Iraqi Islamic Party. Sunni fears that the state was out to get them seemed to be confirmed as Shi'ite death squads began to meld with state security forces. "If the terrorists wear masks and the National Guard wear masks, how can normal people know who is protecting them and who is killing them?," said a Sunni leader in the Doura section of Baghdad (al-Khalidi and Tanner 2006:9). Sometimes the militias didn't bother to take off their police uniforms as they hunted down Sunni extremists, often described in broad-brush by U.S. forces as "Wahabis." A chilling Coalition Forces memo dated July 13, 2005 records that "on 11 July, 12 Wahabi civs were detained by an IP [Iraqi Police] or IA [Iraqi Army] commando unit in Al Rabi. . . . On 12 July, the 12 civs were delivered to the Medical City Morgue with their eyes cut out" ("Civs Killed in Baghdad Zone 2005).

On February 22, 2006, a bomb exploded inside the Al-Askari Mosque in Samarra, wrecking the gilded dome of one of Shiʿite Islam's holiest shrines. The bombing provoked anti-Sunni pogroms across Iraq. Sectarian identities hardened as a wave of attacks and counter-attacks swept across the country (al-Khalidi and Tanner 2007:7). In Baghdad, Sadrists and Sunni gangs set out to create closed Shiʿite and Sunni zones, respectively, expelling members of the other sect and demanding fealty from their own. The groups kept a dungeon's peace, manning checkpoints, dispensing rough justice, militarizing young men, and sometimes forcing non-Muslims to pay a head tax known as a *jizyah*. Molded by threats and violence, the neighborhoods became almost self-sustaining communities, down to social services and trash collection. Some zones became no-go zones for local police and, sometimes, Iraqi and Coalition forces.

Terror was central to the civilian experience of the sectarian war. The Iraqi author and activist Haifa Zangana (2007:108) described Baghdad as "a ghost city," its desperate inhabitants afraid to venture out after dark. Men cowered in their houses and stopped working for fear they'd be snatched off the street. One man, counting the days as he waited for a promised travel document, described a "waking nightmare, a vision in which I would be killed the moment I set foot out the door after getting my visa for Egypt" (Kukis 2011:19–21). "Fear now dictates which market you shop at; where you go to hospital—or even whether you go at all; whether you send your kids to school; what passenger you take in your taxi, and where you are willing to take him; which friends you see," said a 2007 report (al-Khalidi and Tanner 2007:9). If they had to traverse the city, Baghdadis would thread their way along the safest sectarian corridor. Sunni groups dispensed advice on how to pass for a Shiʿite—memorize the names of Shiʿite imams, set a "Shiʿite" ringtone on your cell phone, or adopt a Shiʿite-sounding name (al-Khalidi and Tanner 2006:14). The city of Basra was plagued by rumors that the police were roaming the thoroughfares in a particular Toyota sedan, intent on killing Sunnis and members of the opposition Shiʿite party, the Fadhila. Locals referred to the Toyota (which was black, white, or cream-colored depending on whom you asked) as the *batta*, or duck. When fresh bodies were dumped on the street Basrans would say the *batta* had struck again.

Blogger Faiza Al-Araji says the war left Iraq "buried in backwardness and oppression" (*Iraq War Blog* 2008:70). For all its terror, the Ba'athist system was relatively progressive with regard to women's health and women's rights in matters of employment, education, divorce, and child custody. The women's rights group MADRE said the U.S. war promised democracy but imposed theocracy. Taliban-like "punishment committees" sprang up, and women were forced to adopt the hijab and pressured to quit jobs or drop out of school. Female leaders and activists were targeted. In several instances, acid was thrown on "immodest" women. Female-headed households were especially precarious, driving some women to begging or prostitution. Sexual violence, the abduction of women and girls, forced marriages of girls, and the incidence of "honor" killings all grew. The Shi'ite tradition of "marriages of pleasure" (*muta'ah*) was revived, often as a cover for prostitution and rape. MADRE argued that the Bush administration had "decisively traded women's rights for cooperation from the Islamists it has empowered," noting that the new constitution contained a number of provisions that were more Islamist than prewar laws and rendered gender-based violence more of a private than a political matter (MADRE 2007).

Long persecuted in Iraq, LGBT (lesbian, gay, bisexual, transgender) persons became open targets after the Grand Ayatollah Ali al-Sistani, the country's highest-ranking Shi'ite cleric, issued an online *fatwa* directing that sodomites be "killed in the worst, most severe way possible" (Tatchell 2006). (The fatwa was later removed.) Al-Sistani had been a voice for tolerance between Sunnis and Shi'ite, but his acceptance evidently did not extend to all of Allah's children. Iraqi police and members of the Badr Brigade reportedly tracked down and murdered scores, possibly hundreds, of gay men. According to Ali Hili, who fled persecution under Saddam's regime and from exile in London helped establish a network of safe houses in Iraqi cities, militants were "entrapping gay men via Internet chat rooms. . . . They arrange a date, and then beat and kill the victim. Males who are unmarried by the age of thirty or thirty-five are placed under surveillance on suspicion of being gay, as are effeminate men. They will be investigated and warned to get married." Those who don't change their ways "will be arrested, disappear, and eventually be found dead. The bodies are usually discovered with their hands bound behind their back, blindfolds over their eyes, and bullet wounds to the back of the head" (Tatchell 2006; Otterman et al. 2010:176). "Honor killings" of gays by their own families also surged. More recently, the Madhi Army waged an anti-gay campaign to try to lift its political profile (Human Rights Watch 2009c).

A generation of Iraqi youth was lost in the war. According to the UN, more than 300,000 Iraqi youth between ages ten and eighteen have never attended school. Thousands of homeless children lead subsistence lives of begging, stealing, and scavenging for food (IRIN 2007). Sunni militias, the Mahdi Army, and the Awakening Councils, the Iraqi Sunnis groups backed by the U.S. to fight al-Qaeda in Iraq, all recruited children as fighters or used them in the conduct of hostilities. According to the Iraq Education Ministry, in a 4-month period in 2005–2006, 417 schools were attacked and 311 teachers and ministry officials killed. In 2007, during the terror, only 53 percent of school-age children were enrolled (UN Country Team Iraq 2014; IRIN 2006).

Michael Howard of the *Guardian* described how the violence crept into the innocent lives of children:

> The car stopped at the makeshift checkpoint that cut across the muddy backstreet in western Baghdad. A sentry appeared. "Are you Sunni or Shia?" he barked, waving his Kalashnikov at the driver. "Are you with Zarqawi or the Mahdi army?"
>
> "The Mahdi army," the driver said. "Wrong answer," shouted the sentry, almost gleefully. "Get him!"
>
> The high metal gate of a nearby house was flung open and four gun-toting males rushed out. They dragged the driver from his vehicle and held a knife to his neck. Quickly and efficiently, the blade was run from ear to ear. "Now you're dead," said a triumphant voice, and their captive crumpled to the ground.
>
> Then a moment of stillness before the sound of a woman's voice. "Come inside boys! Your dinner is ready!" The gunmen groaned; the hapless driver picked himself up and trundled his yellow plastic car into the front yard; the toy guns and knives were tossed by the back door. Their murderous game of make-believe would have to resume in the morning. (Howard 2007)

Finally, in cities, a kind of "urbicide" took hold, destroying the built environment but also strangling tolerance and heterogeneity (see Graham 2003). Authors, intellectuals, and journalists were attacked. Museums, universities, and libraries were bombed, looted, or burned. University student bodies fractured along confessional lines. Scientists, doctors, and professors were the targets of "a coordinated liquidation process" (Zoepf 2006). An earlier spasm of violence had targeted Ba'athist professors and university administrators, but the new attacks seemed aimed at liberal thought itself. In 2007, a huge car bomb killed 20 people in the Mutanabi Street book market, a symbol of Baghdad's intellectual life reaching back to the Middle Ages, when the city boasted the Abbasid library, known as the House of Wisdom (Bayt al-Hikma) and considered by many to be the world's first university. "Those terrorists do not represent Islam," said one frequent browser at the book market. "They are fighting science. They hate the light of science" (Wong and Habeeb 2007).

Displacement and Exile

No longer safe in their homes and neighborhoods, families faced the terrible decision to stay or go. Nearly 10 percent of Iraq's 2003 population ended up in exile; another 10 percent have been internally displaced.[3] Most of the exiles joined the Iraqi "near diaspora" in Jordan, Syria, and Lebanon. The initial exodus of Ba'athists and others favored under the old regime, the so-called "Mercedes refugees," was followed by the departure of the professional and managerial class—doctors, scientists, engineers, professors—and, finally, a stream of increasingly impoverished refugees gambling that they would be safer outside of Iraq. About 60 percent of the exiles were Sunni Arabs, 15 percent were Syriac or Chaldean Christians, and the remainder secular Shi'ites, Yazidis, Mandaeans, Faili (Shi'ite) Kurds, Bahá'ís, Shabaks, Palestinians (who were reviled for the privileges they had enjoyed under Saddam's patronage), Roma, and others. Religious persecution was compounded by accusations of being Westernized or showing sympathy to the occupying Multi-National Forces-Iraq (MNF-I). Many Iraqi Christians, for example, had worked as interpreters or support staff for the occupation forces. With no tribe or militia to protect them, more than half of Iraq's non-Muslim population has left the country since 2003 (Taneja 2003). The U.S. Commission on International Religious Freedom (2010:67) notes, "the violence, forced displacement, discrimination, marginalization, and neglect suffered by members of these groups threaten these ancient communities' very existence in Iraq."

The displacements were a byproduct of the war as well as a deliberate strategy to recast the country's demography. Hundreds of thousands of Iraqis were driven from their homes by the Coalition's major offensives in Anbar,

Thi Qar, Basra, and Baghdad provinces. Some were short-term dislocations, while others, in Fallujah, Ramadi, Kufa, Haditha, Al-Qaim, Tal Afar, Samarra, Baghdad, and Basra, were protracted. Those who lived in strategic hotspots were repeatedly displaced (International Medical Corps 2007:7; International Displacement Monitoring Centre 2008:108). Sunni militias drove thousands of Shiʿites out of the "Triangle of Death" south of Baghdad, even from Shiʿite-majority towns like Latifiyah, Mahmudiyah, Yusufiyah, and Iskandariyah. As U.S. forces stepped up raids on Sadr City in 2007 thousands of residents fled south to Najaf and Karbala. The provinces of Diyala and Ninewah (Iraq's second most populous with 2.5 million residents), where Arabs and Kurds, Shiʿites and Sunnis had traditionally lived together, were rocked by violence. As the Islamic State in Iraq and the Levant, or ISIL or ISIS, gathered strength, hundreds of thousands of Chaldean and Assyrian Christians, Yazidis, and Shabaks from Ninewah flocked to the relative calm of Iraq's autonomous Kurdish region.

The sectarian bloodletting in 2006 and 2007 spurred the greatest displacement. At its peak, some 60,000 people a month were pulling up roots and leaving. The International Organization for Migration called the scale of dislocations "transformative" (International Organization for Migration 2008; Fagen 2011). The more mixed the area the greater the violence, as sectarian gangs sought to consolidate power in "their" areas and to dominate the mixed zones. The provinces of Baghdad, Mosul, Salah al-Din, Diyala, Babil, and Basra were hit especially hard. Militias would prepare lists of individuals or families to be expelled or killed. Threats or intimidation—a bullet left on the stoop, a phone call or text message, graffiti scrawled on a gate, "advice" from a friend or neighbor ("this is not a good place for you now," "I was at a meeting and I heard your name mentioned"), or a gunman simply knocking on the front door and telling them to leave—had families cramming their possessions into suitcases and taking flight (al-Khalidi and Tanner 2006:27). Those who tried to protect a friend or neighbor of the other sect could find themselves in danger. Sometimes sectarian strife was wedded to tribal violence, for example as Shiʿites turned on Sunnis of a particular tribe in response to a perceived offense by one of its members. In Basra and Najaf, rivalry between political parties propelled Shiʿite-on-Shiʿite violence as well.

In the end, people made a cold Hobbesian choice to draw closer to their co-religionists for security. "People flee to areas where they feel safer," wrote Victor Tanner and Ashraf al-Khalidi (a pseudonym for an Iraqi researcher fearful for his own safety). "Shiʿa go to Shiʿa areas. Sunnis go to Sunni areas.

Kurds go to the northern provinces and Christians go to parts of Ninewah province. (And most of those who can leave the country do.) The result is that hard-line authorities then hold sway over 'cleansed' territories" (al-Khalidi and Tanner 2006:2). Baghdad's population of 7 million churned as hundreds of thousands of residents moved to sectarian enclaves across the city, decamped for other parts of the country, or fled abroad. They tramped from place to place seeking shelter or squatted in abandoned buildings. Many ended up in squalid conditions in ad hoc clusters around the city. Shi'ites settled in houses recently vacated by Sunnis, and vice versa. The newly displaced competed for housing with some 300,000 returnees who had been driven into exile by Saddam, mostly Shi'ites streaming in from Iran. Families were rent apart, spread out among relatives who could take in one or two of them. According to the Iraqi Red Crescent Organization, more than three-quarters of the displaced were either women (28 percent) or children (48 percent). Male breadwinners often joined armed groups or went underground, compounding the social and economic dislocations of the war (Goldenberg 2007).

With the exception of the Iraqi Red Crescent, the country's major humanitarian aid groups tended to be run by sectarian charitable foundations, or *waqfs*, which sought to monopolize assistance in "their" neighborhoods (Younis and Rosen 2008). With the national government ill-equipped to deliver aid and foreign assistance sidelined by the violence, families were often thrown into the arms of the religious charities, reinforcing sectarian loyalties. By 2007, half of the Iraqi provinces were blocking new arrivals, either to freeze the demographic makeup of the region or to bar the displaced from settling permanently (Ferris 2008:5). Neighboring Jordan also shut the door on new immigrants. Some Iraqis chose "micro-displacements" instead—hiding in one's apartment, sleeping elsewhere, taking a new job, pulling children out of schools, shopping at a market in another, safer neighborhood, and other strategies to survive (al-Khalidi and Tanner 2006:28–29). Couples in mixed (Sunni-Shi'ite) marriages were targeted by militants on both sides. A Sunni artist was told to divorce his Shi'ite wife or else be killed. "We left Dora [a once-mixed neighborhood in Baghdad] now. My wife is staying with her family in Sha'b [a Shi'a neighborhood] and I am staying with my friends in Mansur [a Sunni neighborhood]. I am trying to find a different house but it's difficult now to find a place that accepts both of us in Baghdad" (quoted in al-Khalidi and Tanner 2006: Foreword). Another mixed family moved from Sunni-dominated west Baghdad to a mixed neighborhood in the city center.

Anticipating the partition of Iraq, the wife's Shi'ite parents planned to quit Baghdad and move to southern Iraq, where their daughter's family could not follow. "It's a bitter feeling, to have to choose between my husband and my parents," said the daughter (R. Watson 2006).

Sectarian cleansing is a fact of life in Iraq. The country has never been so sharply divided along Shi'ite, Sunni, and Kurdish lines. Maps comparing Baghdad's sectarian demography in 2003 and 2009 show a growing concentration of Sunnis in a handful of neighborhoods, and, most striking, a wholesale consolidation and expansion of Shi'ite areas at the expense of mixed areas. The historic pluralistic (Shi'ite, Sunni, Christian) neighborhoods in the city center shrank to about a quarter of what they were before the war (BBC 2007). Social relations are similarly Balkanized. With the possible exception of Kurds, Iraqis oppose the idea of partitioning the country into its constituent parts, but sectarian polarization is strong. Only about half of Iraqis said they had a friend from across the sectarian divide, or would support a child marrying into another sect (Ferris 2008:16).

Many Sunnis still look on the war as an American-Shi'ite plot to disenfranchise Sunnis. This wasn't the Coalition's intention though there was poetic justice in handing the country over to its long-suffering Shi'ite majority. Coalition military exercises affected Sunnis disproportionately. Although the ideology of the Ba'athist Party was Pan-Arab rather than sectarian, membership in Iraq was heavily Sunni. De-Ba'athifying the civil service and dismantling the army cleared the way for Shi'ite dominance. The roundups and reprisals against Sunnis grew under Shi'ite rule. Other policies deepened the sectarian divide, politically and spatially. The Coalition Provisional Authority (CPA) appointed members of the Iraqi Governing Council based on sectarian proportionality. Though this was probably unavoidable, Sunnis and Shi'ites began to "sell themselves on the basis of sectarian identity . . . political leaders had to become sectarian entrepreneurs" (Herring and Rangwalla 2006:152). The 2007 "surge" also accelerated the sectarian partition of the country, "driving fearful Iraqis from their homes at much higher rates than before the tens of thousands of additional troops arrived"; the Red Crescent said the surge displaced more than 100,000 people a month (Glanz and Farrell 2007). Desperate to stem the violence, MNF-I troops turned to twelve-foot-high blast walls, Jersey road barriers, and checkpoints. In 2007, the U.S. (without consulting the local municipal council) erected a 3-mile wall around the Baghdad neighborhood of Adhamiyah, a Sunni enclave which had seen some of the city's most intense killing. The blast walls were designed to "freeze the conflict," but they further ghettoized the city and heightened dependence on sectarian militias, soldiers, and police (Damluji 2010:80). Sunnis and Shi'ite alike denounced the barriers, comparing them to Israel's wall blocking off Palestinians in the West Bank. The Adhamiyah wall was still standing in 2015, residents complaining that it was now Shi'ite security forces instead of Shi'ite militias that were harassing and illegally detaining them.

U.S. planning for the war did not seriously consider the question of sectarian violence and displacement. The U.S. has provided more financial support for the internally displaced than any other country by far, though the degree of American responsibility is debated. Former U.S. ambassador to the UN John Bolton said that sectarian violence, not American actions, was to blame, so the crisis was not the responsibility of the United States: "Our obligation . . . was to give them new institutions and provide security. We have fulfilled that obligation. I don't think we have an obligation to compensate for the hardships of war" (Roberta Cohen 2009:317). U.S. processing of Iraqi asylum claims was frozen for the first two years of the war, but between 2007 and 2013, about 85,000 Iraqi refugees were admitted to the U.S., most coming by way of Jordan and Syria, where they first had to register with the UNHCR, which would refer eligible applicants to American officials (U.S. Citizenship and Immigration Services 2013). The U.S. wanted to honor the principle of *non-refoulement*, which forbids sending a refugee or asylum seeker back to a country where he or she will be persecuted or worse on grounds of religion, nationality, social group, or political opinion. But it also hoped as many refugees as possible—especially liberal-minded members of the professional and technocratic classes—would return to Iraq as the security situation stabilized (Ferris 2008:19). Several thousand special immigrant visas have been extended to Iraqis who were employed by or on behalf of the U.S. during the war.

Still, it is clear that "sustainable return," the term favored by humanitarian groups, means more than simply being repatriated or moving back to one's city or neighborhood. Prompted by the United Nations Human Rights Commission, the UN Guiding Principles on Internal Displacement (2004) leaven existing laws with the language and urgency of rights, including the right of return:

> Competent authorities have the primary duty and responsibility to establish conditions, as well as provide the means, which allow internally displaced persons to return voluntarily, in safety and with

> dignity, to their homes or places of habitual residence, or to resettle voluntarily in another part of the country. Such authorities shall endeavor to facilitate the reintegration of returned or resettled internally displaced persons. . . . [those] who have returned to their homes or places of habitual residence or who have resettled in another part of the country shall not be discriminated against as a result of their having been displaced. They shall have the right to participate fully and equally in public affairs at all levels and have equal access to public services. (UN Office of the Commissioner for Humanitarian Affairs 2004)

In 2004, the CPA established the Ministry of Displacement and Migration and a Property Claims Commission. The Commission handles only those claims regarding property seized by the Ba'athist regime. More recent displacement-related disputes often get mired in civil and criminal courts. Homes are frequently looted or damaged in the owner's absence. It is not unusual for returnees to find another family living in their house. The state institutions mediating claims to property tend to be partial, particularly with regard to Sunni- Shi'ite disputes. The process often kowtows to local and national political elites concerned how returns will affect the local balance of sectarian power (Van der Auweraert 2011:14–15). The Iraqi government has touted a cash incentive program to encourage people to return, though a 2010 survey by the UNHCR found that most returnees struggled economically and faced continuing violence and harassment (P. Ali 2011). The longer people are displaced, the less likely they are to try to return. In a 2013 survey, 85 percent of Iraq's internally displaced persons said they planned to integrate in place rather than return (International Organization for Migration 2013:8). Indeed, the fact of returns doesn't necessarily herald national reconciliation. Amid the sectarian fervor, returns are often seen as a provocative act of reclaiming cleansed land (Ferris 2009:9).

Rates of displacement and return are good indicators of the overall security situation. Though, like gasoline prices, the number of people displaced tends to rise quickly and fall slowly. Perhaps a few hundred thousand Iraqis have trickled back since the worst sectarian violence ended in late 2007. At least 50,000 Iraqis have returned from Syria since the war erupted there in 2011, while others, displaced again, have made their way to Jordan, Turkey, or Lebanon, or on to Europe. Of the refugees who returned to Iraq, about 70 percent went back to their place of origin; many of the remaining 30 percent cited poor security or the fear of targeted violence as reasons for settling elsewhere (International Organization for Migration 2013:24). In 2014, renewed strife in Anbar and the rise of the Islamic State, or ISIS, a rebranded version of al-Queda in Iraq, prompted a new wave of displacement. ISIS fighters, including some former Ba'athists whom Donald Rumsfeld had written off as "dead-enders" back in 2003, and other disaffected Sunnis, some of whom had been radicalized at Camp Bucca, seized Haditha, Hit, Ramada, and Fallujah, then quickly overran Tal Afar and Mosul. A frenzied Shi'ite *levée en masse* to counter ISIS threatened to end in a sectarian bloodbath. Since January 2014 more than 3 million Iraqis have been newly displaced, including about 900,000 Assyrian Christians, Turkmen, Shabaks, Yezidis, Mandaeans, and others who fled the provinces of Salahaddin, Diyala, and Ninewah, most for the Kurdish north. It wasn't the country's largest wave of displacement, but it was the fastest. Many were repeat-displaced, who had escaped from central Iraq to the Mosul area during the earlier violence. Now they were fleeing pure barbarism: the destruction of religious shrines, public stonings and beheadings, mass executions of Shi'ite soldiers, and forced conversions to Islam. The chance that many these refugees will ever return seems slim (Wing 2014; Amnesty International 2014b).

Eroding Public Health

Of all the areas of Iraq's human development affected by the war, health care has probably been the hardest hit (IRIN 2013). Iraq is a textbook case of war's double toll on public health, spreading death and disease while upending the delivery of medical care. "Shock and awe" almost immediately overwhelmed the country's emergency medical capacity. Three weeks into the war, one reporter compared the city's Al-Kindi Hospital to a charnel house, where the bodies pile up. The trauma ward

> doesn't have enough medical staff, drugs and equipment; it's running out of body bags and clean water and is dependent on electricity in a city of day-long blackouts. Patients facing emergency surgery can have only 800 milligrams of ibuprofen, the same amount an Australian doctor might prescribe for muscle pain, and there is a critical shortage of anaesthetics. . . . Patients keep arriving in a procession of racing ambulances, muddied utilities and battered taxis. An army of exhausted,

> weepy support staff help them on to trolleys, scattering the flies that feed on the blood of the last patient. . . . Kindi's 12 operating theatres are in use around the clock. A haggard and tearful Dr Tarib Al Saddi stands outside the hospital, trying to have a break. . . . "I have done 12 operations today—crushings, fractures and amputations. You see that these Americans are hitting civilians—their homes, their streets, their cars and even those who walk about. They hit anyone." (McGeough 2003)

Coalition forces made serious efforts to reduce the spillover from dual-use attacks, for example, using carbon-fiber bombs that short out, but don't completely destroy electrical plants. The war nevertheless reverberated across electrical production, water pumping stations, waste treatment, and sanitation. The engineers and technicians who ran the public works either scattered or fled the country. Hospitals and clinics were widely looted. One witness recalled seeing looters with stethoscopes around their necks dragging heavy hospital equipment down the street (Kukis 2011:23). Doctors were targeted for political attacks (membership in the Ba'ath Party was something of a prerequisite for advanced degrees) and for criminal extortion. After 2003 roughly half of Iraq's physicians left the country, and very few have returned. Violence drove medical NGOs out of the country as well. In 2011, Iraq had 7.8 doctors per 10,000 people, a rate 3–4 times lower than its neighboring countries, and closer to that of destitute, conflict-riven countries like Afghanistan, Somalia, and South Sudan. So many doctors were kidnapped or killed that in 2005 the Ministry of Health broadcast this public service announcement: "Dear Citizens, please do not kill doctors—you may need them one day" (Human Rights Watch 2005b:91).

Chaos, graft, and sectarian rivalries probably did more to undermine public health than the shortages of staff and supplies. For years the Iraqi Ministry of Health was controlled by Muqtada al-Sadr's movement. Sectarian militants dispensed medical policy, controlled the delivery of health care, and oversaw the state-run company that imported drugs and medical supplies. Some hospitals were commandeered by militias accompanied by a resident *sayed*, or religious cleric. Together they intimidated doctors and administrators, and sometimes even determined who would be treated and how (Ali 2008). Medicine and medical supplies disappeared by the truckload, and monies reportedly were siphoned off from the Ministry to help fund the Mahdi Army. When the Ministry set up a desperately needed network of community-based primary care facilities, Shi'ite neighborhoods were favored at the expense of Sunni neighborhoods. Sunnis were terrified to go to "Shi'ite" facilities amid rumors of kidnappers dragging patients out of their hospital beds. In 2007, U.S. and Iraqi forces raided the Ministry of Health and arrested the deputy health minister, Hakim al-Zamili, on suspicion of involvement in sectarian kidnappings and killings. (He was later cleared at trial after witnesses failed to come forward.)

With the Ba'athists out and the international sanctions lifted, Iraq's public health challenges shifted markedly. Before 2003, child and maternal health were characterized by malnutrition, drug shortages, and poverty. After 2003, violence (war-related as well as domestic), psychological trauma, infectious diseases, and failing infrastructure were the main culprits (Webster 2013). The chance that a mother will die during childbirth is twice that of neighboring Jordan. Child immunization rates have fallen. Mortality rates for children under 5 are twice that of Jordan and three times that of prewar Syria. Tuberculosis rates are six times that of prewar Syria and 30 times that of Jordan (Webster 2011). At the height of the violence, women were loath to go to hospitals. As the number of unattended home births rose, Iraq's infant mortality grew to one of the highest on earth (75th of 78 countries in the developing world in 2006), tied with Sierra Leone, and better than only Afghanistan and Liberia (Save the Children 2006:12). The social determinants of health—refugees, housing shortages, poor water and sanitation, access to electricity, transportation and road safety, food and agriculture, education, and poverty—remain poor. Cholera, dysentery, hepatitis, and tuberculosis continued to crop up. In 2014, Basra's water supply was still not suitable for human consumption (Rawaf et al. 2014).

The war damaged many Iraqis psychologically as well. "Anything can happen at any moment," said Hashim Zainy, a psychiatrist at Al-Rashid Psychiatric Hospital in Baghdad, the country's only mental health hospital. "You can't plan for the next day or the next hour. You're always afraid, in every waking hour and in your sleep. This chronic stress gives you a deep sense of helplessness, an inability to take charge of your life and make decisions" (Fassihi 2008:177). In two 2006 studies, 14 percent of children surveyed in Baghdad and 30 percent of those in Mosul exhibited symptoms of PTSD. Girls were disproportionately harmed—17 percent of girls and 9 percent of boys in Baghdad, and 32 percent of girls and 26 percent of boys in Mosul, showed symptoms. Forty-seven percent of Baghdad primary school children had been exposed to a major traumatic event in the previous two years (Razokhi et al. 2006).

The 2007 Iraq Mental Health Survey, the first of its kind in the country, detailed the effects of living through the war. Respondents from the Kurdish region (45 percent) and Central/Southern Iraq (66 percent) reported direct war trauma. People in southern and central Iraq were twelve times more likely than those in the Kurdish north to say they'd been refugees, three times as likely to say they'd been internally displaced, and eight times more likely to say they'd been sexually assaulted. They reported much higher levels of exposure to bomb blasts, capture, kidnap or imprisonment, public humiliation, accusations of collaboration, witnessing a killing, the death of a dear one, family member kidnapped, war-related trauma, or other trauma. The researchers estimated that 35 percent of the 9,000 respondents nationwide suffered "significant psychological distress." While many respondents showed signs of PTSD, severe depression, phobias, and anxiety disorders were more dominant. Although men were more likely to be exposed to violent trauma, 40 percent of females and 30 percent of males suffered acute distress—findings in line with studies in Afghanistan, Sudan, Lebanon, and the West Bank and Gaza Strip (World Health Organization Regional Office for the Eastern Mediterranean/Iraq Health Ministry 2009:62, 81, 90).

Not surprisingly, experiences of trauma are pervasive among those who have fled the war. In a 2007 survey of 754 Iraqi refugees in Syria, *100 percent* of the respondents said they'd been exposed to severe trauma:

> Seventy-seven percent of the Iraqi refugees who were interviewed reported being affected by air bombardments and shelling or rocket attacks. Eighty percent reported witnessing a shooting. Sixty-eight percent said they experienced interrogation or harassment by militias or other groups, including receiving death threats, while sixteen percent have been tortured. Seventy-two percent were eye witnesses to a car bombing and seventy-five percent know someone who has been killed. The report highlighted the many forms of torture endured by Iraqi refugees, including beatings, electric shocks, objects being placed under fingernails, burns and rape. Most instances of torture were perpetrated by militias (sixty-nine percent). (UNHCR 2008)

Among Iraqi refugees, social and economic struggles, loss of social and family networks, and fears of repatriation have been shown to prolong depression and PTSD (Shoeb et al. 2007:450).

Iraq was spectacularly ill-equipped to treat the psychological fallout of the war. Mental illness remains a taboo topic, and families often privately bear the burden of caring for patients. The World Health Organization counted as few as 100 psychiatrists nationwide, while the Mental Health Survey found that only 10 percent of Iraqis suffering psychological disorders had ever been treated for their illness. As the years wore on, many Iraqis accepted the trauma as normal and downplayed the symptoms. Indeed, repeated exposure to violence can make a population more psychologically resilient (World Health Organization Regional Office for the Eastern Mediterranean/Iraq Health Ministry 2009:74, 80–81). Religious faith, political commitment, social networks, and psychological preparation for torture have also been shown to defend against psychological damage. Treating psychiatrists say Iraqi war victims blended scientific and indigenous constructs to create a new language of suffering: *dayeg* (rumination, poor concentration, lack of initiative, boredom, sleep problems, etc.), *qalbak maqbound* (sadness, anxiety, insecurity, or uprootedness "squeezing the heart," or *qalb*), *asabi* (nerves, irritability, impatience, anger), *nafsak deeyega* or *makhnouk* (poverty, political repression, or panic constricting the chest), and a form of PTSD known as *nafseetak ta'abana*, or "tired soul" (Shoeb et al. 2007:450, 456–57).

Finally, the war resulted in widespread environmental damage. Bombing, looting, and arson contributed to the worst toxic hotspots, at least some of them "strategic" in nature: a metal plating facility that was bombed, looted, and demolished, leaving tons of cyanide compounds scattered over publicly accessible areas; a pesticides warehouse caked in toxic materials; a petrochemicals warehouse that had been looted and burned; a sulfur mining complex; and a military scrapyard, including tanks, missiles, unexploded ordnance and hazardous chemicals (UNEP 2005:11–12). Children and street cleaners have a right not to be maimed or killed by unexploded cluster bombs. Coalition soldiers were exposed to burn pits, oil spills, and stockpiles of mustard gas and nerve agents left over from the 1980s (Chivers 2014). The right of ordinary Iraqis to live in a safe environment is doubtful, given the toxic munitions, carcinogenic waste, and unexploded ordnance left behind. The *Times* of London discovered that U.S. military contractors had dumped large amounts of oils, acids, filters and batteries in Iraqi scrapyards, which have inflicted rashes, blisters, and burns on workers at the sites, and threaten nearby agricultural lands (August 2010). Scientists are still trying to understand the epidemiology of incendiary white phosphorus and of depleted uranium (DU) weapons, which were widely used in Iraq for their armor-piercing qualities. Laboratory experiments show that exposure to DU can cause genetic mutations, chromosomal damage, and leukemia in mice, but the human effects are unclear (IVK Pax Christi 2013:11–13). Some scientists have pointed to spikes in congenital birth defects in Fallujah and Basra, which they surmise are related to the use of white phosphorus or DU. The Iraqi Ministry of Health could not replicate those findings (Caputi 2012; Iraqi Ministry of Health 2013).

The Damage Done: Learning from Iraq

The obvious lesson from Iraq is that decapitating a regime is much easier than securing a population and protecting its rights. While the consequences of the invasion may have been unintended, they shouldn't have been surprising. The downward spiral was foretold in the arrogance and ignorance of the occupation, the blind exercise of power, the shifting of responsibility amid the rising anarchy. U.S. troops in their ubiquitous dark sunglasses were often parodied as being faceless and hard-hearted, unable to see the agony of ordinary Iraqis. But the military as an institution also wore blinders. The violence was formalized and bureaucratized in blunt policies stretching from shock-and-awe, to counterinsurgency tactics, to detention and interrogation rules. Over the years, the Pentagon improved its efforts to protect civilians, but the sunglasses never really came off. Rules of engagement were modified and checkpoints redesigned to reduce the number of noncombatant casualties. During the Surge U.S. troops assumed greater risks to themselves in order to better protect civilians. Coalition officials tried mightily to contain sectarian killing, and sometimes criticized human rights abuses carried out by Iraqi forces. The biggest doctrinal change to emerge from the war was the U.S. Army's *Civilian Casualty Mitigation* manual. Published in 2012, the "civcas" manual marked a genuine shift in attitude. It advocates using the minimum degree of force necessary, discourages a Wild West "shoot-first" mentality, and recommends tracking rigorously the number and patterns of civilian casualties. Yet, here, too, the terms of restraint—necessity, proportionality, discrimination—are also instrumental terms of engagement that admit a great deal of violence. It's also hard not to notice that the new doctrine took effect after the U.S. had withdrawn from Iraq and as it was planning its departure from Afghanistan. Sparing civilians may be a means to win wars, but it's not clear the Pentagon views sparing civilians as an end in itself (see T. Smith 2014).

The U.S. military's "institutional learning" is cold comfort to those Iraqis (and U.S. soldiers) whose lives were shattered by the war, the disappeared and dislocated, the families left bereft, those caught in irreparable sectarian rifts. It takes a kind of moral myopia to think that tightening rules of engagement or handing out condolence payments frees political and military leaders from their secondary responsibilities for what happened. The war affected almost every facet of private and public life. It ushered in a repressive and often violent Shi'ite regime, deepening Sunni distrust and extremism. According to the Iraqi government, 10,000 people are still missing from the post-2003 period, although officials acknowledge that the actual number is much higher. Estimates that include the disappearances and mass killings under Saddam run as high as 250,000 to 1 million (Williams and al-Sahly 2009; International Commission on Missing Persons 2011). In 2015 there were about 100 security checkpoints in Baghdad. Shi'ite militias still patrol the streets. Levels of violence and displacement remain extremely high. According to the UN, nearly 19,000 Iraqi civilians were killed in between January 2014 and October 2015, most at the hands of ISIS (Office of the UN High Commissioner for Human Rights / United National Assistance Mission for Iraq-Human Rights Office 2016). The human rights balance sheet remains deep in the red. According to the most recent Zogby poll undertaken in Iraq, most respondents say the impact of the war has been negative with respect to personal safety and security (72 percent), economic development and employment (66 percent), and administration of government services (59 percent). Half of Iraqis say the upheaval has undermined political freedom, while a third say political freedom has grown. Nearly half say the impact on education has been negative. Only a quarter say women's rights are more secure. The sole area of (muted) optimism, driven by the Shi'ite majority, is religious freedom (39 percent positive, 36 negative, 14 percent no impact) (Zogby 2011:6–7). The notion that this was a just and legal war is light-years away from the carnage Iraqis themselves have endured.

CHAPTER 4

The Gaza Wars, 2008–2014: Human Rights Agency and Advocacy

> I want to survive, and if I don't, remember that I was not a Hamas man or a fighter. I wasn't used as a human shield, either. I was home.
>
> —tweet from Gaza, July 24, 2014 (Mualem 2014)

Wedged between Israel and Egypt in an area twice the size of Washington, D.C., the Gaza Strip is often compared to an open-air prison, its 1.7 million inhabitants suffocated by an economic blockade, barred from overseas travel by an Israeli overlord and a hostile regime in Cairo, and stifled at home by Hamas (Harakat al-Muqawamah al-Islamiyya, or Islamic Resistance Movement), the political-military faction that won the Palestinian elections in 2006 and has clung to power in Gaza ever since. Since 2005, Hamas's armed wing, the Izz al-Din al-Qassam Brigades, and several smaller militias have showered thousands of rockets on Israel. Before that, Hamas carried out more terror bombings inside the Jewish state than any other Palestinian group. The Israel Defense Forces (IDF) have launched countless raids against Hamas leaders and operatives, including the assassination of the movement's wheelchair-bound spiritual leader, Sheik Ahmed Yassin. Israel and Hamas maintain no political or diplomatic ties. Instead, the two sides carry on a crude dialogue in which arrests, assassinations, and political provocations are met with rockets and missile strikes. These almost weekly exchanges have been punctuated by three major offensives—Operation Cast Lead (2008–2009), Operation Pillar of Defense (2012), and Operation Protective Edge (2014)—which I refer to collectively as the Gaza wars.[1]

Israeli strategists have characterized these operations as "mowing the grass": the routine management of Palestinian threats and violence (Inbar and Shamir 2014). Hamas's capabilities have grown year by year as Gaza's thriving cottage industry in rockets has been supplemented by longer-range weapons imported from China, Syria, and Iran. As the range of Hamas missiles has grown, so has the swath of Israeli civilians traumatized, maimed, and killed. During Cast Lead, most of the rockets landed in southern Israel not far from the Gaza border. During Operation Protective Edge, rockets struck as far north as Haifa and Jerusalem, forcing airlines to suspend flights into Tel Aviv's Ben Gurion Airport. (Some incoming rockets were intercepted by an Israeli anti-missile system known as Iron Dome.) Hamas also built a labyrinth of concrete-reinforced tunnels along the Israeli border, which it used to shelter men and matériel and to launch raids to kill or capture Israelis. But it was Gazans who bore the brunt of the violence. Some 3,600 have been killed and 15,000 injured. Most have been civilians, cut down by IDF artillery or mortar rounds or crushed beneath the wreckage of their own houses in airstrikes. On the Israeli side, 76 soldiers and 11 civilians have died. Hamas has been quick to accuse the IDF of war crimes, but the Islamist group's own actions show contempt for the law. Not only do its erratic rockets make a mockery of discrimination between military and civilian objects, but Hamas fighters launch the rockets from densely populated areas in order to ensure that IDF counterstrikes will kill the requisite number of Palestinian civilians to merit international condemnation of Israel's actions. Civilians are used as "war crimes bait" (Friedman 2014). Israeli missile batteries, F-16 fighter jets, helicopter gunships, naval gunboats, and tank artillery units almost always oblige, pounding civilian areas that the IDF says have effectively been militarized by Hamas. The IDF's callousness toward the immense collateral damage is matched only by Hamas's cynicism in placing civilians in harm's way in the first place.

Israel's military creed is the Spirit of the IDF, which exalts the "supreme value" of human life and espouses the "purity of arms" (*tohar ha'neshek*). Soldiers are enjoined to use only as much force as the mission requires; to maintain their humanity in combat; and to "do all in their power to avoid causing harm to the lives, bodies, dignity, and property" of noncombatants.[2] A quasi-official warrior code geared to fighting terrorism further refines the duties of soldiers (Kasher and Yadlin 2005). And in a kind of hyper-legalism (IHL rather than human rights law), senior IDF officers are assigned dedicated legal counsel in the midst of military operations.[3] These restraints have moderated the IDF's use of force, prompting the Air Force to issue evacuation notices prior to bombing campaigns, for example, or to adjust or abort some airstrikes to avert collateral damage. Nevertheless, for ordinary Gazans, the conflicts have been hugely destructive, ripping at the fabric of society and economy and sending public health into a tailspin. As *Ha'aretz* columnist Amira Hass (2010) wrote of Cast Lead, regardless of the IDF's intentions, the violence "was experienced primarily as a war against civilians."

Under humanitarian law, we can easily indict Hamas for its indiscriminate rocket fire. But it's harder under IHL to get at the moral reality of Israel's campaigns in Gaza. Individual commanders and soldiers breached international law on a number of occasions, but the IDF's core strategy against a determined asymmetric foe seems plausible. Its legal rhetoric of war (no longer occupation) certainly sounds right: self-defense, discrimination, proportionality, counter-forces fire. IDF lawyers vet prospective targets and help select the best legal means of attack. The lawyers have conceded that there are always pressures to be more permissive when "the legal advisor eats, sleeps and runs with the army military," but say they never counseled or condoned illegal behavior (Craig 2013:185). Still, almost inevitably, strategists and lawyers treated the lives of Palestinian civilians as articles of trade to be exchanged for striking the Hamas targets embedded in their midst. Accountability was often reduced to the single question: Did combatants deliberately target civilians as such?

Human rights groups frame Gaza's shattered lives and demolished infrastructure as a rights catastrophe rather than a collateral damage tragedy. Most rights advocates in the region resist the blanket definition of Israeli-Palestinian strife as armed conflict or war, lest the more permissive laws of war eclipse the laws of human rights. Rights groups do rely on IHL to judge major military operations, especially those in Gaza.[4] Yet, while IDF lawyers emphasize the negative duty to refrain from direct, deliberate killing of civilians, human rights lawyers render the law in a more humanitarian, less war-room fashion, focusing on positive duties of due care and accountability and on the obligations of an occupying power. What should combatants have known? What could they have done to protect civilians?[5] The consequence of the violence is as important as the intent of the belligerents. Thus, rights observers generally say that Hamas's wild rocket fire is inherently indiscriminate and therefore illegal. Most also reject the IDF's blame-shifting defense. That defense goes like this: aside from the occasional errant bomb or mortar, Hamas is responsible for the killings in Gaza because it embeds its military apparatus—rocket teams, munitions caches, command and control—within the civilian population, the deeper the better. By "weaponizing" civilian infrastructure Hamas leaders have effectively mooted the IDF's duty to distinguish between military and civilian objects.

Israel's most influential human rights NGO, B'Tselem—The Israeli Information Center for Human Rights in the Occupied Territories—responds that

> Hamas is not—and cannot be—responsible for the extreme damage that Israel caused civilians in Gaza. Holding Hamas responsible for Israel's actions is tantamount to freeing Israel of any restrictions in its response, no matter how horrendous, to violations of the law by Hamas. This position is unjustifiable, either morally or legally: the responsibility for the harsh consequences of Israel's policy . . . lies with Israel's government and top military commanders who authorized it, despite the foreseeable horrific results. (B'Tselem 2014a)

A raft of human rights grievances simmer beneath the surface of any overt violations of IHL that the IDF may have committed in Gaza. Residents of the Strip lived under direct Israeli rule for nearly 40 years, and the abuses and humiliations are still raw. The IDF's conduct and systems of accountability have been shaped by decades of chronic violence. Classic human rights strategies of documenting and publicizing abuses have gone a long way toward framing popular as well as legal views of the wars. Both the IDF and Hamas lost their official monopolies over information, and we often saw the violence from the ground up. In the wake of the conflicts, a few Gazans have been able to lodge formal complaints via Israeli and Palestinian NGOs who could tell their story and act on their behalf. But Palestinians themselves also adopted the language and practices of rights to express and order their experiences. Rights activists in Gaza scrutinized Hamas, too. What Hugo Slim calls the "classic liberal schema of righteous victim and malevolent oppressor" was easy for Gazans to cling to in the context of the occupation, but not when Israel was fighting a regime with innocent blood on its hands (Slim 2009). Palestinian rights groups have criticized Hamas for its attacks on Israeli civilians; for recklessly endangering civilians in Gaza; for attacking Fatah supporters; for executing suspected collaborators with Israel; and for cracking down on free expression and generally trampling the rights of Gazans (see, e.g., Akram and Bronner 2011; and Al Mezan Center for Human Rights 2011). Some of the most damning disclosures about Hamas tactics came from Palestinian activists in Gaza who took far greater personal risks in criticizing Hamas than their counterparts in Israel faced for criticizing the IDF.

From Occupation to War

I noted in Chapter 1 how bureaucratic language and logic can erode basic civilian protections. Many of the effects of the Gaza War can be traced to practices and modes of thought that are the product of nearly fifty years of occupation of the West Bank and the Gaza Strip. The occupation has been marked by chronic violence. The IDF has followed a muscular policy of expulsions; house demolitions; incarceration; curfews, closures, and travel restrictions; "moderate" and "enhanced" "physical pressure" during interrogations; and has authorized lethal force in what are essentially police actions (N. Gordon 2008; Middle East Watch 1990). It has levied broad punishment for narrow offenses, and in recent years has shown a taste for preemption and assassination. If these practices were fit for occupation, they could be redoubled for war. After years of demolishing houses in the West Bank, for example, it seemed natural to do the same thing on a large scale in Gaza. The occupation has humiliated and embittered Palestinians and lent popular legitimacy to calls for violence. It has also hardened the hearts of many Israelis and distorted the country's legal system (Kretzmer 2002; Hajjar 2005). Hebrew University's David Shulman has argued that atrocities are "a natural and enduring part of Israel's military control of the West Bank" (Shulman 2011). He blogged, "I do not believe that a society can disenfranchise, dispossess, and effectively dehumanize large numbers of people living between Jenin and Hebron without this process influencing the way it conducts a war in Gaza" (Shulman 2009).

The NGO Breaking the Silence (BTS), a movement of IDF soldiers who served in the Occupied Territories, has sought to distill the "harsh logic" of the occupation.[6] Since 2004, BTS has collected testimonies from nearly 1,000 IDF veterans or active-duty soldiers. The group emphasizes the day-to-day routines of wielding power over other people. "Standing at a checkpoint you can be nice for the first hour," says BTS's Avner Gvaryahu. "But after four hours of being hungry, or hot or cold, and pissed off, and the only way you can actually control people is by force, that's what you're going to do" ("Israeli Soldiers Breaking the Silence on the Occupation of Palestine" 2012). The founder of BTS, Yehuda Shaul, served 14 months in the flashpoint of Hebron, the largest city on the West Bank, where several hundred Jewish settlers live in what the IDF calls the "Israeli" sector, or H-2, which extends from settlements on the eastern edge of Hebron to the heart of the city, where settlers are clustered in the neighborhood around the Tomb of the Patriarchs. While most of Hebron is under the day-to-day control of the Palestinian Authority, H-2 is under the control of the IDF. Streets are heavily patrolled by Israeli soldiers, and Palestinian residents must pass through military checkpoints and searches every day. The IDF has closed long stretches of the central *casbah*, the city's historical commercial center, ostensibly for security reasons. Settlers and soldiers may walk or drive along the shuttered streets, but Palestinians may not. The IDF welded shut the front doors of hundreds of Palestinian houses and shops that opened onto the blocked streets, and some inhabitants must instead use ladders to climb in and out of their back windows. For BTS, this perversity is part and parcel of occupation. "If your mission is to go down to Hebron and make sure that 850 settlers have rights and that 185,000 Palestinians don't have rights, there's no nice way of doing that," said Shaul. "The only way to rule people against their will is to make them fear you, and once they get used to a level of fear, you have to increase it, and increase it."[7]

A basic technique of the Israeli occupation is "demonstrating a presence" or "searing the consciousness"—constant reminders of the IDF's presence lead to a kind of internalized fear and control of the population. During night patrols, for example,

> Soldiers are sent to patrol the alleys and streets of a town, and they "demonstrate their presence" in a variety of ways: shooting into the air, throwing sound bombs, shooting flares or tear gas, conducting random house invasions and takeovers, and interrogating passersby. Field-level commanders call these "violent patrols," "harassment activity," or "disruption of normalcy." According to the soldiers' testimonies, "demonstrating a presence" is done on a frequent and ongoing basis, and it is not dependent on intelligence about a specific terrorist activity. Missions to "demonstrate a presence" prove that the IDF sees all Palestinians—whether or not they are engaged in opposition—as targets for intimidation and harassment. (Breaking the Silence 2012:22–23)

The mismatch of knowledge and control is nearly absolute. In 2002, during the Second Intifada, chief of staff and now defense minister Moshe Ya'alon said that IDF operations were designed to "etch the consciousness" of the Palestinians so completely that resistance would seem futile (Dahan 2012:32). In 2006 then executive director of B'Tselem Jessica Montell argued that "the suffering of the civilian population is not merely a byproduct of Israel's attacks against militants. . . . It is an intentional part of Israeli policy. . . . The clear intention of the practice is to pressure the Palestinian Authority and the armed Palestinian organizations by harming the entire civilian population." Montell cited the low-flying sorties over Gaza by the Israeli Air Force three or four times each night to create powerful sonic booms. The flights served no military purpose; they were meant to roil the population at large. Prime minister Ehud Olmert explained, "Thousands of residents in southern Israel live in fear and discomfort, so I gave instructions that nobody will sleep at night in Gaza" (Montell 2006).

Since the First Intifada (1987–1993) the IDF's use of violence has been condoned and even encouraged by political leaders. Palestinians still remember Yitzhak Rabin for ordering the IDF to use "force, might, and beatings" to quash the revolt ("Israel Declines to Study Rabin Tie to Beatings" 1990). The use of torture and mistreatment was widespread in lockups. On the ground, Palestinians were forced to undertake dangerous tasks at the behest of IDF soldiers. Soldiers would order civilians to enter buildings to see if they were booby-trapped, have them remove suspicious objects from roads, hold civilians inside or on the porch of a house the troops had commandeered so it would not be attacked, or force them to walk in front of IDF soldiers to protect the soldiers from harm (B'Tselem 2011). During the Second Intifada (2000–2005) this use of civilians was formalized in the "neighbor policy." The procedure was used widely in arrests of suspected militants. Soldiers would select a Palestinian man or teenage boy and order him to enter the house of a suspect to try to coax the occupant to surrender without a fight. The exact procedure varied, but the neighbor would often go room to room, turning on lights and opening windows. The procedure could be disorderly and dangerous, preceded by soldiers yelling, using loudspeakers, throwing stun grenades, or shooting toward the dwelling. The IDF command insisted the device was designed to avoid bloodshed during arrests. But it was also designed—perhaps primarily—to spare IDF soldiers the risks of extracting potentially dangerous suspects.

The neighbor policy was routinized and expanded. At the height of Operation Defensive Shield, in 2002, IDF forces were arresting 200 people a night (Breaking the Silence 2012:33). Human Rights Watch described

> night[s] of panic and terror, including death threats, house demolitions, and wide-scale arrests. In each of these cases, the IDF routinely coerced civilians to perform life-endangering acts that assisted IDF

> military operations. . . . Friends, neighbors, and relatives of "wanted" Palestinians were taken at gunpoint to knock on doors, open strange packages, and search houses in which the IDF suspected armed Palestinians were present. Some families found their houses taken over and used as military positions by the IDF during an operation while they themselves were ordered to remain inside. In one case documented by Human Rights Watch, a civilian was held as a hostage in order to pressure his brother to surrender. (Human Rights Watch 2002:2)

The policy collectivized the hard hand of occupation and transferred risk from soldiers to civilians. It was popular with the IDF's elite "preventive arrest" units, who argued it saved lives on both sides and judged it "better than our ceramic bullet-proof vests" (Samy Cohen 2010:131–32). This instrumental use of civilians led to even more egregious cases of human shielding. Rabbis for Human Rights accused members of the Israeli Border Police of attempting to deter rock-throwers by tying a thirteen-year-old boy to the front of a jeep and driving through a West Bank village (BBC 2004).

In May 2002 a consortium of human rights groups led by Adalah—The Legal Center for Arab Minority Rights in Israel—petitioned the Israeli Supreme Court to ban the neighbor policy. Three months later a man named Nidal Abu Mukhsan was killed in the West Bank village of Tubas as he was being used as a "neighbor" by IDF forces trying to arrest a wanted man. Pressed again by the petitioners, the Court issued a temporary injunction banning the practice. In response, the IDF command issued, for the first time, an order that forbade IDF troops using civilians as "live shields" against gunfire or other attacks, and prohibited use of civilian hostages during the execution of "military acts," or using civilians in ways that might endanger their life or limb (locating or defusing a bomb, e.g.). Soon after, the IDF announced a new policy known as the "early warning" procedure in which Palestinians would be "solicited" to "assist" in arrests. According to the directive, the purpose was "to minimize the danger of wounding innocent civilians and the wanted persons themselves (allowing their arrest without bloodshed)." The procedure would go forward only with the civilian's consent and if the commander determined the operation would not pose any danger to the civilian. The consortium of human rights petitioners responded with a catalog of affidavits from Palestinians who said that in recent months they had been used both as neighbors and as human shields even in live-fire situations.[8]

The Israeli Supreme Court banned the neighbor policy and the early warning procedure in 2005. The president of the court, Justice Aharon Barack, argued that it was impossible to ensure the safety of the volunteers, and even if a civilian had agreed to participate, his or her consent could not be considered genuine. As a soldier's affidavit in the case put it, "No civilian would refuse a 'request' presented to him at 0300 by a group of soldiers aiming their cocked rifles at him" (BBC 2005). Another soldier said, "at 3AM, 2AM, we knock on the door. So the person opening the door sees 5–6 armed soldiers with painted faces, camouflage colors on their faces, asking him to come with them. He won't refuse. No one has ever refused" (Breaking the Silence 2004). The Court went a step farther, however, ruling that even in the absence of open coercion, the stark inequalities of power at work meant consent that appeared to be genuine could still be false.

The fate of the neighbor policy shows the degree to which the IDF remains under civil authority and susceptible to pressures from civil society. The Supreme Court applied human rights ideas in a sophisticated way: Justice Barack sounded outright Foucauldian as he described the coercion inherent in the procedure. "Soliciting the assistance of local residents," as the apprehension protocol put it, was a quaint fiction in the context of occupation. Consent was also doubtful because assisting the IDF might be construed by other Palestinians as collaboration, which could lead to further misery, this time at the hand of Fatah or Hamas. Still, the Supreme Court decision did not end the instrumental use of Palestinians by Israeli soldiers. New risk-shifting methods emerged. In 2006 the IDF introduced the "bulldozer policy." If an arrest target refused to come out of his house, a bulldozer would ram the building, shaking it but not knocking it down (Samy Cohen 2010:132). The physical structures of Palestinian life had been fair game for some time: the Supreme Court approved house demolitions under certain conditions. During Cast Lead, the bulldozer was often the weapon of first resort in extraction and clearing cases.

The neighbor policy also illustrates the sorts of legal entanglements the IDF command meant to avoid in Gaza. The occupation of the West Bank entailed the long-term administration of people following fairly established rules of conduct and entailing some affirmative humanitarian duties. The Gaza campaigns would be quick and conclusive micro-wars featuring heavy firepower and permissive rules of engagement. Commanders were determined not to repeat the mistakes made in 2006 in the Second Lebanon War. Many Israelis regarded the prosecution of that war as timid and indecisive. A government inquest criticized a ground offensive into southern Lebanon that achieved little but left troops bogged down and vulnerable (Israel Ministry of

Foreign Affairs 2008). That lesson was magnified by "Gaza phobia" in Israeli political pronouncements and military planning. Gaza was referred to as "*me'arat nachashim*," a snake pit (Pappé 2009). That image came alive during Protective Edge as the extent of Hamas's secret tunnel system was revealed. Looming over these wars was the specter of another Gilad Shalit, the IDF soldier who was captured by Hamas in 2006 and held captive until 2011, when he was exchanged for 1,027 Palestinian prisoners.[9]

The legal status of Gaza helped clear the way for war. After Israel withdrew all its troops and settlers from Gaza in 2005, international lawyers and the Israeli government wrangled over whether or not the Jewish state still controlled the territory. The question was legally significant. Territorial control would oblige Israel to afford basic protections to the residents of the Gaza, and would lessen the degree of force IDF troops could deploy to maintain public order (Bisharat et al. 2010). According to the Ariel Sharon government's Disengagement Plan, Israeli security forces would continue to guard and monitor land borders, carry out security activities in the sea off the coast of Gaza, and wield "exclusive authority" in Gaza air space. The Strip itself would be "demilitarized" and "devoid of weaponry" (Disengagement Plan of Prime Minister Ariel Sharon 2004). Israeli officials were eager to replace the constraints of occupation with the more permissive *in bello* rules. In 2007 Israel's Security Cabinet designated Gaza as "hostile territory," and vowed to continue "military and counter-terrorist operation against the terrorist organizations in Gaza," a move meant to support Israel's claims of self-defense in its on-going use of force in Gaza while distancing Israel from any human rights duties there (James 2009; Al Haq 2007).

Most human rights groups in the region say Israel has tried to shed its obligations to the people of Gaza—security, health care, education, freedom of movement, basic infrastructure—while maintaining power and control. Gisha—Legal Center for Freedom of Movement—for example, argues that Israel retains certain "post occupation obligations" on the way to "fulfillment of lawful sovereignty" of Palestinians over Gaza (Bashi and Feldman 2011:chap. 3). The Supreme Court ruled in 2007 that after the withdrawal, "the primary obligations imposed on the State of Israel regarding residents of the Gaza Strip are derived from the state of warfare that currently ensues between Israel and the Hamas organization which controls the Gaza Strip," but noted also that "these obligations also stem from the degree of control that the State of Israel has at the border crossings between it and the Gaza Strip; and also from the situation that was created between the State of Israel and the territory of the Gaza Strip after years of Israeli military control in the area, following which the Gaza Strip is now almost totally dependent on Israel for its supply of electricity."[10]

The IDF continued to govern the movement of people and goods in and out of Gaza, maintaining land and sea blockades as well as no-go border zones inside Gaza territory. In agreement with the Palestinian Authority, Israel controlled the population registry for Gaza and approved the issuance of ID cards necessary for travel abroad. Surveillance drones and balloons hovered overhead, while robotic guns policed border zones inside Gaza. Israel claimed that it was bound only to allow the free passage of goods "vital for the survival of the civilian population" and of people only "in humanitarian cases, with an emphasis on urgent medical cases" (Bashi and Feldman 2011:5). Israel continued to provide the lion's share of gas, water, electricity, and telecommunications. After the 2006 election, Israel choked off supplies of electricity and fuel to put pressure on Hamas. The methodical nature of that control became clear when WikiLeaks released a November 2008 cable from the U.S. Embassy in Tel Aviv in which Israeli officials were quoted as saying the blockade would keep Gaza's economy "functioning at the lowest level possible consistent with avoiding a humanitarian crisis" (U.S. Embassy, Tel Aviv 2008; Wright and Robinson 2010).

The social and political backdrop deteriorated as well. The militancy of Hamas primed the IDF and much of Israeli society for a vigorous campaign. Hamas's ideology is incorrigibly racist and anti-Semitic. Its Charter vows to destroy Israel and "raise the banner of Allah over every inch of Palestine."[11] The almost weekly suicide attacks during the Second Intifada had already pushed Israeli society sharply to the right on security issues. The growing power of religious conservatives was increasingly reflected in the IDF's rabbinical unit, which sought to fill soldiers with "yiddishkeit (Jewishness) and a fighting spirit." In crusading language, official pamphlets distributed to soldiers compared Palestinians to Amalekites and Philistines, and implored soldiers to "show no mercy on the cruel." Messianic literature linked to the settler movement also found its way onto IDF bases. One pamphlet rejected basic norms of discrimination: "As for the population, it is not innocent. . . . We call on you to ignore any strange doctrines and orders that confuse the logical way of fighting the enemy."[12] On the opening day of Protective Edge, Givati brigade commander Col. Ofer Winter spurred on his officers, saying, "History has chosen us to spearhead the fighting [against] the terrorist 'Gazan' enemy which abuses, blasphemes and curses the God of Israel's forces" (Friedman 2014).

IDF soldiers, too, were brutalized and desensitized. Most were young conscripts who came of age during the traumas of the Second Intifada. Graffiti left behind in Cast Lead advertised: "Death to the Arabs," "No Arabs, No Attacks," a drawing of a grave inscribed "Arabs 1948–2008"; "Die you all"; and "1 is down, 999,999 to go," "my best Arabic translator is my grenade launcher," and spray-painted insignia of the racist Kach Party, which is banned in Israel for advocating expulsion of Palestinians (International Crisis Group 2009:18; UN Human Rights Council 2009:199; Breaking the Silence 2009:52). Trash-talk and black humor are endemic to war, but these strains of hatred are a fast track to atrocities. During Protective Edge, Israeli politicians and media joined in. Following the murder of three Israeli yeshiva students in the West Bank, a crackdown in the West Bank, and the immolation of a Palestinian boy at the hands of a Jewish gang in Jerusalem, many were baying for blood. Ayelet Shaked, a Knesset member for the Jewish Home Party, called on the Israeli army to destroy the homes of terrorist "snakes," and to murder their mothers as well, so that they would not be able to bring "little snakes" into the world (quoted in Jarbawi 2014). Netanyahu was pressured by the far right wing of his own government to conquer and even re-annex Gaza. Calls to "let the IDF win," or to "go all the way" and eradicate Hamas held out no real plan to excise a deep-rooted social movement other than more bombing. The country's highest circulation newspaper, *Israel Hayom*, called for the Gaza to be "returned to the Stone Age" (Regev 2014).

As in the American case, expectations regarding force protection ran high. Since the First Lebanese War (1982–1983) Israeli society and military have grown increasingly risk-averse. IDF casualties that might once have been considered heroic are now seen as signs of strategic or political incompetence. As a result, political leaders and the IDF command tend to favor stand-off weapons and aerial attacks over ground offensives (Levy 2011). These policy choices are reflected in Israeli-Palestinian casualty ratios: approximately 1:6 (one Israeli soldier to 6 Palestinians) in the First Intifada (1987–1993), 1:9 in the al-Aqsa Intifada (2000–2005), 1:10 in Lebanon (2006); 1:86 in Cast Lead (2009); 1:42 in Pillar of Defense (2012); and 1:26 in Protective Edge (2014).

This shift of risk from soldiers to civilians is evident in the 2004 code of conduct crafted by a team of philosophers and defense officials convened by Tel Aviv University ethicist Asa Kasher and IDF Maj. Gen. Amos Yadlin. The ethic sought to refine the Spirit of the IDF within the context of fighting terrorism. Arguing that "a combatant is a citizen in uniform," Kasher and Yadlin rejected the chivalric ideal that "the duty to minimize casualties among combatants during combat is last on the list of priorities or next to last, if terrorists are excluded from the category of noncombatants." "In Israel, quite often [the citizen-combatant] is a conscript or on reserve duty. His blood is as red and thick as that of citizens who are not in uniform. His life is as precious as the life of anyone else" (Kasher and Yadlin 2005:17). Israelis were thus citizens first, and combatants or noncombatants second. An attack on a soldier becomes an attack on the entire body politic, and the whole framework of distinction starts to topple.

Kasher and Yadlin argue (2005:15) that soldiers owe a duty, in descending order, to ensure:

> (d.1) Minimum injury to the lives of citizens of the state ["same-side" citizens] who are not combatants during combat; (d.2) Minimum injury to the lives of other persons (outside the state) who are not involved in terror, when they are under the effective control of the state;
> (d.3) Minimum injury to the lives of the combatants of the state ["same-side" combatants] in the course of their combat operations;
> (d.4) Minimum injury to the lives of other persons (outside the state) who are not involved in terror, when they are not under the effective control of the state;
> (d.5) Minimum injury to the lives of other persons (outside the state) who are indirectly involved in terror acts or activities;
> (d.6) Injury as required to the liberties or lives of other persons (outside the state) who are directly involved in terror acts or activities.

The novel claim here is that "our" citizen-soldiers (d.3) deserve greater protection than do "their" people who are uninvolved in terror and whom "we" do not effectively control (d.4); or are indirectly involved in terror (d.5); or directly involved in terror (d.6). One can argue within the traditional *jus in bello* framework that combatants have no obligation to protect persons directly, and with less confidence, indirectly involved in terrorism. But the claim that *uninvolved* civilians are less worthy of protection than one's own combatants is flatly anti-chivalric. "Under the control of" is also used in a new fashion. As noted earlier, a number of international tribunals and courts, including the ICJ in its Advisory Opinion regarding Israel's separation barrier ("the wall"), have held that effective control triggers certain human rights obligations. Kasher and Yadlin argue that it triggers only the more modest, IHL-derived protections of "other-side" civilians.

The IDF's legal procedures were also shaped by the occupation. Human rights groups have waged a protracted legal battle over fair trials and adequate investigations in the West Bank and Gaza. From 1987 to 2000 the IDF Military Police Investigation Unit (MPIU) investigated almost every instance in which Palestinians not taking part in hostilities were killed. As the Second Intifada/Al-Asqa Intifada (2000–2005) became increasingly violent, the IDF changed the legal framework from occupation to "armed conflict short of war." Under the new framework, independent investigations would be convened only if a unit-level "operational investigation" found evidence of criminal wrongdoing. The number of homicide investigations plummeted (Stein 2010:6). In 2003, the Association for Civil Rights in Israel (ACRI) and B'Tselem petitioned the Supreme Court to reinstate the earlier policy. The Court did so in 2011, though human rights fact-finding continues to fill in the holes in official investigations. Testifying in the trial of one of his own soldiers accused of abusing a bound detainee, Commander of the Paratroopers Brigade, Colonel Yossi Bechar, noted,

> These incidents are not so rare in number, but there is simply a silence surrounding some of them, and some of them are done in a more sophisticated and criminal way . . . these cases of Palestinian detainees being beaten by soldiers and police are incidents that unfortunately occur from time to time. In many cases no complaint is made, and there are various conspiracies of silence surrounding them, so that sometimes we only know about them years later, and furthermore, through anonymous messages by [the organization] Breaking the Silence and others, through the media or through other means. (Yesh Din 2008)

Destroying Hamasastan

If the occupation foretold a harsh campaign in Gaza, the IDF's means and methods of attack ensured it. The choice of weaponry, the scale of firepower, the doctrine of force protection, the use of heavy covering fire, and limits on humanitarian access were unprecedented in the history of the IDF. Hamas often says that Israel is a militarized society, flush with conscripts and reservists, and has used this as justification for targeting noncombatants. Israeli strategy toward Gaza also conflated a government, a people, and a place.

During Cast Lead Israel's deputy prime minister Haim Ramon said, "We damaged Hamas's capability of ruling. . . . we can't accept the existence of Hamasastan" (quoted in Goodman, Menuchin, and Oron 2009:24). Of course, "Hamasastan" was not just a gang of leaders or a gaggle of ministry buildings. The term identified an organization with a cramped, densely populated space. Attacks were aimed at the parliament building, the prime minister's office, the ministries of education, transportation, finance, foreign affairs, and labor, as well as courts, media outlets, and the Islamic University of Gaza, destroying both the women's college and the science building, which Israeli officials said housed a weapons research center (Bisharat et al. 2010:73–74).

The bombing strategy followed protocols developed in the Second Lebanon War. In that conflict, aerial bombardment flattened the south Beirut neighborhood of Dahiye, a Shiʿite stronghold where Hezbollah had its headquarters. (The before and after satellite photographs that ran on the front page of the *New York Times* were devastating.) In October 2008, with the Gaza campaign brewing, Maj. Gen. Gadi Eisenkott outlined what he called the "Dahiye Doctrine": "What happened in the Dahiye Quarter of Beirut in 2006 will happen in every village from which shots are fired on Israel. We will use disproportionate force against it and we will cause immense damage and destruction" (Wilmshurst 2012:412).

Much of the international law debate about the wars has focused on specific targets struck (hospitals, schools, UN shelters) and on the IDF's reliance on white phosphorus munitions, fletchette and fragmentation bombs, and weapons that emitted toxic heavy metals. But it was the conventional "legal" missile strikes and artillery fire that were the least discriminate and most destructive. General rules of engagement—"only military targets shall be attacked"; "any attack against civilian objectives shall be prohibited"—meant little, given the often crude munitions used in close civilian quarters. During Cast Lead, the IDF fired around 3,500 155 mm shells. Each shell weighs 52 kilograms and can kill people within a 200-meter radius. On the testing ground, soldiers must be at least 250 meters away if they're sheltered in a bunker, 350 meters away if they're exposed. For purposes of civilian protection in Cast Lead, the footprint of the blast was calculated at a mere 50 square meters, with a "safe" distance from buildings of 25 meters. Thus, a strike the IDF considered discriminate was almost guaranteed to have a lethal impact over a large area. "Covering fire" from tank cannons often meant wild shooting. During two weeks in Gaza, one tank operator fired 40–50 shells, 32 boxes of medium size machine gun bullets, 230 bullets per box, 400–500 Browning machine gun bullets, and 19 shells of a 60 mm mortar. In earlier operations, firing even one tank shell required approval of the division, and sometimes brigade, officer. Now, twenty-one-year-old tank gunners were making decisions on the fly.[13] During Protective Edge, the IDF fired a startling 32,000 artillery shells targeting what the IDF identified as 5,226 "terror sites" (Harel and Cohen 2014; B'Tselem 2015b:5).

During the ground invasions in 2009 and 2014 there was very little direct gunfire between IDF soldiers and Palestinian fighters. If the IDF detected rocket fire it would respond with guided missiles or standoff artillery. Anyone on the street in what was deemed a hostile area could be targeted. A soldier who served in Cast Lead recounted his commanding officer's "militant" and "fierce" declaration that "this is war and in war . . . no consideration of civilians was to be taken. You shoot anyone you see" (Breaking the Silence 2009:27). "In urban warfare, anyone is your enemy. No innocents. It was simply urban warfare in every way" (20). "The instruction was explicit—if you're not sure, kill. Fire power was insane. The booms were just mad. The minute we got to our starting line, we simply began firing at suspect places" (20). One soldier was awestruck by the power he wielded: "You feel like a kid playing around with a magnifying glass, burning up ants. Really. A 20-year-old kid should not be doing such things to people" (88).

Hamas rigged schools with explosives, stored weapons in homes and mosques, and launched rockets from schoolyards and children's playgrounds (Israel Ministry of Foreign Affairs 2009a). Some IDF airstrikes were followed by terrific secondary blasts as stores of munitions exploded. Israeli officials stressed that Palestinian fighters had created these "mixed settings," and so it was they, not the IDF, who bore responsibility for civilian losses. That logic was echoed at times by Gazans themselves, who pleaded with Palestinian fighters not to fire rockets from their neighborhoods lest they draw counterstrikes. A resident of Gaza City complained that "Israel destroyed entire buildings around us, in which there were many innocent people, because of what isolated individuals did" (International Crisis Group 2009:2). During Protective Edge, Gazans who lived in the border zones laced with Hamas tunnels quietly criticized Hamas for bringing the wrath of Israel down upon them (Rudoren 2014b). A Hamas representative justified the strategy as classic collateral damage: "That's the way it works with all resistance movements. Yes, some people die, but it's to prevent a bigger loss" (International Crisis Group 2009:3).

The house demolitions during Cast Lead weren't unforeseen collateral damage. Some harm to structures was incidental to the fighting, but most was planned. In the wake of the ground invasion, IDF engineering units moved in. D-9 Caterpillar armored (and armed) bulldozers, smaller Lioness bulldozers designed to traverse narrow alleyways, rigged explosive charges, and engineered airstrikes cleared about 2,100 houses and damaged another 3,200.[14] The demolitions ostensibly served two purposes. First, they were used to demolish houses or other structures connected to Hamas leaders or activists, or suspected of containing booby traps, weapons caches, explosive charges, or tunnels that might endanger IDF troops. Second, they were aimed at "the day after," a reference to securing IDF advantages in tactical position, field of vision, and range of fire in future conflicts." "It was amazing," recounted one soldier. "At first you go in and see lots of houses. A week later, after the razing, you see the horizon further away, almost to the sea. They simply took down all the houses around so the terrorists would have nowhere else to hide" (Breaking the Silence 2009:101). Next time, said another, Palestinian positions would be "more exposed, a state that would afford us better firing and observation conditions, and far greater control" (11). Satellite images show that most of the buildings were demolished after the IDF gained control over the area, many in the final days of the conflict (Human Rights Watch 2010a:4).

Human rights groups have documented a number of cases in which IDF soldiers shanghaied Palestinians into service as human shields. Referred to as "Johnnies" by IDF soldiers, they were forced to enter potentially dangerous houses ahead of Israeli units to make sure they were safe. Following the neighbor policy playbook, "sometimes the force would enter while placing rifle barrels on a civilian's shoulder, advancing into a house and using him as a human shield" (Breaking the Silence 2009:7–8). A man in his sixties was forced to run in front of IDF troops toward an area under fire; "uninvolved" civilians were sent into houses to retrieve militia weapons; children were forced to carry military supplies, to search bags, houses, or people for explosives, or to carry messages to suspects. Children were held inside houses where soldiers had taken up positions to discourage attacks, and were forced to stand or walk near soldiers during confrontations to ward off attacks (Al Mezan Center for Human Rights 2009; Al Mezan Centre for Human Rights and Defence for Children International-Palestine Section 2009:52).

On the Palestinian side, some human shields were coerced. A video clip from Cast Lead shows a Hamas fighter, gun slung over his shoulder, dashing across a street carrying a young boy as a shield against Israeli snipers.[15] In another clip, a militiaman launches a rocket from within a walled compound, and then flees surrounded by a protective entourage of children. In both cases Israeli forces held their fire.[16] Other human shields volunteered for duty. After the IDF would warn residents to evacuate an apartment block or a house, friends and family would sometimes *come to* the address and gather on top of the building to deter air strikes. Israel responded with its "knock on the roof" policy, striking the rooftop with "light" fire or dummy shells a few minutes before the full-blown strike. This was usually enough to drive people out of the building. The IDF was reluctant to strike when the volunteer human shields were around, but it was not paralyzed by their presence. IDF lawyers gave less weight to the "civilian-ness" of human shields than they gave to other noncombatants. If the target was considered important enough, the Israelis would strike, stressing that Hamas's reckless endangerment of civilians was to blame for the damage that ensued. During Protective Edge Hamas's entire strategy was a form of human shielding.

Many of these excesses clearly breached IHL, but others could be ascribed to military necessity or the discretion of commanders. Some IDF misstrikes involved bad intelligence or miscommunication, or were clumsy and careless, but not necessarily reckless or negligent. During Cast Lead many IDF airstrikes hit city centers, but most formed a rough ring around Gaza City, with the heaviest concentration on the east and northeast sectors closest to the Israeli border where Hamas rocket-launchers were most active (UN Environment Program 2009:17). These were technically "counter-force" strikes, albeit in areas with heavy civilian populations. A three-mile stretch of the city of Rafah, along the border with Egypt, was completely leveled by bombing and bulldozing. Rafah is famous for its hundreds of tunnels linking Gaza to Egypt, so this destruction, too, arguably served the military purpose of cutting supply lines (23). During Protective Edge, the worst devastation was in the Gaza City neighborhood of Shujaiyeh where Palestinians rocketeers were active and many of the tunnels originated, and, yet again, in Rafah. However plausible these targets may seem in humanitarian law, the means of attack—the Israeli Air Force dropped more than 100 one-ton bombs on Shujaiyeh in a single day—failed to meet any reasonable standard of proportionality (G. Cohen 2014).

At the same time, IDF tactics deliberately tilted the balance of risk in favor of soldiers and against civilians (see Levy 2011:82, 2012:chap. 6). "We rewrote the rules of war for Gaza," said one Cast Lead commander. The traditional standard was "means and intentions": a Palestinian could be legitimately targeted if he or she brandished a weapon and showed intent to use it. Now fear and suspicion were enough (MacIntyre 2010). The rules were much like those in Iraq at the height of the insurgency. "Shoot if you like," an IDF infantryman described his orders. "If you're afraid, or you see someone, shoot. . . . You don't only shoot when threatened. The assumption is that you constantly feel threatened, so anything there threatens you, you shoot" (Breaking the Silence 2009:24). Ground forces swept into civilian quarters behind a "rolling curtain" of aerial and artillery fire. "Covering fire" and "air support" led to sharp upticks in civilian casualties (Palestinian Centre for Human Rights n.d.:39). "No humanitarian consideration played any role in the army. . . . The goal was to carry out an operation with the least possible casualties for the army, without its even asking what the price would be for the other side" (Breaking the Silence 2009:27). During house-to-house searches, units sometimes blasted holes in the back wall out of fear that the entrances might be booby trapped. A soldier recalled,

> [The battalion commander] said: "not a hair will fall off a soldier of mine, and I am not willing to allow a soldier of mine to risk himself by hesitating. If you are not sure—shoot. If there is doubt then there is no doubt." We understood this and said that it's not because people wanted to kill, to collect hits or glory. It's because they wanted to preserve human lives at any cost. We all know, we're all living in this country and know that the soft belly is casualties in all of the wars, and they simply wanted to stick to this, completely. (Breaking the Silence 2009:20)

Brigade Commander Col. Herzl Halevy ranked the priorities: "first complete the mission, then defend the soldiers' lives and finally minimize the damage to the Palestinian population" (quoted in Goodman, Menuchin, and Oron 2009:14).

During Cast Lead the IDF air-dropped about 2.5 million leaflets, called 165,000 landlines and cell phones, interrupted television and radio broadcasts, and blanketed Gaza with text messages ("IDF Issues Warnings to the Civilians of Gaza" 2009). The first messages sought to drive a wedge between the people and Hamas in all its manifestations—political party, administrative body, provider of social services, military organization. This part of the campaign was largely successful; years of attacks on Hamas assets had taught Gazans to steer clear of political and bureaucratic buildings as well as the homes of prominent Hamas figures. On December 28, 2008, 300,000 leaflets were dropped warning that "the IDF will hit and destroy any building or site containing ammunitions." Anyone harboring munitions "is risking his life and must leave the place for the safety of his own life and that of his family. You have been warned."[17] Flyers included a phone number and a Gmail address for Gazans to report militia activities. Additional messages instructed residents to flee in advance of airstrikes. On January 3 and 4, flyers were dropped on central Gaza City, saying that the IDF was "obliged" to respond to terrorist actions launched from the area, and residents were told they remained behind at their own risk. These were not isolated pockets of violence. During Cast Lead nearly 500,000 civilians—a third of Gazans—were ordered to evacuate their houses at some point during the three-week war (Palestinian Centre for Human Rights n.d.:13).

According to the IDF's blog, 410,000 flyers were air-dropped during Protective Edge warning about strikes on "terror sites" in the neighborhood. Some of the flyers that fluttered down featured maps of suggested evacuation routes. The IDF says it met, and even exceeded, the international law requirement of effective advance warning: "To notify civilians of impending IDF operations and to instruct civilians how to avoid harm, the IDF employed a comprehensive advance warnings system, with multiple, overlapping notification procedures" (State of Israel 2015:170). The fact that the IDF issued warnings was commendable. But the notices also shifted the burden of protection onto civilians, and short circuited the question whether or not the targets were legitimate in the first place. Tom Gregory suggests that the warnings served to delineate "specific geographies of killing, in which the distinction between combatants and noncombatants was considered to be irrelevant." All those who remained within these "sterile combat zones" (the IDF term) were considered combatants regardless of their actual status (Gregory 2015).

The system of warnings might give the impression that the wars were orderly and logical and that Gazans had a hand in their own fate. But on the ground people were often bewildered, unsure when and where to run. Consider this radio announcement made during Cast Lead: "Military announcement to all residents of the area: For your own safety, you are required to leave your homes immediately and move to the city centers—IDF Command" (Garlasco 2009:7). What city centers? What if you're already in the center? What if the streets are not safe? Amnesty International (2009b:3) said the telephone calls were "randomly placed," and thus "caused widespread panic but offered little protection." In some cases Gazans received phone calls ordering them to evacuate, but IDF troops in the area barred them from leaving, and in some cases shot at them. The aerial bombardment of Rafah during Cast Lead was preceded by farcical blunders and miscommunications. Residents were warned to leave by 8:00 a.m. on January 8, but the bombing was under way in earnest by 8:30 p.m. on January 7 (Goodman, Menuchin, and Oron 2009:14). Both sides treated civilians like pawns in a chess match. The IDF ordered residents to evacuate, while Hamas warned them to ignore Israel's "psychological warfare" and stay put. Often people didn't attempt to flee bombing zones until after the attack was underway. The Al Jazeera documentary, *Shujayea: Massacre at Dawn*, which appeared a few days after the razing of the neighborhood on July 20, 2014, shows horrific, chaotic scenes of people fleeing the neighborhood carrying children in their arms or the elderly and crippled on their backs, bombs bursting around them.

Many attacks seemed to materialize out of thin air. The January 5, 2009, strike on the 'Allaw family house in the al-Sha'f section of Gaza City killed Mu'min Mahmoud Talal 'Allaw, age ten; and injured Muhammad 'Allaw, 13; and Iman 'Allaw, 8. Mu'min's mother Nahla described the attacks:

> We were just sitting on the roof. It was cool and there was good weather. After five minutes I told my son I will just sit in the sun and went to the other end of the roof and sat down. Suddenly there was a powerful explosion. The roof was covered in white dust and smoke. I saw Mu'min on the bicycle. His legs were crushed, his chest had tiny small holes in it and blood poured from them. I carried him, crying. I ran to the stairway. He was breathing his last breath. I talked to him, saying, "It's alright my dear." (Garlasco 2009:24)

Family members said there was no fighting in the immediate area, no militias sheltering in the building. In another case, a condolence tent (an Arab tradition when a family member has died), was struck with piercing metal darts from a fletchette bomb that unleashed a thicket of thousands of the projectiles over a broad area. Like white phosphorus and fragmentation bombs, fletchettes are not explicitly banned under humanitarian law. However, many human rights groups consider them inherently indiscriminate and thus absolutely prohibited in populated areas.

B'Tselem compiled a list of names and circumstances of 344 minors killed in Cast Lead. During Protective Edge a B'Tselem radio spot that featured the names of some of the estimated 500 children who died during the offensive was blocked by the Israel Broadcast Authority on grounds that it was inflammatory. The rights group identified a number of sixteen- and seventeen-year-old boys who were involved in hostilities, either directly or as scouts. But the vast majority of those killed were blameless. Most were killed while at home, several apparently in operations that targeted the children's fathers. Others were killed while playing in their yards, traveling in a taxi, sheltering in a school (mortar attacks on the Al-Fakhura school in Beit Lahiya), guiding paramedics to help the wounded, loading oxygen tanks onto a truck, fleeing fighting with their families, passing by a police station that was struck, taking out the garbage, feeding pigeons on the roof, collecting firewood, riding a moped, making their way to the hospital, riding a horse-drawn wagon, or returning home from the grocery store (B'Tselem n.d.b; Al Mezan Centre for Human Rights and Defence for Children International—Palestine Section 2009).

A number of the killings happened during humanitarian ceasefires. The lulls in the fighting were designed to allow emergency vehicles to collect the wounded and to permit humanitarian supplies—including supplies arriving from Israel—to be delivered to medical centers. Combatants on both sides failed to respect the ceasefires. In Cast Lead at least seven different "white flag" incidents were reported, in which IDF soldiers shot at residents who sought safe passage by holding makeshift white flags of surrender (Human Rights Watch 2009f:6; Nissenbaum 2009). Suad (age nine) and Amal (age two) Abed-Rabbo were killed as they made their way to safety with a white-flag group. "My daughter Suad and I were waving the white flags at the two Israeli soldiers who were on top of the tank that was parked at the front door, I saw a third Israeli soldier put his head up and then come out from inside the tank. He then fired his gun at us directly" (Al Mezan Centre for Human Rights and Defence for Children International—Palestine Section 2009:35).

Other cases seemed to combine trigger-happy snipers with poor communication among IDF units. At 10:00 a.m. on January 5, 2009, after a night of shelling around the village of Sayafa, north of Beit Lahiya, IDF soldiers directed a group of nineteen people to evacuate to a nearby UNRWA school. As the group walked toward the school they came under attack. Five-year-old Nada al-Marrdi was shot in the back of the head and died the next day. "We asked them to arrange with the other soldiers not to kill us," said Nada's father, Radwan al-Marrdi. "We gave the kids white flags, made from scarves that we attached to sticks" (Human Rights Watch 2009f:27–28). Human Rights Watch corroborated the story with forensic evidence, interviews, and hospital records. Civilians who ventured out to attend to the wounded and dead were often stranded when ceasefires collapsed. The "Black Friday" attack on Rafah during Protective Edge, unleashed after Hamas fighters captured Givati Brigade reconnaissance officer Hadar Goldin, came soon after residents had received word of a temporary ceasefire and many were on the streets. According to Amnesty International (2015a) about 135 civilians were killed. The Khuza'a neighborhood of Khan Younis came under extraordinarily heavy bombardment. Over the course of July 22–23, 2014, the ICRC tried to coordinate with the IDF to allow the exodus of civilians but was rebuffed. A convoy of several hundred civilians attempting to flee came under direct IDF fire (Bachmann et al. 2014: 82–83).

A resident of Khuza'a scoffed at the notion of "safe" zones:

> Do not sit on the balcony, for they have killed a man in the south who went outside to his balcony to smoke a cigarette. Do not stand on the threshold of the house, for a group of young men who were sitting in front of their homes in Khan Younis were decimated by reconnaissance aircrafts. And do not go to the roof of the house; two children died on the roof of their homes in Gaza, because their mother thought the roof would be a better place to play than in the streets. Don't send them to the park; we all know what happened there. Do not go to the market; twenty martyrs died while purchasing groceries. Do you still own a house? Do not go back. Your neighborhood is probably threatened by more bombardment. If you're injured, do not go to the hospital, because it has lost what actually distinguishes it from other buildings in Gaza. If you are in a terrible situation do not take shelter in schools, how many people died from the bombing of the three schools? I lost count. (Ghanim 2014)

Following Cast Lead, the IDF made some modest adjustments to its urban warfare protocols and pledged better humanitarian access to the wounded. Those improvements were apparent during Pillar of Defense in 2012 but faded in Protective Edge in 2014. During Cast Lead, the IDF targeted a number of private houses in firefights, but the pre-vetted targets were predominantly government buildings, police stations, and other manifestations of Hamas rule. In 2014, the IDF evidently loosened its definition of proportionality, targeting the private homes of police officials, Hamas members, and other militants, sometimes killing entire families. On July 21, Dr. Yasser Abu Jamei, director of the Gaza Community Mental Health Programme, lost 25 relatives, including 19 children and three pregnant women, when his house was struck. The family had gathered for the *iftar*, the Ramadan evening meal. The target ostensibly was a dinner guest who belonged to Hamas's military wing. On July 29, reportedly without warning, the Israeli Air Force bombed a four-story apartment building in central Khan Younis, killing 35 and injuring 27. The target appears to have been Wada Abu'Amer, a political leader of the Democratic Front for the Liberation of Palestine, who lived in the building with his wife and children. According to B'Tselem (2014a), more than 70 residential buildings were targeted in this way. These attacks were mounted in the full knowledge that many innocent people would be killed in the pursuit of a single suspect. Strikes on UN shelters, a crowded marketplace, and other public spaces weren't really accidents either. Rather, IDF tanks fired shells indiscriminantly toward the "origins of fire."[18] There were gaps in intelligence, errant projectiles, and other mistakes, but most civilian killings complied with IDF rules of engagement.

The ground invasion in 2014 was initially limited to destroying Hamas's network of tunnels, but as the Givati Brigade barreled into Shujaiyeh, covering fire from tanks, Apache helicopters, and gunboats offshore, followed by a thundering, hours-long, barrage of one-ton bombs, left the area looking like "a moonscape strewn with bodies" (Hussein 2014). Large swathes of Beit Hanoun, Beit Lahiya, Al-Shaas, 'Abisan Al-Jadida, Khuza'a, and Rafah were also flattened. In all, some 520,000 Gazans were displaced, 270,000 of them packed into 90 UNRWA shelters. Thousands of homes were destroyed or damaged beyond repair, infrastructure was upended, mosques, schools, hospitals and clinics destroyed, factories wrecked, and Gaza's only power plant ruined. The UN estimated the physical damage of Protective Edge at $6 billion (UN Office for the Coordination of Humanitarian Affairs 2014a; Rudoren and Akram 2014). In a parting humiliation, relentless shelling kept many families from burying their dead. With morgues overflowing, corpses were stored in produce cases, or, in the case of the bodies of small children, ice cream freezers.

"Rockets, bombs and shells came from every direction," a doctor based in Gaza said of the opening attacks in Cast Lead, "it was as if the earth was lifting, shifting, and smashing itself into a different configuration" (Abuelaish 2010:160). Another doctor described how his family huddled together in a room during the bombardment so they would all live or die together. He tried to comfort his children by telling stories about the paradise that awaited them in the afterlife.[19] Other families placed their children in different rooms of the house in the Darwinian hope that at least some would survive. In many videos filmed during the attacks one hears the trembling cries of "Allah, Allah," and of Palestinians reciting the *shahada*, the declaration of the Muslim faith, in the face of death.

The physical toll on Gazans was staggering. Civilians constituted at least 70 percent of the casualties in Gaza. Most victims were wounded or killed by crushing and explosions, most often while they were in or close to their homes or the homes of relatives or neighbors. Airstrikes and explosions often claimed multiple members of families, while the "double tap" strikes struck civilians and rescuers alike. Punishingly heavy explosives were used in residential neighborhoods. Emergency medical evacuation was evidently deprioritized (Bachmann 2015). Up close, the violence was hard to fathom. Mads Gilbert, the Norwegian anesthesiologist who volunteered at al-Shifa hospital during Cast Lead and again during Protective Edge, saw the wounded and dead delivered by the carload, the

> incomprehensible chaos of bodies, sizes, limbs, walking, not walking, breathing, not breathing, bleeding, not bleeding humans. HUMANS! Ashy grey faces—Oh no! Not one more load of tens of maimed and bleeding. We still have lakes of blood on the floor in the ER, piles of dripping, blood-soaked bandages to clear out . . . the cleaners, everywhere, swiftly shoveling the blood and discarded tissues, hair, clothes, cannulas—the leftovers from death—all taken away... to be prepared again, to be repeated all over." (quoted in Qumsiyeh 2014)

Physicians for Human Rights-Israel believes the IDF's attitude toward medical relief efforts hardened in Gaza. Before Cast Lead, PHR-I had a cool but working relationship with the Army. Palestinians would sometimes call PHR-I staff directly, who would then coordinate with the ICRC and Army medics to provide assistance or evacuation. Now, even if members of the medical corps seemed sympathetic, commanders often refused access, even in cases where no obvious military threat was looming.[20] The fate of Mohammed Shurrab and his two sons Ibrahim (18) and Qasab (28) during Cast Lead was emblematic of the attitude toward aid to the injured. The three men had taken advantage of a mid-day humanitarian ceasefire on January 16 to travel in a red jeep from their farm in Al-Fukhkhari toward the center of Khan Younis. The IDF had carried out an operation in the area the night before, and the Shurrabs passed a number of tanks and troops along the road without incident. As the jeep navigated around a sand roadblock, the vehicle was hit with a burst of gunfire, and a bullet struck Qasab in the chest. Soldiers ordered the car to stop and yelled at the men to exit the vehicle and lie on the ground. As the men climbed from the car Ibrahim was shot in the leg. Qasab, slumped in the dirt, died soon thereafter. Over the next 12 hours Ibrahim slowly bled to death as his father frantically pleaded with the soldiers to allow a local ambulance to approach, or to let him drive his son to the Gaza European Hospital, a mile away. Several times, he said, the soldiers warned him not to move, and told him to "shut up or we will shoot you." During the evening, the father put his mobile phone to the best use he could, pleading his case on local radio stations, the BBC Arabic Service, and with PHR-I, which tried unsuccessfully to mediate with the Army. Ibrahim died shortly after midnight, as his father was giving an interview with Al Jazeera. The father and the bodies of his two sons were evacuated around noon the following day (Dan Magen 2009:37–38, 63–66).

Human rights groups documented dozens of cases of medical crews coming under attack while rescuing injured persons. The World Health Organization reported that 16 medical personnel were killed and 25 wounded while on duty during Cast Lead (Dan Magen 2009:7). During Protective Edge, five of Gaza's 13 hospitals, and 34 medical clinics, were evacuated after they came under attack.[21] During the fighting the "humanitarian corridors" went only one way, bringing humanitarian supplies into Gaza, but not evacuating the severely wounded to Israel. Opening the corridors might not have helped. During Cast Lead the Palestinian Authority Ministry of Health, in a fit of pride, refused to refer injured patients to Israel for treatment.[22] During Protective Edge, PHR-I said that it reached out to the IDF to try to facilitate the removal of residents who were trapped in the rubble of their homes in Khuza'a, but was met with "a wall of silence" (Physicians for Human Rights-Israel 2014).

"Screaming Household Members"

As the Cast Lead ceasefire took hold, Gazans looked as "if they were waking from a nightmare," said Antoine Grand, head of the local ICRC office (International Committee of the Red Cross 2009b). Thousands of homes were ruined and damaged, government ministries and other administrative buildings leveled, businesses and schools hit, and hospitals and other health facilities damaged. The foundations of everyday life were degraded, with damage to factories, mosques, agricultural production, infrastructure, and electrical production and transmission, with secondary impacts on sewage treatment, water quality, and the delivery of medical care.

A public health survey conducted in Gaza in February 2009 found:

> 346 (48%) of 718 interviewed households had non-household people living with them, 326 (45%) were hosted by other people for at least 24 hours during the Operation Cast Lead, and 342 (48%) had damage to their houses. 354 (49%) had impaired access to health services and 353 (49%) to drugs. 623 (87%) had at least one screaming household member, 620 (86%) cried, 466 (65%) loss of appetite, and 588 (82%) nightmares. 690 (96%) had disruption of electricity for all or most of the time, 249 (35%) disruption of potable water supplies entirely and 257 (36%) for most of the time, 185 (26%) disruption of their landline phone for all or most of the time, and 402 (56%) disruption of waste collection. A loss of income was reported by 233 (32%) of households, and 611 (85%) had food shortages. (Ashour, Ghuneim, and Yaghi 2011)

How many surveys ask about screaming household members? A study of 3,017 Gaza households conducted six months after the war ended found residents suffering "severe psychological injury, stress and grief on broad scale" (Abu-Rmeileh et al. 2012:735). Longitudinal data collected by Médecins sans Frontières show that after Cast Lead the number of patients referred for or seeking mental health care doubled; the interval between the traumatic stressor and time to seek medical attention shortened; and the number of diagnoses of acute post-traumatic stress disorders soared. The most common symptoms for patients under the age of 15 were distress, anxiety, withdrawal, sleep disturbances, bed-wetting, and aggressiveness. Older patients reported sleep disturbances, sadness, crying, intrusive memories, and anxiety. The toll in psychosocial health reflects violence, displacement, and financial loss as well as the erosion of social support networks (Llosa et al. 2012). Every serious mental health survey in Gaza has also identified violence between Palestinian factions as a significant source of distress. An American neurosurgeon who has travelled to Gaza several times as part of a medical brigade told me half-jokingly that one of the biggest public health challenges is not open sewers or infectious disease, but navigating the power struggle between Hamas and Fatah.[23]

The effects of post-traumatic stress disorder (PTSD) remain widespread in Gaza. One study conducted before Protective Edge found that a third of Palestinian children suffered from the disorder (Barnard 2014). Given the open-ended nature of the violence, a better diagnosis is *chronic* trauma and stress.[24] A psychiatrist in Gaza City tallied the impact of the violence:

- Increased incidence rate of psychiatric disorders, especially anxiety disorder, PTSD, depressive disorders, somatoform disorders [experiences of pain that can't be traced to any physical cause], and functional enuresis [uncontrolled urination] among children.
- Increased relapse rate among psychiatric patients.
- Increased levels of aggression.
- Frustration and losing hope.
- Substance abuse and dependence.
- New way of thinking that conflicts are *only* solved by aggression and violence.
- Expectation of transmission of trauma through generations.[25]

This idea of cyclical trauma runs deep in Gaza. War in Gaza is war amid children: 45 percent of the inhabitants of the Strip are under age fourteen. Children were afraid because their parents seemed powerless; parents were ashamed because they couldn't protect their children. War orphans often turned to martyrs and militants as role models (UN Human Rights Council 2009:270). Olivia Watson of Defence for Children International—Palestine described how the children who survived Protective Edge would "emerge to find their previous lives almost unrecognizable, as the families, schools, hospitals and mosques that framed their world are systematically destroyed" (O. Watson 2014). The United Nations Office for the Coordination of Humanitarian Affairs (2014b) estimated that 326,000 children would require specialized psychosocial support. The *Lancet* referred to Gaza's youth as a "broken generation" (McGirk 2009:531).

Mental health professionals in Gaza describe the numbness and detachment of older Gazans scarred by their experiences and facing bleak life choices. Addiction to the opioid pain medicine Tramadol has risen, as has the incidence of depressive disorders and feelings of "helplessness and hopelessness."[26] The chronic nature of the violence makes psychological recovery that much harder. Hadas Ziv from Physicians for Human Rights—Israel compares the prognosis to that of people who have been tortured. Once torture victims are free of their tormentors and reintegrated back into their communities, the chances for rehabilitation are fairly good. But recovery is impossible when the victim knows his or her torturer may reappear at any moment.[27]

During Cast Lead the damage was slighter on the Israeli side but no less real. The Magen David Adom, the Israeli equivalent of the Red Cross, treated 770 civilians harmed by rockets during Cast Lead. In addition to those Israelis physically killed or wounded, another 584 were treated for shock and "anxiety syndrome" (Magen David Adom 2009). Across southern Israel, children were terrorized, Holocaust survivors were retraumatized, and residents of all ages suffered the effects of depression, anxiety, and severe stress. "The fear gets into your blood," said a resident of Sderot, an Israeli city of 24,000 a few miles from the Gaza border that has borne the brunt of Hamas's rocket attacks (Robb 2013). A survey at a middle school in Sderot found that 44 percent of 7th and 8th grade children showed signs of PTSD (Berger, Gelkopf, and Heineberg 2012). Children between ages eighteen months and five years showed multiple symptoms of PTSD, including re-experiencing, disassociation, hypervigilance, and substantial developmental regression (Feldman and Vengrober 2011). Women in Sderot, their lives punctuated by air raid sirens and actual bombs falling, were 32 percent more likely to suffer miscarriage than women in other parts of Israel (Wainstock et al. 2013). As the range of Hamas rockets has expanded, so has the civilian fallout in Israel, with children, teenagers, the elderly, and the handicapped most affected. More than 1,000 Israelis were hospitalized or treated for anxiety attacks during Protective Edge. Hamas's cross-border tunnels were a singular source of terror and fear for Israelis living on the Gaza border (State of Israel 2015:118–29).

Investigations and Impunity: Human Rights as Legal Gadfly

Within days of the Cast Lead ceasefire, Chief of General Staff Lt. Gen. Gabi Ashkenazi ordered five special IDF command investigations into allegations raised by international observers, NGOs, and media organizations. These involved:

- Claims that a large number of civilians not directly participating in the hostilities were harmed;
- Allegations that UN and international facilities were fired upon and damaged during the Gaza Operation;

- Incidents involving shooting at medical facilities, buildings, vehicles and crews;
- Destruction of private property and infrastructure by ground forces; and
- Use of weapons containing phosphorus. (State of Israel 2010:ii)

These investigations were concluded in three months. A three-page statement noted that "a very small number" of "unavoidable" accidents occurred due to unspecified "intelligence or operational errors," but that the war was fought "in accordance with international law" (R. McCarthy 2009). An additional special command investigation was convened in November 2009 in response to three of the incidents outlined in the Goldstone Report: the airstrike on the al-Samouni compound that killed some 29 civilians, the alleged mistreatment of Palestinian detainees, and the attack on the Al-Maquadme Mosque. Several administrative punishments were meted out, but a high threshold for ill intent led to the conclusion that none of the strategic choices was illegal. The IDF refuted the infrastructural claims as well, arguing that the Namar well, which Gazans claimed was targeted as a civilian source of drinking water, was located within a closed Hamas military installation and therefore was a legitimate target; and suggesting that the al-Sheikh Ejlin wastewater treatment plant may have been damaged by Hamas as a ruse; and that the el-Bader flour mill was targeted because it was incorporated into Hamas defenses and was being used as a "strategic high point" (State of Israel 2010:42).

All told, the IDF reportedly conducted some 400 Cast Lead investigations at lower levels. The breakdown is murky, but most were operational debriefings carried out by units in the field. About 50 inquiries were forwarded for criminal investigation. Of those, four led to indictments, and three have ended in convictions (UN Human Rights Council 2010a). An IDF military court convicted and demoted two Givati Brigade staff sergeants for forcing a nine-year old Palestinian boy to open a bag the soldiers suspected might contain explosives. Another staff sergeant was charged with manslaughter for killing two women—Rayya Abu Hajjaj and her adult daughter Majda Abu Hajjaj—who complied with a radio announcement telling residents to evacuate, only to be attacked while holding white flags of safe passage. While the names of the two women and the details of the killings were undisputed, a one-day discrepancy in the original report meant the defendant was charged with involvement in the deaths of "an anonymous figure"; the charge sheet said the defendant aimed at and struck the upper body of "the figure"

("*Ha'aretz* Editorial: When War Criminals Walk Free" 2012). The sergeant eventually pled guilty to "illegal use of a weapon" and "conduct unbecoming" and served 45 days in jail and probation. Another soldier went to jail for stealing a credit card from a Gazan and using it to withdraw money from an automated teller machine. The highest-level investigations involved the attack on the Gaza office of the United Nations Relief and Works Agency (UNRWA) for Palestine Refugees. In that case, Brig. Gen. Eyal Eisenberg and Givati Brigade commander Col. Ilan Malka were reprimanded for firing artillery shells in a populated area (Kershner 2010).

Col. Malka was also involved in the most notorious event of Cast Lead: the killing of more than 20 members of the extended al-Samouni family in the Zeitoun section of Gaza City. The killings unfolded slowly, then explosively, over the course of two days. Before dawn on January 4, 2009, IDF soldiers launched several house raids along what was known as al-Samouni Street where the families lived. In one "wet" entry into a house where 18 people were sheltering, live fire and grenades killed forty-five-year old Ateya al-Samouni and severely wounded four-year old Ahmad al-Samouni. Some family members managed to flee toward the center of Gaza City. IDF soldiers marched other family members, the men handcuffed and blindfolded, to other houses nearby. But most of the displaced families were corralled into a cement block warehouse belonging to Wa'el al-Samouni. By mid-day January 4, around 100 people, mostly women and children, were packed into the building. The soldiers rejected entreaties to allow ambulances to approach to take Ahmad to the hospital. An ambulance dispatched from al-Quds hospital was stopped short of the house. The driver and a nurse were made to strip and lie on the ground, and then the ambulance was turned away. The boy died during the night.

On the morning of January 5, several of the men in Wa'el al-Samouni's house ventured out the front door to gather firewood. IDF troops, or perhaps a drone overhead, responded by shooting several projectiles, killing two of the men. Heavy projectiles were then directed at the house itself. At least two shells struck the house, bringing the roof down on those inside, and showering them with shrapnel. The terror and chaos inside the packed house must have been unbearable. "You couldn't see or hear anything. The air was filled with smoke and pressure and my ears felt like they were shaking," said Salah al-Samouni, whose grandmother and two-year-old daughter died in the attack (Finer 2009). Masouda al-Samouni, whose husband and ten-month old were killed, recalled, "I was screaming and crying. I saw everything, the blood and the brains. There was smoke everywhere" (Palestinian Centre for Human Rights 2009b:57). Survivors inside the house made panicked phone calls to the Palestine Red Crescent Society, the ICRC, and even to B'Tselem's office in Jerusalem seeking help.[28] As a shaken convoy of several dozen survivors fled the house, making their way toward Salah al-Din Road and on to al-Shifa Hospital, an IDF helicopter hovered overhead and soldiers shouted at them to go back and shot over their heads. The intake log at al-Shifa recorded 39 Samounis at the emergency room on January 5. The dead and some of the severely wounded who could not be moved were left behind in the wreckage (Hass 2009; Finer 2009).

The al-Samouni attacks were surprisingly intimate. Palestinian fighters had been active in the vicinity of the compound for several days, and it is possible the IDF wanted to seize control of the area, which sits on a slight elevation, for the strategic advantages it offered. But by the morning of January 4, Israeli troops controlled the scene, commanding the rooftops, patrolling the streets, and establishing a military post some 80 meters from Wa'el al-Samouni's house. Soldiers interacted almost continuously with residents and would-be rescuers. When the Wa'el al-Samouni house was struck, the soldiers watching the house obviously knew a terrible mistake had been made, but they nevertheless continued to bar medical assistance to the survivors. After days of negotiations with the ICRC, the IDF finally allowed ambulances into the neighborhood on the afternoon of January 7, a full 80 hours after the initial raids. When rescuers reached the house they found thirteen family members still alive, several of them children who had been trapped for two and a half days with the bodies of their dead parents and family members.[29] Once the survivors were evacuated, an IDF engineering unit demolished the remainder of the house on top of the corpses left behind. When family members returned to the house two weeks later, they found hands and feet sticking out of the rubble.

The al-Samouni killings were the subject of a command investigation as well as a criminal inquiry by the Military Police Investigation Unit (MPIU), which took testimony from several members of the family. B'Tselem researchers say the army's actions have never been fully explained. On behalf of the family the NGO has requested a copy of the investigation file, which will probably be released with some information redacted. It is possible that Col. Malka misread the location of the house on a drone image when ordering the attack, or that the presence of the family was not communicated up the line. Malka said he did not know the family was in the house when he ordered the strikes.

Whether or not he should have known is still unclear. Unmoved by the intense media coverage of the case, the IDF Military Advocate General's Corps ruled in January 2012 that Malka "did not deviate from the boundaries of discretion that a 'reasonable military commander' operating in similar circumstances possesses," and concluded that the killing lacked the "mental element constituting criminal intent." No criminal indictment was issued. However, for his "professional shortcomings," Malka's promotion was frozen for two years and he was barred from ever holding a command position in an operational setting again (IDF Military Advocate General's Corps 2012).

To the family, of course, this was not a professional shortcoming. It was an arbitrary attack on defenseless people who did what the IDF soldiers asked of them. Such operations are messy, and commanders make mistakes. But the focus on military necessity and a harsh rendering of IHL sidelined basic humanitarian questions: Why use such firepower in the presence of civilians? Why demolish houses in the first place? With the area apparently under IDF control, why were ambulances barred from collecting the wounded? Why did the soldiers not immediately pivot from an offensive operation to a rescue operation? Some victims almost certainly could have been saved had they received medical attention earlier. Yet no IDF military commanders or soldiers have been punished for barring medical aid to the wounded. The Army seemed incapable of drawing even crude humanitarian lessons from its mistakes. The day after the al-Samouni attack, the IDF bombed another packed house in Zeitoun, killing some 20 members of the Al-Dayah family, most of them children.[30]

Without the efforts of human rights groups, the al-Samouni case and others like it might have been swept under the rug. The IDF's initial reaction was a boilerplate statement denying the strike had taken place, but as the facts came to light investigators had to take them seriously. Usually, though, investigations are inadequate, and even when there is compelling evidence, criminal charges are rarely filed.[31] B'Tselem says the system appears to operate normally—"complaints are filed, investigations are opened and decisions are made"—but in fact, the process is "barely functional" (B'Tselem 2013). Cases are cursorily reviewed and often closed without ever talking to survivors of attacks. The reason, of course, is that investigators privilege intent. It is enough to interview the soldier who pulled the trigger; the actual effects on the ground are secondary. The Palestinian Centre for Human Rights (PCHR) (2011) concluded that "rather than uphold the rule of law, the Israeli investigative and judicial system is artfully manipulated to provide an illusion of investigative and judicial rigor, while systematically perpetuating pervasive impunity."

With regard to Protective Edge, Israel again refused to look beyond a handful of violations and consider the strategic sources of human suffering. The focus instead has been on a number of "exceptional incidents." The IDF's General Staff Inquiry task force has reviewed close to 200 such incidents and has ordered the Military Police Investigative Unit to open 22 investigations. So far, three of those have ended in indictments, for looting and obstruction of justice (B'Tselem 2015a). Indeed, criminal responsibility for *any* acts involving harm to Palestinians remains extremely rare. Since 2001, there have been a total of 23 convictions of IDF soldiers or Border Police for any crime involving the treatment of Palestinians.[32] This is a staggeringly low figure, given the huge footprint of the occupation and the many documented cases of abuse.

Hamas has rejected all suggestions that it committed war crimes. In Gaza, a commission headed by Justice Minister Faraj al-Ghoul carried out no investigation at all of Hamas's actions during Cast Lead. Instead, it deflected guilt back toward Israel: "the Palestinian people were the victim and the occupation was the hangman and the criminal must be brought to account" (Beckerman 2010). A Hamas official complained that a Human Rights Watch report accusing the Islamist group of war crimes "exempts the occupation from the crimes it committed," adding that "resistance in all its forms is a legitimate right of the Palestinian people as long as they are under occupation and face state terrorism" (Al Jazeera 2009). On the question of targeting civilians, Hamas tried to have it both ways. A spokesman said that the group had only "primitive weapons, and with such weapons, mistakes are to be expected" (Kershner 2009). Al-Ghoul's committee stated that armed groups in Gaza

> work as hard as possible in order not to expose civilians to any harm, but it shall be known that the Palestinian resistance—even though it is a resistance organization—is not a regular army with technologically advanced weapons, so the resistance might set a military target and the fire deviate a little or a lot and thus might impact near a civilian site, despite the efforts to keep the civilians safe. We assure you that the resistance does not deliberately set civilian targets, and that it deals with unintended incidents. (Human Rights Watch 2010b:14)

Al-Ghoul described "armed resistance" in Gaza as if it were a spontaneous uprising, saying that Palestinian fighters lacked the formal command and control needed to assign criminal responsibility. But these were not partisans in the forest. Hamas's armed wing, the al-Qassam Brigades, was an organized force 7,000–10,000 strong, and often it was they who coordinated the other, smaller, militias (Human Rights Watch 2009d:10–11). Most rockets aimed at Israel were launched by Hamas fighters in any event. These were willful attacks on civilians. An al-Qassam spokesman vowed "to double the number of Israelis under fire," while Hamas leaders said that the IDF's indiscriminate attacks "gave us legitimacy to strike them in the same way" (Human Rights Watch 2010b:8–9). Hamas officials later disclaimed all responsibility for attacks on Israelis, telling the UN fact-finding mission that "they had nothing to do, directly or indirectly, with al-Qassam Brigades or other armed groups and had no knowledge of their tactics" (UN Human Rights Council 2009:134.) Hamas disingenuously said the Cast Lead attacks were meant to send a "political message" to the Israeli people, and called the killing of the three Israeli civilians a "mistake," noting that the intended targets were "military installations inside the Zionist cities" (al-Mughrabi 2010). Al-Qassam has since dropped all pretentions. Its website lists such recent targets as "Tel Aviv," "the Knesset," "Beersheva," "Hirtseilia" [Herzliya], and "the military site Ashkol," that is, Ashkelon, a coastal city of more than 100,000 residents just north of Gaza. During Protective Edge, Hamas spokesman Abu Zuhri declared that "all Israelis have now become legitimate targets" (Toameh 2014).

Human rights groups have consistently condemned Hamas's tactics. B'Tselem (2010) said that "imposing terror on a civilian population" demonstrated Hamas's "shameful disregard for human life." Eleven Palestinian human rights NGOs sent a joint letter to President Mahmoud Abbas in Ramallah and to Prime Minister Ismail Haniyeh in Gaza, urging them to investigate Goldstone's allegations using international standards for independence and fairness (Addameer Prisoner Support and Human Rights Organization. n.d.). NGOs focused on the attacks on Israelis as well as the "domestic" terror Hamas wreaked in Gaza. Under cover of Cast Lead and Protective Edge, Hamas goons maimed scores of Fatah activists by breaking limbs and shooting people in the legs, and carried out gruesome public executions of dozens of Palestinians suspected of collaborating with Israel (Human Rights Watch 2009e; Amnesty International 2015b).

IDF investigators ended up working directly with B'Tselem, Human Rights Watch, Adalah, and Al Mezan to locate and interview Palestinian witnesses in several of the white flag cases from Cast Lead. Unfortunately, human rights investigators were often left in the dark about the disposition of cases they had helped to build. Reparations efforts have faced similar hurdles. While American field commanders in Iraq and Afghanistan had wide discretion to pay claims, Palestinians face the iron bureaucracy of the Israeli Ministry of Defense Compensation Office. The PCHR submitted 1,046 civil "damage applications" on behalf of Gazan families. Usually hearing nothing, lawyers then lodged civil cases in Israeli courts, though these claims face a wide combat exclusion that applies whether or not the military operation is legal, stringent power-of-attorney requirements, and a ruinously expensive "court guarantee" of several thousand dollars that each claimant must pay. Lawyers from Gaza are barred from representing plaintiffs in Israeli courts, while Israeli lawyers who take the cases are not allowed to travel to Gaza to meet their clients. To date, the Israeli government has paid only three claims related to Cast Lead, including $150,000 to the family of Rayya and Majda Hajjaj, the mother and daughter killed in a white-flag case, and $108,000 to the family of the two Sharrub brothers who bled to death while awaiting medical assistance.[33] The practice has become a rite of justice that offers some affirmation for those whose lives were disrupted or destroyed, but little in the way of compensation or policy changes, and even less in terms of accountability. Following Protective Edge, B'Tselem changed tack, refusing to help the IDF investigate alleged war crimes, saying "there is currently no official body in Israel capable of conducting independent investigations of suspected violations of international humanitarian law." B'Tselem contends that the political and military architects of war policies are virtually untouchable; that the military advocate general provides legal counsel regarding the conduct of war and thus is reluctant to investigate potential abuses that follow; and that military investigations lack the independence and rigor that justice demands (B'Tselem 2014b).

Public discourse in the wake of Cast Lead has been dominated by the Goldstone Report, a compilation of factual and legal conclusions prepared by the United Nations fact-finding mission on the Gaza War chaired by South African jurist Richard Goldstone. Israel has long been censured by UN resolutions and pilloried by UN agencies. As noted earlier, the General Assembly's strongest statement ever on human rights in war, that "essential and inalienable human rights should be respected even during the vicissitudes of war," came in 1967 and was directed largely at Israel, which a few weeks earlier had seized the West Bank, Gaza, the Golan Heights, and the Sinai Peninsula in the Six-Day War (UN General Assembly 1967). The first resolution of the 1968 International Conference on Human Rights (the "Tehran Conference") was titled "Respect and Enforcement of Human Rights in the Occupied Territories." The last two special rapporteurs on human rights in the Occupied Territories have been sharply critical. South African lawyer John Dugard often drew parallels to the history of apartheid in his native South Africa. Dugard's successor, international lawyer Richard Falk, has accused Israel of ethnic cleansing and state-sponsored terrorism, and called the siege of Gaza a prelude to "genocide" and "a Holocaust in the making" (Barghouti 2011:193).

The Goldstone report was denounced before it was even released. Shimon Peres, the country's Nobel Laureate president, condemned it as "a mockery of history" (Zohar 2009). Israel's ambassador to the UN, Gabriela Shalev, said the report "was conceived in hate and executed in sin" (Israel Ministry of Foreign Affairs 2009b). U.S. Representative Gary L. Ackerman called the report as "a pompous, tendentious, one-sided political diatribe," and accused Goldstone of living in a "self-righteous fantasy land" (quoted in Zogby 2010:47). The report is unbalanced at least in part because Israel refused to cooperate with the fact-finding mission and barred the group from the Jewish State. Entering from Egypt instead, the investigators found the residents of Gaza eager to share their stories. Goldstone conducted phone interviews with Israelis and relied on secondary accounts of the impact of Hamas rockets on Sderot and other cities, but the Israeli point of view remains sparse. One senses, too, that UN investigators were perhaps more credulous of Palestinian assertions than of Israeli claims. Certain issues of importance to Israel, such as the allegation that Hamas used medical facilities for military purposes, were skirted (PoKempner 2010). These shortcomings were unfortunate because they allowed critics to dismiss its findings, including the detailed charges connected to specific acts.

The report described Cast Lead as "a deliberately disproportionate attack designed to punish, humiliate and terrorize a civilian population" (UN Human Rights Council 2009:525). Its "massive and deliberate destruction" was directed against "the people of Gaza as a whole" as part of "an overall policy aimed at punishing the Gaza population for its resilience and for its apparent support for Hamas" (253, 406). "The destruction of food supply installations, water sanitation systems, concrete factories and residential houses was the result of a systematic policy by the Israeli armed forces." Such attacks served no military purpose, but were designed "to make the daily process of living, and dignified living, more difficult for the civilian population" (195).

Although the mission was dispatched to Gaza by the Human Rights Council, the most contentious claims dealt with the laws of war, particularly the question of intent. The war was devastating for Gazans. But that wasn't enough to make it war crime: the devastation must be intentional. That is perhaps why the report seems to have overreached in its charge that the IDF intentionally targeted civilians. We might like it to be the case that IHL criminalizes broader breaches of human rights as well, but this would defy the past 150 years of legal practice. Rather than inferring intent, the mission's stronger suit was the direct language of human rights and its detailed descriptions of everyday impacts of the war. Hamas's crude weapons and Israel's raw firepower could only have caused immense misery. This approach also avoids turning the issue into one of haves and have-nots, of commending precision weapons while condemning crude ones.

B'Tselem's executive director Jessica Montell said the Goldstone Report raised very serious questions that demanded to be investigated, but that its conclusions were too broad. "I was disturbed by the framing of Israel's military operation as part of 'an overall policy aimed at punishing the Gaza population for its resilience,'" she wrote. "The facts presented in the report would not seem to support such a far-reaching conclusion. In light of the sweeping conclusions regarding Israel, the very careful phrasing regarding Hamas abuses is particularly conspicuous" (Montell 2009). B'Tselem research director Yael Stein noted how meticulously B'Tselem documents its claims, but did not see the same level of care in the Goldstone report, especially regarding the IDF's intent.[34] It was on the question of intent that, in April 2011, Judge Goldstone personally retracted some of the charges in the report, saying that at the time the report was written all the evidence pointed toward deliberate Israeli war crimes (Goldstone 2011). (The other three members of the panel issued a statement saying they stood by the report.) As we will see in the following chapter, the International Criminal Court (ICC) is now scrutinizing the Israeli-Palestinian situation. The Court is widely expected to take up the case of Protective Edge, exposing both Israel and Hamas to possible prosecution.

Agency and Advocacy

IDF policies often end up in the hands of the Israeli Supreme Court. Unlike the U.S. Supreme Court, which weighed in on broad constitutional questions regarding the war on terror, but steered clear of operational matters, Israel's high court has overseen IDF operations in the Occupied Territories for decades, reviewing hundreds of decisions taken by the Military Commander of the Occupied Territories (Weill 2014:145). Human rights litigants often have found the court sympathetic. Nevertheless, skeptics, including some in the rights movement, say the High Court's involvement has perversely humanized and sustained the occupation. David Kretzmer, a prominent law professor and long-time human rights activist, says the Supreme Court has reined in the IDF and strengthened due process and procedural rights, but at the same time has made the military option more palatable (Kretzmer 2002:2). Limor Yehuda of the Association for Civil Rights in Israel (ACRI) contends that the legal strategy has "anesthetize[d]" an Israeli "public that believes that as long as the HCJ [High Court of Justice] is watching, our occupation is enlightened and we can sleep well at night" (Golan and Orr 2012:794–95; and see Sultany 2014).

This strikes me as too much handwringing. The High Court has examined everything from checkpoint protocols, deportations, interrogation techniques, and the security barrier (the wall), to human shields, house demolitions, and targeted assassinations. Some of the decisions have propped up the occupation, but others have rejected torture, tightened detention policies, prohibited using enemy soldiers as hostages, and ended reliance on unit-level "operational investigations." The Court deftly grasped the working of power in the neighbor policy case, and grappled seriously with new wars in the targeted killings case. Where the legal approach has failed to make headway is in reforming the IDF's broader strategies: the Dahiye Doctrine, the rash use of heavy counterforces fire, the denial of humanitarian access. Nor has the Court tackled the occupation directly. While some human rights activists focus on discrete cases or issue areas, others see the problem in the aggregate. Yesh-Din co-founder Michael Sfard argues that one "cannot treat large scale human rights abusing regimes as a random collection of many human rights violating events. The existence of an 'industry' of abuses forces human rights activists and lawyers to fight for the dismantling of the abuses 'factory'" (Sfard 2009:40).

The most fundamental work of human rights is not found in the machinations of these court cases. Documenting, analyzing, and publicizing abuses comes first. These methods have gone a long way toward framing popular and legal views of the Gaza wars. It helped that sophisticated human rights networks were already in place; those groups quickly re-tooled to cover the wars and their impact. The details of rights reporting proved formidable, particularly when married to YouTube, Twitter, and Instagram. Official boilerplate professing adherence to international law sounded feeble compared to the images of what Israeli Prime Minister Benjamin Netanyahu coarsely called "telegenically dead Palestinians" (Samuel 2014). There was no shortage of misinformation and spin. But when specific, verifiable accounts emerged they were hard to ignore. In the wake of Cast Lead, Israeli officials initially stonewalled the UN mission and dismissed the "unreliable witness reports" collected by human rights groups (Human Rights Watch 2009a). But as evidence mounted, one thing led to another and the IDF was drawn into detailed discussions of individual cases. Determined not to be caught flat-footed on the publicity front during Protective Edge, the IDF mounted a media campaign that hinged on videos and photographs, infographics, and cartoon-like animations, backed up by thousands of Hasbara ("explanation") volunteers who carried Israel's message into chat rooms and onto blogs. It was a textbook case of how to shape public opinion in a media age, yet it hardly bested the al-Qassam Brigades savvy Twitter feeds. The hashtag #GazaUnderAttack was wildly popular during the war as a platform both for users in Gaza and for the global commentariat.

In the media flurry, it's easy to forget that Gazans are not just subjects of the high-minded NGOs that champion their cause. They are agents and advocates in their own right. Gazans invoked the more or less universal framework of rights as a way to order their own experience of the war, as a standard for collecting and collating evidence, and as a platform for their political barbs at Israel. It's true that many zealots in Gaza reject human rights out of hand, while other Palestinians have forsaken rights out of cynicism and despair. For a few, violence and rights are intimately related. "They are killing us all anyway—either a slow death by the siege, or a fast one by military attacks. We have nothing left to lose—we must fight for our rights, or die trying," said Um Al Ramlawi (quoted in Manduca et al. 2014:397). Nevertheless, recent survey data show vigorous support among Palestinians for political, socioeconomic, and environmental rights (Webb et al. 2012). Human rights are taught in the curriculum of UNRWA schools (alas, Holocaust education is not included), and are featured in educational, legal, medical, and social work training at universities, including the Islamic University of Gaza. To the irritation—and sometimes censorship—of Hamas, independent Palestinian media cover rights issues daily. Social media in Gaza were steeped in rights-talk: as always in Palestinian discourse, the right to national self-determination and the right to return, but also the right to live in dignity and peace, to work, to play, to learn.[35]

The legwork of this human rights documentation and advocacy was eminently local. In the midst of Protective Edge, Al Haq broadcast nearly hourly field bulletins that covered details down to smaller neighborhoods. Al Mezan published a kind of community diary that tracked the impact of the war day by day. Local knowledge was evident in well-sourced photographs and interviews. Indeed, the causes célèbres publicized by Amnesty or HRW were first brought to light by local investigators. Sometimes even the IDF noticed. As noted, almost all the IDF probes of alleged abuses by its soldiers were conducted from afar, but in several cases MPIU investigators turned to rights groups for information, rather than the other way around. Fieldworkers from Al-Mezan, B'Tselem, and the Palestinian Centre for Human Rights were in the thick of counting and categorizing the dead. They visited bomb sites, consulted local media sources, interviewed relatives, neighbors, and survivors, called on hospitals, clinics, and morgues, and tapped social and family networks to help identify bodies and to distinguish combatants and noncombatants. A team of ten fieldworkers from Al Mezan set out to assemble a dossier on every single attack on Gaza during Protective Edge.[36] The IDF also compiled dossiers (at least for the bank of targets vetted in advance), but Al Mezan hoped to portray the war through the other end of the gun sights.

While the imagery and narrative of the war are deeply shocking, perhaps even more disturbing is the normalcy of the violence in the eyes of the warring parties. Israeli officials went to great lengths to justify their position in humanitarian law, and in some cases took steps to limit civilian damage. While IHL was meant to be the law of exception, shelling of civilians became the rule. Hamas's strategy was infused with more than a little of the anarchists' "propaganda of the deed," drawing attention to the plight of Gazans, but at the expense of Israelis and Gazans alike. "For every Israeli asking himself if Israel didn't go too far in the destruction and suffering it inflicted on Gaza," wrote Amos Harel, *Ha'aretz*'s military correspondent, "there are two or three others who are convinced that the Israel Defense Forces should have hit harder" (Harel 2014). There are no winners here and there are many losers. A human rights framework illuminates the depth of that loss.

CHAPTER 5

Who's Responsible? Justice and Accountability

> Are these things a terrible, mad aberration, or can cause and responsibility be traced?
>
> —Telford Taylor (1970:152)

> Those *most* responsible for wars are usually least involved in the actual killing. Nearly all of the consequences of the actions of state leaders who order armies into combat are mediated by the responses of those who carry out the orders. Those who do the actual killing have little say in the overall enterprise in which they are engaged; they are usually young conscripts who have no part in decision making and little grasp of the issues over which they are asked to fight. Frequently they are lied to by their governments.
>
> —Robert Holmes (1989:185–86)

Political and military leaders accused of war crimes today face not just moral censure and public shaming, but the real possibility of landing in the dock. Human rights provide much of the normative structure of a new kind of atrocity law, while rights advocates shine a light on abuses and galvanize public support for prosecutions. A rights framework stresses individual criminal responsibility in place of a corporate or bureaucratic model of blame. And because human rights courts traditionally judge states rather than individuals, they tend to target the architects of atrocity rather than those who carry out their designs. There are certainly many gaps in accountability, particularly when state actors manage to insulate themselves from international courts. When left to their own devices to investigate and try torture cases from Iraq, U.S. military prosecutors often took a shallow, rank-and-file view of responsibility. They made a shambles of the courts martial in the Haditha killings, widely considered the signature atrocity of the Iraq War. By contrast, the European Court of Human Rights has imposed rigor and independence on British inquiries into unlawful killing, torture, and mistreatment by its troops in Iraq. As we will see, the military trials in the case of Baha Mousa, a hotel receptionist tortured to death by British troops in Basra, fizzled after the regiment closed ranks, but a prominent ECtHR case, two public inquiries, and a hefty payment to Mousa's family made a marked impact on European militaries. The UK is now in the midst of a mammoth effort to take testimony from Iraqi victims, families, and witnesses regarding allegations of possibly thousands of war crimes. While glacially slow, the process has given victims a voice in ways that are certain to raise British standards for civilian protections. The specter of a referral to the ICC has also spurred investigations and prosecutions at the national level, even in cases involving powerful states.

In the age of rights, justice for wartime abuses also means compensation or restitution for victims (see van Dijken et al. n.d.). If we're expecting a meaningful, systematic compensation scheme, the record is discouraging. As noted, claims filed by Gazans with the IDF Compensation Office are largely symbolic, given the slim chance of success. U.S. condolence payments to Iraqis and Afghans proved insulting as compensation and arbitrary as legal practice (Tracy 2007 and Witt 2008). The payments—$2,500 for a death, $1,500 for a serious injury, and $200 for a minor injury—are disbursed at the discretion of officers on the ground and expressly disclaim guilt or liability, indeed responsibility of any kind. A purchase order from the U.S. Army 256th Brigade Combat Team in Iraq, one of hundreds prepared by U.S. troops during the war, is numbingly bureaucratic: "Services: Death of Wife / Qty: 1 / Unit Price: $2,500."[1] Increasingly, however, victims have access to legal remedies no student of *Realpolitik* could have imagined. Individuals can petition regional rights tribunals, sue states directly in national courts, or lodge claims against third parties under the doctrine of universal jurisdiction. The specter of a referral to the International Criminal Court (ICC) looms over state actions, while private military contractors (and their stockholders) also are on the hook in civil and criminal cases.[2] The standing of individuals to pursue claims is now widely recognized even in the absence of any obligation under IHL to compensate victims of war. True, these bottom-up claims often fail under the battle exclusion, sovereign immunity, or other obstacles to justiciability. But behind the scenes belligerents are often keenly aware of their legal exposure, and that risk increasingly influences strategic calculations (see, e.g., Duva and Cuè 2010; Sikkink 2011).

Systemic Crimes, Individual Accountability

Political theorist John Keane notes that "Violence seems increasingly to be mediated by large-scale institutions, like armies equipped with state of the art surveillance and monitoring and killing equipment." Keane continues,

> These institutions of violence have the effect of blurring the intentions and camouflaging the culpable negligence and responsibility of the violent. Those who inflict physical pain and suffering on others do so not because they are thugs and sadists (although they may be this), but because they are trained in the habits and skills of behaving in accordance with the logic and imperatives of the institutional system in which they are operating. Violence tends to become "anonymous." Harm earns the status of a profession. But it remains violence, nonetheless. The victims are still physically or mentally assaulted by actors who act: they programme software, press buttons, tap keyboards, fill out forms, make decisions around tables, load weapons, grease engines and fly aircraft, and they do so with at least some awareness that what they are doing may well, however directly or indirectly, have effects that are regarded by others as violent. (Keane 2004:36–37)

The diffusion of wartime agency can make these look like authorless atrocities. They're not. Still, responsibility can easily fall through the cracks of IHL. Although the act of killing comes at the end of a long train of bureaucratic decisions, the law tends to narrow war crimes to the "guilty mind" of individual soldiers. Neta Crawford argues that the focus on individual responsibility promotes a "bad apple or mad apple" theory of atrocity. We define atrocities as those instances when soldiers go off the rails and deliberately massacre civilians. This kind of carnage commands media headlines and is often investigated and prosecuted. But singling out the bad/mad apples obscures the moral reality of war as a bureaucratic enterprise and criminalizes only the most literal, "tip-of-the-spear" violence. Crawford instead wants us to "add up" individual cases of killing and injury in order to see the patterns of "systemic atrocities." These ordinary killings far outnumber deliberate massacres, but they often go unrecognized because their origins seem so bureaucratically benign. As one soldier in Iraq put it, "It's just the nature of the situation you're in. That's what's wrong. It's not individual atrocity. It's the fact that the entire war is an atrocity" (Crawford 2013:263–64).

Psychological and organizational theories support this structural approach. The psychiatrist Robert Jay Lifton has argued (2004) that soldiers at My Lai, Abu Ghraib, and Haditha faced an "atrocity-producing situation—one so structured, psychologically and militarily, that ordinary people, men or women no better or worse than you or I, can commit atrocities." Individuals who participate in torture or killing are accountable for their behavior, he writes, "but the greater responsibility lies with those who planned and executed the war in Iraq and the 'war on terrorism' of which it is a part, and who created, in policy and attitude, the accompanying denial of the rights of captives (at Abu Ghraib and Guantanamo) and of the humanity of civilians (at Haditha)." Lifton is surely right that the training and conditioning of soldiers underpins many atrocities, though, as his passive phrasing suggests, individual culpability can be brushed off too easily. In an interview with *Esquire* magazine before he was sentenced in the My Lai case, Lt. William Calley described the U.S. army as a "Frankenstein monster":

> America tried to build sort of a superman: a war machine (it may sound ridiculous) that was a peace machine. . . . On paper the Army's a beautiful thing. But remember the story of Dr. Frankenstein? What a good doctor he was, at first? How he would build a superman with the smartest brain and the strongest body? . . . But it became uncontrollable. And it just killed. Do not blame the Frankenstein monster, though. The "people of the United States" did create the U.S. Army. (quoted in French 1998:1)

Deflecting responsibility served Lt. Calley's interests, of course, but the issue of responsibility is surely more complex and *political* than the acts of individual soldiers. The challenge is to apportion institutional and individual responsibility fairly. It's tempting to say that atrocities emerge from a miasma of loose cultural norms that drift from one battlefield to another without any clear, prosecutable, origins (D. Kennedy 2006b:133). Culpability seems to pass elliptically from crafters of doctrine to tactical technicians. Actions seem vaguely rooted in command culture, risk apportionment, ROEs, FRAGOs,

SOPs, training drills, and even "muscle memory." Yet even when training protocols or command culture are implicated, blame usually falls far down the chain of command. Many enlisted soldiers believe they will be prosecuted, while their superiors walk away scot-free. "Different spanks for different ranks," say soldiers. But the most likely outcome is that *no one* will be held responsible. Mark Osiel notes (1999:125), "the environing circumstances have often been accorded legal weight." The bureaucratic origins of atrocities may diminish the responsibility of soldiers, but they're invoked just as frequently by officers in their own defense.

War crimes, like lynchings, are often considered group activities. But while command investigations lean toward an esprit-de-corps model of shared responsibility, rights advocates tend to see abuses as an accumulation of individual acts by military personnel as well as political leaders and apparatchiks. Thirty officers and enlisted men were involved either directly or indirectly in the My Lai massacre andcoverup. So many people were implicated that Pentagon lawyers proposed holding a mass trial of two dozen of the defendants, but the prospect was too reminiscent of the Nuremberg trials and was dropped (Belknap 2002:144). The epidemic of torture cases in the wake of 9/11 similarly unfolded through concrete decisions taken by policymakers. The ACLU flow chart, "The Architects of Torture," traces crisply the directives emanating from the National Security Council, the Office of the President, and the Office of the Vice President (authorized and presided over the program, set up "black sites" overseas, and declared the Geneva Conventions and the Torture Convention moot); to the Department of Justice (fabricated a legal justification for torture); the Department of Defense (approved military programs of torture, and failed to curb abuses); and the Central Intelligence Agency (ran its own torture centers overseas, rendered prisoners to other countries to be tortured, subverted Congressional oversight, destroyed physical evidence of torture). The chart looks like a prosecutor's exhibit in a conspiracy trial, complete with photographs of the key officials involved at each level (ACLU n.d.).

These decisions were nothing if not deliberate. White House counsel Alberto Gonzales wrote that the war against terrorism rendered the Geneva Conventions "quaint." In fairness, Gonzales was referring to "some of its provisions requiring that captured enemy [sic] be afforded such things as commissary privileges, scrip (i.e., advance of monthly pay), athletic uniforms, and scientific instruments" (Gonzales 2002:2). But the administration's overall goal clearly was to strip detainees of basic protections under IHL or human rights. Lawyers at the U.S. Department of Justice provided Gonzales a starkly limited definition of what constituted torture, namely inflicting intense pain equivalent to that of "serious physical injury, such as organ failure, impairment of bodily function, or even death," or exacting psychological suffering that will produce significant harm or is of significant duration, such as "months or even years" (Bybee 2002:1). U.S. interrogators could almost be forgiven for thinking the Geneva Conventions did not apply to the prisoners in their care. A JAG representing a U.S. army private accused of torturing two Afghan prisoners to death at a detention center in Bagram defended his client, saying, "The president of the United States doesn't know what the rules are! The secretary of defense doesn't know what the rules are. But the government expects this Pfc. to know what the rules are?" (Golden 2006).

Most prosecutions for war crimes don't fall short for lack of knowledge about what happened. On January 13, 2004, Spc. Joseph Darby, a military police (MP) soldier at Abu Ghraib Prison, gave the Army's Criminal Investigation Division a CD-ROM containing more than a hundred images of torture and abuse at the prison. Two and half weeks later Maj. Gen. Antonio Taguba was appointed to conduct a formal investigation into the prison's 800th Military Police Brigade. Taguba found that "numerous incidents of sadistic, blatant, and wanton criminal abuses were inflicted on several detainees. This systemic and illegal abuse of detainees was intentionally perpetrated by several members of the military police guard force." The prison was overcrowded, the MPs ill-trained, and the mission short-staffed. There was "virtually a complete lack of detailed SOPs at any of the detention facilities," and those that did exist were never trained or shared with the lower ranks (Article 15-6, Investigation of the 800th Military Police Brigade 2004:16, 31). The MPs were supposed to carry out detention and corrections duties, but were asked instead to prepare prisoners for interrogation. The means were at hand—sleep deprivation, exposure to cold, the use of stress positions, sexual humiliation, dogs—but there were no clear rules in place. A string of officers failed to take any systematic steps to better train the MPs or rein in the abuses.

Taguba blamed the Abu Ghraib scandal on a sweeping failure of detention policies in Iraq in general, and of the prison command structure in particular. With CIA, DOD, and private contract interrogators, often in civilian dress, coming and going it was unclear exactly who was in charge. The solicitation of abuse was often insinuated: "loosen this guy up for us," "make sure he has a bad night," "make sure he gets the treatment" (Article 15-6, Investigation of the 800th Military Police Brigade 2004:19). Taguba singled out one paragraph of Fragmentary Order (FRAGO) 1108 issued on November 19, 2003, for sowing ambiguity on the prison tiers:

> 3.C.8. A. 1. (U) EFFECTIVE IMMEDIATELY COMMANDER 205 MI BDE ASSUMES RESPONSIBILITY FOR THE BAGHDAD CONFINEMENT FACILITY (BCCF) AND IS APPOINTED THE FOB COMMANDER. UNITS CURRENTLY AT ABU GHRAIB (BCCF) ARE TACON TO 205 MI BDE FOR "SECURITY OF DETAINEES AND FOB PROTECTION." (FRAGO 1108 [19NOV03 DTU] to CJTF-7 OPORD 03-036 2003)

Translation: MPs at Abu Ghraib now report to the prison's military intelligence commander rather than the military police commander. (BDE is short for "brigade"; TACON means to be under tactical or operational control; FOB stands for forward operating base, also referring to the prison.) "This is not doctrinally sound," the report noted, "due to the different missions and agendas assigned to each of these respective specialties" (Article 15-6 Investigation of the 800th Military Police Brigade 2004:38). Taguba would later say that the MPs on the tiers "were being literally exploited by the military interrogators. My view is that those kids were poorly led, not trained, and had not been given any standard operating procedures on how they should guard the detainees" (Hersh 2007). This doesn't absolve the MPs for their acts, but responsibility looks more top-down than the courts-martial indicated.

Top Pentagon brass reacted to the Abu Ghraib scandal with studied ignorance. As noted, the army's Criminal Investigation Division received the photographs on January 13, 2004. By February, a number of implicated soldiers and officers had been suspended, and by March the first charges had been filed. Taguba issued his report on April 4, 2004. CBS News ran the first photographs depicting the abuse on April 28, 2004, and the *New Yorker* published additional photographs two days later. Taguba finally met with secretary of defense Donald Rumsfeld on May 6, 2004, the day before the secretary was to testify before Congress about the scandal. At the meeting Rumsfeld claimed he had yet to see either the photographs or the report, which had been circulating for weeks within the Pentagon and Central Command in Tampa, Florida. Other top officials at the meeting sounded equally naïve about the case. "Could you tell us what happened?" asked Rumsfeld's deputy Paul Wolfowitz. Someone else asked, "Is it abuse or torture?" Taguba recalled, "I described a naked detainee lying on the wet floor, handcuffed, with an interrogator shoving things up his rectum, and said, 'That's not abuse. That's torture.' There was quiet." Taguba said that when he tried to get one lieutenant general to look at the photographs, he declined, saying, "I don't want to get involved by looking, because what do you do with that information, once you know what they show?" (Hersh 2007).

Few of Taguba's recommendations were adopted. The only Abu Ghraib officer court-martialed was Army Reserve Lt. Col. Steven Jordan. Jordan, who had come out of retirement to direct the Joint Interrogation Debriefing Center at the prison, was accused of creating a "chaotic situation" (R. Serrano 2004; von Zielbauer 2007). He was ultimately tried for a single instance of cruelty and maltreatment unrelated to any of the photographed abuses, and after an appeal was cleared of all charges. Brig. Gen. Janis Karpinski was relieved of her command of the 800th Military Police Brigade. The highest-ranking military intelligence officers at Abu Ghraib, Col. Thomas Pappas and Capt. Carolyn Wood, were never tried, although Pappas received a letter of reprimand and was fined $8,000. In the end, 11 enlisted soldiers and no officers were convicted or pled guilty to the abuses. Several commanders associated with the scandal were later promoted (E. Schmitt 2005). CIA officers linked to torture flourished, too. An Associated Press analysis concluded, "When people are disciplined, the punishment seems to roll downhill, sparing senior managers even when they were directly involved in operations that go awry" (Goldman and Apuzzo 2011). The U.S. Senate Select Committee on Intelligence report on the CIA post-9/11 detention and interrogation program found that the CIA rarely reprimanded personnel who committed "serious and significant" violations of the agency's own policies. According to internal CIA documents, "The director strongly believes that mistakes should be expected in a business filled with uncertainty" (U.S. Senate Select Committee on Intelligence 2014:14).

When it comes to collateral damage in military operations, officials tend to project blame outward. As we saw in Iraq and Gaza, the Pentagon and the IDF both blamed collateral damage on the terrorists who they said started the war. Rumsfeld said that the Taliban and al-Qaeda were responsible for "every single casualty" in the Afghanistan War, "whether they're innocent Afghans or innocent Americans" (U.S. Department of Defense 2001). I expect most people would agree this is a shallow conception of responsibility. Even if much of the killing was technically unintended, it was the result of fully sanctioned policies, carried out with at least some foresight as to their effects. Strategists are quick to portray crazed atrocities as beyond the pale, thus reinforcing the legitimacy of measured and deliberate uses of force. There is no lack of soul-searching about the My Lais and Hadithas, but less sensational deaths don't evince the same response. Headline-grabbing allegations of murder may even make day-to-day violence seem mundane by contrast. It is these grindingly routine casualties that a human rights perspective helps to illuminate. As Sarah Sewall (2006) notes, "To learn from Haditha is to learn to notice not just the alleged massacres but the steady stream of civilian deaths that for too much of this war have remained invisible."

Through civilian eyes, strategy and atrocity can look very nearly the same. As Kendrick Oliver (2007:115) observes of the U.S. experience in Vietnam, "atrocity mimicked strategy in both its causes and effects." The logic of the war affirmed actions that terrorized and killed large numbers of innocent people. There was no doctrine of atrocity, no deliberate policy of terror. Strategic violence, pursued for the military advantages it ostensibly offered, was enough. "Pacification" programs, the "sanitization" or "sterilization" of villages, free-fire zones, indiscriminate "harass and interdict" fires (later renamed "intelligence targets"), "reconnoiter by fire," the designation of free-fire zones, and the evasive action rule, better known as "shoot if they run," all propelled strategy toward atrocity (Olson and Roberts 1998:7). Gen. William Westmoreland's fixation on body counts and the "kill ratio" as the measure of success rewarded the use of excessive force. Competition among commanders to gin up the stats spurred civilian harm and encouraged the misreporting of dead civilians as dead Viet Cong (Nelson 2008:84–85). Ultimately, the means overcame the ends. As the *New Yorker* editorialized about My Lai, "There can be no doubt that such an atrocity was possible only because a number of other methods of killing civilians and destroying their villages had come to be the rule, and not the exception, in our conduct of the war" (quoted in Belknap 2002:131). Some of the acts were simple murder, but most were routine war crimes. A review of Pentagon records from Vietnam catalogs hundreds of atrocities, "a My Lai each month" (Nelson 2008:73).

The Haditha Killings: Lethal Rules of Engagement?

Atrocity also mimicked strategy at Haditha, a farming town of 100,000 hugging the banks of the Euphrates in western Iraq. On the morning of November 19, 2005, 24 Iraqis, most of them unarmed, were killed by members of

Staff Sgt. Frank D. Wuterich's Squad, Kilo Company, 3rd Battalion, 1st Marines. What many consider the signal atrocity of the Iraq War was sparked when an improvised explosive device (IED) struck a unit supply convoy as it traveled through a lightly populated part of the town. The explosion ripped Lance Cpl. Miguel "T. J." Terrazas in two, instantly killing the twenty-year-old from El Paso, and seriously injured two other Marines. Immediately after the blast the unit reported coming under small arms fire. Drone footage of the area, viewed later, would show likely insurgents fleeing the scene on foot. The Marines raided three houses a hundred yards or so from the road, and also killed the driver and four passengers from a white car they had signaled to move aside as the convoy approached. If the Marines acted in a rampage, as military prosecutors would later claim, it was a deliberate rampage: the raids unfolded over the course of about 45 minutes. Among the dead were four women and six children, some of them toddlers, and a seventy-six-year-old man in a wheelchair who had been shot nine times.

A brief notice issued the following day by the Second Marine Division Headquarters in Ramadi seemed unremarkable:

> A U.S. Marine and 15 Iraqi civilians were killed yesterday from the blast of a roadside bomb in Haditha. Immediately following the bombing, gunmen attacked the convoy with small arms fire. Iraqi Army soldiers and Marines returned fire killing eight insurgents and wounding another. (Second Marine Division, Camp Blue Diamond, Ar Ramadi, Press Release #05-141 2005)

This statement was false. At worst, the unit killed 24 civilians "in cold blood," as U.S. Representative John Murtha of Pennsylvania, who served as a Marine Corps officer in Vietnam, would later allege (J. McIntyre 2006). At best, they blindly followed rules of engagement (ROE) and standard procedures that routinized excessive and indiscriminate violence. Within two days of the attack, commanders in Iraq knew the civilians hadn't been killed by a roadside IED, but they didn't investigate further or revise the earlier statement. An inquiry by U.S. Army Gen. Eldon Bargewell into the killings described command resistance to investigating their Marines as "unwillingness bordering on denial" (White 2007b). They were too credulous, too protective of their troops, even building a "storyboard" that deliberately distorted events. For commanders further up the line, the story did not seem out of the ordinary. When he was interviewed about the killings, U.S. Marine Corps Maj. Gen.

Barry Johnson, then commander of all Multi-National Forces in Western Iraq (MNF-W), explained,

> Even though it was a significant event . . . I didn't feel I had information at that point in time that would cause me to go back and look at it. . . . It happened all the time, not necessarily in MNF-West all the time, but throughout the whole country.
>
> So, you know, maybe—I guess maybe if I was sitting here at Quantico and heard that 15 civilians were killed, I would have been surprised and shocked and gone—done more to look into it. But at that point in time, I felt that that was—had been, for whatever reason, part of that engagement, and felt that it was just a cost of doing business on that particular engagement. (Major General Johnson, USMC Commanding General, MNF-W n.d.)

Hadithans themselves knew perfectly well the official line was false. The town council presented U.S. military officials with a formal written complaint accusing the Marines of war crimes, but were rebuffed. The town mayor (whom the U.S. considered sympathetic to the insurgency) and an entourage of elders visited a nearby Marine camp and asked for an official inquiry, also to no avail. The killings would probably never have been investigated save for the efforts of Taher Thabet, co-founder of a human rights start-up called the Hammurabi Human Rights Organization. Though based in Baghdad, Thabet happened to be visiting family in Haditha the day of the killings. The following morning he videotaped the corpses in their U.S. military-issue body bags at the local morgue, and the blood-washed rooms inside the houses. The Hammurabi group circulated the video to Western media outlets, which were wary of what looked like it could have been fabricated al-Qaeda propaganda. After viewing the videotape and interviewing several Haditha residents, *Time* magazine Baghdad bureau chief Tim McGuirk approached U.S. military officials with a list of questions about the killings (McGuirk 2006).

Multiple investigations ensued, first by U.S. Army Col. Gregory Watt, then by U.S. Army Gen. Eldon Bargewell, and finally by a 60-agent team from the Naval Criminal Investigative Services. Investigators interviewed Iraqi witnesses as well as Marines up and down the chain of command. Survivors of the raids described deliberate killings of people who were praying or trying to shield their children with their bodies. An Iraqi soldier who had accompanied the Kilo squad that morning said the five men who were rousted from the white car did not try to run, as the Marines claimed, but were shot on the spot. As the investigations snowballed, some Marines admitted that they had lied when first questioned. Photographs of the victims taken by Marines on the scene came to light. A trove of supposedly deleted photographs turned up on a Sony Playstation memory stick. One Marine said he had seen some of the images set to music on another Marine's laptop computer. While the forensic evidence was inconclusive, the photographs suggested that many of the victims had been slain execution-style, shot in the head and chest at close range. Lance Cpl. Andrew A. Wright, who helped remove the bodies, held on to a set of pictures he took. "Even though there was no investigation at the time," Wright told investigators, "I felt that the photographs would be evidence if anything came up in the future. In my opinion, the people that I photographed had been murdered" (White 2007a).

Several Kilo Company members faced charges of unpremeditated murder, negligent homicide, and assault. Four higher-level officers were charged with dereliction of duty for failing to investigate or report the incident. By the end, however, the case was a ghost of its former self. None of the Haditha Marines was charged with murder. There were two courts-martial. An intelligence officer, Lt. Andrew Grayson, was tried and acquitted on charges of ordering a subordinate to destroy evidence and to lie about what happened. Several officers received letters of censure for their lack of due diligence, but none were put on trial. All charges were dropped against two other officers. Of the eight Marines who carried out the raids, only Staff Sgt. Wuterich was tried, on reduced charges of aggravated assault, reckless endangerment, dereliction of duty, and obstruction of justice. After two weeks, the trial was halted and Wuterich pled guilty to a single count of "negligent dereliction of duty" for telling his squad to "shoot first and ask questions later." At his sentencing, he apologized for the killings, adding "even with the best intentions, sometimes combat actions can cause tragic results" (Slosson 2012). Wuterich was demoted and had his salary slashed, but served no jail time. Soon afterward, he left the military under a general discharge "with honorable conditions"—one notch below an honorable discharge.

Experts in military law were stunned. The Hammurabi video and the soldiers' photographs were chilling. The media coverage was intense. Investigators managed to cut through most of the lies and closing of ranks that plagued scrutiny of other incidents (after a 2006 firefight in which civilians were killed, a Marine captain was caught on audio telling his charges to "CYA" [cover your ass] by telling investigators they were responding to "muzzle flashes")

(K. Johnson 2007). Perhaps we shouldn't be surprised that the case unraveled. Even when they become public, remarkably few cases of civilian casualties in Iraq ended in convictions. Commanders in Iraq seemed almost allergic to courts-martial, preferring administrative punishments including reprimands, fines, demotions, bans on internet usage, and allowing soldiers to avoid prosecution if they admit guilt and agree to leave the military (Moffeit and Kane 2004). Gary Solis, a law professor and former military judge, thought there were "fewer prosecutions in Iraq than one might expect," given the levels of violence and the number of well-publicized abuses. Eugene R. Fidell, president of the National Institute of Military Justice, noted that the United States and other countries were "having trouble getting convictions and accountability," and characterized the punishments being handed down as "kind of modest" (White et al. 2006). Even in detainee abuse cases, punishments tended to be light. Three New York-based human rights groups compiled evidence of detainee abuse that involved 600 military personnel and 460 detainees. Less than 10 percent of those alleged to be involved were ever convicted by court martial (Center for Human Rights and Global Justice, Human Rights First, and Human Rights Watch 2006:2). A lieutenant colonel who carried out a mock execution of a detainee was spared a court martial. The rates of prosecutions rose under the tenure of Gen. Peter Chiarelli, who took command of forces in Iraq in 2006. But for soldiers on the ground, it was hard to dial back permissive practices.

The number of condolence and "solatia" (solace) payments to Iraqis also increased under Gen. Chiarelli. The Pentagon considers the payments "expressions of remorse and sympathy" for death, injury, or property damage caused by U.S. forces in the course of combat operations, but not admissions of guilt.[3] They are made at the discretion of commanders on the ground. The U.S. spent a total of $51 million in condolence payments in Iraq, likely covering thousands of cases (Bowen 2013:66). Chiarelli described the practice as a culturally appropriate way of making amends "common in this part of the world. It means a death payment, a death gratuity, so to speak. It is part of life over here" (Bender 2006). As noted earlier, while the program was meant to build good will among Iraqis, many were insulted by the paltry sums offered. The amounts and circumstances varied widely, but taken as a whole they appear calibrated to mitigate the most intense, indiscriminate, violence after the fact rather than trying to avoid casualties in the first place. As the payments soared in 2006, a U.S. Marine Corps official said the sum "reflects the high operational tempo" of Marine units operating in Anbar Province (Cloud

2006). Commanders distributed $38,000 to the families of fifteen of the people killed in Haditha. A year later another $7,500 was disbursed.

Particularly after the Haditha killings, many of the systematic explanations for atrocities pointed to troops stretched thin, struggling to manage the civilian population, and under pressure to kill terrorists. Multiple tours and longer deployments were correlated with declining mental health and rising abuses. American officials were disturbed by a 2007 Department of Defense survey of 1,320 U.S. Army soldiers and 447 Marines in Iraq, which found that only 44 percent of the marines and 55 percent of the soldiers would report a fellow service member for killing or injuring an innocent Iraqi. Acute stress, anxiety, and depression were found to be more common among troops with multiple deployments, and soldiers who exhibited these symptoms were nearly twice as likely to mistreat civilians ("Not All Troops Would Report Iraq Abuse" 2007).

None of the Haditha Marines resorted to these kinds of psychological arguments. Instead, they made the rules and norms of engagement the centerpiece of the defense. They argued that they were well trained in the rules of engagement. As one U.S. Marine who served near Haditha put it, "We received ROE [rules of engagement] and LOAC [law of armed conflict] training monthly, though it seemed like weekly" (Bargewell 2006:69). They said they cleared the houses by the book, that these practices had been drilled down the ranks. Lawyers for the accused said that if this was a problem, it was the commanders who crafted the regulations, not the marines who implemented them, who bore the blame. "The collateral civilian deaths were absolutely tragic," said one of Sgt. Wuterich's lawyers, "but occurred as a result of legally justified actions that routinely occur during time of war" (von Zielbauer 2006).

Were these "normal" house clearings or were they revenge killing? From the evidence it was hard to tell the difference. Lt. Col. Paul Ware, a seasoned military judge, conducted the Article 32 evidentiary hearings, the military equivalent of a grand jury, in three of the Haditha cases, including Wuterich's. In his recommendations to Lt. Gen. James N. Mattis, the commander of the 1st Marine Division who would ultimately decide whether or not to court martial the Marines, Ware argued that individual responsibility was diminished by the nature of Kilo Company's training and experience. Many members of the unit were veterans of the house-to-house fighting in Fallujah. The city was treated as something of a free-fire zone after civilians were ordered to evacuate. Despite the different circumstances, the squad approached the

Haditha houses in the same fashion. They believed that once a house was declared "hostile," they were not required to positively identify targets they encountered inside the dwelling. Regardless of the formal ROE in place at the time, "clearly this unit's training and leadership either received different training, or came up with its own form of MOUT [military operations in urban terrain] tactics for clearing a house." "The ROE are not applied in the same manner," wrote Ware. Even if the term "hostile house" did not exist in the JAG training manuals, "clearly it exists in the minds of the Marines who are expected to be facing the enemy at the tip of the spear." "Once a house is declared hostile, you can 'blow it up,' 'lead with grenades and gunfire,' or call in indirect fire to destroy the structure" (Ware 2007:19–20).

Although two Marine captains testified that the rules were not nearly so loose, Ware found that this maxim was understood throughout the company and probably the battalion. The Marines should have been able to distinguish between combatants and noncombatants in the house raids. But Ware said they didn't get that from the Marine Corps. The prosecution presented no evidence of training exercises, situational "vignettes," lectures, PowerPoint presentations, or simulations that involved discrimination inside a room (Ware 2007:19–20). Media interviews with other Marines supported this reading of the ROE. One noted that "running and gunning" was not unusual; when threatened, soldiers were allowed to spray rooms with gunfire. "It may be a bad tactic, but it works." "It keeps you alive" (White 2006). Another explained, "you've got to do whatever it takes to get home. If it takes clearing by fire where there's civilians, that's it" (Broder 2006).

A lawyer for one of Marines said that "Haditha will be the case that causes the military to come to grips with the rules of insurgency combat in a way they've never had to before" (Myers 2008). It wasn't. Instead, we are left with a dizzying sense that the Marines followed the rules of engagement *and* they murdered innocent civilians. Unleashing a rampage of unobserved gunfire and grenades in civilian quarters, or resorting to virtual free-fire tactics in the midst of noncombatants, was reasonably seen as falling within the ROE, however terrifying and indiscriminately lethal the attacks were from the perspective of their victims. Criminal, or near-criminal, tactics had risen to the level of standard operating procedures. As far as Lt. Col. Ware was concerned, individual culpability was subsumed in collective training. The Marines' mental and physical memory took over, and they ceased to be autonomous moral or legal agents. More troubling, however, is that Ware was unable to draw a red line between strategy and atrocity. Despite the gap between the formal rules of engagement and the actual norms and standard procedures that had been constituted and condoned through doctrine and practice, no one has ever been called to task for establishing the battalion's social milieu and fighting tactics. Iraqis, meanwhile, perhaps weren't surprised at the outcome. An Iraqi lawyer named Waleed Mohammed told the *Washington Post* that they expected "the sentence will be like one for someone who killed a dog in the United States . . . because Iraqis have become like dogs in the eyes of Americans" (Knickmeyer 2006).

"Tactical Questioning": The Case of Baha Mousa

On the morning of September 14, 2003, British soldiers from the 1st Queen's Lancashire Regiment raided the Ibn Al-Haitham Hotel in Basra, Iraq. The raid uncovered three Kalashnikov assault rifles and two Beretta submachine guns, two grenades, bags full of Iraqi dinars, and three identity cards from a company that provided interpreters to the U.S. military (the ID cards turned out to be fake). Nine men connected to the hotel, among them twenty-six-year-old receptionist Baha Mousa, were arrested and delivered to the 1st QLR headquarters where they were subjected to two days of what the British Army called "conditioning" and "tactical questioning." The men were double- and even triple-hooded with burlap sandbags in temperatures over 120° Fahrenheit. Their wrists were bound with plastic handcuffs. They were forced into painful stress positions, deprived of food, water, and sleep, and repeatedly, brutally, punched and kicked. The soldiers said the powerfully built Mousa had been combative during his 36 hours in detention and twice had managed to remove his hood and handcuffs. In a vicious final assault by several soldiers, Mousa's head appears to have been slammed into a wall and smashed against the concrete floor. He lay sprawled face down on the floor not breathing, the sandbag still cinched tightly around his neck. Regiment medics frantically attempted to resuscitate Mousa, but failed. The pathologist who conducted the post-mortem six days later said the cause of death was a combination of strangulation, postural asphyxia, and multiple injuries. The autopsy identified 93 external injuries to the body. Mousa had fractured ribs, a broken nose, and swelling of the brain. Mousa's wife had died of cancer six months earlier, leaving him to care for his two children. According to the other Al-Haitham detainees, Mousa's final, muffled, words were "I will die, I have children, I have a dead wife" (*Baha Mousa Public Inquiry Report* 2011:1:93).

Mousa's case was taken seriously. Within 30 minutes of the official time of death, the special Investigation Branch of the Royal Military Police was informed of a death in custody. Within hours nearly the entire battalion command had been notified. Within a day or two, defense officials, civil servants, and politicians in London learned of the case, and the media began asking for details. Investigators in Iraq, however, were slow to grasp the importance of the incident, which seemed to grow with each interview they conducted. The soldiers involved weren't saying much, or were actively lying. A crime scene analysis wasn't conducted until six days after the killing. The trail might have gone cold had investigators not uncovered a one-minute video taken inside the detention rooms during the "conditioning" of the prisoners. The video showed Cpl. Donald Payne "beasting" several hooded prisoners, screaming "get up, you fucking ape," and forcing them to hold the "ski" position, knees bent, backs against the wall, arms shackled and stretched out in front. As the men slide toward the floor Payne drags them back into position.[4] The video was filmed about an hour and twenty minutes into the ordeal, and already the men were groaning and panting in distress. As the hours wore on, Payne invented a game he called "the chorus" or "the choir." He would stand the men on their knees and then proceed down the line kicking each prisoner in the kidneys, making them cry out or shriek in unison. Payne along with other soldiers did this many times, often for the amusement of soldiers who dropped by the detention rooms. The soldiers "play[ed] us like musical instruments," one prisoner testified (*Baha Mousa Public Inquiry Report* 2011:1: 85). The boot kicks left an identical pattern of bruises, scrapes, and contusions on each man's lower back and torso, lurid evidence of deliberate, well-aimed assaults. The kicks contributed to Mousa's death. A second detainee nearly died from renal failure (he was hospitalized for two months). A third was inflicted with serious kidney damage. Soldiers competed to see who could kick a detainee the farthest. They also practiced rugby tackles on the prisoners, forced the men to dance "like Michael Jackson," and threatened to burn them by pushing them against a pulsing generator. There was at least one mock immolation. Gasoline was waved under the nose of a hooded detainee and water poured over his head to make him think he was being doused with petrol. A lighter was then ignited in front of the man's face (167). The prisoners believed they were going to be killed.

The condition of the detainees deteriorated rapidly. Lance Cpl. Redfearn witnessed their monstrous transformation after 24 hours of "conditioning":

> When the detainees were originally arrested they were tidily dressed and not in any kind of distress. The next time I saw them . . . on the Monday morning they all looked like they had been in a car crash. The majority of their clothes were ripped and most if not all of them had had heavy bruising across their abdomens and upper arms. This was visible through their ripped clothing. The bruising that I saw was not just simple round bruises that you might normally see. The bruises I saw ran in a line across the detainees' stomachs and were perhaps five inches wide. The detainees also looked exhausted. When I started my guard shift and removed the detainees' hoods I could see that at least two of them had bloody noses and bruising around their eyes. I remember that Baha Mousa was one of those with a bloody nose. During my shift I had called out for a medic to come, but none ever did. (2011: 1:175)

The torture was carried out openly. The prisoners were held in a squalid single-story building consisting of three small rooms. The rooms were missing their doors, and the windows were open onto the grounds of the compound. The building sat a few yards away from the camp's main housing unit and a stone's throw from the regiment headquarters and medical aid station. Like the cook at U.S. Camp Mercury, soldiers would visit the rooms to abuse prisoners. The Gage Inquiry identified 19 soldiers who perpetrated some form of assault on the prisoners (Williams 2012:287). An additional 20 or more soldiers and officers saw evidence of abuse—lacerations, contusions, bloody noses, bruises around the eyes, lips and nose, bruises across the torso, a bulging groin hernia, torn clothing, detainees writhing in pain, or curled in the fetal position, detainees who had soiled themselves—but did nothing to stop it (2011:1:120–28). Several soldiers said they didn't report the abuse because their superiors had already seen it. Four soldiers said they saw Father Peter Madden, the Roman Catholic priest, or "padre," attached to the regiment, inside the detention facility. "There was no one in that camp . . . that I could have told," Lance Cpl. Redfearn would later testify. "Even the padre had been in there. If you can't turn to the padre, who can you turn to, sir?"[5]

Perversely, prisoners who collapsed during the beatings were taken to the medical unit to recuperate. One of those examined was Detainee 001, probably in his fifties. His legs were shaking uncontrollably, his heart racing, and his breathing labored. He said his hood was removed and he was examined by a man with a stethoscope. Afterward, the hood was replaced and he was sent back to the rooms where the beatings resumed (2011:1:85). The regiment medical officer, Dr. Derek Keilloh, testified that he saw no signs of abuse at all during the 48 hours. During the 20–30 minutes he spent trying to revive Mousa, he noticed only a dab of dried blood in one of Mousa's nostrils. Even after Mousa died, the doctor didn't go to check on the condition of the remaining prisoners. Instead, several hours after Mousa's death, two of the detainees were brought to the aid station, where they were examined, given injections, and returned to the hands of their abusers. Although he escaped court martial, Dr. Keilloh was later drummed out of the medical profession in Britain for failing to protect the prisoners in his charge.

Seven members of the 1st Queen's Lancashire Regiment, including Cpl. Payne and battalion commander Jorge Mendonça, were court-martialed. The six-month trial followed the letter of the law but delivered little justice. Several of the victims were flown to Britain to testify. They saw it as a chance to speak their piece and repair their suffering. But their testimonies were confused and contradictory, and the fact that the prisoners had been hooded most of the time made it difficult to identify any particular assailants. They were treated roughly during cross examination (Williams 2012:214–16). Many of the soldiers, participants as well as bystanders, were stricken by amnesia. Justice McKinnon, the judge advocate who oversaw the court martial, said derisively that many of the soldiers who beat the men were not prosecuted "because there is no evidence against them as a result of a more or less obvious closing of ranks" (2011:1). In the end, no one was held responsible for killing Baha Mousa. McKinnon ruled that the government had failed to make its case against the soldiers, including a manslaughter charge against Cpl. Payne: there was "no case to answer." The two intelligence officers, Maj. Michael Peebles and Warrant Officer Mark Davies, mounted a defense and were acquitted. Payne pleaded guilty to inhuman treatment at the beginning of the trial and was sentenced to 12 months in prison and discharged from the army.

The court martial seemed to confirm the old saw that military justice is to justice what military music is to music. As a human rights case, however, the death of Baha Mousa has had a long half-life. In 2004, Mousa's father, along with relatives of five other Iraqis who had been killed by British troops during street patrols, filed a lawsuit in the UK seeking an independent review of the killings and demanding that the government admit liability and compensate the families of the dead. The case, *Al-Skeini et al v. Secretary of State for Defence*, sought to apply the UK Human Rights Act of 1998 (which allowed violations of the ECHR to be remedied in British courts) in instances where British troops exercised "effective control" over overseas territory. The case eventually reached the Appellate Committee of the House of Lords, which ruled in 2007 that Britain *did* control the detention center where Baha Mousa died, but *did not* control the city streets, buildings, and outdoor areas where the five other killings occurred. The Appellate Committee dismissed the "battlefield" cases, but ordered a new inquiry into the Mousa killing.[6] This was the impetus for the exhaustive public inquest convened in 2008 by Sir William Gage, a retired Court of Appeal judge. The inquiry heard evidence from 388 witnesses. It was a quest for the truth, not a criminal trial. Gage's brief was to examine the circumstances surrounding Mousa's death, to determine how the regiment had adopted such abusive conditioning and interrogation practices, and to make recommendations.

In 2011, the ECtHR overturned the Appellate Committee's decision in *Al-Skeini*. The Court said the UK exercised effective control in all six deaths, not just the death in custody. As noted earlier, this was a novel human rights theory of effective control. Effective control now meant control over the bodies of the victims rather than control over the territory they inhabited. The substance of the petition dealt with the investigations undertaken by the army. Most of the inquiries had been conducted at the command level and had determined within a day or two of each incident that the soldiers responsible had acted within the rules of engagement. The judges acknowledged the obstacles to investigating homicides in a war zone, but nevertheless found the command inquiries wanting under the Convention. As the ECtHR argued in the *Güleç* case, "neither the prevalence of violent armed clashes nor the high incidence of fatalities can displace the obligation under Article 2 to ensure that an effective, independent investigation is conducted into deaths arising out of clashes involving the security forces."[7] The court did applaud the thoroughness of the Baha Mousa Public Inquiry, which was wrapping up its work at the time the *Al-Skeini* decision was announced, and the judges agreed with the British government that the public inquiry had met the Convention's requirements.[8]

This was a dramatic intervention by the ECtHR on jurisdiction as well as substance, extending the court's reach into battle zones abroad and questioning fundamentally the military's ability to police itself. In previous rulings, the ECtHR had addressed the British Army practice of detainee "conditioning," that ill-defined, violence-begging term. Conditioning had migrated from one British counterinsurgency to the next: Palestine, Malaysia, Kenya, Cyprus, Brunei, Aden (Yemen), and other areas. In Northern Ireland, the practice was formalized in the "five techniques" to be used during "in-depth interrogations": 1) hooding detainees; 2) using stress positions; 3) depriving prisoners of sleep; 4) withholding food; and 5) subjecting detainees to deafening "white noise" such as a generator running in an enclosed space. In August 1971, hundreds of Catholic men in Northern Ireland were rounded up by British troops and Royal Ulster constables. The men were accused of being affiliated with the Irish Republican Army and were interned without trial. Fourteen of the internees were chosen to be subjected to the five techniques at a secret Army interrogation center at Ballykelly in Northern Ireland. In 1972, after the Government of Ireland petitioned the European Commission on Human Rights on behalf of the 14 "hooded men," as they became known, British Prime Minister Edward Heath banned the five techniques "with reference to any future operation." In a 1978 ruling the ECtHR said the UK's techniques constituted inhumane and degrading treatment in violation of Article 3 of the European Convention of Human Rights. But the Court did not think they rose to the level of torture.[9]

Thirty-six years later, in December 2014, the Republic of Ireland announced that it would ask the ECtHR to reopen the case of the "hooded men" after newly declassified British government documents showed that UK officials knew at the time that several of the men had developed serious, long-lasting, mental illness as a result of the treatment. Had this evidence come to light earlier, the court might have ruled that the techniques did in fact constitute torture. This is significant not least because the ECtHR's reluctance to label the British methods torture was cited prominently in the post-9/11 U.S. Justice Department memos that sought to justify an aggressive definition of what constituted torture (McCaffrey 2013). It's worth noting, too, that the al-Haitham detainees who were tortured alongside Baha Mousa have all been diagnosed with various psychological disorders: PTSD, panic and mood disorders, isolation, flashbacks, nightmares, deteriorating quality of life, severe depression, and in one case "psychiatric emergency" and risk of suicide—all likely the result of their abuse at the hands of the 1st Queen's Lancashire Regiment (*Baha Mousa Public Inquiry Report* 2011:1:103–14).

Edward Heath and the ECtHR notwithstanding, the five techniques (plus a few more) were used by every British battle group in Iraq. Basic detainee protections withered in the Iraqi heat. It is not clear if the hooding ban got lost in the bureaucratic mists of the Ministry of Defence (MOD) or if it was deliberately flouted. The ban vanished from the training manuals sometime in the 1990s. Some officers who were familiar with the ban thought it applied only in Northern Ireland. Red Cross officials privately told UK commanders in

Basra that hooding, or "bagging," as the troops called it, was illegal. But the Army nevertheless retained the practice as a tool to disorient prisoners and maintain "the shock of capture." The practice may or may not have produced better intelligence: that assumption went untested. It was certainly a way to impose the captor's will on his detainees. Like the American "no blood, no foul" motto, it was an article of faith among many British soldiers that psychological duress was allowed even if physical torture was not. Training materials developed in 2005 and 2008 recommended using crude, Abu Ghraib-style, methods. "Get them naked," said one Powerpoint presentation for interrogators in training. "Keep them naked if they do not follow commands." A 2008 manual recommended using blindfolds or blacked-out goggles to disorient and pressure detainees, noting that such sensory deprivation was lawful as long as it was used for "valid operational reasons" (European Center for Constitutional and Human Rights and Public Interest Lawyers 2014:30–31).

Judge Gage believed this expedient treatment of detainees could have been nipped in the bud. Instead, legal uncertainty about hooding and other tactics was allowed to fester. Army lawyers and intelligence officers wrangled over detainee policy in a battle of FRAGOs. In May 2003, after the deaths in battlegroup custody of several prisoners, Lt. Col. Nicholas Mercer, the UK's chief military lawyer in Iraq, barred arresting units from initiating interrogations. Mercer also tightened reporting on where detainees were being held, and shortened the interval before they had to be remanded to the Royal Military Police. Mercer addressed the Heath Ban directly in FRAGO 152 (May 20, 2003), which iterated that "under no circumstances should [detainees'] faces be covered as this might impair breathing." Chairman Gage commended Mercer's efforts to "design out" the risks of prisoner abuse. Here was proof that such abuse was not only foreseeable, "but it had actually been foreseen" (*Baha Mousa Public Inquiry Report* 2011:2: 893, 903). The follow through was poor, however. The 1st QLR's legal team was briefed on the hooding ban, but division headquarters staff, high-level intelligence officers, and even the head of the military police—much less the squaddies in the trenches—all claimed they'd never heard of the ban (Bennett 2012:186). The court martial established that the 1st Queen's Lancashire probably never received FRAGO 152.[10] In any event, in June most of Mercer's initiatives were reversed by 1st Division FRAGO 29. Intelligence gathering was made the clear priority. In a preview of what would happen at Abu Ghraib, the intelligence branch was given control of the overall internment program. A designated battlegroup officer would begin the interrogation almost immediately after the arrest. The time that arresting units could detain prisoners was extended to 14 hours (2011:903–4).

The Public Inquiry seized on these and other policies that made hooding seem plausible to so many of those involved. Gage blamed the loss of institutional or "corporate" knowledge of the Heath ban on the chaotic transition from invasion to occupation. One consequence of FRAGO 29 was that new rotations of intelligence officers were briefed on detention policies by outgoing officers who themselves had only a few weeks of experience handling detainees. Official apathy made it all possible. The high point of the 28-week inquiry dealt not with the ravages of torture but rather with the bureaucratic banalities of the MOD. On the stand, Lt. Col. Mercer described a pattern of deaths in custody brought about by indifference as reflected in training and budget priorities. Here, Mercer is questioned by Queen's Counsel Gerard Elias:

> Q. Moving on, can I take you, please, to . . . your statement, under the heading "Conclusion," in which you say: "The issue of prisoners (of all categories) was a constant battle. . . . there was a general indifference to prisoners which was reflected, initially, in the lack of manpower and resources provided." . . . Do you mean indifference brought about by a lack of resources or indifference demonstrated in other ways?
>
> A. I think by this stage this went wider. I think actually the lack of resources reflected a general lack of consideration for what was going to be a massive issue and indeed it was. And I found that the prisoner issue overall was a constant battle and that every time we tried to put in proper review procedures . . . we found ourselves fighting some sort of legal war.
>
> Q. You reflect that, don't you, in paragraph 100, where you say: "I am still amazed that we had to fight so hard for even basic Geneva Convention rights for prisoners."
>
> A. That's correct.
>
> Q. You say: "This indifference, of course, was exacerbated by the total strategic failure to plan for occupation and the vacuum it created. . . . In my view, if the issue of prisoners had been properly resourced and

we had been allowed to implement a proper reviewing and oversight mechanism (and had this been sustained) then the tragedy which unfolded might never have happened."

A. Yes, I agree with that.[11]

Mercer said the MOD had failed to properly educate and train soldiers how to handle detainees, and that soldiers themselves lost their moral bearings, turned a blind eye, or fell silent. The Gage Inquiry couldn't remedy all these ills, but it did make 73 different recommendations covering almost every aspect of the military's detention and interrogation policies, inter alia, to ban "harsh" interrogation practices, to improve training, inspections, and audits, and to describe in clear language what is permitted and what is not, avoiding open-ended phrases like "restraint positions" and "prolonging the shock of capture," and banishing altogether the "dangerously ambiguous" term "conditioning" (*Baha Mousa Public Inquiry Report* 2011: 3:1267–86).

A second major British inquest known as the Al-Swedy Inquiry found that British troops had mistreated Iraqis in custody but roundly rejected claims that the troops had murdered civilians, as many Iraqis believed (Forbes 2014). The findings of these public inquiries, including the exculpatory findings, are widely viewed as authoritative. Framed by the ECtHR rulings, they have had a greater institutional impact than the cosmetic reforms the British Army adopted on its own. The MOD's official soul-searching about the abuses in Iraq yielded only a modest report issued by Brig. Robert Aitken in 2008. Aitken criticized the failure to plan for the occupation and dutifully condemned the five techniques, but he sidestepped the issue of responsibility, insisting that the number of allegations of abuse in Iraq had been "tiny," and smoothly suggesting there was "no evidence of fundamental flaws in the Army's approach to preparing for or conducting operations" (*Aitken Report* 2008: 5, 25). The MOD seemed incapable of serious self-criticism. Phil Shiner, whose law firm Public Interest Lawyers represented Baha Mousa's family and has led the effort to hold the British military accountable, blamed the "huge structural problems with the military system of investigating itself." He said the courts-martial system "lacks independence, rigor [and] a strong rationale to get to the bottom of this type of incident" (Vasagar 2006).

In Britain, independent scrutiny for high-profile cases is probably here to stay. Routine cases increasingly are given their due, too. The ECtHR's rulings on jurisdiction and effective investigation opened the door for individual

Iraqis to bring claims against the British military under the Human Rights Act of 1998. Virtually all of these allegations are brought forward not through military channels, but by private human rights lawyers. Several British law firms now specialize in such cases. All this scrutiny has cost British taxpayer considerable sums. The MOD expects to spend $150 million on public inquiries and investigations related to Iraq and Afghanistan. Several hundred cases of illegal detention and torture have been settled with cash payments averaging about $100,000 per complaint. The civil case brought by Baha Mousa's father, Daoud, and the other al-Haitham detainees was settled after the Government admitted to "substantive breaches" of the ECHR, publicly apologized, and paid damages of $6 million.[12] Some critics of the process have suggested that the MOD will have "to call on the Treasury Reserve to fight legal as well as military action, or risk having procurement and other commitments compromised" (Tugendhat and Laura Croft 2013:36).

In November 2010, the MOD convened the Iraq Historic Allegations Team (IHAT) to investigate killings and abuse of civilians. The IHAT was designed explicitly to meet the UK's human rights obligations. To be sure, the process hasn't scrutinized the full spectrum of rights trampled in Iraq, but it has nudged humanitarian law investigations toward the standards of human rights. About 125 civilian investigators are reportedly looking into more than 1,300 allegations of unlawful killing, rendition, torture, and abuse. Interviewers have set up shop in a "safehouse" in a city in southeastern Europe. Working alongside interpreters, psychologists, advocates, and lawyers for the claimants, they have taken testimony from a stream of Iraqi claimants and witnesses. About 100 Iraqis have been interviewed thus far, a fraction of the total who will need to be interviewed in the coming years (Williams 2014). British investigators are also scouring some 2,600 videotaped interrogations looking for evidence of abuse (Cobain 2014).

The IHAT process is likely to produce a number of criminal prosecutions and civil claims. Most of the cases involve assault or ill treatment during detention. But there are also at least 240 cases alleging unlawful killing. Some of them involve suspicious deaths in custody or even a drowning at the hands of British soldiers. But many others involve the kind of classic collateral damage so often brushed aside as the inevitable byproduct of war: a girl killed while playing near her home in broad daylight, a bus driver shot while returning from a market, a man shot after backing his car out of a queue at a gas station and knocking over a British soldier. What is most striking about the process is the attention it affords alleged victims and the venue it offers for them to tell their stories. Alleged perpetrators, to the extent that they can be identified, have no voice, and none have been offered amnesty in exchange for coming clean. It's the reverse image of a court-martial, in which soldiers face discipline by military officers over military rules of engagement. Now the accusers command the stage.

What Can the ICC Really Do?

Quite a lot, it seems. In 2006, the International Criminal Court (ICC) found evidence to believe that British troops had committed a range of war crimes in Iraq, but chose not to pursue the case because it didn't regard the allegations as grave enough to be admissible under Article 17 of the Rome Statute. In 2014, however, ICC prosecutor Fatou Bensouda reopened the investigation after receiving a thick dossier from the European Center for Constitutional and Human Rights and Public Interest Lawyers. The dossier contained allegations by hundreds of Iraqis involving possibly thousands of instances of unlawful killing, torture, or cruel, inhuman, or degrading treatment, many of them already under investigation by IHAT. The human rights lawyers argued that abuses had been "ordered, sanctioned or enabled by higher level officers within the military chain of command, and with the knowledge of higher level civilian officers." They said MOD investigations targeted soldiers at the bottom of the chain of command and "systematically shielded from prosecution those bearing the greatest responsibility for the crimes, thereby enabling the persistence of impunity instead of securing criminal accountability" (European Center for Constitutional and Human Rights and Public Interest Lawyers 2014:250, 7). A number of human rights groups have since pressed the ICC to take up the case in full. Human Rights Watch noted that the last time Britain had held a senior political or military official responsible for the war crimes of its armed forces was in 1651, during the English Civil War! (Baldwin 2014).

Iraq isn't the only war the ICC has in its sights. The ICC addresses "widespread and systematic" atrocities, specifically, genocide, crimes against humanity, serious breaches of the laws and customs of war, and aggression. The court upholds individual criminal responsibility whether or not one is acting in an official capacity or on superior orders and whether or not violations are committed in international or in internal conflicts, during humanitarian missions, or during peacetime. No nexus with interstate war is required (see T. Smith 2002a). Nevertheless, atrocities on this scale tend to happen in wars, and the court's docket consists largely of cases linked to armed conflict: Uganda, Congo, Darfur, Central African Republic, Côte d'Ivoire, and Mali. The court is designed to complement rather than replace sovereign courts, trying only those cases that national courts are unwilling or unable to prosecute. Not only does the ICC envision these matters being adjudicated at the national level, but it furnishes states with a legal model to emulate.

The "widespread and systematic" threshold also means that the ICC is likely to examine atrocities driven by deliberate state policies, not the misdeeds of a few bad apples. As a rule, the capacity for states to kill or maim is far greater than that of informal armed forces. ICC relations with target governments are often adversarial, but there is also more diplomatic give and take than one might expect. For example, in 2014 a delegation from the ICC met with members of IHAT and the MOD's Service Prosecuting Authority to communicate directly the court's expectations regarding the rigor and independence of the Iraq investigations. The hope on both sides is that the UK will manage to head off a full referral (ICC, Office of the Prosecutor 2014). Even Washington has managed to find common ground with the court. The Rome Statute was signed by the Clinton administration and then, infamously, unsigned by the Bush administration. Behind the scenes the U.S. tried to chip away at the authority of the ICC, reportedly reaching bilateral immunity agreements with over 100 countries not to refer each other's citizens to the court. The American Service-Members Protection Act of 2002 prohibited the United States from cooperating with or funding the ICC. A provision in the act giving the president the right to take "all necessary measures" to repatriate U.S. citizens detained by the court earned it the nickname "The Hague Invasion Act." Still, U.S. government lawyers do not dismiss the ICC lightly. After 9/11, White House Counsel Gonzales asked the Justice Department's John Yoo if enhanced interrogation methods would violate the Torture Convention, but also if they would warrant prosecution by the ICC. Yoo's response followed a circular, sovereign, logic: because the president had already ruled that since captured al-Qaeda members were not POWs, their treatment was not an issue for the ICC. Yoo warned that the Hague court was an activist and unhinged institution and that a "rogue prosecutor or judge" might nevertheless pursue the case (Yoo 2002).

Anti-ICC bluster still issues from Washington, but the court isn't the bête noire it used to be. American actions in Iraq were insulated from the ICC, given that the U.S. and Iraq weren't parties to the Rome Treaty and that the Americans could effectively block any referral by the UN Security Council.

Alarmist fears have receded as it has grown clearer that the ICC cannot seize American soldiers on a political or legal whim. U.S. diplomats know that the ICC bolsters some of the most pressing human rights goals of American foreign policy. Categorical opposition is counterproductive. In fact, there is considerable signaling and accommodation between Washington and The Hague (Schiff 2008:176; Bosco 2014). The United States helped the Office of the Prosecutor secure an arrest warrant (yet to be executed) for Sudanese president Omar al-Bashir for alleged war crimes and crimes against humanity in Darfur. The State Department's Rewards for Justice Program now includes suspects indicted by the ICC, and the U.S. helped secure the surrender of Bosco "The Terminator" Ntaganda to The Hague, where he is now on trial for rape, murder, recruitment of child soldiers, and sexual slavery in the Democratic Republic of Congo. The State Department praised the ICC when the court won its first conviction, of Congolese warlord Thomas Lubanga for recruiting and exploiting child soldiers (Kersten 2014). In 2014 the U.S. lobbied for a Security Council resolution referring the situation in Syria to the ICC, but the resolution was blocked by China and Russia.

The ICC has been criticized for picking low-hanging fruit. The awkward fact that the Court has prosecuted only African suspects prompted a nasty diplomatic row with the African Union, which outright accused the court of being racist. Increasingly, however, the ICC is addressing protracted, politically fraught, cases, including some, like British involvement in Iraq and Russian encroachment on Ukraine, that involve major powers. The Office of the Prosecutor is currently examining the situation in Afghanistan based on evidence of abuses by the Taliban (attacking civilians, targeting girls' education, recruiting child soldiers, including child suicide bombers), as well as Afghan military and intelligence personnel and U.S. armed forces (torture, humiliating and degrading treatment, civilian casualties caused by air strikes, night raids, and escalation-of-force incidents, and the use of "enhanced interrogation techniques") (ICC, Office of the Prosecutor 2014:20–23). The ICC has also examined allegations from Honduras (unlawful killing, illegal imprisonment and torture, rape and sexual violence, deportation and transfer), Colombia (unlawful killing, torture and cruel treatment, outrages upon personal dignity, rape and other forms of sexual violence), Georgia (forcible transfer, pillaging, destroying civilian property), the Korean Peninsula (the sinking of a South Korean warship and the shelling of Yeonpyeong Island by North Korean artillery), and Ukraine (mass killings, illegal occupation, forced displacement, and destruction of infrastructure).

The court is now eyeing the Israeli-Palestinian conflict. In December 2014, President Mahmoud Abbas of the Palestinian Authority signed the Rome Statute over strenuous protests from the U.S. and Israel that Palestine was not a state and thus did not qualify for membership. The Office of the Prosecutor rejected those challenges and quickly opened a preliminary examination of the situation in the Occupied Territories. In June 2015, Palestinian Authority foreign minister Riyad al-Maliki presented the prosecutor with files of evidence and legal argument related to Protective Edge as well as conditions in the West Bank and East Jerusalem. That filing reportedly contained charges of "Apartheid," "targeting of civilians," and the denial of due process rights for Palestinian detainees prosecuted under the Israeli military code (Deger 2015). In October 2015, amid a spike in violence in Israel and the West Bank, President Abbas hand delivered to Prosecutor Bensouda further materials alleging "summary executions, collective punishments, house demolitions and ethnic cleansing" (Patel 2015). It is now widely expected that Protective Edge will land on the court's docket, exposing Israelis as well as Palestinians to charges of war crimes or crimes against humanity.[13] The case against Hamas might be easier to make, given the Islamist organization's refusal to try any of its combatants for war crimes. Hamas officials say they are willing to run that risk if it means getting Israel's actions in front of the ICC. The Netanyahu government has responded to the ICC's scrutiny with a full-bore public relations campaign. Foreign minister Avigdor Lieberman called the court an anti-Israel institution that "embodies hypocrisy and grants a tailwind to terrorism," and vowed that Israel's allies would defund the ICC and cut off aid to the Palestinian Authority (Israel punished Abbas's government by withholding $400 million in tax receipts it had collected on behalf of the Palestinian Authority) (Gladstone and Kershner 2015).

This is the Israeli government's almost Pavlovian response to international condemnation of its human rights practices. Behind the scenes, however, many officials distinguish the credible law of the ICC from the nonbinding politics of the Human Rights Council and other critics. Prosecutor Bensouda's stock rose among some Israel watchers after she declined to open a criminal investigation into the 2010 *Mavi Marmara* flotilla raid, saying the allegations did not meet the threshold of gravity required by the court. Prime Minister Netanyahu still rejects ICC jurisdiction and denies the basis of Palestinian claims—"no state, no standing, no case" (Keinon and Toameh 2015). But he shows little sign of resorting to his UN playbook of freezing out rapporteurs, haranguing critics, and lambasting conclusions as biased and foregone. The aim instead is to preempt the ICC by engaging its doctrine of complementarity. If Israel can convince the Prosecutor's Office that the Jewish state is willing and able to hold its own soldiers to account, this could stave off prosecution in The Hague (Harel and Cohen 2015). Four days after the ICC opened its preliminary investigation, Israel's government watchdog, the State Comptroller, announced that he would scrutinize decisions political and military leaders took during Protective Edge and also review the IDF's procedures for investigating itself (Kershner 2015). Five senior operational officers, including one colonel and four lieutenant colonels, have recently been questioned in several prominent cases. And in July 2015 Netanyahu dispatched a team of government officials to The Hague to present the Israeli position to representatives of the ICC. B'Tselem, Yesh Din, and other rights groups say this is all a Potemkin strategy to cover up the "severe structural flaws" inherent in IDF investigations (B'Tselem 2015). Certainly it's a tall order, given the ICC's rigorous standards for investigations and prosecutions and the IDF's lax record in these areas. Nevertheless, even in this thorniest of cases the ICC is becoming a normal part of world politics.

CHAPTER 6

"Kind-Hearted Gunmen": Human Rights and Humanitarian Intervention

> Humanitarian action is more than simple generosity, simple charity. It aims to build spaces of normalcy in the midst of what is abnormal. More than offering material assistance, we aim to enable individuals to regain their rights and dignity as human beings.
>
> —James Orbinski, President of Médecins sans Frontières, Nobel Prize speech, December 10, 1999.

> We're just living on the edge of life. We're always nervous, we're always afraid.
>
> —Mariam Akash, a mother of nine in Aleppo, Syria, whose husband was killed by a sniper. (BBC 2014)

Instead of prosecuting war crimes in the wake of conflicts, why not stop them from happening in the first place? This chapter takes up the vexing issue of military intervention in the name of human rights. At its heart is what international lawyer Ian Brownlie (1973) called the problem of "kind-hearted gunmen." Can armed violence wedded to good intentions achieve humanitarian ends? More concretely, can Tomahawk cruise missiles and Mirage fighter jets promote the cause of human rights, as the UN Security Council wagered they would when it authorized intervention in Libya in 2011? Can intervention in Syria bring an end to the agony there? Even if the odds are long, does the international community have a duty to try?[1] What's at stake is not just grasping the full weight of war on civilians, but the real prospect of rescuing innocent people from death and destruction. Despite the urgency, human rights groups tend to duck the debate over whether or not to intervene and focus instead on the conduct of war. "We do not get involved in geopolitical posturing," an Amnesty International UK staffer blogged about the prospects of intervention in Syria. "What we do is focus on protecting civilian lives" (Amnesty International UK Blogs 2013). Still, if pressed, most human rights groups would probably agree that securing rights sometimes requires muscular, even military, means.

The age of rights has also been the age of intervention. Critics say the human rights movement has promoted a kind of "military humanitarianism" that unites state strategy and humanitarian assistance under the banner of an "ethical" or "moral" foreign policy (see Chandler 2001). At times, human rights organizations have advocated intervention. Human Rights Watch, for example, supported the deployment of international ground forces in Bosnia, the creation of a Kurdish safe haven in northern Iraq, and intervention in Rwanda and Somalia. But rights groups are more at home in the peaceable realm of prevention and advocacy. A common refrain is that the international community wouldn't find itself teetering on the brink of war if it had promoted human dignity and well-being in the first place. After years of neglect, sending in troops or ordering airstrikes seems like the last best hope. Others in the movement try to reimagine humanitarian intervention altogether. The president of the International Rescue Committee, former British foreign minister David Miliband, is not categorically opposed to intervention in Syria, and indeed has fought to keep the option on the table. But he points out that "none of the military options being canvassed . . . promises a decisive shift in the course of the conflict," adding that the most realistic route is to redouble efforts to provide a steady supply of food, medicine, and clean drinking water, and to keep borders open to fleeing refugees (Miliband 2013). Here, amid the clamor for armed intervention, is a clarion call of rights.

"Soldiers in the Name of Human Rights"

The idea that the use of military force is permissible, even morally required, under certain circumstances seems fairly settled. As geopolitical constraints have fallen and the humanitarian tide has risen, intervention seems increasingly plausible. Many liberal theorists have lined up behind the idea. John

Rawls (1999:98–99) and Michael Walzer (1977:251), for example, each has argued that liberal states have a duty to intervene militarily to protect human rights in the midst of "supreme emergencies." Walzer contends that the defense of rights isn't just *a* reason to go to war; it's the *only* reason to go to war. His willingness to override the bedrock principle of nonintervention reflected "deep and valuable, though in their applications difficult and problematic, commitments to human rights" (Walzer 1977:108).

"Do-something" activists across the political spectrum support humanitarian intervention. The activist view recalls the soaring British internationalism of the nineteenth century, carried along by faith in free trade and the harmony of interests. Today's interventionists are similarly high-minded. Some are steely liberals who have vowed to stop atrocities by force if necessary. Others are neoconservatives convinced that a muscular foreign policy can help spread freedom around the globe. The new interventionism is seen to fulfill the duty of liberal states to secure global human rights (see, e.g., Tesón 2003; Cushman 2005; Weiss 2007); to recast international law in a more activist and humanitarian mold (see, e.g., Franck 2003; Glennon 2003); or to foster a stronger international society (e.g., Wheeler 2000). Weaving together several of these strands, the critical theorist Jürgen Habermas endorsed NATO intervention in Yugoslavia to stop the ethnic cleansing of Kosovar-Albanians. Even without UN approval, he argued, intervention "could signify a leap from the classical international law of states to a cosmopolitan law of a global civil society" (Habermas 1999:264).

Human rights groups, however, have been conspicuously quiet about whether or not to intervene. As I've noted, there is nothing inherently pacifist about human rights. The rights rank and file are often in the forefront of advocates of intervention. But the official position of most mainline human rights groups is not to take a position. None have been more steadfastly agnostic than Amnesty International. This stance rests on a long tradition of neutrality. Launched in 1961, at the nadir of the Cold War, Amnesty was determined to remain nonaligned, and studiously balanced its portfolio of prisoners of conscience between East and West. The organization mastered a kind of apolitical politics that kept the spotlight on the prisoners themselves despite the geopolitical theater surrounding them. In the early 1970s, Amnesty went through a long internal debate about joining the burgeoning movement to try to apprehend and prosecute human rights violators. Some worried the new direction would politicize Amnesty's efforts and shift too much attention to perpetrators. Neutralists argued that groups such as the UN Committee against Torture or the International Committee of Jurists might be better suited for such legal work (Power 2001:112–13). Eventually, of course, Amnesty became a leader in international atrocity law, working not just to free prisoners of conscience, but to hold perpetrators accountable and to seek remedies for victims.

Amnesty International has undergone no such evolution with regard to humanitarian intervention. As a matter of policy, the group skirts the "political" question of whether or not it is just to launch a war and instead focuses on the conduct of hostilities. This stance is driven largely by the practicalities of politically neutral advocacy. It would be impossible to support one intervention over another without seeming partial. Support for intervention would also mean backing the Western powers that invariably are leading the charge. But the decision also reflects a deep ambivalence about violence itself. Amnesty isn't pacifist, but it has always refused to advocate on behalf of political prisoners who either use or espouse violence, with the exception of self-defense or symbolic acts like tearing down flags or defacing political posters. Amnesty adopted Nelson Mandela as a "forgotten prisoner" in 1962, but dropped him two years later because of his support for armed struggle against apartheid in South Africa (Larsen 1978:24). For a group whose stock in trade is sending polite letters to public officials, military intervention is a radical proposition indeed.

In a 2000 essay titled "Soldiers in the Name of Human Rights?," Amnesty secretary general Pierre Sané asked, "Are invasion and bombardment by foreign forces justifiable in the name of human rights? And have external military interventions succeeded in winning respect for human rights?" His answer, largely, was no. Sané conceded that protecting people from human rights abuses and bringing perpetrators to justice might sometimes require the use of force, even lethal force. But he urged Amnesty to stand apart "from the clamour for armed action," even in the face of immediate suffering. "We do not call for military action, nor do we oppose it, but we do campaign on how such interventions should be conducted" (Sané 2000:5). Sané was justifiably suspicious of the motives of the states calling for intervention in the very places where they had previously coddled tyrants or become inured to the suffering. "If government decisions to intervene are motivated by the quest for *justice*, why do they allow the situation to deteriorate to such unspeakable injustice?" He noted that in Yugoslavia, Somalia, Angola, and Haiti, the interveners used up their enthusiasm and money on the invasion, and failed to carry out the long-term commitment of repairing strife-torn societies (8–9).

Sané agreed in the abstract that then UN secretary general Kofi Annan's criteria for UN Security Council authorization for armed intervention were reasonable. The decision would be governed by the scale and nature of the breaches of human rights and humanitarian law; the unwillingness or inability of local authorities to secure the population or, indeed, their complicity in atrocities; the exhaustion of peaceful remedies; the ability of the Security Council to monitor operations; and the demand to use limited and proportionate force. But Sané found these criteria hazy in practice, particularly with regard to civilian protections. "Perhaps the most difficult criterion, and probably the most difficult to evaluate, is the last—the impact on the civilian population, the very people on whose behalf the action is being taken" (Sané 2000:7).

Above all, Sané thought that invasion or inaction was a false choice. After years of turning a blind eye to human rights abuses, military intervention was the only option left. The crisis might have been averted through preventive human rights work: pressing governments to ratify treaties and to amend and enforce their laws; confronting impunity with truth and justice, investigating abuses and bringing violators to account; and working to end discrimination and to ensure the promises of the Universal Declaration. Usually human rights groups and others had identified these calamities years before they happened. "The problem is not lack of early warning, but lack of early action. Only by protecting human rights everywhere, every day, will we render the debate over humanitarian action obsolete" (Sané 2000:8). Of course, prevention never seemed as urgent as a humanitarian emergency. The international community generally recognized the need to forestall imminent harm, but it was a long way from embracing prevention, even if it was more effective and less costly than waiting for a crisis to erupt.

This "no-position position," as Stephen Hopgood (2006:144) calls it, offends liberal interventionists and antiwar activists alike. Interventionists dislike its indiscriminate neutrality. Prevention is well and good, they say, but it is unconscionable to stand aloof as a humanitarian catastrophe unfolds. Confronted with mass atrocities, it's not enough to draw attention to the plight of victims. There is a kind of realism here: when the range of strategic choices narrows moral agents may have to dirty their hands. Silence might also provide political cover to governments that are already reluctant to intervene out of concern for their own soldiers or their own standing in domestic politics.

The antiwar wing of the human rights movement is even more frustrated with neutrality. Silence looks like acquiescence. The same holds true for adherents of just war theory. Forget the *ad bellum* criteria for right authority, proportionality, and last resort: war is acceptable as long as it doesn't harm too many innocent people. During the Iraq War, the house rules at many human rights shops were to condemn the consequences of the war, but not the war as such. Many activists chafed under this Jesuitical distinction. They considered neutrality worse than a moral dodge. For an organization of Amnesty's stature and reach, it was a missed opportunity to denounce an aggressive war that was indiscriminately harming civilians. It didn't help that staff members at Amnesty's London headquarters who were involved in the UK Stop the War Coalition were instructed to behave themselves at rallies lest they jeopardize Amnesty's impartiality. They ended up marching under the generic banner, "Human rights workers against the war" (Hopgood 2006:198–99).

Most rights groups have remained neutral despite the pressures of public opinion and political correctness. As the Iraq War unfolded, rights organizations set out to persuade Coalition officials to mitigate civilian harm rather than stop the war. As Human Rights Watch executive director Kenneth Roth put it, "We use as our legal framework the Geneva Conventions, which do not prohibit war; they regulate war" (Papenfuss 2003). A year into the deeply unpopular conflict, Amnesty likewise kept its cool: "There are many different—and passionate—views on whether and when it is legitimate to use violence to achieve change or to confront state power. Amnesty International takes no position on this issue—we do insist, however, that groups which resort to force respect minimum standards of international humanitarian justice and humanity. Armed groups, no less than governments, must never target civilians, take hostages, or practice torture or cruel treatment, and they must ensure respect for basic human rights and freedoms in territory they control" (Amnesty International 2004). Oxfam managed to have it both ways: "Oxfam opposes a military strike on Iraq at this time because we fear that it could create a massive humanitarian crisis. But because of that grave concern, we are also preparing for it" (Oxfam 2007).

Human rights groups have campaigned tirelessly on behalf of civilians mired in the Syrian war, but most take no position on whether or not to intervene. Only Médecins sans Frontières (MSF) has categorically rejected military strikes. Human Rights Watch hasn't advocated or opposed intervention, but did insist that "any armed intervention should be judged by how well it protects all Syrian civilians from further atrocities." Physicians for Human Rights has called on the actors to follow IHL and to "ensure that the injured and the wounded are taken care of, without discrimination." Amnesty has maintained its agnosticism, "tak[ing] no position on the legality or moral basis for any such action" (Rogers 2013). The Syrian Observatory for Human Rights (2015) has neither condemned nor condoned the Coalition airstrikes, which appear to have been highly effective, killing at least 1800 ISIS combatants. But the London-based group has harshly censured the killing of some 70 civilians in those same airstrikes. There is a certain sophistry in clinging to these two positions simultaneously. Like the global rights groups, the Syrian Observatory hopes that the country's war crimes will be referred to the ICC or that a special court will be established to try perpetrators on all sides of the conflict.

It would be easier to oppose interventions if they were all naked displays of hegemonic power. But they aren't. Most are launched with the blessing of the UN Security Council, which has authorized peacekeepers to use "all necessary means" to protect civilians in Somalia, Rwanda, Haiti, the Democratic Republic of Congo, Sudan, Liberia, Sierra Leone, Burundi, Côte d'Ivoire, and Libya. Many operations unfold at the regional level and involve few Western soldiers. In some cases humanitarian and military functions are lashed together, making it difficult to take a position on one but not the other. Rights groups generally appreciate these nuances. In May 2003, while refusing to take a side in the Iraq War, Human Rights Watch and Amnesty International issued a joint letter calling for a UN rapid-reaction force to be sent to the Ituri region of the Democratic Republic of Congo. "Deployment of troops with a clear and robust mandate to protect civilians" was a "critical test" of the Security Council's resolutions to prevent mass killings and protect civilians caught in war (Human Rights Watch and Amnesty International 2003). Even antiwar human rights activists can be receptive to this kind of UN-based armed humanitarianism.

Médecins sans Frontières deserves special mention. MSF observes strict neutrality with regard to the provision of medical care. At the same time, it loudly condemns the political underpinnings of human suffering. The organization was started by doctors disillusioned by the ICRC's steadfast neutrality during the Biafra War in the late 1960s. Rejecting "blind and dumb" humanitarian relief, the founders set out to expose the roots of the conflict (Brauman 1993:205). As the organization's president James Orbinski noted in accepting the Nobel Prize on behalf of MSF in 1999, "we act not in a vacuum, and we speak not into the wind, but with a clear intent to assist, to provoke change, or to reveal injustice. Our action and our voice is an act of indignation, a refusal to accept an active or passive assault on the other" (Orbinski

1999). Former U.S. executive director Joelle Tanguy called the tactic "vocal impartiality: refusing not only to take sides but also to keep silent in the face of massive violations of human rights and humanitarian law." Otherwise, said Tanguy, humanitarianism becomes a fig leaf for political inaction and hinders meaningful, long-term, solutions (Tanguy 2000).

Over the years, MSF has focused its attention on open violence as well as the quieter carnage of injustice and inequality. As former MSF France president Jean-Hervé Bradol put it,

> Is it enough to isolate war as a distinct social field, the natural territory of humanitarian organisations? . . . In our opinion, no. The distinction between war and peace depends less on the use or otherwise of violence and more on differences between overt violence and hidden violence—the kind that is integrated into the routine reproduction of the social order. . . . This is primarily the case with the infectious diseases responsible for the greater part of global mortality. The task of humanitarian organisations entails exposing the hidden lethality of the political order and proving through action that there are ways—if not the political will—to limit the number of deaths and reduce the suffering caused by epidemics and endemic diseases. (Bradol 2004:8–9)

This is model human rights framing of public health. Because MSF focuses on the nonmilitary roots of abuses, it staunchly opposes any blurring of military and humanitarian efforts. "New age 'military interventions'—defined as deployments of military might undertaken in situations involving mass crime or terror—may be at times not only appropriate, but necessary, required, just, desirable, maybe even effective; they could also become legitimate and accountable with a little help. But that does not make them humanitarian" (Tanguy 2000). If soldiers and aid workers are seen to be collaborating, this jeopardizes the humanitarian mission. Nor should humanitarians necessarily try to stop the war. MSF considers it arrogant of outsiders to think they can succeed where local efforts have failed. The goal rather is to carve out a neutral humanitarian space at the heart of the conflict where aid can be rendered.

Not surprisingly, MSF is adamantly anti-interventionist. The one exception in the group's history was the genocide in Rwanda. In May 1994, MSF called on French authorities to use their influence to stop the killings, and then went before the UN Commission on Human Rights, hoping to trigger state action. MSF's field hospitals in Rwanda were overrun by militias who would cart off patients and kill them. Many in-country medical staff were murdered. In June, 1994 MSF ran a full-page appeal in *Le Monde* calling for a "radical, immediate response . . . using arms to protect the population from danger," and urging the UN Security Council to authorize military action. The message, in bold, was clear: **"On n'arrête pas un génocide avec des médecins!"—"You can't stop a genocide with doctors!"** It was a rare admission that there were limits to humanitarian work (Médecins sans Frontières 2014).

Finally, nothing rankles human rights groups more than seeing belligerents cloak their national interests in the finery of universal rights. Kenneth Roth of Human Rights Watch roundly rejected the assertion that the Iraq War was a humanitarian intervention. He thought the Bush administration was not motivated primarily, or even largely, by the desire to save Iraqis from mass killing. The Coalition's lack of concern for Iraqi civilians was evident in the indiscriminate tactics they used. Roth warned that enlisting human rights in the service of regime change would give intervention a bad name and make it harder to mount future campaigns to save the lives of people in truly desperate straits. Roth set these criteria for intervention: Is genocide or mass slaughter underway or imminent? Is intervention the last reasonable option to stop the killing? Are the motives for intervening predominately humanitarian? Does the use of force comply with humanitarian law? Will the intervention leave things better or worse? Ideally, but not always, the UN Security Council should approve the use of force (Roth 2004).

In September 2002, Amnesty International advised the Bush administration not to try to repackage the looming invasion of Iraq in terms of rights. Amnesty pointed out the hypocrisy of selectively invoking rights, as well as the civilian harm the war would inevitably bring. "As the debate on whether to use military force against Iraq escalates, the human rights of the Iraqi people, as a direct consequence of any potential military action, is sorely missing from the equation," said Amnesty. "Life, safety and security of civilians must be the paramount consideration in any action taken to resolve the current human rights and humanitarian crisis. The experience of previous armed intervention in the Gulf has shown that, all too often, civilians become the acceptable casualties of war" (Amnesty International 2002).

In December 2002, the British Foreign Office published a dossier, *Saddam Hussein: Crimes and Human Rights Abuses*, which relied on evidence from Amnesty, Human Rights Watch, the U.S. Committee for Refugees, the

International Alliance for Justice, and British government sources. The dossier looked very much like the human rights reports it was based on. Photographs of victims and copies of chilling security directives leapt off the page. A 1987 memorandum to a field commander quoted Ali Hasan al-Majid, commander of the Northern Organization Bureau: "there is no objection to beheading traitors. But it would have been preferable had you also sent them to Security for the purpose of interrogating them" first. The report described a secret "casket prison" in a basement of the Directorate of General Security building in Baghdad. More than 100 political prisoners were allegedly entombed in rows of steel mortuary boxes, held there until they either confessed or died of torture or terror. Other prisoners were reportedly kept in metal canisters shaped like oversized milk jugs. The list of torture techniques included eye-gouging, acid baths, mock executions, and piercing hands with an electric drill (UK Foreign and Commonwealth Office 2002:13).

"The dossier makes for harrowing reading, with accounts of torture, rape and other horrific human rights abuses," said British foreign secretary Jack Straw in a speech to the Atlantic Partnership that was part of the roll-out of the document. "The aim is to remind the world that the abuses of the Iraqi regime extend far beyond its pursuit of weapons of mass destruction in violation of its international obligations." Incensed, Amnesty denounced the dossier and the public relations drive as a cynical attempt to ramp up support for regime change. "This . . . is nothing but a cold and calculated manipulation of the work of human rights activists," said Secretary-General Irene Khan. "Let us not forget that these same governments turned a blind eye to reports of widespread violations in Iraq before the Gulf War." The humanitarian justification was especially hard to credit, given the fact that Saddam's crimes had peaked years earlier. His most shocking act—the killing of thousands of civilians with poison gas in the Kurdish city of Halabja—happened in March 1988, nearly fifteen years earlier. At the time, British officials downplayed the killings and continued high-level contacts with Saddam's government (Beeston 2002).

Human Rights and the Responsibility to Protect

The prime mover behind humanitarian intervention today is the "responsibility to protect," or "R2P." Over the past decade this principle has reframed the concept of civilian protection, exchanging the prickly "right to intervene" for the more palatable "responsibility to protect" (G. Evans 2008). According to the International Commission on Intervention and State Sovereignty, which midwifed the idea into existence, "where a population is suffering serious harm . . . and the state in question is unwilling or unable to avert it, the principle of non-intervention yields to the international responsibility to protect." The cornerstone of R2P is the insistence that a state's sovereignty is conditioned on its duty to protect its citizens, not on its right to rule as it pleases. "The case for thinking of sovereignty in these terms is strengthened by the ever-increasing impact of international human rights norms," noted the International Commission. "International organizations, civil society activists and NGOs use the international human rights norms and instruments as the concrete point of reference against which to judge state conduct" (International Commission on Intervention and State Sovereignty 2002:xi).

The idea was formalized at the 2005 United Nations World Summit. The closing document enunciated three pillars to R2P: 1) States have a responsibility to protect their own populations from genocide, war crimes, ethnic cleansing, and crimes against humanity; 2) the international community has a duty to assist individual states and help them build capacity to protect their citizens; and 3) "should peaceful means be inadequate and states manifestly fail to protect their populations," the international community shall take "collective action, in a timely and decisive manner" within the framework of the UN Security Council (UN General Assembly 2005:30). While the enumeration of crimes leaves little doubt about what's covered, implementation and enforcement are still up for debate. What does it mean for a state to "manifestly fail" its responsibilities? What level of enforcement is demanded in each case? Is the Security Council the only source of right authority? Tethering enforcement to the Security Council lends legitimacy to the process, but may also drag it into great-power politics.

These questions have done little to derail the norm. In remarkably short order R2P has become common currency on the world stage, "to the point where it is harder to do nothing in the face of atrocities" (Chesterman 2011:279). An array of international actors have invoked the principle in crises as disparate as genocide in Sudan, post-election violence in Kenya, Cast Lead and Protective Edge in Gaza, war crimes in Sri Lanka, and famine in North Korea. While R2P evokes images of humanitarian armies dispatching evildoers, here, as in the case of the ICC, complementarity is the rule. External involvement is triggered only if national implementation fails. Moreover, the norm envisions a range of interventions, from local reforms to international diplomacy to use of military force. Much like Pierre Sané's vision of rights promotion, prevention is supposed to be king.

The UN Security Council has explicitly sanctioned armed force by UN troops in the name of R2P only twice: in Côte d'Ivoire (2010) and Libya (2011). But since these watershed cases, the idea has frequently been woven into the language and practice of the Security Council. The advent of R2P marks a genuine departure in the history of humanitarianism. Alex Bellamy has identified 24 instances of genocide or mass atrocity between 1990 and 2005 (when R2P was adopted), and finds that the Security Council formally addressed only about half of those episodes, and even then civilian protections were seldom a priority. The Security Council made specific provisions for civilian protections on only four occasions. Worst of all, in Angola, Bosnia, and Rwanda, peacekeepers became spectators to mass killings that they were neither mandated nor equipped to respond to (Bellamy 2015:163–64).

Today, however, the spirit of R2P is summoned freely. According to the Global Centre for the Responsibility to Protect (2015), since 2006 the idea of R2P has underpinned 38 different Security Council resolutions, covering the world's worst humanitarian hotspots: Democratic Republic of Congo, Burundi, Darfur, South Sudan, Libya, Côte d'Ivoire, Yemen, Mali, Central African Republic, and Syria. Since the Libya intervention in 2011 the UN almost routinely views the plight of civilians through the R2P lens. The idea is embedded in agencies across the UN system, allowing the organization to mount multifaceted strategies to protect civilians. The level of controversy associated with the practice also dropped off dramatically. As we've seen, the precise meaning of civilian protection is still debated, and there are still failings of political will, but when the Security Council fails its R2P role it is reproached by the General Assembly and the Human Rights Council. In 2013 Secretary-General Ban Ki Moon launched the "Human Rights Up Front" initiative to make early warning and early action a core responsibility across the UN system. Member states have followed suit, devoting resources, including military forces, for the explicit goal of halting atrocities and protecting civilians (Bellamy 2015:165–66).

The widest gap between the theory and practice of R2P is seen in the international response to the war in Syria. The Security Council could have authorized intervention based on either the predations of the Bashar Al-Assad regime, or the implosive forces of a vast civil war. Yet, despite years of well-publicized suffering, at least 250,000 dead, and more than half the population internally displaced (7.6 million) or driven from the country (4.5 million),

R2P has failed to jolt the Security Council out of its great-power paralysis. Putting the best face on failure, Tom Weiss (2014:13) suggested that in Syria "mainly the moral dimensions of R2P have been apparent." It was not until February 2014 that the Security Council adopted a resolution calling on all parties to the Syrian conflict to "take all appropriate steps to protect civilians, including members of ethnic, religious, and confessional communities." The resolution added that the "primary responsibility to protect its population lies with the Syrian authorities," which is true enough but rings hollow given that it is the Assad regime which has carried out most of the killing. Only the terrifyingly rapid rise of the Islamic State, or ISIS, prompted the recent airstrikes in Syria. Those attacks were launched without UN authorization, despite the fact that all the permanent members of the Security Council except China have carried out bombings. These raids were retroactively legalized by a unanimous Security Council resolution in November 2015. Although the Pentagon and other defense ministries categorized these strikes as "humanitarian operations," they were framed in terms of fighting terrorists rather than protecting civilians.

Of course, the idea can be invoked too easily. This was Brownlie's slippery slope fear that normalizing intervention would grant "a general license to vigilantes and opportunists" (Brownlie 1973:148). Moscow recited R2P back to its promoters when Russian troops entered Georgia in August 2008, ostensibly to defend their ethnic kin in the Caucasus. This was widely viewed as a misappropriation of the norm. So was the appeal the same year by France's foreign minister, Bernard Kouchner (co-founder of MSF), for intervention in Myanmar after a cyclone killed more than 100,000 people and left a million and a half homeless. Although it was in over its head, Myanmar's ruling junta rejected foreign aid and opposed intervention. China, ASEAN, and others were flatly opposed to extending R2P to cover a natural disaster over the opposition of the target government. The British Foreign Office called the move "incendiary" (Bellamy 2010:152).

In other cases, R2P can look like an excuse for great powers to meddle in the affairs of other countries. This is the so-called "Trojan horse" model. During the Libya crisis, the Brazilian representative to the Security Council warned against "excessively broad interpretations of the protection of civilians, which could link it to the exacerbation of conflict, compromise the impartiality of the United Nations, or create the perception that it is being used as a smokescreen for intervention or regime change." The Venezuelan representative claimed that "powerful countries are manipulating the concept . . .

to impose their strategic interests on the world. The responsibility for protecting civilians lies solely with States. The assistance that the international community can offer in this regard should be in support of national efforts at the request of the State concerned" (International Coalition for the Responsibility to Protect 2011:1,5). One is reminded of Richard Falk's (1999:370) felicitous line that intervention is like the Mississippi: it only flows from north to south.

Even if partly or even largely true, such rhetoric too easily reduces R2P to humanitarian intervention redux. This doesn't do justice to the nonviolent, but still coercive, side of the norm. R2P has fared best in cases short of armed intervention, where it has helped to galvanize peacebuilding and diplomacy, and to open up humanitarian access. Perhaps its most successful effort came amid post-election violence in Kenya in 2007. About 1,500 people were killed and 300,000 displaced before officials from the African Union and former UN Secretary General Kofi Annan managed to persuade Kenyan president, Mwai Kibaki, and his main opponent, Raila Odinga, to craft a power-sharing agreement that likely forestalled wider bloodletting and displacement. Annan later said he had viewed the crisis through "the R2P prism with a Kenyan government unable to contain the situation or protect its people. I knew that if the international community did not intervene, things would go hopelessly wrong. The problem is when we say 'intervention,' people think military, when in fact that's a last resort. Kenya is a successful example of R2P at work" (Bellamy 2010:154).

This non-military impulse seems right. The temptations to use disproportionate violence, the arbitrary death and destruction, the spillover from intended targets to unintended ones, the tendency for good wars to turn bad: these are all too common. There has been enough bad behavior on the part of UN troops to warrant a new corollary to R2P: "responsibility *while* protecting."[2] (UN troops enjoy a kind of diplomatic immunity during deployment, and there are disincentives for them to be prosecuted by their home countries.) It's worth noting that in the two cases where the Security Council sanctioned military intervention, the outcomes weren't noticeably better than those of pre-R2P interventions. As violence spread in Côte d'Ivoire following a disputed presidential election, an existing UN peacekeeping mission was rechristened as a civilian protection force in the mold of R2P. But as peacekeeping degenerated into street battles with government troops, R2P started to look like a pretext for regime change. NATO's ouster of Muammar Qaddafi in Libya wedded R2P to the latest in stand-off weaponry: cruise missiles, fighter jets, B-2 bombers, helicopter gunships, naval destroyers, attack submarines, and so on. NATO's campaign is at least partly to blame for what increasingly looks like a failed state in Libya (see M. Serrano 2011).

Michael Walzer has noted (2004:70) how seductive intervention scenarios can be: dispatching a bloody tyrant lording over a mass of victims. But, he asks, "what if the trouble is internal, the inhumanity locally and widely rooted, a matter of political culture, social structures, historical memories, ethnic fear, resentment, and hatred?" The invasion of Iraq succeeded in dethroning the Ba'athists, but was so blind to local conditions and culture that it failed in nearly everything else. R2P floundered in Darfur because that was a complex, layered conflict, and it was wrong-headed to try to "save" the population through military action that only superficially addressed conditions driving the conflict in the first place (de Waal 2007). Sometimes military might is simply too crude a tool to work the levers of local power.

If the pursuit of humanitarian ends lifts our moral imaginations, this question of means brings us back to earth. "Violence," writes Catherine Lu, "is an unpredictable teacher." "Even if one endorses the claims of common humanity, embraces the interpretation of 'sovereignty as responsibility' to protect basic humanitarian interests, and deems authoritative current international mechanisms for adjudicating uses of force by states for humanitarian purposes, the question remains whether military force can ever be effectively employed in the name of common humanity" (Lu 2006:153). Focused on the high politics of ends, it is easy to lose sight of the daily grind of means. Wars are launched with only the roughest prediction of the consequences. It is fairly easy to project a rosy future.

The contradictions of kind-hearted gunmen are still with us. Tony Lang argues that interventionists have yet to shake the "the conflict between the recurrent need to provide aid in times of civil war and famine, and the inability of armed intervention to accomplish these aims without trampling the political rights and freedoms of those being aided" (Lang 2002:187). Indeed, the reliance on war-like methods can itself lower expectations for civilian protections. It was the U.S.'s own ham-fisted tactics that scuttled its legitimacy in Iraq. In Gaza, the IDF stuck to a technical legal script even as the human costs soared. NATO had good intentions in Libya, but seemed incapable of shouldering full responsibility for its conduct. In one meeting with human rights representatives, NATO officials insisted the organization wasn't a party to the conflict, even as it rained down high explosives. NATO's worst accident in Libya was the bombing of several civilian houses in Majer, a farming village on the outskirts of Misrata. A follow-up strike minutes later killed rescuers who were frantically digging victims from the rubble. Journalists, human rights groups, and UN researchers reported 34 civilians dead and 38 wounded. Unmoved, NATO said it knew of no "confirmed" civilian casualties and announced that it wasn't obligated to investigate the incident. The organization saw itself as literally above the conflict and above the law.[3]

Even if military intervention can stop the immediate killing without harming innocent people, the odds are long that intervention will usher in a liberal, rights-based, society. Jürgen Habermas had fervently hoped that the intervention in Yugoslavia would herald a new cosmopolitanism, buoyed by international society rather than domestic political actors. In Iraq, Habermas saw more clearly the contradictions of war in the name of human rights:

> The more that political power (understood in its role as a global civilizing force) is exercised in the dimensions of the military, secret security services, and the police, the more it comes into conflict with its own purposes, endangering the mission of improving the world according to the liberal vision. . . . There was a time when liberal nationalism saw itself justified in promulgating the universal values of its own liberal order, with military force if necessary, throughout the entire world. This arrogance doesn't become any more tolerable when it is transferred from nation-states to a single hegemonic state. It is precisely the universalistic core of democracy and human rights that forbids their unilateral realization at gunpoint. (Habermas 2005:24–25)

Militarizing Human Rights?

A more radical critique is that militarism and humanitarianism have become indistinguishable, that human rights have been "securitized," and defined essentially as a military problem. David Kennedy suggests that the language and legitimacy of human rights have been militarized. "Humanitarians increasingly provide the terms in which global power is exercised. We speak the same language as those who plan and fight wars, the language of humanitarian objectives and proportional, even humane means" (Kennedy 2006a:132). The rhetorical turn renders "humanitarian" war morally unassailable. Costas Douzinas (2007:61) witheringly calls this the "military-humanitarian complex" and pronounces human rights dead.

This idea of "death by humanity" gained traction after NATO's high-flying bombing campaign in Yugoslavia (Shinko 2010). The call to war invoked ideals more than interests. As British prime minister Tony Blair argued, it was "a just war, based not on any territorial ambitions but on values." French prime minister Jacques Chirac called the intervention "a battle for the rule of law and for human dignity," adding, "what is at stake today is peace on our soil, peace in Europe" (Sané 2000:5). For some, the rhetoric of intervention recalled the crusader ethos that the American historian Charles Austin Beard labeled "perpetual war for perpetual peace" (see Barnes 1953). Others echoed the icy realism of the conservative legal theorist Carl Schmitt: "Whoever invokes humanity wants to cheat" (Schmitt 2007:54): Like E. H. Carr or Hans Morgenthau, Schmitt expected states to conflate their particular interests with universal moral values, but he found the practice fraught with moral hazards. Waging war for "humanity" rendered one's enemy "an outlaw of humanity" and allowed you to do terrible things to him (Luban 2011:465). Indeed, imperialist and racist campaigns have always employed low methods for high ends. British commanders in India were infamous for their punitive "butcher and bolt" raids, referred to in Raj bureaucratese as "administrative massacres" (Arendt 1973:221).

Skeptics such as David Rieff and Michael Barnett say that humanitarianism has never been as pure as it appears. Many aid groups work hand in glove with militaries and other state agents. With the exception of the Quaker American Friends Service Committee, humanitarian organizations were instrumental in the U.S. "hearts and minds" campaign in Vietnam. Catholic Relief Services and CARE were generously funded by the American government, and heavily supported the reactionary regime in Saigon. Ardently anticommunist in a country with a large Catholic following, Catholic Relief's interests coincided neatly with those of the U.S. Both Catholic Relief and CARE supported American ideas and institutions, and participated in social and economic initiatives, refugee services, and the civil side of village "pacification" programs. Both were instrumental in U.S. food distribution schemes aimed at families of men who had joined the anti-communist movement (see Rieff 2010; Barnett 2011:147–48).

Since the 1990s, humanitarian-military relations have evolved from an "integrated approach" that involves coordination of military, diplomatic, development, and humanitarian assistance, to a "comprehensive approach" in which militaries themselves take on humanitarian tasks. Military recruiters were not shy about marketing the image of soldiers as first responders in "complex humanitarian disasters." One observer noted that adverts in the UK made the British Army look like "the military wing of Oxfam" (Chandler 2002:49).

The global war on terror has brought back integration with a vengeance, tightening coordination between officers and aid workers, and synching public and private humanitarian activities (S. Gordon 2004). After the invasion of Afghanistan, secretary of state Colin Powell (2001) assured humanitarian and human rights groups that they were "force multipliers," and "part of our combat team. . . . [We are] all committed to the same, singular purpose to help human kind." In the run-up to the Iraq War, staff-level planners at the Department of Defense, the National Security Council, and the U.S. Agency for International Development reached out to UN agencies and to a range of humanitarian and human rights NGOs, soliciting suggestions for Iraqi sites that should be considered off limits in the event of war (Woodward 2004:276–77). Eventually several thousand no-strike and restricted-strike targets were identified, an exercise that left some human rights advocates worried that they would be reduced to humanitarian-law adjuncts, rejecting some targets, but giving their stamp of approval to others. Either way, they'd be complicit in the war (Bennoune 2004:228). In some cases, U.S. officials didn't merely exhort civil society to play for the American side, but attached concrete expectations to participation and access. In 2003, the head of the U.S. Agency for International Development (USAID), Andrew Natsios, told humanitarian NGOs that if they wished to continue receiving federal funds they should emphasize their connections to the U.S. government. Some USAID grants included explicit language linking NGO efforts to the U.S. military's counterinsurgency strategy (Rieff 2010).

MSF's Rony Brauman and Pierre Salignon acidly suggested (2004:271) that American NGOs had become handmaids of the state, politically compliant and fearful they'd lose humanitarian "market share" to private contractors. In fact, a number of groups did lose market share because they pushed back against Washington's demands or declined to participate in the early reconstruction efforts. Their concerns were both principled and practical. When U.S. commanders in Iraq pressed NGO staff to wear Pentagon-issued identification, the groups protested that this would compromise their neutrality. Mary E. McClymont, chief executive of InterAction, an umbrella organization of aid groups, said operating "under DoD jurisdiction complicates our ability to help the Iraqi people and multiplies the dangers faced by relief workers in the field" (Sanger 2003).

In some ways working under "DoD jurisdiction" is a fact of life for humanitarian groups who rely on military access and security in order to do their jobs. In places like Iraq, many aid workers and reconstruction experts fled the country. Those who stayed behind became modern-day camp-followers. Much of the time they shared the Pentagon's priorities. Conor Foley, who worked in Afghanistan for the International Rescue Committee and the Norwegian Refugee Council, said his humanitarian colleagues complained about the "mixing of military and humanitarian mandates," but that in many ways the two were identical. "We both wanted to strengthen law and order, weaken the warlords, combat corruption and support human rights." These were worthy objectives, but they were also intensely political tasks that required taking sides in the war (Foley 2008:111). In the gray zones of contemporary conflicts, even some civilians can appear more innocent or more deserving of aid than others (Bruderlein 2001:225).

If humanitarian groups are tempted to take sides or dive into advocacy, human rights groups tend to be more deliberate. Still, they have no shortage of critics. Stephen Hopgood has argued recently that the authenticity and spontaneity of local and transnational networks of activists, which he refers to as "human rights" (lower-case initial letters), is being swallowed up in a hegemonic empire of laws, courts, norms, and organizations that he calls "Human Rights" (upper-case initial letters). While human rights is rooted in the concrete details of life, Human Rights is unhinged from reality. It proselytizes for intervention, crushes domestic organizing, and smothers local adaptations of human rights (Hopgood 2013). The global rights movement is not as hegemonic as Hopgood suggests. There are crusading moralists in the pack, but the mainline groups rarely flaunt intervention. As we've seen, they're more likely to be fending off state leaders trying to usurp rights in the name of war. While Amnesty International and Human Rights Watch may have enviable resources and reach, human rights remain a two-way street, albeit with most of the traffic rushing from north to south. Nevertheless, it's still possible to find vibrant local manifestations of rights.

Human rights is also the thread that runs from *jus in bello* to *jus post bellum*, or justice in the wake of war. There is no simple equation between human rights and peace. Violations of human rights can give rise to grievances that spill over into armed violence. War itself is a meta-human rights violation; and those abuses can further exacerbate grievances, rendering conflicts more intractable and peace more elusive. Post-war accountability for human rights abuses can help as well as hinder peace efforts (Sriram, Martin-Ortega, and Herman 2009). Recent empirical studies, however, show that human rights reporting and attention may help shorten the duration of wars and help fuel more vigorous peacemaking efforts. Focusing attention on rights is thought to interject moral reasoning and political mobilization, to shame the conflicting parties into improving human rights conditions; and to clear the way for third parties to broker peace deals (Burgoon et al. 2015).

The immediate hazard facing human rights advocates is not that they'll be swept up in a global crusade, but rather that they will uncritically adopt the language and assumptions of generals and judge advocates. Today's liberal armies say that *all* their wars are humanitarian wars. On their face, these are plausible claims. Modern armies as a rule do take seriously their commitments under IHL. "Avoiding civilian casualties" is more than an empty mantra. Still, as I've argued, the role of human rights is not just to prize ever greater civilian protections out of IHL. Much of human rights practice is technical and legal, examining munitions and weapons systems, citing the line and verse of IHL, or probing targeting decisions. Engaging the military on these terms garners human rights activists relevance in the eyes of policymakers and real, if limited, influence over the conduct of war. But such a strategy makes it harder to counter the unexamined premises of armed conflict, or to highlight the long-term, indirect, even nonmilitary, repercussions of war.

This is not to suggest that the human rights community should abandon the field to the military experts. Military matters are squarely within the remit of rights. The scope and intensity of human rights abuses in war demand that this be the case. Rights NGOs have expanded their portfolios to cover munitions and weapons systems, arms transfers, terrorism, insurgency, and other traditional "military" fields. Already, official spin meets clarity in the quality and volume of data compiled by researchers in these areas. There is always a risk that military-talk and rights-talk will start to converge, but such experience and expertise probably open more doors than they close. During the Russian incursion in Georgia in 2008, Marc Garlasco, the former Defense Intelligence Agency chief of high-value targets who "switched sides" and joined Human Rights Watch, found himself standing in a field in Georgia littered with illegal cluster munitions (both sides used them), taking phone calls from Congressional offices in Washington. Legislators who had previously shown little enthusiasm for human rights were eager for first-hand, expert, knowledge about the conflict.[4]

Nor should human right activists and militaries be locked in a low-intensity conflict of their own. There is a great deal of distrust on both sides. And when the human rights leadership seeks out common ground the rank and file tends to protest. Amnesty International USA executive director Suzanne Nossel sparked a minor firestorm when she suggested that NATO's presence in Afghanistan benefited the rights of Afghan women. Amnesty ran an advertising campaign during NATO's summit in Chicago in 2012: "Human Rights for Women and Girls in Afghanistan; NATO: Keep the Progress Going." It's hard to image that Afghan women would be better off under the thumb of the Taliban, but the message certainly simplified the issue. Protesters called Nossel a "feminist war hawk" and a shill for NATO's wars (J. Evans 2012). It's probably impossible to bridge these worlds, but there are critical areas of overlap. When she was the Pentagon's deputy assistant secretary for peacekeeping and humanitarian assistance, Sarah Sewall was by all accounts a humane voice amid the military brass. Later, as director of the Carr Center for Human Rights Policy at Harvard University, she helped fashion the new—and definitely improved—U.S. counterinsurgency field manual. No doubt the Pentagon gained some Ivy-League moral cover, but on balance it's better for the sides to engage rather than ignore each other. Bonnie Docherty, a senior researcher in the Arms Division at Human Rights Watch who also teaches at Harvard Law School, noted, "We don't want to be co-opted by the military . . . but I think there can be an important dialogue between the two groups" (P. Cohen 2007).

The Way Forward

A commitment to human rights does not completely shut the door on military intervention. In exceptional cases the demands of rights tip the scale toward intervention and even violence. Sending in armed forces is always a leap of faith, however. As Kantian deontologists are quick to point out, we can never really know in advance the consequences, intended or otherwise, of our actions. The moral hazards of an act as sweeping and potentially violent as armed intervention are especially high. The large-scale use of military power is bound to produce unintended collateral effects. Kind-hearted gunmen often lose their way when the abstract idea of intervention collides with the complex realities on the ground. Interveners cut deals with unsavory local militias, misread the local balance of power, ignore local expertise, or find themselves mired in violence and looking for the door. These shortcomings will hopefully improve as the culture of R2P matures. But even in the best of circumstances intervention can take on a bureaucratic logic of its own at odds with the needs of the civilians it is meant to protect. It should come as no surprise that the connection between humanitarian intervention and human rights is so tenuous. In many cases interventions fail to secure even basic rights; sometimes they make matters worse (Kernot 2006).

On balance, human rights vigilance and non-military solutions may produce better outcomes for civilians. The coercive but non-violent face of R2P also holds promise. But in rare cases there is no avoiding the use of armed force. Rescuing desperate people from widespread atrocities or genocidal destruction is surely just cause to intervene. As in the case of Médecins sans Frontières' frantic appeal to save Rwandans from mass murder, such instances will involve actual or looming violations of rights, not the generalized evil of a despot. While there is always one more diplomatic initiative that could be pursued, reasonable peaceful measures will be exhausted. The means employed will take effective safeguards to minimize civilian harm, even if this translates into greater risk to soldiers. Compliance will be measured not by how closely the interveners hew to humanitarian law, but by the actual effects on civilians. As difficult as it is to gauge, there will be a reasonable chance of success.

As this book went to press, the Syrian conflict cried out for a full-blown, boots-on-the-ground intervention. But at the same time prudence militated against it. Most of the killing in Syria has been carried out by Bashar Al-Assad's government forces. But there are also as many as 1,000 different militias engaged in a byzantine contest for power and control: Hezbollah forces from Iran, Kurdish separatists, Islamist rebels, village and tribal fighters, and peripatetic jihadists who have flocked from every corner of the earth to join the Islamic State, or ISIS. The slaughter of civilians, thousands of them killed by crude barrel bombs dropped from planes or helicopters; the use of siege warfare and starvation tactics; the indiscriminate roundups of military-aged males; the chaos and terror; the marauding and pillaging have remade the country in the Hobbesian image of a war of every man against every man. ISIS has carried out mass killings of rival militia members, Ba'athist armed forces, and religious minorities; it has enforced its rule with public executions, amputations and lashings, beheadings of infidels and apostates, and kidnappings and extortion. The group seems intent on erasing Yazidis, Syriacs, and Chaldeans from the map, targeting culture, religion, and even bloodline. Men are forced to convert or be killed. Women and girls are kidnapped, raped, and sexually enslaved. ISIS has recently stepped up suicide and car bombs in Shi'ite neighborhoods in Damascus and other cities. General violence as well as this targeted sectarian cleansing have displaced more than half the population of Syria. Millions of Syrian refugees now languish in camps in Turkey and Jordan or are dispersed in cities and towns across the region, particularly in Lebanon. A stream of others, over 1 million in 2015 alone, have made their way along a GPS-guided underground railroad to Europe. Many of the refugees have little hope of returning home.

It's hard to imagine a clearer case of widespread and systematic crimes against humanity, and in the case of ISIS even genocide. Armed intervention is probably the only way to quell the atrocities, to separate and weaken warring factions, and to block the advance of ISIS fighters, but there is no certainty that it will accomplish any of these goals. The U.S., UK, France, Australia, and other states conducted humanitarian missions in Ninewah Province in Iraq, airlifting food, water, and medicine to the Yazidi besieged by ISIS fighters at Mount Sinjar. Russia dropped humanitarian supplies into the city of Deir Ezzor in eastern Syria. But the options for containing, much less ending, the broader conflict are severely limited. A number of Syrian and Syrian diaspora groups –The Syrian Observatory for Human Rights, The Syrian Center for Statistics and Research, The Syrian Network for Human Rights, the Syrian Center for Policy Research, and the Violations Documentation Centre—have worked overtime to document, verify, and cross-check atrocities. But none of the local or global rights groups has endorsed full-blown intervention to stop the terror. As noted earlier, R2P has meant remarkably little in this case. Humanitarian donors are fatigued. Refugees have worn out their welcome in Europe. By early 2016, Turkey had curtailed its open-border policy, barring entry to tens of thousands of people fleeing the fighting. Legal options have come too late as well. Neither Syria nor Iraq is a party to the Rome Treaty, so the prosecutor couldn't bring a case against ISIS directly. In May 2014, a Security Council resolution referring the Syria situation to the ICC was vetoed by Russia and China, blocking that path to prosecution. In April 2015 Prosecutor Bensouda (2015) considered opening a preliminary investigation into atrocities committed by the Islamic State, based on the fact that many ISIS fighters hail from ICC member states, but in the end decided this was too narrow a basis on which to stake jurisdiction.

In the summer of 2013 the British coalition government made a plausible case for intervening in Syria in the wake of Assad's use of "barrel bombs" freighted with the chemical agent sarin. The proposed criteria were rigorous and restrained and avoided the war hype of 2003. Military intervention would be justified as long as there was "convincing evidence of extreme humanitarian distress on a large scale requiring immediate and urgent relief"; that it was "objectively clear" that there was "no practicable alternative"; and that the use of force was "necessary and proportionate to the aim of relief of humanitarian need" (Office of the Prime Minister 2013). In a bruising battle, the House of Commons, fearing another Iraq, rejected the government's proposal. The specter of intervention did help to convince Assad to accept a UN-backed initiative to rid the country of its chemical weapons stockpiles. Since then, new evidence of appalling torture and state murder has emerged. But so has the growing realization that regime change would likely mean state collapse and absolute levels of human misery. As Syria expert Joshua Landis (2015) argues, "the West falsely believes that it can separate the regime from the state." In fact, "destroying the regime means destroying the state. The price of regime change is chaos." Even some of Assad's sharpest critics now grudgingly advocate a political settlement that will keep the state intact—and Assad in power—at least in the medium term.

The British criteria seem better suited for intervening against ISIS than against Assad. Even in the absence of UN approval, those measures are well underway as the U.S., Britain, France, Russia, Turkey, Saudi Arabia and other countries have been drawn inexorably into the conflict. Well, not completely into the conflict. Here again we see the temptations of airpower with its low risk to the attackers despite the extreme violence and high likelihood of collateral damage. Since September 2014, the U.S. and a growing list of other countries have carried out thousands of airstrikes and cruise missile attacks against targets in Syria. Turkey and Russia have intervened at cross-purposes with their supposed allies. The Turkish Air Force not only struck ISIS positions but also unleashed a barrage of missiles to halt advances of the Syrian Kurdish militias knows as the People's Protection Units (YPG), who make up the backbone of the ground campaign against ISIS. Ankara simultaneously stepped up air assaults on PKK forces in southeastern Turkey and in northern Iraq. Russia has sided squarely with the Assad regime, targeting some of the opposition forces being backed by the U.S. and providing close air support for Syrian ground troops. The bombings have tended to focus on areas in which there are heavy concentrations of ISIS fighters, but many civilians have also been killed. Turkey, Russia, and France escalated airstrikes after their respective citizens were targeted in mass killings by ISIS terrorists. This doesn't justify lashing out clumsily in retaliation; the conduct of those raids should be every bit as rigorous with regard to civilian damage as any other airstrike. Raqqa, the de facto capital of the Islamic State and the bullseye for bombers, remains a sizeable Euphrates city with tens of thousands of civilian residents who are unable to flee even if they wanted to (Hisham 2016).

While it's no exemplar of neutral humanitarian intervention, there is a crude ethic of rescue to crushing ISIS. Still, a final, cautionary, note is necessary. Recent empirical research points to the highly unpredictable consequences of intervening in the midst of the sort of splintering factionalism that we see in Syria. Lounsbery, Pearson, and Klotz (2015:17–18) suggest that external arms supplies, strategic funding, and air attacks can affect the choices and even identities of the protean militias on the ground, leading to "changed group strategies, to arms flowing from group to group and from more to less trusted recipients, to group retaliation and efforts to weaken opposing state coalitions, to consolidation of group held territory, dispersal of warrior concentrations, cross-border fighting and attacks on rival groups. Group identities can themselves change, through merger, renaming, shifting loyalties, splintering, and side deals with outside patrons, other insurgents, or governmental authorities." It's a pipedream to think intervention will necessarily favor Western-leaning forces, which in Syria are the weakest and most inept militias in any case. Intervention will more likely bolster the "more extreme, militant, experienced and better organized fighters." Clearly, nonviolent coercions should be redoubled, heading off radicalization of would-be jihadists, slowing the influx of foreign fighters, and drying up the financial lifeblood of the Caliphate. No doubt the airstrikes will continue to pound ISIS-held territory. But in the remainder of Syria, much more can be done to end the misery. It will probably take an international ground force under UN mandate to staunch the killing and clear the way for a brokered settlement, even partition, if that will save the lives of Syrians.

CONCLUSION

Ours is an age in which the wartime state of exception seems permanent and many people have become inured to the regular recourse to armed conflict in the name of humanity. It's a good time to reflect on war from the perspective of its collateral victims. This book has tapped into the conceptual framework and moral urgency of human rights to set at center stage the experience of those who are terrorized or killed or have their lives upended by war. I have sought to show that human rights don't simply enjoin combatants to observe the rights of noncombatants. They also anchor humanitarian expectations by defining the status of civilians and the protections they are owed. The specificity and concreteness of rights bores into the details of civilian life, vividly exposing and enumerating the hard hand of war. Rights empower individuals to make legitimate claims in their own cause, but they also affirm the value of civilians as civilians, not simply as noncombatants. This vantage, I have argued, is crucial as we assess the justification and conduct of modern wars.

According rights pride of place requires that we put to rest the convention that human rights is the law of peace and humanitarian law is the law of war. Given the prevalence of war and chronic warlike violence, the separation of the two regimes cannot and ought not be sustained. As far as the victims of war are concerned the distinction is moot. I have tried to show that rights have purchase on a range of armed violence committed by state armies as well as non-state rebels, militias, and terrorists. The time of more or less chivalrous armies facing off on the battleground is long gone. Much of today's armed violence unfolds in a gray zone between war and peace. Informal warfare is the rule. This is true in the case of religious crusaders and ethnic *genocidaires* as well as modern militaries that remotely fire drone-based missiles or dispatch special operations teams to achieve their missions around the globe. The more these conflicts depart from the traditional assumptions of the laws of war the more relevant rights become.

At the same time, human rights stand as an independent, extramural, source of war norms. The rigor of rights distinguishes them from the more utilitarian laws of war and steels decision makers against the inevitable pleas of strategy and necessity. The comparative advantage of rights is not to do a better job of applying the laws of war, or to hold belligerents to ever more rigorous readings of the Geneva Conventions. What human rights do uniquely well is to draw attention to civilians and civilian protections, bringing the immediate as well as indirect and long-term impacts of war into focus. Rights highlight the terrorization of populations even by lawful attacks, promote accountability for indiscriminate war policies, expose hypocrisies in the exercise of violence, offer alternatives to ticking time-bomb narratives, and raise basic questions about the militarization of societies and economies.

The late Louis Henkin (1990:193) called human rights "the idea of our time." "There is now a working consensus that every man and woman, between birth and death, counts, and has a claim to an irreducible core of integrity and dignity," Henkin wrote. "In that consensus, in the world we have and are shaping, the idea of human rights is the essential idea." Neglecting that essential idea in the midst of war has profound and lasting effects. The human rights promises of the Iraq War are in deep arrears. Regime change ushered in an era of heightened blood-letting and tribalism and continues to feed fanaticism and violence in the region today. Over the past year Gazans have returned to a kind of stifling normalcy in the clutches of Hamas and under the de facto control of Israel. Large pockets of the Gaza Strip lie in wreckage. The few construction supplies Israel will allow into Gaza, paired with the dispiriting prospect of another war, have left the rebuilding effort inching along. With Palestine teetering on the brink of a possible third Intifada, Gazans and Israelis alike wonder anxiously what the future holds.

Finally, at several junctures in this book I have taken a pragmatic view of rights as a tool to improve incrementally the conduct of war and the protection of civilians. Pragmatism has its limits, however. As the historian Lynn Hunt notes, the greatest strength of human rights has always been its passion, "the feelings, convictions, and actions of multitudes of individuals, who demand responses that accord with their inner sense of outrage" (Hunt 2007:213). Rights increasingly shape the perception and sometimes the practice of war, but there is still plenty of room for outrage. Victims still struggle to be heard, crude terror and counterterror tactics go unchecked, torturers elude responsibility for their crimes, prisoners of war are detained indefinitely. Atrocity law has made impressive strides, but impunity is still common. The rights of refugees and asylum seekers are imperiled every day. Enthusiasm for R2P aside, interveners can still lose sight of the welfare of those they seek to save. What the movement needs now is not a politic version of human rights with the sharp edges rounded off, but a full-throated defense of rights that illuminates the heavy human costs of war and leads the way to a just peace.

NOTES

Chapter 1. Human Rights and the Norms of Modern Warfare

1. Convention (IV) Respecting the Laws and Customs of War on Land and its annex: Regulations Concerning the Laws and Customs of War on Land. The Hague, 18 October 1907, Preamble.

2. According to the Office of the UN High Commissioner for Human Rights, "*Human rights protection is not a specific tool or approach, but rather refers to a desired outcome—where rights are acknowledged, respected and fulfilled by those under a duty to do so, and as a result of which dignity and freedom is enhanced*" (2005:para. 34), emphasis original.

3. The Swiss NGO Geneva Call has spearheaded this effort. The agreements focus on observing minimal human rights standards, submitting to monitoring with regard to the use and stockpiling of land mines, protecting children from the effects of war, and improving protection of women and girls caught in war. The deeds of commitment are available at http://www.genevacall.org/resources/deed-of-commitment/deed-of-commitment.htm. The UN is developing similar initiatives to reach out to non-state actors.

4. On the distinction between battle deaths and non-battle deaths see Lacina and Gleditsch 2005. They rightly suggest that estimating war deaths "is an exercise of obvious importance but surprising complexity" (146). The 3:1 ratio is from the UN. The 4:1 ratio is from Geneva Declaration Secretariat, Global Burden of Armed Violence, 2008, http://www.genevadeclaration.org/fileadmin/docs/Global-Burden-of-Armed-Violence-full-report.pdf. The more controversial 9:1 ratio is suggested by C. J. L. Murray et al. (2002).

5. Conventions Respecting Laws and Customs of War on Land (Art. 32).

6. Human rights advocates are less enthusiastic about "human security," whose more survivalist approach to rights has led some to call it "human rights lite" or "securitizing human rights." See Oberleitner 2005 and Petrasek 2004. Rhoda Howard-Hassmann argues (2012:103,105–6) that the concept demotes human rights "to merely a subset of human security concerns, and as such less worthy of attention than they have heretofore been." She adds that the security of "the people" has a collectivist air to it that makes it a "quasi-realist substitute for the liberal internationalist perspective on human rights."

7. In 2003, the UN Human Rights Commission's special rapporteur called a lethal U.S. drone strike in Yemen "a clear case of extrajudicial killing." See UNHRC 2003. Human Rights Watch (2013:88) says that the U.S. targets people based on "overly elastic interpretations of the imminent threat to life that they pose."

8. My gratitude to Anthony Chase of Occidental College for helping me to clarify this point.

9. See European Commission of Human Rights, *Greece v. The United Kingdom and Northern Ireland*, Case No. 176/56, Report (26 Sept. 1958).

10. See Duffy 2008. The practice outsources torture. Typically a prisoner is handed over to another country's intelligence service along with a list of questions to be answered. See Human Rights Watch (2012).

11. The glaring exception arose in the context of the NATO intervention in Yugoslavia. Relatives of several employees of Radio-Television Serbia who were killed in the attack on the studios filed suit with the ECtHR, charging those NATO countries that are parties to the European Convention on Human Rights with violation of Art. 2 (right to life), Art. 10 (free expression), and Art. 13 (right to effective remedy). The Court ruled that the case, *Banković v. Belgium* No. 52207099, was inadmissible because Article 1 of the convention obliges contracting parties to respect human rights only within their own jurisdictions.

12. See *Al-Saadoon and Mufdhi v. The United Kingdom*, Application No. 61498/08, Judgment, March 2, 2010.

13. *Al-Skeini and Others v. The United Kingdom*, Application No. 55721/07, Judgment, July 7, 2011; and *Al-Jedda and Others v. The United Kingdom*, Application No. 27021/08, July 7, 2011.

14. *Al-Skeini and Others v. The United Kingdom*, para. 136. The Court took a similar tack in a 2007 decision involving seven Iranians who were killed by a Turkish helicopter gunship attack along the border between Iran and Turkey. Ankara's admission that it was responsible for the killings was enough to establish "that the victims of the impugned events were within the jurisdiction of Turkey at the material time." Whether the victims were on Iranian or Turkish soil was immaterial. See *Pad et al. v. Turkey*, Admissibility, para. 54. In *Alejandre v. Cuba* the Inter-American Commission ruled that jurisdiction obtained when a Cuban Air Force craft shot down two unarmed civilian planes in international airspace, killing four men (see Cerone 2005).

15. *Al-Skeini and Others v. The United Kingdom*, para. 147, 149. Marko Milanović (2012:121) says the Al-Skeini case is "set to become the leading Strasbourg authority on the extraterritorial application of the ECtHR." Barbara Miltner (2012:697, 746) finds the case more sobering. She accuses the Court of "cherry-picking Convention rights," and says "extraterritorial jurisdiction may be forcibly judicially recognized in ad hoc situations."

16. *Tablada Case*, Argentina, Report No 55/97, Case No. 11.137 (1997).

17. Bennoune 2004:179. See, e.g., *Abella v. Argentina*, Report No. 55/97, Case 11.137, 18 November 1997 (involving charges that during an attempted military putsch government forces denied the insurgents quarter and employed incendiary weapons which caused superfluous and unnecessary suffering); *Avilán et al. v. Colombia*, Report No. 26/97, Case 11.142, 30 September 1997 (important for applying human rights during an internal conflict where the application of IHL was unclear); and *Coard v. United States of America*, Report No. 109/99, Case 10.951, 29 September 1997 (involving arrests and detentions during the 1983 invasion of Grenada in violation of the American Declaration of the Rights and Duties of Man). The U.S. claimed, unsuccessfully, that the petitioners were "civilian detainees held briefly for reasons of military necessity," para. 32.

18. Declaration of Turku. 1995. Declaration of Minimum Humanitarian Standards, reprinted in Report of the Sub-Commission on Prevention of Discrimination and Protection of Minorities on its Forty-sixth Session, Commission on Human Rights, 51st Sess., Provisional Agenda Item 19, at 4, U.N. Doc. E/CN.4/1995/116 (1995) (Declaration of Turku), Preamble and art. 16.

19. Anticipating the Additional Protocols, the Teheran Conference took the same tack, calling for "additional humanitarian international conventions or for possible revision of existing Conventions to ensure the better protection of civilians, prisoners and combatants in all armed conflicts and the prohibition and limitation of the use of certain methods and means of warfare." See Final Act of the International Conference on Human Rights, Teheran, 22 April–13 May 1968, A/CONF.32/41, 18.

20. The Human Rights Council now says that "its jurisprudence runs largely parallel" to that of European and inter-American human rights regimes (UN Human Rights Council 2010).

21. These are rough estimates. Data on battle deaths and war-related deaths (two very different things) tend to split over numbers derived by collating death reports and retrospective mortality surveys or models. See Spagat et al. 2009. Michael Brzoska 2007 underscores the paucity of data on indirect war deaths. According to the Human Security Centre at Simon Fraser University (2011:105),

"the number of indirect deaths generated by today's wars remains mostly unmeasured—and thus unknown."

22. Wagnsson et al. 2010:2 note that scholars, too, "tend to assign only a limited set of roles to [civilians], most commonly the roles of victim, passive subject, or threat, or treat them as irrelevant to political processes in order that they remain nonpoliticized."

23. See Archibald and Richards 2002. On the "vernacularization" of human rights see Merry 2006.

24. "The Real Terrorists Bomb a Mosque in Iraq!" (YouTube, 15 September 2007), accessed December 13, 2007.

25. The video is available at http://www.youtube.com/watch?v=nuFZzQS01HQ.

26. The video and commentary are available at http://www.collateralmurder.com/.

Chapter 2. Humanizing the Laws of War

1. *Prosecutor v. Zoran Kupreskic*, Judgement of Trial Chamber, IT-95-16-T (January 14, 2000), para. 529.

2. *The Prosecutor v. Tadic*, Case No. IT-94-AR72, Appeals Chamber (October 2, 1995), para. 97.

3. See T. Smith 2008. Soldiers certainly have rights, but they also have obligations, chief among them looking after civilians, especially those who are threatened by the soldiers' own actions. See Rockel 2009:10–11.

4. The European Convention, for example, allows the right to life to be set aside when "absolutely necessary" "(a) in defence of any person from unlawful violence; (b) in order to effect a lawful arrest or to prevent the escape of a person lawfully detained; (c) in action lawfully taken for the purpose of quelling a riot or insurrection." Convention for the Protection of Human Rights and Fundamental Freedoms, 1950 (Art. 2).

5. International Court of Justice, *Legality of the Threat or Use of Nuclear Weapons*, Advisory Opinion, 8 July 1996, *ICJ Reports* 1996, para. 25.

6. International Court of Justice, *Legal Consequences of the Construction of a Wall in the Occupied Palestinian Territory*, Advisory Opinion, 9 July 2004, *ICJ Reports 2004*, para. 95–100, 107. The rulings found that the International Covenant on Civil and Political Rights (1966), the International Covenant on Economic, Social and Cultural Rights (1966), and the UN Convention on the Rights of the Child (1989), all ratified by Israel, were applicable in the Occupied Territories, subject to derogation.

7. *Democratic Republic of the Congo v. Uganda*, International Court of Justice, Judgment (19 Dec. 2005), para. 216.

8. The United States Oral Response to the Questions Asked by the Committee Against Torture (May 8, 2006), http://www.state.gov/j/drl/rls/68562.htm.

9. See *Hamdan v. Rumsfeld, Secretary of Defense et al.* 548 U.S. 557 (2006). The *Hamdan* ruling is 185 pages long. The terms "law of war" or "laws of war" appear 241 times; the term "human rights" appears zero times, not even in casual use. It's as if it were scrubbed from the opinion. The Court avoided the ambiguous "international humanitarian law" as well. Nor did the words "human rights" appear even once in the 134-page *Boumediene* decision, which granted Guantánamo detainees access to U.S. courts. *Boumediene et al. v. Bush et al.* 553 U.S. 723 (2008).

10. Convention on the Rights of the Child, Adopted and opened for signature, ratification and accession by General Assembly resolution 44/25 of 20 November 1989, entry into force 2 September 1990. Also see Amnesty International 2011; and Human Rights Watch 2003b.

11. ECtHR, *Ergi v. Turkey*, Case No. 23818, Judgment, 28 July 1998, para. 86, 79.

12. ECtHR, *Isayeva, Yusupova, and Bazayeva v. Russia*, Case No. 57947/00, 57948/00 and 57949/00, Judgment, 24 February 2005, para. 178, 199.

13. ECtHR, *McCann and Others v. the United Kingdom*, Case No. 17/1994/464/545, Judgment, 27 Sept. 1995, para. 200, 212.

14. *The Public Committee against Torture in Israel, et al v. The Government of Israel, et al.*, HCJ 769/02 (2006), para. 40.

15. Amnesty International noted in 2004 that under customary law, "basic human rights norms (directed for the most part at states) might apply to armed groups where they exercise de facto control over territory and take on responsibilities analogous to a government." Quoted in Clapham 2006:49. See also Sassòli 2011:57. Non-state actors often engage in state-like behavior—levying taxes, policing people, conscripting recruits. See Mampilly 2011.

16. Spaight 1911:120, quoting British historian and journalist Henry Sutherland Edwards.

17. See the Lawfare Project at http://www.lawfareblog.com/about/.

18. See http://www.youtube.com/watch?v=vFy1TXp9VyI.

Chapter 3. The Implosion of Iraq: "Shock and Awe," Insurgency, and Sectarian Terror

1. Burnham et al. 2006. Non-peer-reviewed surveys by ORB International, a London-based polling firm, resulted in estimates of more than one million excess deaths from the war. For an overview of the various surveys—and the politics of the numbers—see Burkle and Garfield 2013.

2. Convention (IV) Relative to the Protection of Civilian Persons in Time of War. Geneva, August 12, 1949, Art. 78.

3. The exact numbers are difficult to know, since the displaced have tended to melt into urban environments. See Margesson et al. 2009 and Internal Displacement Monitoring Centre 2014.

Chapter 4. The Gaza Wars, 2008–2014: Human Rights Agency and Advocacy

1. The IDF coins both a Hebrew and an English-language name for its operations. The names tend to sound more belligerent in Hebrew than in English, "Mighty Cliff" in place of "Protective Edge," for example. Other names contain Biblical references. "Pillar of Cloud" ("Pillar of Defense" in English), refers to a passage in Exodus that recounts how divine intervention shielded the Israelites from Egyptian arrows and catapults. Palestinian names for the wars tend to stress the ongoing and lopsided nature of the violence. The Gaza Wars have been referred to variously as "The Israeli War of Aggression," "The Gaza Massacre," and "The Battle of Al-Furqan." *Furqan* meant "criterion" or "standard" in Arabic, and refers to a Koranic verse regarding the discernment of good and evil.

2. See IDF Code of Ethics (Spirit of the IDF). http://www.idfblog.com/about-the-idf/idf-code-of-ethics/.

3. Thanks to Yaakov Garb of Ben Gurion University of the Negev for pointing this out to me.

4. B'Tselem tends to categorize participants in the Gaza Wars according to IHL criteria, distinguishing between those people who took part in hostilities and those who did not. The NGO recently abandoned the involved/uninvolved distinction with regard to events in the West Bank, since there had been virtually no incidents there in years that would rise to the level of armed conflict, but continues to apply the distinction as appropriate to Gaza. See B'Tselem (n.d.a). Many thanks to B'Tselem's Itamar Barack for walking me through the process of data collection and classification.

5. Author interview with Yael Stein, Jerusalem, May 7, 2014.

6. Breaking the Silence 2012. Most of the accounts are given anonymously following a structured interview format. Serious charges like homicide are corroborated by other witnesses before they are published.

7. Author interview with Yehuda Shaul, Jerusalem, May 5, 2014.

8. See *Adalah et al. v. Yitzhak Eitan, Commander of the Israeli Army in the West Bank et al.* H. C. 3799/02 Decision, October 6, 2005.

9. See Levy 2010. The Gilad Shalit case highlights the enormous propaganda as well as exchange value of captured IDF soldiers (or their remains). Following hugely lopsided prisoner swaps between Israel and the PLO in 1983 and 1985 Israel adopted the "Hannibal Directive," which called for vigorous military efforts to foil the abduction of IDF soldiers even if the attacks might harm the soldier they were meant to save. The idea is deeply disturbing to many Israelis because it seems to be designed to sacrifice IDF soldiers if necessary in order to avoid costly prisoner exchanges. The directive may have been invoked during Protective Edge after Hamas fighters reportedly dragged an Israeli soldier named Hadar Goldin into a tunnel along the Rafah Border with Egypt. It is not clear if Goldin was dead or alive at the time, and his body has never been recovered. The IDF responded with one of the most ferocious attacks of the entire war, known as "Black Friday," killing an estimated 135 civilians including 75 children (Margalit 2014; Amnesty International 2015a).

10. See *HCJ 9132/07 Gaber v. Prime Minister* [2008] IsrSC 8, http://www.mfa.gov.il/NR/rdonlyres/938CCD2E-89C7-4E77-B071-56772DFF79CC/0/HCJGazaelectricity.pdf.

11. Covenant of the Islamic Resistance Movement (Hamas), August 18, 1988, Art. 6, http://avalon.law.yale.edu/20th_century/hamas.asp.

12. See Harel 2009; Breaking the Silence 2009:40–42; and Levy 2014. This burgeoning religiosity is anathema to many traditionalists who say serving in the IDF forges an Israeli identity that transcends the religious-secular divide.

13. Author interview with Yehuda Shaul, Jerusalem, May 5, 2014.

14. Palestinian Centre for Human Rights n.d.:125. Satellite imagery collected by the United Nations Environment Program identified 2,692 buildings and 180 greenhouses destroyed or severely damaged during Cast Lead. See UN Environment Program 2009:6).

15. The video is available at http://www.youtube.com/watch?v=nuFZzQS01HQ.

16. "Cast Lead Video: Hamas Terrorist Uses Children as Human Shields," http://www.youtube.com/watch?v=2vHDyuSTneA. The video was posted by the IDF, which says the incident happened January 6, 2009.

17. http://www.psywarrior.com/GazaPSYOP.html.

18. After 19 people sheltering in a Beit Hanoun school were killed, the IDF claimed the school had been "completely empty" when a "single errant mortar" landed. See Reed 2014.

19. Physician questionnaire (April 2014), in the author's possession.

20. Author interview with Hadas Ziv, Tel Aviv, May 8, 2014. Also see Van As et al. 2009:9–20.

21. See Oxfam n.d.; Amnesty International 2014a. Israel said al-Wafa Hospital in Shujaiyeh had been used to store and launch munitions.

22. Author interview with Hadas Ziv, Tel Aviv, May 8, 2014. Also see Dan Magen 2009:3.

23. Author interview with Dr. Donald Mellman, Tampa, FL, February 25, 2014.

24. Some public health scholars prefer a "social suffering" model of trauma rooted in social justice rather than the clinical diagnosis of PTSD. See Tawil 2013; Giacaman 2011.

25. Verbatim quotation from Physician questionnaire (April 2014), in the author's possession.

26. Physician questionnaire (April 2014), in the author's possession.

27. Author interview, Tel Aviv, May 8, 2014.

28. Author interview with Yael Stein, Jerusalem, May 7, 2014.

29. Al-Haq n.d. The case elicited a rare public rebuke from the ICRC: "Israeli soldiers posted at a military position some 80 meters away from this house ordered the rescue team to leave the area which they refused to do. There were several other positions of the IDF nearby as well as two tanks." Pierre Wettach, ICRC head of delegation for Israel and the Occupied Palestinian Territories, said, "the Israeli military must have been aware of the situation but did not assist the wounded. Neither did they make it possible for us or the Palestine Red Crescent to assist the wounded" (International Committee of the Red Cross 2009a).

30. Palestinian Centre for Human Rights 2009a. The IDF said this "tragic event was the result of an operational error." The airstrike erroneously targeted the Al-Dayah house instead of the house next door, which the IDF said contained a cache of weapons. The IDF said it telephoned the house next door to tell the inhabitants to leave, but that it did "knock on the roof" of the Al-Dayah house before the strike. "This is the kind of mistake that can occur during intensive fighting in a crowded environment, against an enemy that uses civilian neighbourhoods as cover for its operations. IDF forces did not intentionally target civilians. This lack of unlawful intent has been a critical factor, in past incidents involving operational mistakes by other armies (such as NATO's erroneous bombing of the Chinese Embassy in the former Yugoslavia), in determining that no violation of the Law of Armed Conflict occurred. Similarly, although its attack on the Al-Daia residence was a tragic error, it did not constitute a violation of the laws of war" (State of Israel 2009:7–8).

31. In the well-documented human shield case at the Abed Rabbo house, for example, IDF military advocate General Avichai Mandelblit privately told the U.S. ambassador in Tel Aviv that the IDF soldiers appeared to have been "out of line," but no criminal case was pursued. See McIntyre 2009; Cunningham 2010.

32. Thanks to B'Tselem data coordinator Itamar Barack for this compilation of legal cases. Informal administrative punishments are not included in these data.

33. CNN 2011 and Almeghari 2012. In 2002, the Knesset exempted the State of Israeli from civil claims brought by Palestinians in the occupied territories, even in cases where it was proved that the damages were the result of war crimes committed by Israeli security forces. The Israeli Supreme Court overturned the law in 2006, but only as regards non-combat-related claims. Chief Justice Aharon Barak wrote that the law had disproportionately violated Palestinian rights to life, dignity, and property. See H.C. 8276/05, *Adalah v. The Minister of Defense*. Israel did pay the United Nations $10.5 million for damage incurred at UN facilities during the offensive.

34. Author interview with Yael Stein, Jerusalem, May 7, 2014.

35. Social media analysis prepared by Tamara Sakijha (August 7, 2014). In the author's possession.

36. Author correspondence with Muhammad Sabah, B'Tselem fieldworker in Gaza (June 2, 2014). Also see Rudoren 2014a.

Chapter 5. Who's Responsible? Justice and Accountability

1. ACLU FOIA document Army 000254-000257, https://www.aclu.org/sites/default/files/webroot/natsec/foia/pdf/Army0205_0207.pdf. Also see Witt (2008:1455).

2. In October 2014, four former guards with the defense contractor Blackwater International were found guilty in a U.S. federal court of murder, manslaughter, and other charges in the killings of 14 Iraqi civilians and wounding of 17 others in a 2007 rampage in Baghdad's Nisour Square. Former detainees who claim they were tortured and mistreated at Abu Ghraib have sued two private military contractors who oversaw interrogations at the prison. The lawsuits, against L-3 Services/Engility Holdings and CACI International, Inc., were filed in U.S. federal district court under the Alien Torts Statute. One of the cases was recently settled for $5.3 million; the other is currently being challenged on jurisdiction.

3. Copies of several of the condolence payment vouchers are available on the Defend Our Marines website's Haditha "evidence room," http://warchronicle.com/TheyAreNotKillers/DefendOurMarines/TopicIndex/EvidenceRoom.htm.

4. The video is available at https://www.youtube.com/watch?v=zqL6N3r3WiA.

5. Baha Mousa Inquiry Transcript, Testimony of Lance Corporal Redfearn (November 11, 2009), 191–92, http://webarchive.nationalarchives.gov.uk/20120215203912/http://www.bahamousainquiry.org/linkedfiles/baha_mousa/hearings/transcripts/20091111day30fullday.pdf.

6. House of Lords, Opinions of the Lords of Appeal for Judgment in the Cause, *Al-Skeini and Others v. Secretary of State for Defence* (June 13, 2007).

7. ECtHR, *Güleç v. Turkey*, Application No. 21593/93, Judgement, July 27, 1998, iii.

8. ECtHR, *Al-Skeini and Others v. The United Kingdom*, Application No. 55721/07, Judgment, July 7, 2011.

9. ECtHR, *Ireland v. The United Kingdom*, Application No. 5310/71, Judgment, January 18, 1978, para. 168.

10. Baha Mousa Inquiry Transcript, Presentation of QC Gerard Elias (March 16, 2010), 145–46; http://webarchive.nationalarchives.gov.uk/20120215203912/http://www.bahamousainquiry.org/linkedfiles/baha_mousa/hearings/transcripts/transcript_210709.pdf.

11. Baha Mousa Inquiry Transcript, Testimony of Nicholas Justin Mercer (March 16, 2010), 102–4.

12. See Ashton 2013; Burns 2008. In 2013, under threat of a lawsuit, the UK paid $31 million to 5,000 elderly Kenyans who were tortured and abused by British forces during the Mau Mau uprising in the 1950s.

13. Meanwhile an Israeli NGO, Shurat-Hadin Israel Law Center, lodged a communication with the ICC alleging that Abbas himself committed war crimes in his capacity as chairman of the Central Committee of Fatah, whose Al-Aksa Martyrs' Brigade carried out deliberate attacks on Israeli civilians (see Shurat-HaDin Israel Law Center 2014). Additional third-party NGO complaints are expected to be filed.

Chapter 6. "Kind-Hearted Gunmen": Human Rights and Humanitarian Intervention

1. The leading overview of the ethical issues surrounding intervention is M. Smith 1998.

2. See Letter dated 9 November 2011 from Permanent Representative of Brazil to the United Nations addressed to the Secretary-General, General Assembly, Security Council. UN doc. A/66/551-S/2011/701.

3. Author interview with Marc Garlasco, March 16, 2015; also see Garlasco 2012.

4. Author interview with Garlasco.

REFERENCES

Abresch, William. 2005. "A Human Rights Law of Internal Armed Conflict: The European Court of Human Rights in Chechnya." *European Journal of International Law* 16 (4): 741–67.

Abuelaish, Izzeldin. 2010. *I Shall Not Hate: A Gaza Doctor's Journey on the Road to Peace and Dignity.* New York: Walker.

Abu-Rmeileh, Niveen M. E. et al. 2012. "Health-Related Quality of Life of Gaza Palestinians in the Aftermath of the Winter 2008–09 Israeli Attack on the Strip." *European Journal of Public Health* 22 (5): 732–37.

ACLU. n.d. "[Infographic] The Torture Architects." https://www.aclu.org/national-security/ infographic-torture-architects.

Addameer Prisoner Support and Human Rights Organization. n.d. "Joint NGO Letters to President Mahmoud Abbas and Prime Minister Ismail Haniyeh: Calling for Immediate Commencement of Internal Investigations in Compliance with UN GA Resolution A/RES/64/10."

Agamben, Giorgio. 2005. *State of Exception.* Trans. Kevin Attell. Chicago: University of Chicago Press.

Akram, Fares and Ethan Bronner. 2011. "Militants Put Gazans in Danger, Group Says." *New York Times*, March 30.

The Aitken Report: An Investigation into Cases of Deliberate Abuse and Unlawful Killing in Iraq in 2003 and 2004. 2008. January 25. London: Ministry of Defence.

Al Haq. 2007. "'Enemy Entity': A Deliberate Attempt by Israel to Obscure Its Continued Occupation of the Gaza Strip." September 22. http://www.alhaq.org/advocacy/topics/gaza/151-enemy-entity-a-deliberate-attempt-by-israel-to-obscure-its-continued-occupation-of-the-gaza-strip.

———. n.d. "The Plight of the Al Samouni Family in Gaza: In Their Own Voices." http://www.alhaq.org/advocacy/topics/gaza/447-the-plight-of-al-samouni-family-in-gaza-in-their-own-voices.

Al Jazeera. 2009. "Report Accuses Hamas of War Crimes." August 13.

Al Mezan Center for Human Rights. 2009. "Hiding Behind Civilians: April 2009 Update Report; The Use of Palestinian Civilians as Human Shields by the Israeli Occupation Forces." September 4. http://www.mezan.org/en/post/8632.

———. 2011. "Gaza Government Executes Two Persons: Al Mezan Calls for Respect for Law." July 26. http://www.mezan.org/en/post/12379.

Al Mezan Centre for Human Rights and Defence for Children International-Palestine Section. 2009. *Bearing the Brunt Again: Child Rights Violations During Operation Cast Lead.* http://www.dci-palestine.org/sites/default/files/bearingthebruntagain.pdf.

Ali, Perveen. 2011. "The Challenges of Repatriation for Iraqi Refugees." JURIST-Dateline, January 22.

Ali, Sarmad. 2008. "At Iraq's Undersupplied, Overcrowded Hospitals, a Deeper Trouble." *Wall Street Journal*, April 16.

al-Khalidi, Ashraf and Victor Tanner. 2006. *Sectarian Violence: Radical Groups Drive Internal Displacement in Iraq: The Brookings Institution-University of Bern Project on Internal Displacement.* Washington, D.C.: Brookings Institution.

———. 2007. "Iraq Bleeds: The Remorseless Rise of Violence and Displacement." *Forced Migration Review* (June): 6–9.

Almeghari, Rami. 2012. "Family of Cast Lead Victims Wins 'Compromise, Not Compensation' from Israel." *Electronic Infitada*, September 26.

al-Mughrabi, Nidal. 2010. "Hamas Says Killed Israeli Civilians by Mistake." Reuters, January 28.

Alston, Philip, Jason Morgan-Foster, and William Abresch. 2008. "The Competence of the UN Human Rights Council and its Special Procedures in Relation to Armed Conflicts: Extrajudicial Executions in the 'War on Terror.'" *European Journal of International Law* 19 (1): 183–209.

al-Taee, Awadh and Steve Negus. 2005. "Sunnis Feel Full Force of Lightning Strike." *Financial Times*, June 29.

Amnesty International. 1992. "Bosnia-Herzegovina: Gross Abuses of Basic Human Rights." EUR63/001/1992/en.

———. 1994. "Central and Southwest Bosnia-Herzegovina: Civilian Population Trapped in a Cycle of Violence." EUR63/001/1994/en.

———. 1996a. "Bosnia-Herzegovina: To Bury My Brothers' Bones." EUR63/015/1996/en.

———. 1996b. *Israel-Lebanon: Unlawful Killing During Operation "Grapes of Wrath."* London: Amnesty International.

———. 2000. *Federal Republic of Yugoslavia (FRY)/NATO: "Collateral Damage" or Unlawful Killings? Violations of the Laws of War by NATO During Operation Allied Force.* London: Amnesty International.

———. 2002. "USA/Iraq: Not in the Name of Human Rights." September 12. MDE 14/009/2002.

———. 2004a. "Stop Violence Against Women: 'It's in Our Hands.'" March 4. ACT 77/001/2004.

———. 2004b. *Colombia: Scarred Bodies, Hidden Crimes: Sexual Violence Against Women in the Armed Conflict.* London: Amnesty International.

———. 2004c. *Lives Blown Apart: Crimes Against Women in Times of Conflict.* London: Amnesty International.

———. 2009a. "Child Soldiers Fighting in the DRC." http://www.amnestyusa.org/news/multimedia/child-soldiers-fighting-in-the-drc.

———. 2009b. *Israel/Gaza: Operation Cast Lead: 22 Days of Death and Destruction.* London: Amnesty International.

———. 2010. *New Order, Same Abuses: Unlawful Detentions and Torture in Iraq.* London: Amnesty International.

———. 2011. *In the Line of Fire: Somalia's Children Under Attack.* London: Amnesty International.

———. 2013. "*Will I Be Next?" US Drone Strikes in Pakistan. London: Amnesty International.*

———. 2014a. "Document: Israel and the Occupied Palestinian Territories: Evidence of Medical Workers and Facilities Being Targeted by Israeli Forces in Gaza." August 7. MDE 15/023/2014/en.

———. 2014b. "Ethnic Cleansing on a Historic Scale: Islamic State's Systematic Targeting of Minorities in Northern Iraq." MDE14/011/2014/en.

———. 2015a. *Black Friday: Carnage in Rafah During 2014 Israel/Gaza Conflict.* London: Amnesty International.

———. 2015b. "Gaza: Palestinians Tortured, Summarily Killed by Hamas Forces During 2014 Conflict." May 27.

Amnesty International UK Blogs. 2013. "Military Intervention in Syria: The Human Rights Perspective." August 29.

Andén-Papadopoulos, Kari. 2009. "Body Horror on the Internet: US Soldiers Recording the War in Iraq and Afghanistan." *Media, Culture & Society* 31 (6): 921–38.

Anderson, Kenneth. 1990. *Yugoslavia, Crisis in Kosovo: A Report from Helsinki Watch and the International Helsinki Federation for Human Rights.* New York: Helsinki Watch Committee.

Archibald, Steven and Paul Richards. 2002. "Converts to Human Rights? Popular Debate About War and Justice in Rural Central Sierra Leone." *Africa* 72 (3): 339–67.

Arendt, Hannah. 1973. *The Origins of Totalitarianism*. New York: Harcourt Brace Jovanovich.

Article 15-6 Investigation of the 800th Military Police Brigade. 2004. [The Taguba Report on the Treatment of Abu Ghraib Prisoners in Iraq]. http://www.npr.org/iraq/2004/prison_abuse_report.pdf.

Ashour, Majdi, Nedal Ghuneim, and Aed Yaghi. 2011. "Civilians' experience in the Gaza Strip During the Operation Cast Lead by Israel." July 5. http://www.thelancet.com/pb/assets/raw/Lancet/abstracts/palestine/palestine2011-1.pdf.

Ashton, John. 2013. "Iraqis Seek Public Inquiry at the High Court over UK Troops 'acts of brutality.'" *The Independent*, January 29.

Associated Press. 2003. "U.S. Military Pounds Iraqi Targets with One-Ton Bombs." November 19.

August, Oliver. 2010. "Blisters, rashes and toxic waste: the U.S. Army's dirty little secret in Iraq." *The Times* (London), June 14.

Ayata, Bilgin. 2011. "The Politics of Displacement: A Transnational Analysis of the Forced Migration of Kurds in Turkey and Europe," Ph.D. Dissertation, Johns Hopkins University.

Aylwin-Foster, Nigel. 2005. "Changing the Army for Counterinsurgency Operations," *Military Review* (November/December): 2–15.

B'Tselem. 2010. "24 February 2010: Hamas Report to UN Shamefully Evades Responsibility." May 6.

———. 2011. "Background on Human Shields." January 1.

———. 2013. "B'Tselem Position Paper: Turkel Commission Report on Israel's Mechanisms for Investigating Complaints of Violations of International Humanitarian Law."

———. 2014a. "Death Foretold: The Inevitable Outcome of Bombing Homes and Inhabited Areas in Gaza." August 12.

———. 2014b. "Israeli Authorities Have Proven They Cannot Investigate Suspected Violation of International Humanitarian Law by Israel in the Gaza Strip." September 5.

———. 2015a. "ICC Jurisdiction Cannot be Denied on Israel's Façade of Investigation." July 16.

———. 2015b. *Black Flag: The Legal and Moral Implications of the Policy of Attacking Residential Buildings in the Gaza Strip, Summer 2014*. Jerusalem: B'Tselem.

———. n.d.a. "Explanation of Statistics on Fatalities."

———. n.d.b. "Statistics: Palestinian Minors Killed by Israeli Security Forces in the Gaza Strip During Operation Cast Lead."

Bachmann, Jutta et al. 2015. *Gaza 2014: Findings of an Independent Medical Fact-Finding Mission*. Tel Aviv: Physicians for Human Rights-Israel, Al Mezan Center for Human Rights-Gaza, Gaza Community Mental Health Programme, Palestinian Center for Human Rights-Gaza.

Badkhen, Anna. 2006. "Critics Say 600,000 Iraqi Dead Doesn't Tally; But Pollsters Defend Methods Used in Johns Hopkins Study." *San Francisco Chronicle*, October 12.

The Baha Mousa Public Inquiry Report. 2011. 3 vols. London: Stationery Office.

Baldwin, Clive. 2014. "Why the ICC Needed to Reopen the Iraq Abuse Case." Human Rights Watch, May 19.

Banks, William C. 2011. "Toward an Adaptive International Humanitarian Law: New Norms for New Battlefields." In *New Battlefields, Old Laws: Critical Debates on Asymmetric Warfare*, ed. William C. Banks, 1–20. New York: Columbia University Press.

Bargewell, Gen. Eldon. 2006. AR 15-6 Investigative Report on Haditha (15 June 2006) [The Bargewell Report].

Barghouti, Omar. 2011. *Boycott, Divestment, Sanctions: The Global Struggle for Palestinian Rights*. Chicago: Haymarket.

Barnard, Anne. 2014. "In Fatal Flash Gaza Psychologist Switches Roles, Turning into a Trauma Victim." *New York Times*, August 4.

Barnes, Harry Elmer, ed. 1953. *Perpetual War for Perpetual Peace: A Critical Examination of the Foreign Policy of Franklin Delano Roosevelt and its Aftermath.* Caldwell, Ida.: Caxton.

Barnett, Michael. 2011. *Empire of Humanity: A History of Humanitarianism.* Ithaca, N.Y.: Cornell University Press.

Barnidge, Robert Perry. 2011. "The Principle of Proportionality Under International Humanitarian Law and Operation Cast Lead." In *New Battlefields/Old Laws*, ed. William C. Banks, 171–89. New York: Columbia University Press.

Bashi, Sari and Tamar Feldman. 2011. *Scale of Control: Israel's Continued Responsibility in the Gaza Strip.* Tel Aviv: Gisha.

Bass, Gary J. 2004. "Jus Post Bellum." *Philosophy & Public Affairs* 32 (4): 384–412.

BBC. 2004. "Israel Faces Human Shield Claim." April 23.

———. 2005. "Israel Bans Use of Human Shields." October 6.

———. 2007. "Iraq: Four Years On; Baghdad: Mapping the Violence."

———. 2014. "Syria Conflict: The Suffering Civilians of West Aleppo." October 9.

Beckerman, Gal. 2010. "Israel, Hamas Respond Differently to Goldstone." *Jewish Daily Forward*, February 3.

Beeston, Richard. 2002. "Human Rights Groups Scorn Dossier on Saddam Brutality." *The Times* (London), December 3.

Beitz, Charles. 2009. *The Idea of Human Rights.* New York: Oxford University Press.

Belknap, Michal R. 2002. *The Vietnam War on Trial.* Lawrence: University of Kansas Press.

Bellamy, Alex J. 2010. "The Responsibility to Protect: Five Years On." *Ethics & International Affairs* 24 (2): 143–69.

———. 2015. "The Responsibility to Protect Turns Ten." *Ethics & International Affairs* 29 (2): 161–85.

Benard, Cheryl et al. 2011. *The Battle Behind the Wire: U.S. Prisoner and Detainee Operations from World War II to Iraq.* Santa Monica, Calif.: RAND.

Bender, Bryan. 2006. "Condolence Payments to Iraqis Soar; Military Gave Nearly $20m to Families of Civilians." *Boston Globe*, June 8.

Benison, Audrey I. 1999. "War Crimes: A Human Rights Approach to a Humanitarian Law Problem at the International Criminal Court." *Georgetown Law Journal* 88 (1): 141–75.

Ben-Naftali, Orna and Keren R. Michaeli. 2003a. "Justice-Ability: A Critique of the Alleged Non-Justiciability of Israel's Policy of Targeted Killings." *Journal of International Criminal Justice* 1 (2): 368–405.

———. 2003b. "We Must Not Make a Scarecrow of the Law: A Legal Analysis of the Israeli Policy of Targeted Killings." *Cornell International Law Journal* 36 (2): 233–92.

Ben-Naftali, Orna and Yuval Shany. 2003. "Living in Denial: The Application of Human Rights in the Occupied Territories." *Israel Law Review* 37 (1): 17–118.

Bennett, Huw. 2012. "Baha Mousa and the British Army in Iraq." In *The British Approach to Counterinsurgency: From Malaya and Northern Ireland to Iraq and Afghanistan*, ed. Paul Dixon, 173–204. Basingstoke: Palgrave Macmillan.

Bennoune, Karima. 2004. "Toward a Human Rights Approach to Armed Conflict: Iraq 2003." *University of California, Davis Journal of International Law & Policy* 11 (1): 171–228.

Bensouda, Fatou. 2015. Statement of the Prosecutor of the International Criminal Court, Fatou Bensouda, on the alleged crimes committed by ISIS. April 8. https://www.icc-cpi.int/en_menus/icc/press%20and%20media/press%20releases/Pages/otp-stat-08-04-2015-1.aspx.

Benvenisti, Eyal. 2006. "Human Dignity in Combat: The Duty to Spare Enemy Civilians." *Israel Law Review* 39 (2): 81–109.

Berger, Rony, Marc Gelkopf, and Yotan Heineberg. 2012. "A Teacher-Delivered Intervention for Adolescents Exposed to Ongoing and Intense Traumatic War-Related Stress: A Quasi-Randomized, Controlled Study." *Journal of Adolescent Health* 51 (5): 453–61.

Berkowitz, Peter. 2010. "The Goldstone Report and International Law." *Policy Review* 162 (August–September).

Best, Geoffrey. 1980. *Humanity in Warfare*. New York: Columbia University Press.

Bhatia, Michael V. 2005. "Fighting Words: Naming Terrorists, Bandits, Rebels and Other Violent Actors." *Third World Quarterly* 26 (1): 5–22.

Bill, Brian J. 2010. "Detention Operations in Iraq: A View from the Ground." In *The War in Iraq: A Legal Analysis*, ed. Raul A. "Pete" Pedrozo, 411–55. International Law Studies 86. Newport, R.I.: Naval War College.

Bisharat, George E. et al. 2010. "Israel's Invasion of Gaza in International Law." *University of Denver Journal of International Law and Policy* 38 (1): 41–114.

Bosco, David. 2014. *Rough Justice: The International Criminal Court's Battle to Fix the World, One Prosecution at a Time*. New York: Oxford University Press.

Bowen, Stuart W., Jr. 2013. *Learning from Iraq: A Final Report from the Special Inspector General for Iraq Reconstruction*. Printed for the Committee on Foreign Affairs. Washington, D.C.: Government Printing Office.

Bowring, Bill. 2008. *The Degradation of the International Legal Order: The Rehabilitation of Law and the Possibility of Politics*. New York: Routledge-Cavendish.

———. 2009. "Fragmentation, *Lex Specialis* and the Tensions in the Jurisprudence of the European Court of Human Rights." *Journal of Conflict & Security Law* 14 (3): 485–98.

Bradol, Jean-Hervé. 2004. "The Sacrificial International Order and Humanitarian Action." In *In the Shadow of "Just Wars": Violence, Politics, and Humanitarian Action*, ed. Fabrice Weissman, 1–22. Ithaca, N.Y.: Cornell University Press.

Brauman, Rony. 1993. "The Médecins sans Frontières Experience." In *A Framework for Survival: Health, Human Rights, and Humanitarian Assistance in Conflicts and Disasters*, ed. Kevin A. Cahill, 202–20. New York: Basic Books/Council on Foreign Relations.

Brauman, Rony and Pierre Salignon. 2004. "Iraq: In Search of a 'Humanitarian Crisis.'" In *In the Shadow of "Just Wars": Violence, Politics, and Humanitarian Action*, ed. Fabrice Weissman, 269–85. Ithaca, N.Y.: Cornell University Press.

Bravin, Jesse and Gary Fields. 2003. "How Do U.S. Interrogators Make a Captured Terrorist Talk?" *Wall Street Journal*, March 4.

Breaking the Silence, eds. 2012. *Our Harsh Logic: Israeli Soldiers' Testimonies from the Occupied Territories*. New York: Henry Holt.

———. 2004. "04 May 11: Neighbors Didn't Refuse." http://www.breakingthesilence.org.il/testimonies/videos/39659.

———. 2009. *Soldiers' Testimony from Operation Cast Lead, Gaza 2009*. Jerusalem: Breaking the Silence.

Brett, Rachel. 1998. "Non-Governmental Human Rights Organizations and International Humanitarian Law." *International Review of the Red Cross* 80 (September): 531–36.

Broder, John M. 2006. "Contradictions Cloud Inquiry into 24 Iraqi Deaths." *New York Times*, June 17.

Brownlie, Ian. 1973. "Thoughts on Kind-Hearted Gunmen." In *Humanitarian Intervention and the United Nations*, ed. Richard B. Lillich, 139–48. Charlottesville: University Press of Virginia.

Bruderlein, Claude, 2001. "The End of Innocence: Humanitarian Protection in the Twenty-First Century." In *Civilians in War*, ed. Simon Chesterman, 221–35. Boulder, Colo.: Lynne Rienner/International Peace Academy.

Brzoska, Michael. 2007. "Collective Violence Beyond the Standard Definition of Armed Conflict," *SIPRI Yearbook 2007: Armaments, Disarmament, and International Security*, 94–106. New York: Oxford University Press/Stockholm International Peace Research Institute.

Burgoon, Brian et al. 2015. "From Media Attention to Negotiated Peace: Human Rights Reporting and Civil War Duration." *International Interactions* 41 (2): 226–55.

Burgorgue-Larsen, Laurence and Amaya Úbeda de Torres. 2011. "'War' in the Jurisprudence of the Inter-American Court of Human Rights." *Human Rights Quarterly* 33 (1): 148–74.

Burke, Anthony. 2007. *Beyond Security, Ethics and Violence: War Against the Other.* London: Routledge.

Burkle, Frederick and Richard Garfield. 2013. "Civilian Mortality After the 2003 Invasion of Iraq." *The Lancet* 381 (March 16): 877–79.

Burnham, Gilbert et al. 2006. "Mortality After the 2003 Invasion of Iraq: A Cross-sectional Cluster Sample Survey." *The Lancet* 368 (October 21): 1421–28.

Burns, John F. 2005a. "To Halt Abuses, U.S. Will Inspect Jails Run by Iraq." *New York Times*, December 14.

———. 2005b. "U.S. Checkpoints Raise Ire in Iraq." *New York Times*, March 7.

———. 2008. "Iraqis to Get Settlement from Britain over Abuse." *New York Times*, July 11.

Bybee, Jay S. 2002. *Memorandum for Albert R. Gonzales, Counsel to the President, Re: Standards of Conduct for Interrogation Under 18 U.S.C. §§ 2340-2340A.* August 1. http://www.justice.gov/sites/default/files/olc/legacy/2010/08/05/memo-gonzales-aug2002.pdf.

Callwell, Maj. C. E. 1903. *Small Wars: Their Principles and Practice.* London: Harrison and Sons.

Caputi, Ross. 2012. "The Victims of Fallujah's Health Crisis Are Stifled by Western Silence." *The Guardian*, October 25.

Cardenas, Sonia. 2010. "The Geneva Conventions and the Normative Tenor of International Relations." In *The Geneva Conventions Under Assault*, ed. Sarah Perrigo and Jim Whitman, 1–17. London: Pluto.

Carmola, Kateri. 2007. "The Concept of Proportionality: Old Questions and New Ambiguities." *Just War Theory: A Reappraisal*, ed. Mark Evans, 93–113. Edinburgh: University of Edinburgh Press.

Carpenter, Charli. 2012. "Hide in Plain Sight: Rethinking 'Invisible' Wars." *World Politics Review* (July 24).

Carr Center for Human Rights Policy. 2002. "Understanding Collateral Damage Workshop, June 4–5." Washington, D.C.: Project on the Means of Intervention.

Casas, Bartolomé de las. 1552. *A Brief Account of the Destruction of the Indies.* Project Gutenberg. http://www.archive.org/details/abriefaccountoft20321gut.

Çelik, Ayşe Betül. 2005. "Transnationalization of Human Rights Norms and Its Impact on Internally Displaced Kurds." *Human Rights Quarterly* 27 (3): 967–97.

Center for Human Rights and Global Justice, Human Rights First, and Human Rights Watch. 2006. *By the Numbers: Findings of the Detainee Abuse and Accountability Project.* Special Issue *Human Rights Watch* 18 (2).

Cerone, John. 2005. "The Application of Regional Human Rights Law Beyond Regional Frontiers: The Inter-American Commission on Human Rights and U.S. Activities in Iraq." *ASIL Insights*, October 25.

———. 2006. "Human Dignity in the Line of Fire: The Application of International Human Rights Law During Armed Conflicts, Occupation, and Peace Operations." *Vanderbilt Journal of Transnational Law* 39 (5): 1447–1510.

Chandler, David. 2001. "The Road to Military Humanitarianism: How the Human Rights NGOs Shaped a New Humanitarian Agenda." *Human Rights Quarterly* 23 (3): 678–700.

———. 2002. *From Kosovo to Kabul: Human Rights and International Intervention.* London: Pluto.

Chesterman, Simon. 2011. "'Leading from Behind': The Responsibility to Protect, the Obama Doctrine, and Humanitarian Intervention After Libya." *Ethics & International Affairs* 25 (3): 279–85.

Chivers, C. J. 2014. "The Secret Casualties of Iraq's Abandoned Chemical Weapons." *New York Times*, October 14.

Ciezadlo, Annia. 2005. "What Iraq's Checkpoints Are Like." *Christian Science Monitor*, March 7.

"Civs Killed in Baghdad Zone." 2005. July 13. WikiLeaks / *New York Times* Secret Dispatches from the War in Iraq. http://www.nytimes.com/interactive/world/iraq-war-logs.html#report/6283F839-33F3-4B6A-8688-27504B1E5ECC.

CJT-F U.S. ROE Card. n.d. Frontline: Rules of Engagement. http://www.pbs.org/wgbh/pages/frontline/haditha/etc/roecard.pdf.

Clapham, Andrew. 2006. *Human Rights Obligations of Non-State Actors*. New York: Oxford University Press.

Clark, Ann Marie. 2001. *Diplomacy of Conscience: Amnesty International and Changing Human Rights Norms*. Princeton, N.J.: Princeton University Press.

Cloud, David S. 2006. "Compensation Payments Rising, Especially by Marines." *New York Times*, June 10.

CNN. 2011. "Israel to Make Payment for 'Cast Lead' Deaths."

Coady, C. A. J. 2008. *Morality and Political Violence*. New York: Cambridge University Press.

Cobain, Ian. 2014. "Films of UK Army Interrogations in Iraq 'Show the Good, the Bad, and the Ugly.' " *The Guardian*, May 13.

Cockburn, Andrew. 2015. *Kill Chain: The Rise of the High-Tech Assassins*. New York: Macmillan.

Cockburn, Patrick. 2008. "Who Is Whose Enemy?" *London Review of Books*, March 6.

Cohen, Gili. 2014. "IDF: Bloodiest Battle in Gaza Could Have Been Much Worse." *Ha'aretz*, July 28.

Cohen, Joshua. 2004. "Minimalism About Human Rights: The Most We Can Hope For?" *Journal of Political Philosophy* 12 (2): 190–213.

Cohen, Noam. 2010. "Through Soldiers' Eyes, 'The First YouTube War.' " *New York Times*, May 23.

Cohen, Patricia. 2007. "Scholars and the Military Share a Foxhole, Uneasily." *New York Times*, December 22.

Cohen, Roberta. 2009. "Iraq's Displaced: Where to Turn?" *American University International Law Review* 24 (2): 301–40.

Cohen, Roger. 2009. "New Tweets, Old Needs." *New York Times*, September 9.

Cohen, Samy. 2010. *Israel's Asymmetric Wars*. New York: Palgrave Macmillan.

Conte, Alex. 2013. "Human Rights Beyond Borders: A New Era in Human Rights Accountability for Transnational Counter-Terrorism Operations?" *Journal of Conflict & Security Law* 18 (1): 233–58.

Cornish, Paul. 2007. "The Ethics of Effects-Based Warfare: Crowding Out of *Jus in Bello*?" In *The Price of Peace: Just War in the Twenty-First Century*, ed. Charles Reed and David Ryall, 179–200. Cambridge: Cambridge University Press.

Coward, Martin. 2009. "Network-Centric Violence, Critical Infrastructure and the Urbanisation of Security." *Security Dialogue* 40 (4/5): 399–418.

Craig, Alan. 2013. *International Legitimacy and the Politics of Security: The Strategic Deployment of Lawyers in the Israeli Military*. Lanham, Md.: Lexington.

Cranston, Maurice. 1967. "Human Rights, Real and Supposed." In *Political Theory and the Rights of Man*, ed. D. D. Raphael, 43–53. Bloomington: Indiana University Press.

Crawford, Neta C. 2013. *Accountability for Killing: Moral Responsibility for Collateral Damage in America's Post-9/11 Wars*. New York: Oxford University Press.

Cryer, Robert. 2010. "The Interplay of Human Rights and Humanitarian Law: The Approach of the ICTY." *Journal of Conflict and Security Law* 14 (3): 511–27.

Cunningham, U.S. Ambassador James B. 2010. "IDF MAG Mandelblit on IDF Investigations into Operation Cast Lead." February 23. http://www.wikileaks.org/plusd/cables/10TELAVIV417_a.html.

Cushman, Tom. 2005. *A Matter of Principle: Humanitarian Arguments for War in Iraq*. Berkeley: University of California Press.

Dagher, Sam. 2010. "Report Details Torture at Secret Baghdad Prison." *New York Times*, April 27.

Dahan, Michael. 2012. "The Gaza Strip as Panopticon and Panspectron: The Disciplining and

Punishing of a Society." In *Proceedings, Cultural Attitudes Towards Technology and Communication*, ed. M. Strano et al., 25–37. Murdoch, Australia: Murdoch University.

Damluji, Mona. 2010. "'Securing Democracy in Iraq': Sectarian Politics and Segregation in Baghdad, 2003–2007." *Traditional Dwellings and Settlements Review* 21 (2): 71–87.

Daniszewski, John. 2005. "'OK, There Were Signs of Torture,' Iraqi Says." *Los Angeles Times*, November 18.

Darcy, James and Sarah Collinson. 2009. "Introduction: The Uncertain Benefits of Protected Status." In *Realising Protection: The Uncertain Benefits of Civilian, Refugee and IDP Status*, ed. Sarah Collinson et al., 1–9. Humanitarian Policy Group Report 28. London: Humanitarian Policy Group, Overseas Development Institute.

Davies, Nick. 2010. "Iraq War Logs: Secret Order That Let US Ignore Abuse." *The Guardian*, October 22.

de Montesquiou, Alfred and Deb Riechmann. 2010. "Troops: Strict War Rules Slow Afghan Offensive." Associated Press, February 15.

de Waal, Alex. 2007. "Darfur and the Failure of the Responsibility to Protect." *International Affairs* 83 (6): 1039–54.

Deger, Allison. 2015. "Exclusive: Palestine Seeks to Charge Israel with 'Apartheid' and War Crimes at The Hague." Mondoweiss (June 25).

Dershowitz, Alan. 2004. "The Present International Rules of War Enable and Protect Terror." *Baltimore Sun*, May 28.

———. 2006a. "Arithmetic of Pain." *Wall Street Journal*, July 19.

———. 2006b. "'Civilian Casualty'? That's a Gray Area: Those Who Support Terrorists Are Not Entirely Innocent." *Los Angeles Times*, July 22.

"Disengagement Plan of Prime Minister Ariel Sharon." 2004. *Ha'aretz*, April 16.

Docherty, Bonnie and Marc Garlasco. 2003. *Off Target: The Conduct of the War and Civilian Casualties in Iraq*. Washington, D.C.: Human Rights Watch.

Donnelly, Jack. 2003. *Universal Human Rights in Theory and Practice*. Ithaca, N.Y.: Cornell University Press.

Doswald-Beck, Louise. 2004. "Human Rights and Humanitarian Law: Are There Some Individuals Bereft of All Legal Protection?" *American Society of International Law Proceedings* 98: 353–58.

———. 2006. "The Right to Life in Armed Conflict: Does International Humanitarian Law Provide All the Answers?" *International Review of the Red Cross* 88 (December): 881–904.

———. 2013. *Human Rights in Times of Conflict and Terrorism*. New York: Oxford University Press.

Doswald-Beck, Louise and Sylvain Vité. 1993. "International Humanitarian Law and Human Rights Law." *International Review of the Red Cross* 33 (April): 94–113.

Douzinas, Costas. 2007. *Human Rights and Empire: The Philosophy of Cosmopolitanism*. Abington: Routledge-Cavendish.

Draper, G. I. A. D. 1998. *Reflections on Law and Armed Conflict: The Selected Works on the Laws of War by the Late Professor Colonel G. I. A. D. Draper, OBE*. New York: Springer.

Droege, Cordula. 2008. "Elective Affinities? Human Rights and Humanitarian Law." *International Review of the Red Cross* 90 (September): 501–48.

Duffy, Helen. 2008. "Human Rights Litigation and the 'War on Terror.'" *International Review of the Red Cross* 90 (September): 573–97.

Dunlap, Maj. Gen. Charles J., Jr. 2008. "Lawfare Today: A Perspective." *Yale Journal of International Affairs* 3 (1): 146–54.

Dunoff, Jeffrey L. and Joel P. Trachtman. 1999. "The Law and Economics of Humanitarian Law Violations in Internal Conflicts." *American Journal of International Law* 93 (2): 394–409.

Duva, Jesús and Carlos E. Cué. 2010. "Worried Washington Has Eyes on Garzón." *El País*, May 12.

Dworkin, Anthony. 2006. "The Laws of War in the Age of Asymmetric Conflict." In *The Barbarization of Warfare*, ed. George Kassimeris, 220–37. New York: New York University Press.

Dworkin, Ronald. 1978. *Taking Rights Seriously.* Cambridge, Mass.: Harvard University Press.

Eck, Kristine and Lisa Hultman. 2007. "One-Sided Violence Against Civilians in War: Insights from New Fatality Data." *Journal of Peace Research* 44 (2): 233–46.

European Center for Constitutional and Human Rights and Public Interest Lawyers. 2014. *Communication to the Office of the Prosecutor of the International Criminal Court, the Responsibility of Officials of the United Kingdom for War Crimes Involving Systematic Detainee Abuse in Iraq from 2003–2008.* January 10.

Evans, Gareth. 2008. *The Responsibility to Protect: Ending Mass Atrocities Once and for All.* Washington, D.C.: Brookings Institution.

Evans, Jodie. 2012. "Why I Had to Challenge Amnesty International-USA's Claim that NATO's Presence Benefits Afghan Women." *Alternet*, July 12.

Fagen, Patricia Weiss. 2011. "Refugees and IDPs After Conflict: Why They Do Not Go Home." Special Report 268. Washington, D.C.: U.S. Institute of Peace.

Falk, Richard. 1999. "An Alternative to Geopolitics." *Peace Review* 11 (3): 369–77.

Fassihi, Farnaz. 2008. *Waiting for an Ordinary Day: The Unraveling of Life in Iraq.* New York: Public Affairs.

Feldman, Ruth and Adva Vengrober. 2011. "Posttraumatic Stress Disorder in Infants and Young Children Exposed to War-Related Trauma." *Journal of the American Academy of Child & Adolescent Psychiatry* 50 (7): 645–58.

Fellmeth, Aaron Xavier. 2008. "Questioning Civilian Immunity." *Texas International Law Journal* 43 (3): 453–97.

Fenrick, William J. 2001. "Targeting and Proportionality During the NATO Bombing Campaign Against Yugoslavia." *European Journal of International Law* 12 (3): 489–502.

Ferris, Elizabeth G. 2008. "The Looming Crisis: Displacement and Security in Iraq." Brookings Policy Paper 5. Brookings Institution.

———. 2009. "Going Home? Prospects and Pitfalls for Large-Scale Return of Iraqis." Paper presented at the International Association for the Study of Forced Migration, Nicosia, Cyprus, June 28–July 2, 2009.

Filkins, Dexter. 2003. "A Region Enflamed: Strategy; Tough New Tactics by U.S. Tighten Grip on Iraq Towns." *New York Times*, December 7.

Final Act of the International Conference on Human Rights, Teheran, 22 April–13 May 1968. New York: United Nations, A/CONF.32/41.

Finer, Jonathan. 2009. "At a Flashpoint in Gaza, a Family's Deadly Ordeal." *Washington Post*, January 27.

"1st Photos of Viet Mass Slaying." 1969. *Cleveland Plain Dealer*, November 20.

Foley, Conor. 2008. *The Thin Blue Line: How Humanitarianism Went to War.* London: Verso.

Fontan, Victoria. 2008. *Voices from Post-Saddam Iraq: Living with Terrorism, Insurgency, and New Forms of Tyranny.* Santa Barbara, Calif.: ABC-CLIO.

Forbes, Sir Thayne. 2014. *The Report of the Al Swedy Inquiry*, vol. 1. London: Stationery Office.

FRAGO 1108 [19NOV03 DTU] to CJTF-7 OPORD 03-036. 2003. November 19. https://www.aclu.org/sites/default/files/torturefoia/released/a31.pdf.

Franck, Thomas, M. 2003. "Interpretation and Change in the Law of Humanitarian Intervention." In *Humanitarian Intervention: Ethical, Legal, and Political Dilemmas*, ed. J. L. Holzgrefe and Robert O. Keohane, 204–31. Cambridge: Cambridge University Press.

Freeman, Colin. 2013. "Iraq Ten Years On: Baghdad's 'Cinema of Death.'" *Telegraph*, March 19.

French, Peter A. 1998. "The Responsibility of Monsters and Their Makers." In *Individual and Collective Responsibility*, 2nd ed., ed. Peter A. French, 1–12. Rochester, Vt.: Schenkman.

Friedman, Thomas L. 2014. "Dear Guests: Revelations in the Gaza War." *New York Times*, August 5.

Gaggioli, Gloria and Robert Kolb. 2007. "A Right to Life in Armed Conflicts? The Contribution of the European Court of Human Rights." *Israel Yearbook of Human Rights* 37: 115–63.

Garfield, Richard, Claudia Patricia Llantén Morales, and Elissa Dresden. 2003. "Addressing

Collective Violence: An Epidemiologic Context for Human Rights Promotion." *Health and Human Rights* 7 (1): 144–57.
Garlasco, Marc E. 2009. *Precisely Wrong: Gaza Civilians Killed by Israeli Drone-Launched Missiles.* Washington, D.C.: Human Rights Watch.
———. 2012. "NATO's Lost Lessons from Libya." *Washington Post*, June 11.
Garraway, Charles. 2010. " 'To Kill or Not to Kill?': Dilemmas on the Use of Force." *Journal of Conflict & Security Law* 14 (3): 499–510.
Geertz, Clifford. 2008. *Local Knowledge: Further Essays in Interpretive Anthropology.* New York: Basic.
Gettleman, Jeffrey. 2004. "As U.S. Detains Iraqis, Families Plead for News." *New York Times*, March 7.
Ghanim, Ahmad. 2014. Resident of Khuza'a, Younis Khan, Gaza Strip, Facebook post, July 31. Trans. Tamara Sakijha.
Ghobarah, Hazem, Paul Huth, and Bruce Russett. 2002. "Civil Wars Kill and Maim People: Long After the Shooting Stops." *American Political Science Review* 97 (2): 189–202.
Giacaman, Rita et al. 2011. "Mental Health, Social Distress and Political Oppression: The Case of the Occupied Palestinian Territory." *Global Public Health: An International Journal for Research, Policy and Practice* 6 (5): 547–59.
Gilligan, Emma. 2010. *Terror in Chechnya: Russia and the Tragedy of Civilians in War.* Princeton, N.J.: Princeton University Press.
Gladstone, Rick. 2015. "UNICEF Warns of Lost Generation of War Children Out of School." *New York Times*, September 2.
Gladstone, Rick and Isabel Kershner. 2015. "Court to Look into Possible Israeli War Crimes in Palestinian Territories." *New York Times*, January 17.
Glanz, James and Stephen Farrell. 2007. "More Iraqis Said to Flee Since Troop Rise." *New York Times*, August 24.
Glennon, Michael J. 2003. *Limits of Law, Prerogatives of Power: Interventionism After Kosovo.* New York: Palgrave Macmillan.
Global Centre for the Responsibility to Protect. 2015. "UN Security Council Resolutions Referencing R2P." http://www.globalr2p.org/resources/335.
Global Coalition to Protect Education from Attack. 2012. *Lessons in War: Military Use of Schools and Other Education Institutions During Conflict.* New York: Global Coalition to Protect Education from Attack.
Global Justice Center. 2008. "Q & A on the Iraq High Tribunal (IHT) and the Global Justice Center's Monitoring of Gender Justice as of August 2008." http://www-tc.pbs.org/weta/crossroads/incl/trial_IHT_gender_issues.pdf. Accessed January 31, 2016.
Global Policy Forum. 2007. "Public Attitudes in Iraq: Four Years On," *Opinion Research Business*, March.
Golan, Daphna and Zvika Orr. 2012. "Translating Human Rights of the 'Enemy': The Case of Israeli NGOs Defending Palestinian Rights." *Law & Society Review* 46 (4): 781–814.
Golden, Tim. 2006. "Years After 2 Afghans Died, Abuse Case Falters." *New York Times*, February 13.
Goldenberg, Suzanne. 2007. "Refugees in Their Own Land: 2m Iraqis Forced to Flee Their Homes." *The Guardian*, September 19.
Goldman, Adam and Matt Apuzzo. 2011. "AP Impact: At CIA, Grave Mistakes, Then Promotions." Associated Press, February 9.
Goldstone, Richard. 2011. "Reconsidering the Goldstone Report on Israel and War Crimes." *Washington Post*, April 1.
Gonzales, Alberto R. 2002. Memorandum for the President; Decision Re Application of the Geneva Convention on Prisoners of War to the Conflict with Al Qaeda and the Taliban. January 25.
Goodman, Graeme, Ishai Menuchin, and Assaf Oron. 2009. "No Second Thoughts: The Changes in

the Israeli Defense Forces' Combat Doctrine in Light of 'Operation Cast Lead.'" Public Committee Against Torture in Israel. Jerusalem, November.

Goodman, Ryan. 2010. "Controlling the Recourse to War by Modifying *Jus in Bello*." *Yearbook of International Humanitarian Law* 12: 53–84.

Gordon, Neve. 2008. *Israel's Occupation*. Berkeley: University of California Press.

———. 2014. "Human Rights as a Security Threat: Lawfare and the Campaign Against Human Rights NGOs." *Law & Society Review* 48 (2): 311–44.

Gordon, Stuart. 2004. "Military-Humanitarian Relationships and the Invasion of Iraq (2003): Reforging Certainties?" *Journal of Humanitarian Assistance* (July 6).

———. 2010. "Civilian Protection: What's Left of the Norm?" In *The Geneva Conventions Under Assault*, ed. Sarah Perrigo and Jim Whitman, 74–98. London: Pluto.

Graham, Stephen. 2003. "Lessons in Urbicide." *New Left Review* (January/February): 63–78.

Gray, Colin. 2005. *Another Bloody Century: Future Warfare*. London: Weidenfeld & Nicolson.

Greenberg, Karen J. and Joshua L. Dratel, eds. 2005. *The Torture Papers: The Road to Abu Ghraib*. New York: Cambridge University Press.

Gregory, Tom. 2015. "Civilian Casualties and Operation Protective Edge." Duck of Minerva Blog (July 11).

Griffin, James. 2008. *On Human Rights*. New York: Oxford University Press.

Grimes, Maj. Derek I., Maj. John Rawcliffe, and Cpt. Jeannine Smith, eds. 2006. *Operational Law Handbook 2006*. Charlottesville, Va.: International and Operational Law Department, Judge Advocate General's Legal Center and School, U.S. Army.

Gross, Michael L. 2010. *Moral Dilemmas of Modern War: Torture, Assassination, and Blackmail in an Age of Asymmetric Conflict*. New York: Cambridge University Press.

"*Ha'aretz*. Editorial: When War Criminals Walk Free." *Ha'aretz*, August 14.

Habermas, Jürgen. 1999. "Bestiality and Humanity: A War on the Border Between Legality and Morality." *Constellations* 6 (3): 263–72.

———. 2005. "Interpreting the Fall of a Monument." In *Globalizing Critical Theory*, ed. Max Pensky, 19–26. Lanham, Md.: Rowman & Littlefield.

Hagopian, Amy et al. 2013. "Mortality in Iraq Associated with the 2003–2011 War and Occupation: Findings from a National Cluster Sample Survey by the University Collaborative Iraq Mortality Study." *PLOS Medicine* 10 (10).

Hajjar, Lisa. 2005. *Courting Conflict: The Israeli Military Court System in the West Bank and Gaza*. Berkeley: University of California Press.

Hammond, Philip. 2002. "Moral Combat: Advocacy Journalism and the New Humanitarianism." In *Rethinking Human Rights: Critical Approaches to International Politics*, ed. David Chandler, 176–95. New York: Palgrave.

Harel, Amos and Gili Cohen. 2014. "Massive Artillery Shelling May Have Caused Numerous Civilian Fatalities in Gaza." *Ha'aretz*, August 16.

———. 2015. "Top IDF Attorney: 'I Will Never Call IDF the Most Moral Army in the World.'" *Ha'aretz*, April 9.

Harel, Amos. 2009. "IDF Rabbinate Publication During Gaza War: We Will Show No Mercy on the Cruel." *Ha'aretz*, January 26.

———. 2014. "Real Test for Gaza Truce Still Lies Ahead." *Ha'aretz*, August 30.

Hart, H. L. A. 1955. "Are There Any Natural Rights?" *Philosophical Review* 64 (2): 175–91.

Hass, Amira. 2009. "Death in the Samouni Compound." *Ha'aretz*, September 24.

———. 2010. "In Gaza, Cast Lead Felt Like a War on Civilians." *Ha'aretz*, July 7.

Hedges, Chris and Laila Al-Arian. 2008. *Collateral Damage: America's War Against Iraqi Civilians*. New York: Nation Books.

Heintze, Hans-Joachim. 2004. "On the Relationship Between Human Rights Law Protection and

International Humanitarian Law." *International Review of the Red Cross* 86 (December): 789–814.
Helsinki Watch. 1986. *Violations of the Helsinki Accords, Yugoslavia: A Report Prepared for the Helsinki Review Conference, Vienna, November 1986*. New York: Helsinki Watch.
———. 1991. "Yugoslavia: Human Rights Abuses in the Croatian Conflict." August 31.
Henckaerts, Jean-Marie and Louise Doswald-Beck. 2005a. *Customary International Humanitarian Law*. Vol. 1, *Rules*. Cambridge: International Committee of the Red Cross/Cambridge University Press.
———. 2005b. *Customary International Humanitarian Law*. Vol. 2, *Practice*. Cambridge: International Committee of the Red Cross/Cambridge University Press.
Henkin, Louis. 1990. *The Age of Rights*. New York: Columbia University Press.
Herring, Eric and Glen Rangwala. 2006. *Iraq in Fragments: The Occupation and Its Legacy*. Ithaca, N.Y.: Cornell University Press.
Hersh, Seymour M. 2007. "The General's Report." *New Yorker*, June 25.
Hills, Alice. 2006. "Fear and Loathing in Fallujah." *Armed Forces & Society* 32 (4): 623–39.
Hisham, Marwan. 2016. "Living Under the Sword of ISIS in Syria." *New York Times*, January 14.
Holland, Joseph. 2004. "Military Objective and Collateral Damage: Their Relationship and Dynamics." *Yearbook of International Humanitarian Law* 7: 35–78.
Holmes, Robert L. 1989. *On War and Morality*. Princeton, N.J.: Princeton University Press.
Homer. 1866. *The Iliad of Homer*. New York: Charles Scribner.
Hopgood, Stephen. 2013. *The Endtimes of Human Rights*. Ithaca, N.Y.: Cornell University Press.
———. 2006. *Keepers of the Flame: Understanding Amnesty International*. Ithaca, N.Y.: Cornell University Press.
Howard, Michael. 2007. "The Children of War: The Generation Traumatised by Violence in Iraq." *The Guardian*, February 5.
Howard-Hassmann, Rhoda. 2012. "Human Security: Undermining Human Rights?" *Human Rights Quarterly* 34 (1): 88–112.
Hsiao-Hicks, Madelyn and Michael Spagat. 2008. "The Dirty War Index: A Public Health and Human Rights Tool for Examining and Monitoring Armed Conflict Outcomes." *PLOS Medicine* 5 (12): 1658–64.
Hsiao-Rei Hicks et al. 2011. "Violent Deaths of Iraqi Civilians, 2003–2008: Analysis by Perpetrator, Weapon, Time, and Location" *PLOSMedicine* 8 (2).
Human Rights First. 2013. "How to Ensure That the U.S. Drone Program Does Not Undermine Human Rights: Blueprint for the Next Administration." Policy Brief. http://www.humanrightsfirst.org/wp-content/uploads/pdf/blueprints2012/HRF_Targeted_Killing_blueprint.pdf.
Human Rights in Armed Conflicts. Resolution XXIII adopted by the International Conference on Human Rights, Teheran, 12 May 1968.
Human Rights Watch. 1991. *Human Rights Watch World Report 1992; Events of 1991*. New York: Human Rights Watch.
———. 1997. "Israel/Lebanon: Operation 'Grapes of Wrath': The Civilian Victims."
———. 1998a. "Human Rights Watch Letter to NATO Secretary-General Javier Solana."
———. 1998b. "Proxy Targets: Civilians in the War in Burundi."
———. 1998c. *War Without Quarter: Colombia and International Humanitarian Law*. New York: Human Rights Watch.
———. 2002. *In a Dark Hour: The Use of Civilians During IDF Arrest Operations*. April 2.
———. 2003a. "Everyday Victims: Civilians in the Burundian War."
———. 2003b. *"You'll learn not to cry": Child Combatants in Colombia*. Washington, D.C.: Human Rights Watch.
———. 2003c. *We'll Kill You if You Cry": Sexual Violence in the Sierra Leone Conflict*. Washington, D.C.: Human Rights Watch.

———. 2004a. "New Global Survey Analyzes War and Human Rights. https://www.hrw.org/news/2004/01/25/new-global-survey-analyzes-war-and-human-rights.

———. 2004b. *World Report 2004: Human Rights and Armed Conflict.*

———. 2005a. "Iraq: Torture Continues at Hands of New Government." January 25.

———. 2005b. *A Face and a Name: Civilian Victims of Insurgent Groups in Iraq.* New York: Human Rights Watch.

———. 2005c. *Leadership Failure: Firsthand Accounts of Torture of Iraqi Detainees by the U.S. Army's 82nd Airborne Division.* New York: Human Rights Watch.

———. 2006. *"No Blood, No Foul": Soldiers' Accounts of Detainee Abuse in Iraq.* New York: Human Rights Watch.

———. 2009a. "Israel: Gaza 'White flag" Deaths Inquiry a Step Forward." September 10.

———. 2009b. "Soldiers Who Rape, Commanders Who Condone: Sexual Violence and Military Reform in the Democratic Republic of Congo."

———. 2009c. *"They Want Us Exterminated": Murder, Torture, Sexual Orientation and Gender in Iraq.* New York: Human Rights Watch.

———. 2009d. *Rockets from Gaza: Harm to Civilians from Palestinian Armed Groups' Rocket Attacks.* New York: Human Rights Watch.

———. 2009e. *Under Cover of War: Hamas Political Violence in Gaza.* April 20.

———. 2009f. *White Flag Deaths: Killing of Palestinian Civilians During Operation Cast Lead.* New York: Human Rights Watch.

———. 2010a. *"I Lost Everything": Israel's Unlawful Destruction of Property During Operation Cast Lead.* New York: Human Rights Watch.

———. 2010b. *Turning a Blind Eye: Impunity for Laws-of-War Violations During the Gaza War.* New York: Human Rights Watch.

———. 2011. *Schools and Armed Conflict: A Global Survey of Domestic Laws and State Practice Protecting Schools from Attack and Military Use.* Washington, D.C.: Human Rights Watch.

———. 2012. *Delivered into Enemy Hands: U.S.-led Abuse and Rendition of Opponents of Gaddafi's Libya.* Washington, D.C.: Human Rights Watch.

———. 2013. *Between a Drone and al-Qaeda: The Civilian Cost of U.S. Targeted Killings in Yemen.* Washington, D.C.: Human Rights Watch.

———. n.d. "Frequently Asked Questions." http://www.hrw.org/en/node/75138.

Human Rights Watch and Amnesty International. 2003. "Letter to the U.N. Security Council." May 21. http://www.genocidewatch.org/images/D.R._Congo_21_ May_03_Congo_U.N._ Should_Deploy_a_Rapid_Reaction_Force_in_Ituri.pdf.

Human Security Centre. 2011. *Human Security Report 2009/2010: The Causes of Peace and the Shrinking Costs of War.* Oxford: Oxford University Press/Human Security Report Project, Simon Fraser University.

Hunt, Lynn. 2007. *Inventing Human Rights: A History.* New York: Norton.

Hussein, Sara. 2014. "Gaza's Shejaiya: A Moonscape Strewn with Bodies." *Agence France-Presse*, July 20.

"IDF Issues Warnings to the Civilians of Gaza." 2009. http://www.mfa.gov.il/MFA/Government/Communiques/2009/IDF_warns_Gaza_population_7-Jan-2009.htm.

IDF Military Advocate General's Corps. 2012. "MAG Legal Opinion: Al-Samouni Family Incident." January 5. http://www.law.idf.il/163-5080-en/Patzar.aspx.

Inbar, Efraim and Eitan Shamir. 2014. "'Mowing the Grass': Israel's Strategy of Protracted Intractable Conflict." *Journal of Strategic Studies* 37 (1): 65–90.

Internal Displacement Monitoring Centre. 2008. *Iraq: Challenges of Forced Displacement Within Iraq.* Geneva: Internal Displacement Monitoring Centre.

———. 2014. "Iraq." http://www.internal-displacement.org/middle-east-and-north-africa/iraq/.

International Coalition for the Responsibility to Protect. 2011. "Security Council Debate: Protection of Civilians in Armed Conflicts Excerpted RtoP Statements." May 10. http://responsibilitytoprotect.org/RtoP%20Statements_docMS.pdf.

International Commission of Jurists. 2009. *Assessing Damage, Urging Action: Report of the Eminent Jurists Panel on Terrorism, Counter-Terrorism, and Human Rights.* Geneva: International Commission of Jurists.

International Commission on Intervention and State Sovereignty. 2002. *The Responsibility to Protect.* Ottawa: International Development Research Centre.

International Commission on Missing Persons. 2011. "ICMP Meets with Iraq Minister for Human Rights to Discuss Future of Missing Persons Process." February 10.

International Committee of the Red Cross. 2000. *The People on War Report: ICRC Worldwide Consultation on the Rules of War.* Geneva: ICRC.

———. 2008. *Enhancing Protection for Civilians in Armed Conflict and Other Situations of Violence.* Geneva: ICRC.

———. 2009a. "Gaza: ICRC Demands Urgent Access to Wounded as Israeli Army Fails to Assist Wounded Palestinians."

———. 2009b. "Gaza: Massive Devastation Calls for Vast Humanitarian Effort." January 20.

International Criminal Court, Office of the Prosecutor. 2014. "Report on Preliminary Examination Activities 2014" (December 2).

International Crisis Group. 2009. "Gaza's Unfinished Business." *Middle East Report* 85, April 23.

International Human Rights and Conflict Resolution Clinic (Stanford University Law School) and Global Justice Clinic (New York University School of Law). 2012. *Living Under Drones: Death, Injury, and Trauma to Civilians from U.S. Drone Practices in Pakistan.* September.

International Medical Corps. 2007. *Iraqis on the Move: Sectarian Displacement in Baghdad.* Santa Monica, Calif.: International Medical Corps.

International Organization for Migration. 2008. "Five Years On, More People Displaced than Ever Before." March 17.

———. 2013. "Iraq: The Impact of the Syria Crisis." Geneva: International Organization for Migration.

International Organization for Migration-Iraq. 2013. *Internal Displacement in Iraq: Barriers to Integration.* Baghdad: International Organization for Migration-Iraq.

"Iraq: Human Rights Watch Interviews Detainees from Secret Prison." 2010. *Los Angeles Times*, April 28.

Iraq Body Count. 2004. "No Longer Unknowable: Falluja's April Civilians Toll Is 600." October 26. https://www.iraqbodycount.org/analysis/reference/press-releases/9/.

———. 2005. *A Dossier of Civilian Casualties 2003–2005.* Oxford: Oxford Research Group.

Iraqi Ministry of Health. 2013. "Summary of the Prevalence of Reported Congenital Birth Defects in 18 Selected Districts in Iraq." September 11. http://www.emro.who.int/irq/iraq-news/summary-report-on-the-congenital-birth-defects-study-in-iraq.html.

The Iraq War Blog. 2008. Nashville, Tenn.: Second Chance Publishing.

IRIN: Humanitarian News and Analysis. 2005. "Iraq: Death in Falluhjah Rising, Doctors Say." January 4.

———. 2006. "Increased Protection for Children Following Attacks." March 5.

———. 2007. "Iraq: Child Beggars Proliferate in Baghdad." February 11.

———. 2013. "Iraq 10 Years On: War Leaves Lasting Impact on Healthcare." May 2.

"Israel Declines to Study Rabin Tie to Beatings." 1990. *New York Times*, July 12.

Israel Ministry of Foreign Affairs. 2008. "Winograd Committee Submits Final Report," January 30.

———. 2009a. "Hamas Exploitation of Civilians." January 13. http://www.mfa.gov.il/MFA/Terrorism-+Obstacle+to+Peace/Terror+Groups/Hamas_Exploitation_Civilians_Jan_2009.htm.

———. 2009b. Statement by Amb Shalev to UN General Assembly on report of the Human Rights Council. November 4.

"Israeli Soldiers Breaking the Silence on the Occupation of Palestine." 2012. http://www.youtube.com/watch?v=RYXdoipaqnY, accessed August 9, 2015.

IVK Pax Christi. 2013. *In a State of Uncertainty: Impact and Implications of the Use of Depleted Uranium in Iraq.* Utrecht: IVK Pax Christi.

Jacobsen, Anette Faye, ed. 2008. *Human Rights Monitoring: A Field Mission Manual.* Leiden: Nijhoff.

James, Carey. 2009. "Commentary: Mere Words: The 'Enemy Entity' Designation of the Gaza Strip." *Hastings International and Comparative Law Review* 32 (2): 643–67.

Janega, James. 2007. "Security Payoff in Fallujah." *Chicago Tribune*, October 14.

Jarbawi, Ali. 2014. "Israel's Colonialism Must End." *New York Times*, August 4.

Jochnick, Chris af and Roger Normand. 1994. "The Legitimation of Violence: A Critical History of the Laws of War." *Harvard International Law Journal* 35 (1): 49–95.

Johnson, James Turner. 1981. *Just War Tradition and the Restraint of War: A Moral and Historical Inquiry.* Princeton, N.J.: Princeton University Press.

———. 2000. "Maintaining the Protection of Non-Combatants." *Journal of Peace Research* 37 (4): 421–48.

Johnson, Kimberly. 2007. "Recording Sparks Investigation of Shootout." *Marine Corps Times*, November 18.

Judge Advocate General's Legal Center and School. 2009. *Rule of Law Handbook: A Practitioner's Guide for Judge Advocates.* Charlottesville: Judge Advocate General's Legal Center and School, U.S. Army Center for Law and Military Operations.

Kaempf, Sebastian. 2013. "The Mediatisation of War in a Transforming Global Media Landscape." *Australian Journal of International Affairs* 67 (5): 586–604.

Kaldor, Mary. 2001. *New and Old Wars: Organized Violence in a Global Era.* Stanford, Calif.: Stanford University Press.

———. 2009. "Gaza: The "New War." OpenDemocracy.net (February 18).

Kandela, Peter. 1991. "Bomb Now, Die Later." *The Lancet* 337 (April 2): 967.

Kasher, Asa and Amos Yadlin. 2005. "Military Ethics of Fighting Terror: An Israeli Perspective." *Journal of Military Ethics* 4 (1): 3–32.

Keane, John. 2004. *Violence and Democracy.* New York: Cambridge University Press.

Keck, Margaret E. and Kathryn Sikkink. 1998. *Activists Beyond Borders: Advocacy Networks in International Politics.* Ithaca, N.Y.: Cornell University Press.

Keinon, Herb and Khaled Abu Toameh. 2015. "Netanyahu: ICC Decision to Launch Inquiry Against Israel is 'Absurd.'" *Jerusalem Post*, January 17.

Kennedy, David. 2006a. "Reassessing International Humanitarianism: The Dark Sides." In *International Law and Its Others*, ed. Anne Orford, 131–55. Cambridge: Cambridge University Press.

———. 2006b. *Of War and Law.* Princeton, N.J.: Princeton University Press.

Kennedy, Liam. 2009. "Soldier Photography: Visualising the War in Iraq." *Review of International Studies* 35 (4): 817–33.

Kernot, Sarah. 2006. "Humanitarian Intervention: Humanitarian Assistance Versus Human Rights." *Global Peace, Change & Security* 18(1): 41–55.

Kershner, Isabel. 2009. "Israel Rejects Call for Gaza Inquiry." *New York Times*, September 16.

———. 2010. "Israel Rebukes 2 for U.N. Gaza Compound Shelling." *New York Times*, February 1.

———. 2015. "Israeli Government Watchdog Investigates Military's Conduct in Gaza War." *New York Times*, January 20.

Kersten, Mark. 2014. "Did the Senate Just Open the U.S. up to ICC Prosecution?" *Washington Post*, December 10.

Kinsella, Helen M. 2011. *The Image Before the Weapon: A Critical History of the Distinction Between Combatant and Civilian.* Ithaca, N.Y.: Cornell University Press.

Kippenberg, Juliane. 2005. *Seeking Justice: The Prosecution of Sexual Violence in the Congo War.* Washington, D.C.: Human Rights Watch.

Knickmeyer, Ellen. 2006. "In Haditha, Memories of a Massacre." *Washington Post*, May 27.

Koller, David S. 2005. "The Moral Imperative: Toward a Human Rights-Based Law of War." *Harvard International Law Journal* 46 (1): 231–64.

Kretzmer, David. 2002. *The Occupation of Justice: The Supreme Court of Israel and the Occupied Territories.* Albany: State University of New York Press.

———. 2005. "Targeted Killing of Suspected Terrorists: Extra-Judicial Executions or Legitimate Means of Defence?" *European Journal of International Law* 16 (2): 171–212.

———. 2009. "Symposium on Complementing International Humanitarian Law: Exploring the Need for Additional Norms to Govern Contemporary Conflict Situation: Rethinking the Application of IHL in Non-international Armed Conflicts." *Israel Law Review* 42 (1): 8–45.

Kristof, Nicholas D. 2009. "Tear Down This Cyberwall!" *New York Times*, June 18.

Kritsiotis, Dino. 2004. "When States Use Armed Force." In *The Politics of International Law*, ed. Christian Reus-Smit, 45–79. New York: Cambridge University Press.

Kukis, Mark. 2011. *Voices from Iraq: A People's History, 2003–2009.* New York: Columbia University Press.

Lacina, Bethany and Nils Petter Gleditsch. 2005. "Monitoring Trends in Global Combat: A New Dataset of Battle Deaths." *European Journal of Population* 21 (2/3): 145–66.

Lagouranis, Tony and Allen Mikaelian. 2008. *Fear Up Harsh: An Army Interrogator's Dark Journey Through Iraq.* New York: Penguin.

Lamp, Nicolas. 2011. "Conceptions of War and Paradigms of Compliance: The 'New War' Challenge to International Humanitarian Law." *Journal of Conflict and Security Law* 16 (2): 225–62.

Landis, Joshua. 2015. "'Regime-Change Without State Collapse Is Impossible in Syria,' Landis Interviewed by RT's Sophie & Co." Syria Comment, November 9.

Lang, Anthony F. 2002. *Agency and Ethics: The Politics of Military Intervention.* Albany: State University of New York Press.

Larsen, Egon. 1978. *A Flame in Barbed Wire: The Story of Amnesty International.* London: Frederick Muller.

Lauterpacht, Hersch. 1954. "The Problem of the Revision of the Law of War." *British Yearbook of International Law* 29: 360–82.

"'Lawfare' Loses Big: The ACLU Loses Its Nasty Suit Against Former Defense Officials." 2012. *Wall Street Journal*, January 28.

Leigh, David and Maggie O'Kane. 2010. "Iraq War Logs: U.S. Turned Over Captives to Iraqi Torture Squad." *The Guardian*, October 24.

Leigh, David. 2010. "Iraq War Logs: Apache Crew Killed Insurgents Who Tried to Surrender." *The Guardian*, October 22.

Levy, Yagil. 2010. "The Tradeoff Between Force and Casualties in Israel's Wars in Gaza, 1987–2009." *Conflict Management and Peace Science* 27 (4): 386–405.

———. 2011. "How Casualty Sensitivity Affects Civilian Control: The Israeli Experience." *International Studies Perspectives* 12 (1): 68–88.

———. 2012. *Israel's Death Hierarchy: Casualty Aversion in a Militarized Democracy.* New York: New York University Press.

———. 2014. "The Theocratization of the Israeli Military." *Armed Forces & Society* 40 (2): 269–94.

Lifton, Robert Jay. 2004. "Conditions of Anarchy." *The Nation*, May 31.

Llosa, Augusto E., et al. 2012. "Short and longer-term psychological consequences of Operation Cast Lead: documentation from a mental health program in the Gaza Strip." *Conflict and Health* 6 (8).

Lounsbery, Marie Olson, Frederic S. Pearson, and Gaia Klotz. 2015. "International Intervention and the Consequences for Insurgent Strategy in Civil Conflict." Paper presented at Annual Meeting of the International Studies Association-South, Tampa, October.

Lu, Catherine. 2006. *Just and Unjust Interventions in World Politics: Public and Private*. New York: Palgrave Macmillan.

Luban, David. 2008. "Lawfare and Legal Ethics in Guantanámo." *Stanford Law Review* 60 (6): 1981–2026.

———. 2011. "Carl Schmitt and the Critique of Lawfare." *Case Western Reserve Journal of International Law* 43 (1/2): 457–71.

Lubell, Noam. 2005. "Challenges in Applying Human Rights Law to Armed Conflict." *International Review of the Red Cross* 87 (December): 737–54.

Lutz, Catherine. 2013. "U.S. and Coalition Casualties in Iraq and Afghanistan." February 21. http://costsofwar.org/sites/default/files/articles/10/attachments/USandCoalition.pdf.

Maass, Peter, 2005. "The Way of the Commandos." *New York Times Magazine*, May 1.

MacIntyre, Donald. 2010. "Israeli Commander: 'We Rewrote the Rules of War for Gaza.'" *The Independent*, February 3.

Mackinlay, W. G. L. 2007. "Perceptions and Misconceptions: How Are International and UK Law Perceived to Affect Military Commanders and Their Subordinates on Operations?" *Defence Studies* 7 (1): 111–60.

MADRE. 2007. "Promising Democracy, Imposing Theocracy: Gender-Based Violence and the U.S. War on Iraq." http://www.madre.org/index/resources-12/human-rights-reports-56/promising-democracy-imposing-theocracy-gender-based-violence-and-the-us-war-on-iraq-86.html.

Magen David Adom. 2009. "MDA Statistics: Cast Lead Operation." February 4. http://mdais.com/316/4155.htm.

Magen, Dan. 2009. *"Ill Morals": Grave Violations of the Right to Health During the Israeli Assault on Gaza*. Tel Aviv: Physicians for Human Rights-Israel.

Mahr, Krista. 2009. "Neda Agha-Soltan." *Time*, December 8.

"Major General Johnson, USMC Commanding General, MNF-W." n.d. Hadith Selected Testimony. http://www.nytimes.com/interactive/2011/12/15/world/middleeast/haditha-selected-documents.html?ref=middleeast#document/p18/a41205.

Mampilly, Zachariah Cherian. 2011. *Rebel Rulers: Insurgent Government and Civilian Life During War*. Ithaca, N.Y.: Cornell University Press.

Manduca, Paola et al. 2014. An Open Letter for the People in Gaza. *The Lancet* 384 (August): 397–98.

Margalit, Ruth. 2014. "Hadar Goldin and the Hannibal Directive." *New Yorker*, August 6.

Margesson, Rhoda, Andorra Bruno, and Jeremy M. Sharp. 2009. "Iraqi Refugees and Internally Displaced Persons: A Deepening Humanitarian Crisis?" Washington, D.C.: Congressional Research Service.

Martin, Rex. 1980. "Human Rights and Civil Rights." *Philosophical Studies* 37 (4): 391–403.

Marx, Andrew and Samuel Goward. 2013. "Remote Sensing in Human Rights and International Humanitarian Law Monitoring: Concepts and Methods." *Geographical Record* 109 (1): 100–111.

Matheson, Michael. 1997. "The Opinions of the International Court of Justice on the Threat or Use of Nuclear Weapons." *American Journal of International Law* 91 (3): 417–35.

Mazower, Mark. 2006. "An International Civilization? Empire, Internationalism, and the Crisis of the Mid-Twentieth Century," *International Affairs* 82 (3): 553–66.

McCaffrey, Barry. 2013. "New Call for Answers over the Scandal of Northern Ireland's 'Hooded Men.'" Thedetail.tv, August 6.

McCarthy, Conor. 2008. "Legal Conclusion or Interpretative Process? *Lex Specialis* and the Applicability of International Human Rights Standards." In *International Humanitarian Law and*

Human Rights Law: Towards a New Merger in International Law, ed. Roberta Arnold and Noëlle Quénivet, 101–20. Leiden: Nijhoff.

McCarthy, Rory. 2009. "Israel's Military Says It Fought Gaza War in Line with International Law." *The Guardian*, April 22.

McGeough, Paul 2003. "Descent into a Charnel-House Hospital Hell." *Sydney Morning Herald*, April 10.

McGirk, Jan. 2009. "Gaza's Health and Humanitarian Situation Remains Fragile." *The Lancet* 373 (February 14): 531.

McGuirk, Tim. 2006. "One Morning in Haditha." *Time*, March 19.

McIntyre, Donald. 2009. "My Terror as a Human Shield: The Story of Majdi Abed Rabbo." *The Independent*, January 30.

McIntyre, Jamie. 2006. "Lawmaker Says Marines Killed Iraqis 'in Cold Blood.'" CNN, May 19.

McNeal, Gregory S. 2014. "Targeted Killing and Accountability." *Georgetown Law Journal* 102 (3): 680–794.

Médecins sans Frontières. 2014. "Dossier: Rwanda, 20 ans après." April 13. http://msf.fr/actualite/dossiers/rwanda-20-ans-apres.

"Medical Officer/Preventive Medical Officer Interview Questions." 2004. April 3. DOD 016679-016703. http://www1.umn.edu/humanrts/OathBetrayed/DOD%20016679-016703.pdf.

Mégret, Frédéric. 2006. "From 'Savages' to 'Unlawful Combatants': A Postcolonial Look at IHL's 'Other.'" In *International Law and Its Others*, ed. Anne Orford, 265–317. New York: Cambridge University Press.

———. 2012. "Where Does the Critique of International Human Rights Stand? An Exploration in 18 Vignettes." In *New Approaches to International Law: The European and the American Experiences*, ed. José María Beneyto and David Kennedy, 3–40. The Hague: Asser.

Meltzer, Nils. 2009. *Interpretive Guidance on the Notion of Direct Participation in Hostilities Under International Humanitarian Law.* Geneva: ICRC.

Meron, Theodor. 1995. "Extraterritoriality of Human Rights Treaties." *American Journal of International Law* 89 (1): 78–82.

———. 2006. *The Humanization of Humanitarian Law.* Leiden: Nijhoff/The Hague Academy of International Law.

Merry, Sally Engle. 2006. "Transnational Human Rights and Local Activism: Mapping the Middle." *American Anthropologist* 108 (1): 38–51.

Meyer, Aaron Eitan. 2010. "'Lawfare': Weaponizing Human Rights." July 10. http://bigpeace.com/aemeyer/2010/07/10/lawfare-weaponizing-human-rights/

Middle East Watch. 1990. *The Israeli Army and the Intifada: Policies That Contribute to the Killings.* New York: Middle East Watch.

Milanović, Marko. 2011a. "Norm Conflicts, International Humanitarian Law, and Human Rights Law." In *International Humanitarian Law and International Human Rights Law*, ed. Orna Ben-Naftali, 95–125. New York: Oxford University Press.

———. 2011b. *Extraterritorial Application of Human Rights Treaties: Law, Principles, and Policy.* New York: Oxford University Press.

———. 2012. "*Al-Skeini* and *Al-Jedda* in Strasbourg." *European Journal of International Law* 23 (1): 121–39.

Miliband, David. 2013. "Syria is Following the Same Script as Afghanistan." *Financial Times*, September 3.

Mill, John Stuart. 1859. *On Liberty.* London: Parker and Son.

Miltner, Barbara. 2012. "Revisiting Extraterritoriality After *Al-Skeini*: The ECtHR and Its Lessons." *Michigan Journal of International Law* 33 (4): 693–747.

Moffeit, Miles and Arthur Kane. 2004. "Iraq GIs Allowed to Avoid Trials." *Denver Post*, August 22.

Moir, Lindsay. 2003. "Decommissioned? International Humanitarian Law and the Inter-American Human Rights System." *Human Rights Quarterly* 25 (1): 182–212.

Montell, Jessica. 2006. "A Form of Collective Punishment." Bitterlemons.org (July 17). http://www.bitterlemons.org/previous/bl170706ed28.html#isr2.

———. 2009. "A Time for Soul-Searching." *Jerusalem Post*, September 30.

Morris, Maj. Scott R. 1997. "The Laws of War: Rules by Warriors for Warriors." *Army Lawyer* (December): 4–13.

Moss, Michael. 2006. "How Iraq Police Reform Became Casualty of War." *New York Times*, May 22.

Mualem, Mazal. 2014. "Tweets from Gaza Show Israel Other Side of War." Al-Monitor, July 25.

Murray, C. J. L. et al. 2002. "Armed Conflict as a Public Health Problem." *British Medical Journal* 324: 346–49.

Myers, Gary. 2008. Interview for PBS Frontline Show On Haditha Killings, "Rules of Engagement." February 19.

Nabulsi, Karma. 1999. *Traditions of War: Occupation, Resistance and the Law.* Oxford: Oxford University Press.

"National Defense Strategy of the United States of America." 2005. Global Security.org.

Nelson, Deborah. 2008. *The War Behind Me: Vietnam Veterans Confront the Truth About War Crimes.* New York: Basic Books.

Nickels, James W. 2007. *Making Sense of Human Rights.* 2nd ed. Malden, Mass.: Blackwell.

Nissenbaum, Dion. 2009. "Israeli Troops Killed Gaza Children Carrying White Flag, Witnesses Say." McClatchy Newspapers, January 27.

"Not All Troops Would Report Iraq Abuse, Study Says." 2007. *New York Times*, May 5.

O'Connell, Mary Ellen. 2012. "Unlawful Killing with Combat Drones: A Case Study of Pakistan, 2004–2009." In *Shooting to Kill: Socio-Legal Perspectives on the Use of Lethal Force*, ed. Simon Bronitt, Miriam Gani, and Saskia Hufnagle, 263–91. Portland, Ore: Hart.

O'Flaherty, Michael and George Ulrich. 2010. "The Professionalization of Human Rights Fieldwork." *Journal of Human Rights Practice* 2 (1): 1–27.

Oberleitner, Gerd. 2005. "Porcupines in Love: The Intricate Convergence of Human Rights and Human Security." *European Human Rights Law Review* 6: 588–606.

———. 2015. *Human Rights in Armed Conflict: Law, Practice, Policy.* New York: Cambridge University Press.

Office of the UN High Commissioner for Human Rights/United National Assistance Mission for Iraq-Human Rights Office 2016. 2016. Report on the Protection of Civilians in the Armed Conflict in Iraq 1 May–30 October 2015. http://www.ohchr.org/Documents/Countries/IQ/UNAMIReport1May31October2015.pdf.

Office of the Prime Minister. 2013. Chemical Weapon Use by Syrian Regime: UK Government Legal Position. August 29.

Oliver, Kendrick. 2007. *The My Lai Massacre in American History and Memory.* Manchester: Manchester University Press.

Olson, James S. and Randy Roberts. 1998. *My Lai: A Brief History with Documents.* Boston: Bedford.

Onishi, Norimitsu. 2013. "For Most Young Refugees From Syria, School Is as Distant as Home." *New York Times*, December 21.

Orbinski, James. 1999. "Nobel Lecture." December 10. Nobel Prize.org.

Orend, Brian. 2000. *War and International Justice.* Waterloo, Ont.: Wilfrid Laurier University Press.

Osiel, Mark J. 1999. *Obeying Orders: Atrocity, Military Discipline and the Law of War.* New Brunswick, N.J.: Transaction.

———. 2009. *The End of Reciprocity: Terror, Torture, and the Law of War.* New York: Cambridge University Press.

Otterman, Michael, Richard Hil, and Paul Wilson. 2010. *Erasing Iraq: The Human Costs of Carnage*. London: Pluto.

Owens, Patricia. 2003. "Accidents Don't Just Happen: The Liberal Politics of High-Technology Humanitarian War." *Millennium: Journal of International Studies* 32 (3): 595–616.

———. 2007. *Between War and Politics: International Relations and the Thought of Hannah Arendt*. New York: Oxford University Press.

Oxfam. 2007. "Rising to the Humanitarian Challenge in Iraq." Briefing Paper 105.Oxfam. n.d. "Medical Staff in Gaza Struggle to Cope with Rising Casualties." http://www.oxfam.org/en/emergencies/gaza/medical-staff-struggle-cope-rising-casualties.

Packer, George. 2005. *Assassin's Gate: America in Iraq*. New York: Farrar, Straus and Giroux.

Palestinian Centre for Human Rights. 2009a. "6 January 2009: Al-Dayah Family."

———. 2009b. *Through Women's Eyes: A PCHR Report on the Gender-Specific Impact and Consequences of Operation Cast Lead*. PCHR: Gaza City.

———. 2011. "Human Rights Council Votes in Favour of Justice for Victims of Gaza Conflict: EU Abstains." March 25.

———. n.d. *Targeted Civilians: A PCHR Report on the Israeli Military Offensive Against the Gaza Strip (27 December 2008–18 January 2009)*. Gaza City: PCHR.

Paley, Amit R. 2008. "In Iraq, 'a Prison Full of Innocent Men.'" *Washington Post*, December 6.

Papenfuss, Mary. 2003. "Building a Better War," Salon.com, March 6.

Pappé, Ilan. 2009. "Israel's Message." *London Review of Books*, January 14.

Partlow, Joshua. 2007. "Soldiers Shift to Baghdad Outposts: Smaller Bases Expand Troop Presence in Capital But Also Pose New Risks." *Washington Post*, March 1.

Patel, Romil. 2015. "Palestinian Leader Mahmoud Abbas Meets ICC Over Israeli War Crimes." *International Business Times*, October 30.

Patterson, Eric. 2012. *Ethics at War's End*. Washington, D.C.: Georgetown University Press.

Perry, Michael J. 1998. *The Idea of Human Rights: Four Inquiries*. New York: Oxford University Press.

Petrasek, David. 2004. "Human Rights 'Lite'? Thoughts on Human Security." *Disarmament Forum* 3 (2): 59–62.

Physicians for Human Rights-Israel. 2014. "Three Days and Nights of Despair: PHR-Israel Team Worked to Facilitate the Evacuation of Six Residents of Khuza'a." July 27.

PoKempner, Dinah. 2010. "Valuing the Goldstone Report." *Global Governance* 16 (2): 144–59.

PoKempner, Dinah, Marc Garlasco, and Bonnie Docherty. 2003. "Off Target on the Iraq Campaign: A Response to Professor Schmitt." *Yearbook of International Humanitarian Law* 6: 111–25.

Powell, Colin. 2001. "Remarks to the National Foreign Policy Conference for Leaders of Non-Governmental Organizations, U.S. Department of State." October 26.

Power, Jonathan. 2001. *Like Water on Stone: The Story of Amnesty International*. Boston: Northeastern University Press.

Price, Richard. 1998. "Reversing the Gun Sights: Transnational Civil Society Targets Land Mines." *International Organization* 52 (3): 613–44.

Proclamation of Teheran, Final Act of the International Conference on Human Rights, Teheran, 22 April–13 May 1968, UN Doc A/CONF 32/41.

Provost, René. 2002. *International Human Rights Law and Humanitarian Law*. New York: Cambridge University Press.

Quénivet, Noëlle. 2008. "Introduction: The History of the Relationship Between International Humanitarian Law and Human Rights Law." In *International Humanitarian Law and Human Rights Law: Towards a New Merger in International Law*, ed. Roberta Arnold and Noëlle Quénivet, 1–12. Leiden: Nijhoff.

Qumsiyeh, Mazin. 2014. "From Gaza with Pain—and Dignity." *San Francisco Bay View*, July 23.

Rabkin, Jeremy. 2004. "Lawfare: The International Court of Justice Rules in Favor of Terrorism." *Wall Street Journal*, September 17.

Rawaf, Salman et al. 2014. "Living Conditions in Iraq: 10 Years After the U.S.-Led Invasion." *Journal of the Royal Society of Medicine* 107 (5): 187–93.

Rawls, John. 1999. *The Law of Peoples*. Cambridge, Mass.: Harvard University Press.

Rayment, Sean. 2004. "U.S. Tactics Condemned by British Officers." *The Telegraph*, November 4.

———. 2006. "British Troops in Iraq Are Afraid to Open Fire, Secret MoD Report Confirms." *The Telegraph*, April 29.

Razokhi, Ali H. et al. 2006. "Mental Health of Iraqi Children." *The Lancet* 368 (September 2): 838–39.

Reed, John. 2014. "Dozens Die in Gaza School and Market Attacks." *Financial Times*, July 30.

Refugees International. 2013. "DR Congo: Outdated Approach, Misplaced Priorities." http://www.refintl.org/sites/default/files/032613_DR_Congo_Outdated%20letterhead.pdf.

Regev, Amos. 2014. "Return Gaza to the Stone Age." *Israel Hayom*, July 9.

Reiss, Hans. 1970. *Kant's Political Writings*. New York: Cambridge University Press.

Rejali, Darius. 2009. *Torture and Democracy*. Princeton, N.J.: Princeton University Press.

Reus-Smit, Christian. 2011. "Obligation Through Practice." *International Theory* 3 (2): 339–47.

Reynolds, Jefferson D. 2005. "Collateral Damage on the 21st Century Battlefield: Enemy Exploitation of the Law of Armed Conflict, and the Struggle for the Moral High Ground." *Air Force Law Review* 56 (1): 1–108.

Rieff, David. 2010. "How NGOs Became Pawns in the War on Terrorism," *New Republic*, August 3.

Risse, Thomas and Kathryn Sikkink. 1999. "The Socialization of International Human Rights Norms into Domestic Practices: Introduction." In *The Power of Human Rights*, ed. Thomas Risse, Stephen C. Ropp, and Kathryn Sikkink, 1–38. New York: Cambridge University Press.

Riverbend. 2005. *Baghdad Burning: Girl Blog from Iraq*. New York: Feminist Press at the City University of New York.

———. 2006. "Baghdad Burning: Wednesday, October 18, 2006." http://riverbendblog.blogspot.com/2006_10_01_archive.html.

Rivkin, David B., Jr., and Lee A. Casey. 2007. "Lawfare." *Wall Street Journal*, February 26.

Roach, Steven C. 2006. *Politicizing the International Criminal Court: The Convergence of Politics, Ethics, and Law.* Lanham, Md.: Rowman & Littlefield.

Robb, Chris. 2013. "The Fear Gets into Your Blood." *Ottawa Citizen*, November 11.

Roberts, Adam. 2006. "Transformative Military Occupation: Applying the Laws of War and Human Rights." *American Journal of International Law* 100 (3): 580–622.

———. 2009. "The Civilian in Modern War." *Yearbook of International Humanitarian Law* 12: 13–52.

Roberts, Adam and Richard Guelff. 1982. *Documents on the Laws of War.* Oxford: Clarendon.

Rockel, Stephen J. 2009. "Collateral Damage: A Comparative History." In *Inventing Collateral Damage: Civilian Casualties, War, and Empire*, ed. Stephen J. Rockel and Rick Halpern, 1–93. Toronto: Between the Lines.

Rockwood, Lawrence P. 2007. *Walking Away from Nuremberg: Just War and the Doctrine of Command Responsibility.* Amherst: University of Massachusetts Press.

Rogers, Alex. 2013. "Human Rights Groups Divided over Potential Syria Intervention." *Time*, August 30.

Rorty, Richard. 1993. "Human Rights, Rationality, and Sentimentality." In *On Human Rights: The Oxford Amnesty Lectures*, ed. Steven Shute and Susan Hurley, 111–34. New York: Basic.

Roth, Kenneth. 2004. "War in Iraq: Not a Humanitarian Intervention." http://www.hrw.org/wr2k4/3.htm.

Rothbart, Daniel. 2012. "The Politics of Civilian Identity." In *Civilians and Modern War: Armed Conflict and the Ideology of Violence*, ed. Daniel Rothbart, Karina V. Korostelina, and Mohammed D. Cherkaoui, 115–29. New York: Routledge.

Rothbart, Daniel and Karina V. Korostelina, eds. 2011. *Why They Die: Civilian Devastation in Violent Conflict.* Ann Arbor: University of Michigan Press.

Rothbart, Daniel, Karina V. Korostelina, and Mohammed D. Cherkaoui. 2012. "The Place and Plight of Civilians in Modern War." In *Civilians and Modern War: Armed Conflict and the Ideology of Violence*, ed. Daniel Rothbart, Karina V. Korostelina, and Mohammed D. Cherkaoui, 1–16. New York: Routledge.

Rubin, Alissa J. 2008. "U.S. Remakes Jails in Iraq, But Gains Are at Risk." *New York Times*, June 2.

Rudoren, Jodi. 2014a. "Civilian or Not? New Fight in Tallying the Dead from the Gaza Conflict." *New York Times*, August 5.

———. 2014b. "In Gaza, Grief, Anger—and No Small Measure of Pride." *New York Times*, August 10.

Rudoren, Jodi and Fares Akram. 2014. "Conflict Leaves Industry in Ashes and Gaza Reeling from Economic Toll." *New York Times*, August 6.

Samuel, Sigal. 2014. "Netanyahu: Hamas Want to Pile Up 'Telegenically Dead Palestinians.'" *Jewish Daily Forward*, July 20. http://forward.com/articles/202436/netanyahu-hamas-wants-to-pile-up-telegenically/.

Sandholtz, Wayne. 2008. "Dynamics of International Norm Change: Rules Against Wartime Plunder." *European Journal of International Relations* 14 (1): 101–31.

Sané, Pierre. 2000. "Soldiers in the Name of Human Rights." In *Amnesty International Report 2000*, 5–9. London: Amnesty International.

Sanger, David. 2003. "Plans for Post-War Iraq are Re-Evaluated." *New York Times*, April 2.

Sassòli, Marco. 2011. "The Role of Human Rights and International Humanitarian Law in New Types of Armed Conflicts." In *International Humanitarian Law and International Human Rights Law*, ed. Orna Ben-Naftali, 34–94. New York: Oxford University Press.

Sassòli, Marco and Laura M. Olson. 2008. "The Relationship Between International Humanitarian and Human Rights Law Where It Matters: Admissible Killing and Internment of Fighters in Non-International Armed Conflicts." *International Review of the Red Cross* 90 (September): 599–627.

Save the Children. 2006. *The State of the World's Mothers 2006: Saving the Lives of Mothers and Newborns*. Washington, D.C.: Save the Children.

Scarborough, Rowan. 2010. "Afghan Rules Need Changes." *Human Events*, June 30.

Schabas, William A. 2007. "*Lex Specialis*? Belt and Suspenders? The Parallel Operation of Human Rights Law and the Law of Armed Conflict, and the Conundrum of *Jus ad Bellum*." *Israel Law Review* 40 (2): 592–613.

———. 2010. "Gaza, Goldstone, and Lawfare." *Case Western Reserve Journal of International Law* 43 (1/2): 307–12.

Schiff, Benjamin N. 2008. *Building the International Criminal Court*. New York: Cambridge University Press.

Schmitt, Carl. 2007. *The Concept of the Political*. Trans. George Schwab. Chicago: University of Chicago Press.

Schmitt, Eric. 2005. "Army Moves to Advance 2 Linked to Abu Ghraib." *New York Times*, June 29.

Schmitt, Eric and Carolyn Marshall. 2006. "In Secret Unit's 'Black Room,' a Grim Portrait of U.S. Abuse." *New York Times*, March 19.

Schmitt, Eric and Thom Shanker. 2005. "U.S., Citing Abuse in Iraqi Prisons, Holds Detainees." *New York Times*, December 25.

Schmitt, Michael N. 2012. "Discriminate Warfare; the Military Necessity-Humanity Dialectic of International Humanitarian Law." In *Protecting Civilians During Violent Conflict: Theoretical and Practical Issues for the 21st Century*, ed. David W. Lovell and Igor Primoratz, 85–102. Burlington, Vt.: Ashgate.

———. 2007. "The Law of Targeting." In *Perspectives on the ICRC Study on Customary International Humanitarian Law*, ed. Elizabeth Wilmshurst and Susan Breau, 133–68. Cambridge: Cambridge University Press.

Second Marine Division, Camp Blue Diamond, Ar Ramadi. 2005. Press Release #05-141, November 20. http://www-tc.pbs.org/wgbh/pages/frontline/haditha/etc/release.pdf.

Sengupta, Somini. 2015. "60 Million People Fleeing Chaotic Lands." *New York Times*, June 18.

Serrano, Monica. 2011. "The Responsibility to Protect: Libya and Côte d'Ivoire." *Amsterdam Law Forum* 3 (3): 92–101.

Serrano, Richard A. 2004. "The Conflict in Iraq; Interrogation Center Chief Created 'Chaotic Situation.'" *Los Angeles Times*, August 27.

Serwer, Adam. 2009. "Can Human Rights Win the War?" *American Prospect*, October 29.

Sewall, Sarah. 2006. "Blinded by Haditha." *New York Times*, June 13.

Sfard, Michael. 2009. "The Price of Internal Legal Opposition to Human Rights Abuses." *Journal of Human Rights Practice* 1 (1): 37–50.

Shadid, Anthony. 2005. *Night Draws Near: Iraq's People in the Shadow of America's War*. New York: Henry Holt.

Shah, Sikander Ahmed. 2014. *International Law and Drone Strikes in Pakistan: The Legal and Socio-Political Aspects*. New York: Routledge.

Shamsi, Hina and Deborah Pearlstein. 2006. *Command's Responsibility: Detainee Deaths in U.S. Custody in Iraq and Afghanistan*. New York: Human Rights First.

Shaw, Martin. 2004. "Risk-Transfer Militarism and the Legitimacy of War After Iraq." *Foreign Policy in Focus*, June 30.

Shinko, Rosemary. 2010. "Death by Humanity: A Postmodern Reading of the War in Iraq." International Studies Association Conference, New Orleans.

Shoeb, Marwa, Harvey Weinstein, and Richard Mollica. 2007. "The Harvard Trauma Questionnaire: Adapting a Cross-Cultural Instrument for Measuring Torture, Trauma and Posttraumatic Stress Disorder in Iraqi Refugees." *International Journal of Social Psychiatry* 53 (5): 447–63.

Shue, Henry. 2008. "Do We Need a 'Morality of War'?" In *Just and Unjust Warriors: The Moral and Legal Status of Soldiers*, ed. David Rodin and Henry Shue, 87–111. Oxford: Oxford University Press.

Shulman, David. 2009. "Israel Without Illusions: What Goldstone Got Right," *New York Review of Books*, November 17.

———. 2011. "'And No One Wants to Know': Israeli Soldiers on the Occupation." *NYR Blog*, January 9.

Shurat-HaDin Israel Law Center. 2014. Communication to the Prosecutor of the International Criminal Court regarding war crimes committed by Mahmoud Abbas also known as Abu Mazen, November 11.

Sikkink, Kathryn. 2011. *The Justice Cascade: How Human Rights Prosecutions Are Changing World Politics*. New York: Norton.

Skerker, Michael. 2004. "Just War Criteria and the New Face of War: Human Shields, Manufactured Martyrs, and Little Boys with Stones." *Journal of Military Ethics* 3 (1): 27–39.

Slim, Hugo. 2003. "Why Protect Civilians? Innocence, Immunity and Enmity in War." *International Affairs* 79 (3): 481–501.

———. 2008. *Killing Civilians: Method, Madness, and Morality in War*. New York: Columbia University Press.

———. 2009. "NGOs in Gaza: Humanitarianism vs. Politics." *Open Democracy*, January 30.

Sliwinski, Sharon. 2011. *Human Rights in Camera*. Chicago: University of Chicago Press.

Slosson, Mary. 2012. "Marine Spared from Jail Time in Iraq Killings." *Reuters*, January 25.

Smallman-Raynor, M. R. and A. D. Cliff. 2004. *War Epidemics: An Historical Geography of Infectious Diseases in Military Conflicts and Civil Strife, 1850–2000*. Oxford: Oxford University Press.

Smith, Michael Joseph. 1998. "Humanitarian Intervention: An Overview of the Ethical Issues." *Ethics & International Affairs* 12: 63–79.

Smith, Rupert. 2007. *The Utility of Force: The Art of War in the Modern World*. New York: Knopf.

Smith, Thomas W. 2002a. "Moral Hazard and Humanitarian Law: The International Criminal Court and the Limits of Legalism." *International Politics* 39 (2): 175–92.

———. 2002b. "The New Law of War: Legitimizing Hi-Tech and Infrastructural Violence." *International Studies Quarterly* 46 (3): 355–74.

———. 2008. "Protecting Civilians . . . Or Soldiers? Humanitarian Law and the Economy of Risk in Iraq." *International Studies Perspectives* 9 (2): 144–64.

———. 2010. "Can Human Rights Build a Better War?" *Journal of Human Rights* 9 (1): 24–44.

———. 2014. "*Accountability for Killing: Moral Responsibility for Collateral Damage in America's Post-9/11 Wars* by Neta C. Crawford (review)." *Human Rights Quarterly* 36 (4): 958–61.

Sontag, Susan. 2003. *Regarding the Pain of Others*. New York: Picador.

Spagat, Michael et al. 2009. "Estimating War Deaths: An Area of Contestation." *Journal of Conflict Resolution* 53 (6): 934–50.

Spaight, James Maloney. 1911. *War Rights on Land*. London: Macmillan.

Spiro, Peter J. 1996/1997. "New Global Potentates: Nongovernmental Organizations and the 'Unregulated' Marketplace.'" *Cardozo Law Review* 18 (3): 957–69.

Sriram, Chandra Lekha, Olga Martin-Ortega, and Johanna Herman. 2009. *War, Conflict and Human Rights: Theory and Practice*. New York: Routledge.

Stahn, Carsten. 2007. "'Jus ad bellum,' 'Jus in bello' . . . 'Jus post bellum'? Rethinking the Conception of the Law of Armed Force." *European Journal of International Law* 17 (5): 921–43.

State of Israel. 2010. *Gaza Operation Investigations: An Update*. Jerusalem: State of Israel.

———. 2015. *The 2014 Gaza Conflict 7 July–26 August 2014: Factual and Legal Aspects*. Jerusalem: State of Israel.

Steele, Jonathan. 2004. "'Shells and Rockets Were Falling like Rain.'" *The Guardian*, April 11.

Stein, Yael. 2010. *Void of Responsibility: Israel Military Policy Not to Investigate Killings of Palestinians by Soldiers*. Jerusalem: B'Tselem.

Steinberg, Gerald M. 2006. "Soft Powers Play Hardball: NGOs Wage War Against Israel." *Israel Affairs* 12 (4): 748–68.

Stepanova, Ekatarina. 2009. "Trends in Armed Conflict: One-Sided Violence Against Civilians." In Stockholm International Peace Research Institute, *Yearbook 2009: Armaments, Disarmament, and International Security*, 39–68. New York: Oxford University Press.

Stephens, Dale. 2010. "The Age of Lawfare." In *International Law and the Changing Character of War*, ed. Raul A. "Pete" Pedrozo and Daria P. Wollschlaeger, 327–57. Newport, R.I.: Naval War College Press.

Sultany, Nimer. 2014. "Activism and Legitimation in Israel's Jurisprudence of Occupation." *Social & Legal Studies* 23 (3): 315–39.

"Suspected Detainee Abuse in Husaybah." 2006. WikiLeaks. https://wikileaks.org/irq/report/2006/06/IRQ20060626n4296.html.

Suter, Keith. 1976. "Human Rights in Armed Conflicts." *Military Law and Law of War Review* 15 (3/4): 393–439.

Syrian Observatory for Human Rights. 2015. "About 2000 including women and children, killed and wounded in 6 months of coalition air strikes." March 23. http://syriahr.com/en/2015/03/about-2000-including-women-and-children-killed-and-wounded-in-6-months-of-coalition-air-strikes/.

Taback, Nathan and Robin Coupland. 2005. "Towards Collation and Modelling of the Global Cost of Armed Violence on Civilians." *Medicine, Conflict and Survival* 21 (1): 19–27.

Taneja, Preti. 2007. *Assimilation, Exodus, Eradication: Iraq's Minority Communities Since 2003*. London: Minority Rights Group International.

Tanguy, Joelle. 2000. "Intervention, Protection, and Humanitarian Assistance at a Crossroads." Speech, World Affairs Council, San Francisco, March 27.

Tatchell, Peter. 2006. "Crime and Punishment: Grand Ayatollah al-Sistani Urges Death to Gay People." *The Guardian*, April 4.

Tawil, Shireen. 2013. "No end in sight: moving towards a social justice framework for mental health in continuous conflict settings." *Intervention* 11 (1): 24–36.

Taylor, Telford. 1970. *Nuremberg and Vietnam: An American Tragedy.* Chicago: Quadrangle.

Teitel, Ruti G. 2002. "Humanity's Law: Rule of Law for the New Global Politics." *Cornell International Law Journal* 35 (2): 355–87.

———. 2011. *Humanity's Law.* New York: Oxford University Press.

Tesón, Fernando R. 2003. "The Liberal Case for Humanitarian Intervention." In *Humanitarian Intervention: Ethical, Legal, and Political Dilemmas*, ed. J. L. Holzgrefe and Robert O. Keohane, 93–129. Cambridge: Cambridge University Press.

"They Are Just Covering Their Ass." 2001. *The Guardian*, October 9.

Thomas, Ward. 2001. *The Ethics of Destruction: Norms and Force in International Relations.* Ithaca, N.Y.: Cornell University Press.

Thoms, Oskar N. T. and James Ron. 2007. "Public Health, Conflict and Human Rights: Toward a Collaborative Research Agenda." *Conflict and Health* 1 (1).

Thucydides. 1881. *Thucydides Translated into English*, ed. Benjamin Jowett. Oxford: Clarendon.

Toameh, Khaleh Abu. 2014. "Hamas: All Israelis Now Targets for Missile Attacks." *Jerusalem Post*, July 8.

Tomaskovic-Devey, Anna, Charli Carpenter, and Kyle Brownlie. n.d. "Agenda-Setting in Transnational Networks: Findings from Consultations with Human Security Practitioners." http://people.umass.edu/charli/networks/CPPA_Report.pdf.

Torchin, Leshu. 2006. "*Ravished Armenia*: Visual Media, Humanitarian Advocacy, and the Formation of Witnessing Publics." *American Anthropologist* 108 (1): 214–20.

Tracy, Jonathan. 2007. "Responsibility to Pay: Compensating Civilian Casualties of War." *Human Rights Brief* 15 (1): 16–19.

Trimble, Philip R. 1990. "International Law, World Order, and Critical Legal Studies." *Stanford Law Review* 42 (3): 811–45.

Trinquier, Roger. 1964. *Modern Warfare: A French View of Counterinsurgency.* New York: Praeger.

Tsouras, Peter G. 2005. *The Book of Military Quotations.* Minneapolis: Zenith Press.

Tugendhat, Thomas and Laura Croft. 2013. *The Fog of Law: An Introduction to the Legal Erosion of British Fighting Power.* London: Policy Exchange.

Turney-High, Harry. 1991. *Primitive War: Its Practice and Concepts.* Columbia: University of South Carolina Press.

UK Foreign & Commonwealth Office. 2002. *Saddam Hussein: Crimes and Human Rights Abuses* London: Foreign & Commonwealth Office.

UN Country Team Iraq, Iraq Facts and Figures. 2014. http://iq.one.un.org/Facts-and-Figures.

UN Educational, Scientific, and Cultural Organization [UNESCO]. 2013. "Children Still Battling to Go to School." Education for All Global Monitoring Report, Policy Paper 10, July. http://unesdoc.unesco.org/images/0022/002216/221668e.pdf.

UN Environment Programme [UNEP]. 2005. *Assessment of Environmental "Hotspots" in Iraq.* Nairobi: UNEP.

———. 2009. *Environmental Assessment of the Gaza Strip Following the Escalation of Hostilities in December 2008–January 2009.* Nairobi: UNEP.

UN General Assembly. 1967. UNGA 2252 (ES-V) Humanitarian Assistance, July 4.

UN General Assembly. 2005. Resolution adopted by the General Assembly 60/1. 2005 World Summit Outcome (October 24). http://www.un.org/womenwatch/ods/A-RES-60-1-E.pdf.

UN High Commissioner for Refugees [UNHCR]. 2008. "Trauma Survey in Syria." January 22. http://www.unhcr.org/4795e6222.html.

———. 2013. "The Future of Syria: Refugee Children in Crisis." December 10. http://unhcr.org/FutureOfSyria/index.html.

UN Human Rights Commission. 2003. "Civil and Political Rights, Including the Questions of Disappearances and Summary Executions-Extrajudicial, Summary and Arbitrary Executions." Report of the Special Rapporteur, Asma Jahangir (E/CN.4/2003/3) submitted to UN Economic and Social Council Commission on Human Rights (January).

UN Human Rights Committee. 2004. UN Human Rights Committee, General Comment 31, "The Nature of the General Legal Obligation Imposed on States Parties to the Covenant," March 29. CCPR/C/21/Rev.1/Add.13, of 26 May 2004.

UN Human Rights Council. 2009. *Human Rights in Palestine and Other Occupied Arab Territories; Report of the United Nations Fact Finding Mission on the Gaza Conflict* A/HRC/12/48, September 15. [Goldstone Report]. http://www2.ohchr.org/english/. bodies/hrcouncil/specialsession/9/docs/UNFFMGC_Report.pdf.

UN Human Rights Council. 2010a. Report of the Committee of Independent Experts in International Humanitarian and Human Rights Laws to Monitor and Assess Any Domestic, Legal or Other Proceedings Undertaken by Both the Government of Israel and the Palestinian Side, in the Light of General Assembly Resolution 64/254, Including the Independence, Effectiveness, Genuineness of These Investigations and Their Conformity with International Standards. September 23. A/HRC/50.

———. 2010b. Report of the Special Rapporteur on Extrajudicial, Summary or Arbitrary Executions, Philip Alston: Study on Targeted Killings. May 28.

——— 2011. Report of the Committee of independent experts in international humanitarian and human rights law established pursuant to Council resolution 13/9, A/HRC/16/24. 2011. (May 5).

UNICEF Iraq. 2008. *Iraq's Children 2007: A Year in Their Life.* Amman: UNICEF Iraq.

UN Office for the Coordination of Humanitarian Affairs. 2014a. "Occupied Palestinian Territory: Gaza Emergency Situation Report (as of 5 August, 0800 hours). http://www.ochaopt.org/documents/ocha_opt_sitrep_05_08_2014.pdf.

———. 2014b. "Occupied Palestinian Territory: Gaza Emergency Situation Update (as of 2 August 2014, 1500 hours)." http://www.ochaopt.org/documents/ocha_opt_sitrep_03_08_2014.pdf.

UN Office of the High Commissioner for Human Rights. 2005. *OHCHR Plan of Action: Protection and Empowerment.* Geneva: Office of the High Commissioner for Human Rights.

UN Office of the Commissioner for Humanitarian Affairs (OCHA). 2004. "Guiding Principles on Internal Displacement." http://www.brookings.edu/~/media/Projects/idp/GPEnglish.pdf.

UN Security Council. 1999. Report of the Secretary-General to the Security Council on the Protection of Civilians in Armed Conflict. http://www.refworld.org/docid/4ae9acc5d.html.

The United States' Oral Response to the Questions Asked by the Committee Against Torture. 2006. http://www.state.gov/j/drl/rls/68562.htm.

U.S. Army. 1956. *The Law of Land Warfare* (Field Manual 27-10).

———. 2004. *Counterinsurgency Operations (FMI 3-07.22)*, October 2. usacac.army.mil/CAC/milreview/download/English/NovDec05/aylwin.pdf, pp. 4-4, 1–3.

U.S. Army National Ground Intelligence Center. 2004. "Complex Environments: Battle of Fallujah I, April 2004." http://file.wikileaks.org/file/fallujah.pdf.

U.S. Citizenship and Immigration Services. 2013. "Iraqi Refugee Processing Fact Sheet." http://www.uscis.gov/humanitarian/refugees-asylum/refugees/iraqi-refugee-processing-fact-sheet.

U.S. Commission on International Religious Freedom. 2010. *United States Commission on International Religious Freedom Annual Report 2010.* Washington, D.C.: U.S. Commission on International Religious Freedom.

U.S. Department of the Army. 2004. *Counterinsurgency Operations.* FMI 3-07.22. https://fas.org/irp/doddir/army/fmi3-07-22.pdf.

U.S. Department of Defense. 2001. "DoD News Briefing- Secretary Rumsfeld and Gen. Myers." December 4. http://www.defense.gov/transcripts/transcript.aspx?transcriptid=2598.

———. 2003. DoD News Briefing, Secretary Rumsfeld and Gen. Myers. April 11. http://www.defense.gov/transcripts/transcript.aspx?transcriptid=2367.

———. 2005. "News Briefing with Secretary of Defense Donald Rumsfeld and Gen. Peter Pace." November 29. http://www.defense.gov/transcripts/transcript.aspx?transcriptid=1492.

U.S. Department of Defense, Office of General Counsel. 2015. *Department of Defense Law of War Manual.* Washington, D.C. U.S. Department of Defense.

U.S. Department of State, Bureau of Democracy, Human Rights, and Labor. 2010. *2009 Human Rights Report: Iraq*, March 11. Washington, D.C.: U.S. Department of State, Bureau of Democracy, Human Rights, and Labor.

U.S. Embassy, Tel Aviv. 2008. "Cashless in Gaza?" November 3. https://wikileaks.org/plusd/cables/08TELAVIV2447_a.html.

U.S. Senate Select Committee on Intelligence. 2014. *The Senate Select Committee's Study of the Central Intelligence Agency's Detention and Interrogation Program, Executive Summary. http://www.nytimes.com/interactive/2014/12/09/world/cia-torture-report-document.html*

Van As, Sebastian et al.. 2009. *Final Report: Independent Fact-Finding Mission into Violations of Human Rights in the Gaza Strip During the Period 27.12.2008–18.01.2009.* Brussels: Physicians for Human Rights-Israel and Palestinian Medical Relief Society.

Van der Auweraert, Peter. 2011. "Displacement and National Institutions: Reflections on the Iraqi Experience." Middle East Institute, Fondation pour la Recherche Stratégique. http://www.refugeecooperation.org/publications/Iraq/08_auweraert.php.

van Dijken, Sophie, Suzanne Knijnenburg, and Rabia el Morabet Belhaj. n.d. *Monetary Payments for Civilian Harm in International and National Practice.* Amsterdam: Amsterdam International Law Clinic/Center for Civilians in Conflict.

Vasagar, Jeevan. 2006. "Soldiers Cleared of Iraqi Teenager's Manslaughter." *The Guardian*, June 6.

Verdirame, Guglielmo. 2008. "Human Rights in Wartime: A Framework for Analysis." *European Human Rights Law Review* 6: 689–705.

von Zielbauer, Paul. 2006. "At Least Five Marines Are Expected to be Charged in Haditha Deaths." *New York* Times, December 6.

———. 2007. "Colonel Is Acquitted in Abu Ghraib Abuse Case." *New York Times*, August 29.

Wagnsson, Charlotte, Maria Hellman, and Arita Holmberg. 2010. "The Centrality of Non-Traditional Groups for Security in the Globalized Era: The Case of Children." *International Political Sociology* 4 (1): 1–14.

Wainstock, Tamar et al. 2013. "Prenatal Stress and Risk of Spontaneous Abortion." *Psychosomatic Medicine* 75 (3): 228–35.

Waldron, Jeremy. 1987. *"Nonsense upon Stilts": Bentham, Burke, and Marx on the Rights of Man.* London: Methuen.

Walzer, Michael. 1977. *Just and Unjust Wars: A Moral Argument with Historical Examples.* New York: Basic.

———. 2004. *Arguing About War.* New Haven, Conn.: Yale University Press.

Ware, Lt. Col. Paul J. 2007. *Investigating Officer's Report (Of Charges Under Article 32, UCMJ and R.C.M. 405, Manual for Courts-Martial) [Staff Sgt. Frank D. Wuterich, accused]*, October 2. http://warchronicle.com/TheyAreNotKillers/SSgtWuterich/Art 32 Report ICO Wuterich.pdf.

Waters, Christopher P. M. 2008. "Is the Military Legally Encircled?" *Defence Studies* 8 (1): 26–48.

Watkin, Kenneth. 2004. "Controlling the Use of Force: A Role for Human Rights Norms in Contemporary Armed Conflict." *American Journal of International Law* 98 (1): 1–34.

———. 2005. "Assessing Proportionality: Moral Complexity and Legal Rules." *Yearbook of International Humanitarian Law* 8: 3–55.

Watson, Olivia. 2014. "How Will Gaza's Children Carry Their Scars into Adulthood." *972*, August 8. http://972mag.com/how-will-gazas-children-carry-their-scars-into-adulthood/.

Watson, Robert. 2006. "'Where Can We Live Safely as Sunni-Shia Husband and Wife?'" *The Telegraph*, November 12.

Webb, Raymond Jet al. 2012. "Human Rights Among Muslims and Christians in Palestine and Germany." In *Tensions Within and Between Religions and Human Rights*, ed. Johannes A. van der Ven and Hans-Georg Ziebertz, 177–201. Leiden: Brill.

Webster, Paul C. 2011. "Iraq's Health System Yet to Heal from Ravages of War." *The Lancet* 378 (September 3): 863–66.

———. 2013. "Roots of Iraq's Maternal and Child Health Crisis Run Deep." *The Lancet* 381 (March 16): 891–94.

Weill, Sharon. 2014. *The Role of National Courts in Applying International Humanitarian Law*. New York: Oxford University Press.

Weiss, Thomas G. 2007. *Humanitarian Intervention: Ideas in Action*. Cambridge: Polity.

———. 2014. "Military Humanitarianism: Syria Hasn't Killed It." *Washington Quarterly* 37 (1): 7–20.

Welch, Michael. 2010. "Detained in Occupied Iraq: Deciphering the Narratives for Neocolonial Internment." *Punishment & Society* 12 (2): 123–46.

Whetham, David. 2012. "Remote Killing and Drive-By Wars." In *Protecting Civilians During Violent Conflict: Theoretical and Practical Issues for the 21st Century*, ed. David W. Lovell and Igor Primoratz, 199–214. Burlington, Vt.: Ashgate.

Wheeler, Nicholas J. 2000. *Saving Strangers: Humanitarian Intervention in International Society*. New York: Oxford University Press.

White, Josh. 2006. "Marine Says Rules Were Followed; Sergeant Describes Hunt for Insurgents in Haditha." *Washington Post*, June 11.

———. 2007a. "Marines' Photos Provide Graphic Evidence in Haditha Probe." *Washington Post*, January 7.

———. 2007b. "Report on Haditha Condemns Marines." *Washington Post*, April 21.

White, Josh, Charles Lane, and Julie Tate. 2006. "Homicide Charges Rare in Iraq War: Few Troops Tried for Killing Civilians." *Washington Post*, August 28.

Whitty, Noel. 2010. "Soldier Photography of Detainee Abuse in Iraq: Digital Technology, Human Rights and the Death of Baha Mousa." *Human Rights Law Review*10 (4): 689–714.

Wigham, J. T. 1939. "War, Famine and Pestilence." *Irish Journal of Medical Science* 14 (2): 49–58.

Williams, Andrew. 2012. *A Very British Killing: The Death of Baha Mousa*. London: Jonathan Cape.

———. 2014. "British Soldiers Accused of Torture and Abuse During Iraq Occupation." *Newsweek*, December 17.

Williams, Timothy and Suadad al-Sahly. 2009. "Fate of Missing Iraqis Haunts Those Left Behind." *New York Times*, May 24.

Wilmshurst, Elizabeth. 2012. *International Law and the Classification of Conflicts*. New York: Oxford University Press.

Wing, Joel. 2014. "Iraq's New Refugee Crisis." Musings on Iraq: Iraq News, Politics, Economics, Society. http://musingsoniraq.blogspot.com/2014/07/iraqs-new-refugee-crisis.html.

Winter, Yves. 2011. "The Asymmetric War Discourse and Its Moral Economies: A Critique." *International Theory* 3 (3): 488–514.

Witness. 2011. *Cameras Everywhere: Current Challenges and Opportunities at the Intersection of Human Rights, Video and Technology*. Brooklyn, N.Y.: Witness.

Witt, John Fabian. 2008. "Form and Substance in the Law of Counterinsurgency Damages." *Loyola of Los Angeles Law Review* 41 (4): 1455–81.

Wong, Edward and Wissab A. Habeeb. 2007. "Baghdad Car Bomb Kills 20 on Booksellers' Row." *New York Times*, March 6.

Woodward, Bob. 2004. *Plan of Attack*. New York: Simon & Schuster.

World Health Organization Regional Office for the Eastern Mediterranean/Iraq Health Ministry. 2009. *Iraq Mental Health Survey 2006/7*. Cairo: World Health Organization.

Wright, Fiona and Sara Robinson. 2010. *"Humanitarian Minimum": Israel's Role in Creating Food and Water Insecurity in the Gaza Strip*. Tel Aviv: Physicians for Human Rights- Israel.

Yesh Din—Volunteers for Human Rights. 2008. *Exceptions: Prosecution of IDF Soldiers During and After the Second Intifada, 2000–2007*. http://www.yesh-din.org/sys/images/File/Exceptions%5BEng%5D%5B1%5D.pdf.

Yoo, John C. 2002. Letter from John C. Yoo, Office of Legal Counsel, to Alberto R. Gonzales, Counsel to the President, August 1. http://www.justice.gov/sites/default/files/olc/legacy/2010/08/05/memo-gonzales-aug1.pdf.

Younis, Kristele and Nir Rosen. 2008. *Uprooted and Unstable: Meeting Urgent Humanitarian Needs in Iraq*. Washington, D.C.: Refugees International.

Zangana, Haifa. 2007. *City of Widows: An Iraqi Woman's Account of War and Resistance*. New York: Seven Stories Press.

Zegveld, Liesbeth. 2002. *Accountability of Armed Opposition Groups in International Law*. New York: Cambridge University Press.

Zehfuss, Maja. 2011. "Targeting: Precision and the Production of Ethics." *European Journal of International Relations* 17 (3): 543–66.

———. 2012. "Killing Civilians: Thinking the Practice of War." *British Journal of Politics and International Relations* 14 (3): 423–40.

Zoepf, Katherine. 2006. "Iraqi Academics Are Marked for Death, Human-Rights Groups Say." *Chronicle of Higher Education*, July 7.

Zogby, James. 2010. *Arab Voices: What They Are Saying to Us, and Why It Matters*. New York: Palgrave Macmillan.

———. 2011. *Iraq: The War, Its Consequences and the Future*. Washington, D.C.: Zogby Research Services/JZ Analytics.

Zohar, Shalhavet. 2009. "Peres: Goldstone Report Mocks History." *Jerusalem Post*, September 18.

INDEX

ACKNOWLEDGMENTS

I've been toiling on this book for several years, and there many people I want to thank for their help along the way. First are those who offered encouragement and criticism, clarified parts of the argument, or served as discussants on conference panels where I presented papers drawn from this project. Thanks to: Zehra Arat, Robert Barnidge, Karima Bennoune, Jay Boda, Daniel Brunstetter, Michael Byers, Chip Carey, Anthony Chase, Amy Eckert, Sebastian Kaempf, Phillip Kasaija, Joshua Landis, Felipe Mantilla, Muhamad Olimat, Ido Oren, Steven Roach, Stephen Rockel, Michael Joseph Smith, Ty Solomon, Ward Thomas, Ajay Verghese, and Nikos Zahariades. A special thanks to my colleague, the philosopher Hugh Lafollette, who helped me whip the book's argument into shape. I'm grateful to the denizens of the Snell House at the University of South Florida St. Petersburg for providing such a congenial working atmosphere. Thanks to Ray Arsenault, Chris Meindl, Michael Francis, Sudsy Tschiderer, Daun Fletcher, and Veronica Matthews.

I am deeply indebted to Penn Press's editor-in-chief Peter Agree and Human Rights series editor Bert Lockwood for their encouragement and editorial direction. Many thanks to those human rights researchers and activists who so freely shared their time and insights with me. Thanks to Itamar Barack (B'Tselem), Gerrie Haynes (Physicians for Social Responsibility), Dr. Donald Mellman, Muhammad Sabah (B'Tselem), Yehuda Shaul (Breaking the Silence), Yael Stein (B'Tselem), Hadas Ziv (Physicians for Human Rights-Israel), and a number of medical professionals who live and work in Gaza and asked to remain anonymous. I'm grateful to Yagil Levy of the Open University of Israel for his assistance with the Gaza chapter. Thanks to Andrew Williams of the University of Warwick for shedding light on the Baha Mousa case and to Marc Garlasco for walking me through the human rights advocacy process in Washington, D.C. A special thanks to Jacqueline Inman for research assistance and to Tamara Sakijha for collecting and translating Arabic-language social media related to the Gaza wars.

Research for this book was funded in part by a grant from the University of South Florida St. Petersburg Internal Research Grant Fund. A section of Chapter 1 was first published in my article, "Can Human Rights Build a Better War?" *Journal of Human Rights* 9 (2010): 24–44. It is reprinted here with permission.

On a personal note, I want to thank my mother, Cornelia W. Smith, for her enduring love and support. My father, Dr. James A. Smith, Jr., passed away while I was working on this manuscript. I hope some of his clarity of thought and passion for social justice is reflected in these pages. An exuberant thank you to my in-laws, George and Pola Alexopoulos, who provided me a warm and inviting home and abundant, delectable, Greek food during a sabbatical in Chicago in the fall of 2014.

I dedicate this book to my wife, the Russian historian Golfo Alexopoulos. Golfo is, as the Greeks say, my *anthropo*, my "person." She, along with our amazing daughters, Athena and Sophia, has filled my life with love and joy.

CPSIA information can be obtained
at www.ICGtesting.com
Printed in the USA
LVHW091528211020
669425LV00017B/496/J